Continual Service Improvement

London: TSO

Published by TSO (The Stationery Office) and available from:

Online
www.tsoshop.co.uk

Mail, Telephone, Fax & E-mail
TSO
PO Box 29, Norwich, NR3 1GN
Telephone orders/General enquiries: 0870 600 5522
Fax orders: 0870 600 5533
E-mail: customer.services@tso.co.uk
Textphone 0870 240 3701

TSO Shops
123 Kingsway, London, WC2B 6PQ
020 7242 6393 Fax 020 7242 6394
16 Arthur Street, Belfast BT1 4GD
028 9023 8451 Fax 028 9023 5401
71 Lothian Road, Edinburgh EH3 9AZ
0870 606 5566 Fax 0870 606 5588

TSO@Blackwell and other Accredited Agents

Published for the Office of Government Commerce under licence from the Controller of Her Majesty's Stationery Office.

First published 2007

ISBN 978 0 11 331049 4

Printed in the United Kingdom for The Stationery Office

Contents

List of figures

All diagrams in this publication are intended to provide an illustration of ITIL Service Management Practice concepts and guidance. They have been artistically rendered to visually reinforce key concepts and are not intended to meet a formal method or standard of technical drawing. The ITIL Service Management Practices Integrated Service Model conforms to technical drawing standards and should be referred to for complete details. Please see www.best-management-practice.com/itil for details.

List of tables

OGC's foreword

Since its creation, ITIL has grown to become the most widely accepted approach to IT Service Management in the world. However, along with this success comes the responsibility to ensure that the guidance keeps pace with a changing global business environment. Service Management requirements are inevitably shaped by the development of technology, revised business models and increasing customer expectations. Our latest version of ITIL has been created in response to these developments.

This publication is one of five core publications describing the IT Service Management practices that make up ITIL. They are the result of a two-year project to review and update the guidance. The number of Service Management professionals around the world who have helped to develop the content of these publications is impressive. Their experience and knowledge have contributed to the content to bring you a consistent set of high-quality guidance. This is supported by the ongoing development of a comprehensive qualifications scheme, along with accredited training and consultancy.

Whether you are part of a global company, a government department or a small business, ITIL gives you access to world-class Service Management expertise. Essentially, it puts IT services where they belong – at the heart of successful business operations.

Peter Fanning

Acting Chief Executive

Office of Government Commerce

Chief Architect's foreword

ITIL service management practices are based on a solid framework of concepts, processes, functions and activities that exert positive outcomes on business value. One of the constant features of these practices is the objective to improve in maturity and therefore service excellence in every possible way.

No matter what we do in our daily lives, we are constantly assessing how we can improve the quality and meaningfulness in all we achieve. We look to experiences of our peers to learn and measure how we perform in that context.

Continual Service Improvement surrounds the ITIL service lifecycle by exerting influence in every aspect of service management to improve our performance, capability and business value as service providers.

The most important aspect of understanding how to improve is in knowing what to measure and how those measures can be assessed, analysed and used as a basis for improvements.

This publication forms part of an overall lifecycle of service management practices and guides the reader in understanding service measurement, how to assess the overall service management health and maturity, and then what to do to make it better.

The guidance in *Continual Service Improvement* is based around the view of improvement from the business perspective of service quality.

As service providers, what we think of our service quality is important, but what our business customers think is paramount to our survival.

Service providers who are serious about paying more than lip service to service improvement need to own and use the practices in this publication.

Sharon Taylor

Chief Architect, ITIL Service Management Practices

Preface

The ethos behind the development of ITIL is the recognition that organizations are increasingly dependent upon IT to satisfy their corporate aims and meet their business needs. This growing dependency leads to growing needs for quality IT services – quality that is matched to business needs and user requirements as they emerge.

This is true no matter what type or size of organization, be it national government, a multinational conglomerate, a decentralized office with either a local or centralized IT provision, an outsourced service provider or a single office environment with one person providing IT support. In each case there is the requirement to provide an economical service that is reliable, consistent and fit for purpose.

IT service management (ITSM) is concerned with delivering and supporting IT services that are appropriate to the business requirements of the organization. ITIL provides a comprehensive, consistent and coherent set of best practices for IT service management processes, promoting a quality approach to achieving business effectiveness and efficiency in the use of information systems. ITIL service management processes are intended to be implemented so that they underpin but do not dictate the business processes of an organization. IT service providers will be striving to improve the quality of the service, but at the same time they will be trying to reduce the costs or, at a minimum, maintain costs at the current level.

The best-practice processes promoted in this publication both support and are supported by the ISO Standard for IT Service Management (ISO/IEC 20000) and the ISO quality standard ISO 9000.

This is a volume of principles, practices and methods that can be collectively applied towards an approach to continual service improvement, both in industry and government. The guidance in this publication has been written for managers and practitioners at all levels, whether they be senior executives providing leadership and direction through objectives, policies and strategies; or consultants, experts and practitioners who carry out programmes and operations that will ultimately realize the objectives. This publication is about effective continual service improvements. It is to be noted that the improvements will range in scope and scale. Depending on the nature of their business, readers may be interested in one or more of the above perspectives, either in sequence or combination.

The context of this publication is set by the ITIL® which today is the most popular framework worldwide among organizations seeking to develop and improve their capabilities in IT service management.

The drafts of this publication have been reviewed by consultants, experts, practitioners and business managers with tough criteria for what can be considered best practice. This includes customers and providers of IT services facing some difficult problems that they hope would be easier to solve with right type of knowledge. A guiding principle has been that management decisions, practices and methods should be based on hard evidence rather than untested opinions, popular notions and insufficient information. In other words, this publication provides evidence-based service management that can be useful and relevant for creating and delivering value to their customers in the form of services. Without being either too prescriptive or too generic, this publication aims to strike a balance by providing robust principles, practices and methods that can be applied under varying organizational contexts and business scenarios.

CSI is, as its name implies, an ongoing activity woven into the fabric of an organization as opposed to a reactive response to a specific situation or a temporary crisis. These quick-fix initiatives are heralded with laments of:

- 'Oh my, the network keeps going down, then up, then down again. We need an instant stability programme.'
- 'The servers just blew up! We need to start managing availability ... this minute!'
- 'Sadly, because the network keeps going up and down and the servers are blowing up, IT staff morale is in the toilet. We need a quick turnaround team-building programme.'

This approach is far too common in today's organizations and has little to do with the discipline of CSI. Implementing CSI will force major change for many organizations. This change initiative as well as the full breadth of service improvement is the focus of this publication.

Continual versus continuous

The Wikipedia Online Dictionary differentiates between the two terms.

- 'Continuous' is the stronger word, and denotes that the continuity or union of parts is absolute and uninterrupted; as, a continuous sheet of ice; a continuous flow of water.
- 'Continual', in most cases, marks a close and unbroken succession of things, rather than absolute continuity. Thus we speak of continual showers, implying a repetition with occasional interruptions.

Hence the decision to use the word 'continual' for the title of this publication as well as throughout this publication has been made. An IT organization will not be 'continuously' improving itself seamlessly, but rather it will be cyclical in nature: there will be a period of stability followed by more improvements, then a new level of stability followed by more improvements and so on.

Contact information

Full details of the range of material published under the ITIL banner can be found at www.best-management-practice.com/itil

For further information on qualifications and training accreditation, please visit www.itil-officialsite.com. Alternatively, please contact:

APMG Service Desk
Sword House
Totteridge Road
High Wycombe
Buckinghamshire
HP13 6DG
Tel: +44 (0) 1494 452450
Email: servicedesk@apmg.co.uk

Acknowledgements

Chief Architect and authors

Sharon Taylor (Aspect Group Inc)	Chief Architect
Gary Case (Pink Elephant)	Author
George Spalding (Pink Elephant)	Author

ITIL authoring team

The ITIL authoring team contributed to this guide through commenting on content and alignment across the set. So thanks are also due to the other ITIL authors, specifically Jeroen Bronkhorst (HP), David Cannon (HP), Ashley Hannah (HP), Majid Iqbal (Carnegie Mellon University), Shirley Lacy (ConnectSphere), Vernon Lloyd (Fox IT), Ivor Macfarlane (Guillemot Rock), Michael Nieves (Accenture), Stuart Rance (HP), Colin Rudd (ITEMS) and David Wheeldon (HP).

Mentors

Alan Nance and James Siminoski.

Further contributions

A number of people generously contributed their time and expertise to *Continual Service Improvement*. Jim Clinch, as OGC Project Manager, is grateful to the support provided by Pink Elephant; to the authoring team on the development of this publication; and to the support of Jenny Dugmore, Convenor of Working Group ISO/IEC 20000; Janine Eves, Carol Hulm, Aidan Lawes and Michiel van der Voort.

The authors would also like to thank Pierre Bernard, Anil Dissanayake, Troy DuMoulin, Isabel Feher-Watters, Bill Irvine, Shane Johnson, Glen Notman, Frances Price, Jack Probst and Marianna Ruocco of Pink Elephant; Rick Joslin of Help Desk Institute; and Bill Powell of IBM.

In order to develop ITIL v3 to reflect current best practice and produce publications of lasting value, OGC consulted widely with different stakeholders throughout the world at every stage in the process. OGC would also like to thank the following individuals and their organizations for their contributions to refreshing the ITIL guidance:

The ITIL Advisory Group

Pippa Bass, OGC; Tony Betts, Independent; Signe-Marie Hernes Bjerke, Det Norske Veritas; Alison Cartlidge, Xansa; Diane Colbeck, DIYmonde Solutions Inc; Ivor Evans, DIYmonde Solutions Inc; Karen Ferris, ProActive; Malcolm Fry, FRY-Consultants; John Gibert, Independent; Colin Hamilton, RENARD Consulting Ltd; Lex Hendriks, EXIN; Carol Hulm, British Computer Society-ISEB; Tony Jenkins, DOMAINetc; Phil Montanaro, EDS; Alan Nance, ITPreneurs; Christian Nissen, Itilligence; Don Page, Marval Group; Bill Powell, IBM; Sergio Rubinato Filho, CA; James Siminoski, SOScorp; Robert E. Stroud, CA; Jan van Bon, Inform-IT; Ken Wendle, HP; Paul Wilkinson, Getronics PinkRoccade; Takashi Yagi, Hitachi.

Reviewers

Roger Appleby, HM Revenue & Customs; Ben de Backker, Atos Origin NL; Simon J.J Bos, Bos & Cohen Strategy Advisors; Lee Cross, Computacenter Services; Alejandro Debenedet, Business IT; John Donoghue, HP; Brian Helstrom, IBM; Mike Ellis, Ministry of Social Development, New Zealand; Daniel Ernst, IBM; Joseph Forte, Forte Services Conseils Inc; William Giotto, HP; Ashley Hanna, HP; Michael Holderness, ICore Ltd; Kevin Holland, NHS Connecting for Health; Gary Holmes, ITSM Solutions Ltd; Lou Hunnebeck, CCN Inc; John Jasinski, Accenture; Albert Lau Tsz Ming, IBM; Paul Leenards, Getronics PinkRoccade; Martin Lewis, Unisys West; Colin Lovell, HP; Goran Lundqvist, LDC, Lunds University; Ian Macdonald, Barclays Bank; Ian MacLeod, HP; Steven McReynolds, Microsoft Canada; Nick Metropoulos, IBM; Karan Mishra, Deloitte Consulting LLP; Patrick Musto, STB; Karen Navoy, IBM; Peter Ober, HP; Alejandro Pestchanker, Microsoft; Valor Poland, Pultorak & Associates; Bill Powell, IBM; Ron Richard, Inherent Quality; Liesbeth Riekwel, Germeente Rotterdam, ICT Services; Sameer Sahay, Providence Health and Services; Rudolf Salinger, IBM; Frances Scarff, OGC; Elka Schrijver, Canadian Natural Resources Ltd; Arivarasu Selvaraj, Wipro Technologies Ltd; Gabriel Stefan, Independent; H P Suen, The Hong Kong Jockey Club; Wilbert Teunissen, Sogeti Nederland B.V; Leo van Selm, ProRail; David Whapples, Link Interchange Networks; Julian White, NHS Connecting for Health; Paul Wilkinson, Getronic PinkRoccade; Alan Yamamoto, IBM; Frank Zielke, Inforora GmgH.

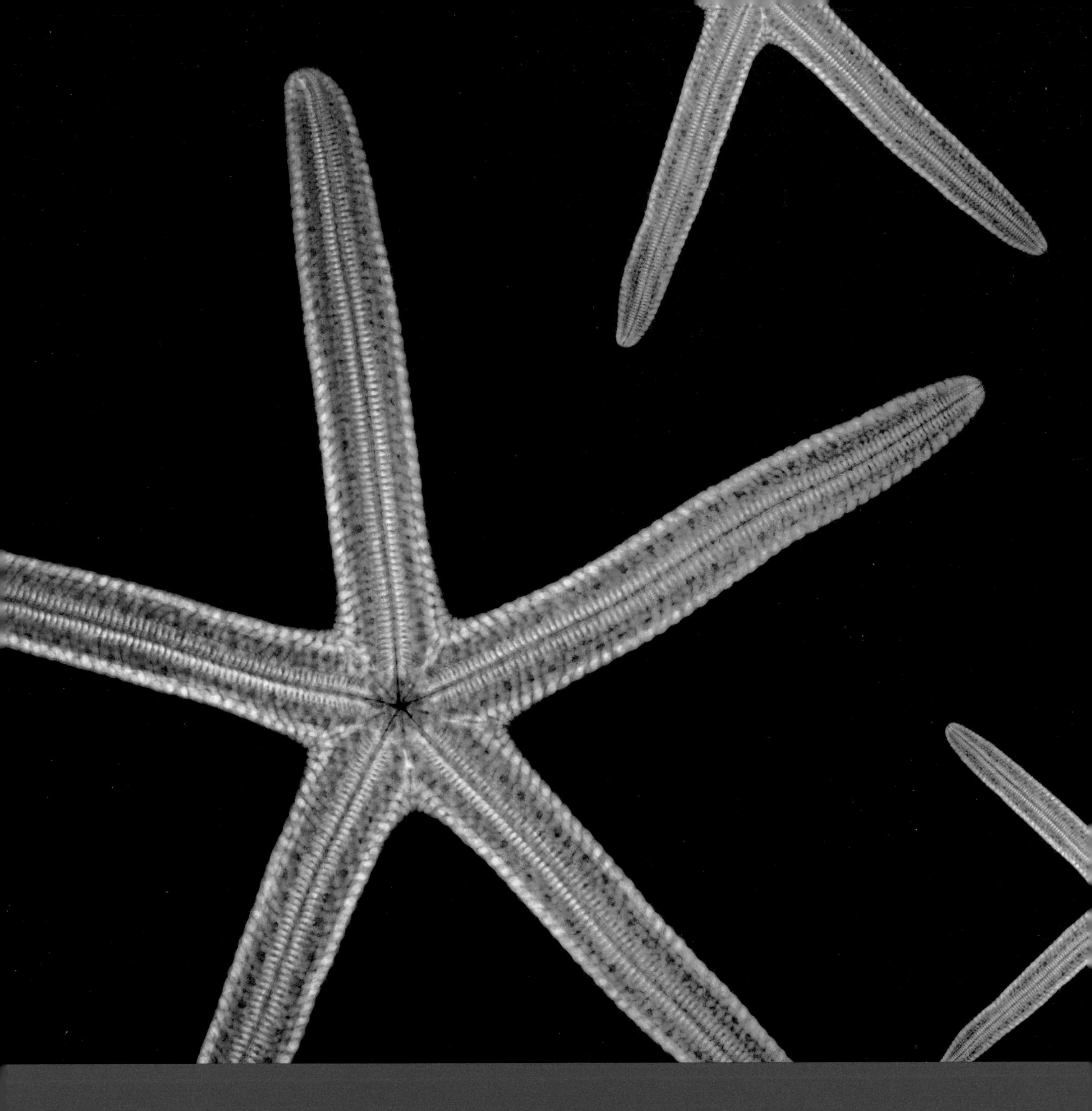

1 Introduction

1 Introduction

1.1 OVERVIEW

Continual Service Improvement (CSI) is not a new concept. Organizations have talked about it for many years but for most the concept has not moved beyond the discussion stage. For many organizations, CSI becomes a project when something has failed and severely impacted the business. When the issue is resolved the concept is promptly forgotten until the next major failure occurs.

Once an organization has gone through the process of identifying what its services are, as well as developing and implementing the IT service management (ITSM) processes to enable those services, many believe that the hard work is done. How wrong they are! The real work is only just beginning. How do organizations gain adoption of using the new processes? How do organizations measure, report and use the data to improve not only the new processes but to continually improve the services being provided? This requires a conscious decision that CSI will be adopted with clearly defined goals, documented procedures, inputs, outputs and identified roles and responsibilities. To be successful CSI must be embedded within each organization's culture.

A distinction must be made upfront regarding tools. Throughout this publication the word 'tool' applies to software tools such as integrated service management tools, monitoring tools, discovery tools, software repository and distribution tools and the like. When the authors talk about ways of doing things this will be referred to as 'methods and techniques', although these could be automated as well.

1.2 CONTEXT

1.2.1 Service management

'Information technology' is a commonly used term that changes meaning with context. From the first perspective, IT systems, applications and infrastructure are components or sub-assemblies of a larger product. They enable or are embedded in processes and services.

From the second perspective, IT is an organization with its own set of capabilities and resources. IT organizations can be of various types such as business functions, shared services units and enterprise-level core units.

From the third perspective, IT is a category of services utilized by business. They are typically IT applications and infrastructure that are packaged and offered as services by internal IT organizations or external service providers. IT costs are treated as business expenses.

From the fourth perspective, IT is a category of business assets that provide a stream of benefits for their owners, including but not limited to revenue, income and profit. IT costs are treated as investments.

1.2.2 Good practice in the public domain

Organizations operate in dynamic environments with the need to learn and adapt. There is a need to improve performance while managing trade-offs. Under similar pressure, customers seek advantage from service providers. They pursue sourcing strategies that best serve their own business interest. In many countries, government agencies and non-profit organizations have a similar propensity to outsource for the sake of operational effectiveness. This puts additional pressure on service providers to maintain a competitive advantage with respect to the alternatives that customers may have. The increase in outsourcing has particularly exposed internal service providers to unusual competition.

To cope with the pressure, organizations benchmark themselves against peers and seek to close gaps in capabilities. One way to the close such gaps is the adoption of good practices in wide industry use. There are several sources for good practices including public frameworks, standards and the proprietary knowledge of organizations and individuals (Figure 1.1).

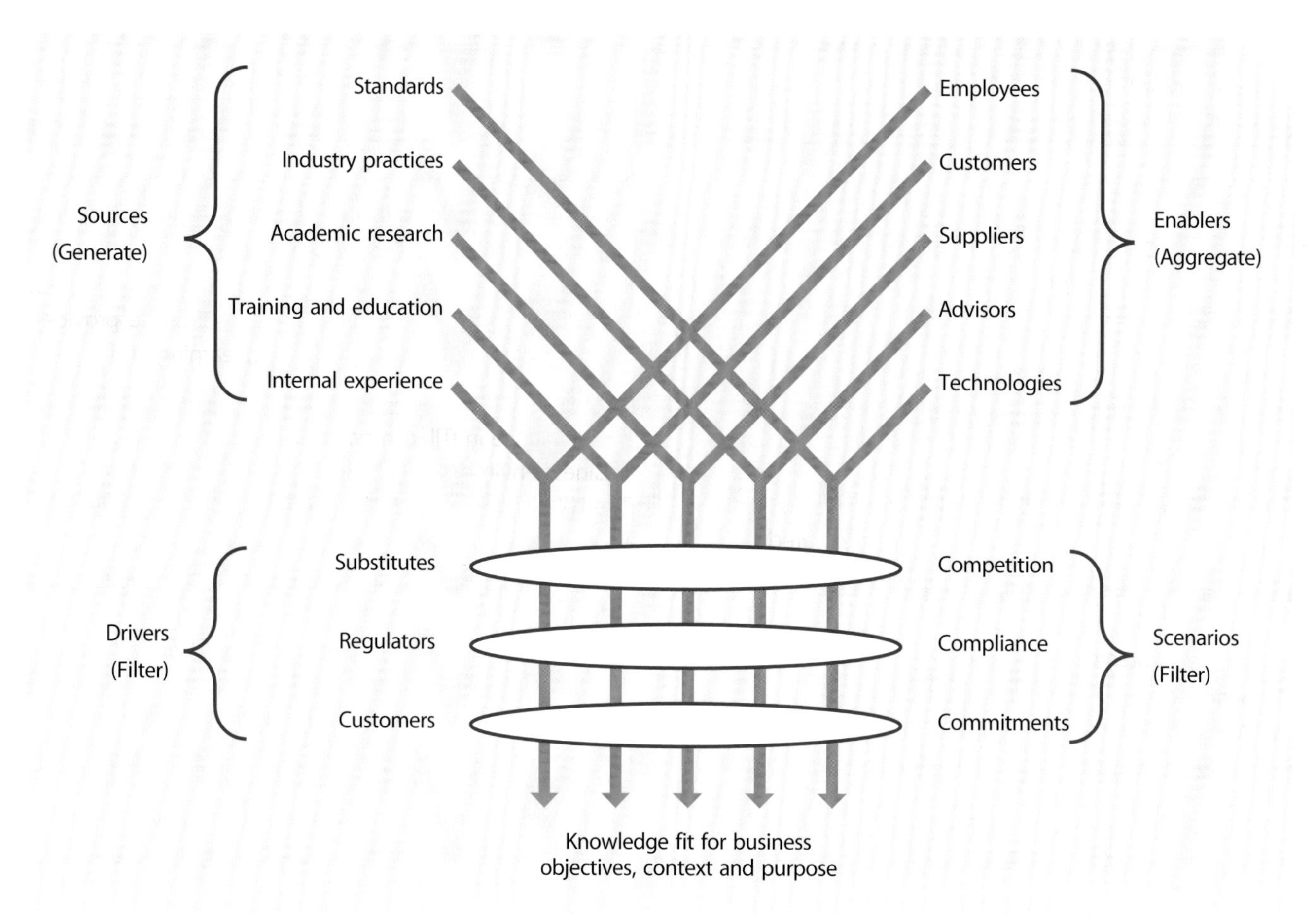

Figure 1.1 Sourcing of service management practice

Public frameworks and standards are attractive when compared with proprietary knowledge:

- Proprietary knowledge is deeply embedded in organizations and therefore difficult to adopt, replicate, or transfer even with the cooperation of the owners. Such knowledge is often in the form of tacit knowledge which is inextricable and poorly documented.
- Proprietary knowledge is customized for the local context and specific business needs to the point of being idiosyncratic. Unless the recipients of such knowledge have matching circumstances, the knowledge may not be as effective in use.
- Owners of proprietary knowledge expect to be rewarded for their long-term investments. They may make such knowledge available only under commercial terms through purchases and licensing agreements.
- Publicly available frameworks and standards such as ITIL, COBIT, CMMI, eSCM-SP, PRINCE2, ISO 9000, ISO/IEC 20000 and ISO/IEC 27001 are validated across a diverse set of environments and situations rather than the limited experience of a single organization. They are subject to broad review across multiple organizations and disciplines. They are vetted by diverse sets of partners, suppliers and competitors.
- The knowledge of public frameworks is more likely to be widely distributed among a large community of professionals through publicly available training and certification. It is easier for organizations to acquire such knowledge through the labour market.

Ignoring public frameworks and standards can needlessly place an organization at a disadvantage. Organizations should cultivate their own proprietary knowledge on top of a body of knowledge based on public frameworks and standards. Collaboration and coordination across organizations are easier on the basis of shared practices and standards.

1.2.3 ITIL and good practice in service management

The context of this publication is the ITIL framework as a source of good practice in service management. ITIL is used by organizations worldwide to establish and improve capabilities in service management. ISO/IEC 20000 provides a formal and universal standard for organizations seeking to have their service management capabilities audited and certified. While ISO/IEC 20000 is a standard to be achieved and maintained, ITIL offers a body of knowledge useful for achieving the standard.

ITIL has the following components:

- The **ITIL Core** – Best practice guidance applicable to all types of organizations who provide services to a business.
- The **ITIL Complementary Guidance** – A complementary set of publications with guidance specific to industry sectors, organization types, operating models and technology architectures.

The ITIL Core consists of five publications (Fig 1.2). Each provides the guidance necessary for an integrated approach as required by the ISO/IEC 20000 standard specification:

- *Service Strategy*
- *Service Design*
- *Service Transition*
- *Service Operation*
- *Continual Service Improvement.*

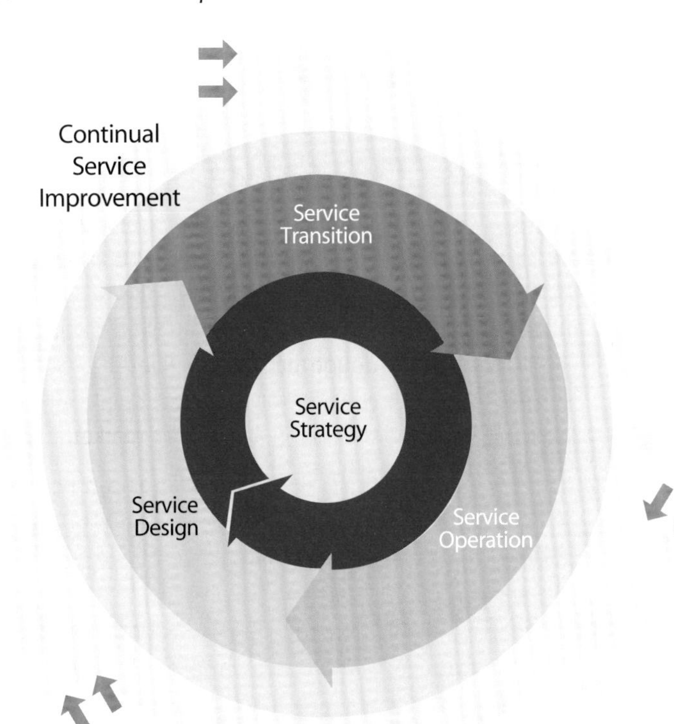

Figure 1.2 ITIL Core

Each publication addresses capabilities having direct impact on a service provider's performance. The structure of the core is in the form of a lifecycle. It is iterative and multidimensional. It ensures organizations are set up to leverage capabilities in one area for learning and improvements in others. The ITIL Core is expected to provide structure, stability and strength to service management capabilities with durable principles, methods and tools. This serves to protect investments and provide the necessary basis for measurement, learning and improvement.

The guidance in ITIL can be adapted for use in various business environments and organizational strategies. The ITIL Complementary Guidance provides flexibility to implement the Core in a diverse range of environments. Practitioners can select Complementary Guidance as needed to provide traction for the Core in a given business context, much like tyres are selected based on the type of automobile, purpose and road conditions. This is to increase the durability and portability of knowledge assets and to protect investments in service management capabilities.

Service Strategy

The Service Strategy volume provides guidance on how to design, develop and implement service management not only as an organizational capability but as a strategic asset. Guidance is provided on the principles underpinning the practice of service management which are useful for developing service management policies, guidelines and processes across the ITIL service lifecycle. Service Strategy guidance is useful in the context of Service Design, Service Transition, Service Operation and Continual Service Improvement. Topics covered in Service Strategy include the development of markets, internal and external, service assets, service catalogue and implementation of strategy through the service lifecycle. Financial Management, service portfolio management, organizational development and strategic risks are among other major topics.

Organizations use the guidance to set objectives and expectations of performance towards serving customers and market spaces, and to identify, select and prioritize opportunities. Service Strategy is about ensuring that organizations are in position to handle the costs and risks associated with their service portfolios, and are set up not just for operational effectiveness but for distinctive performance. Decisions made with respect to Service Strategy have far-reaching consequences including those with delayed effect.

Organizations already practising ITIL use this volume to guide a strategic review of their ITIL-based service management capabilities and to improve the alignment between those capabilities and their business strategies. This volume of ITIL encourages readers to stop and think about why something is to be done before thinking of how. Answers to the first type of questions are closer to the customer's business. Service Strategy expands the scope of the ITIL framework beyond the traditional audience of IT service management professionals.

Service Design

The Service Design volume provides guidance for the design and development of services and service management processes. It covers design principles and methods for converting strategic objectives into portfolios of services and service assets. The scope of Service Design is not limited to new services. It includes the changes and improvements necessary to increase or maintain value to customers over the lifecycle of services, the continuity of services, achievement of service levels and conformance to standards and regulations. It guides organizations on how to develop design capabilities for service management.

Service Transition

The Service Transition volume provides guidance for the development and improvement of capabilities for transitioning new and changed services into operations. This publication provides guidance on how the requirements of Service Strategy encoded in Service Design are effectively realized in Service Operation while controlling the risks of failure and disruption. The publication combines practices in release management, programme management and risk management and places them in the practical context of service management. It provides guidance on managing the complexity related to changes to services and service management processes; preventing undesired consequences while allowing for innovation. Guidance is provided on transferring the control of services between customers and service providers.

Service Operation

The volume embodies practices in the management of Service Operation. It includes guidance on achieving effectiveness and efficiency in the delivery and support of services so as to ensure value for the customer and the service provider. Strategic objectives are ultimately realized through Service Operation, therefore making it a critical capability. Guidance is provided on how to maintain stability in Service Operation, allowing for changes in design, scale, scope and service levels. Organizations are provided with detailed process guidelines, methods and tools for use in two major control perspectives: reactive and proactive. Managers and practitioners are provided with knowledge allowing them to make better decisions in areas such as managing the availability of services, controlling demand, optimizing capacity utilization, scheduling of operations and fixing problems. Guidance is provided on supporting operations through new models and architectures such as shared services, utility computing, web services and mobile commerce.

Continual Service Improvement

This volume provides instrumental guidance in creating and maintaining value for customers through better design, introduction and operation of services. It combines principles, practices and methods from quality management, Change Management and capability improvement. Organizations learn to realize incremental and large-scale improvements in service quality, operational efficiency and business continuity. Guidance is provided for linking improvement efforts and outcomes with service strategy, design and transition. A closed-loop feedback system, based on the Plan-Do-Check-Act (PDCA) model specified in ISO/IEC 20000, is established and capable of receiving inputs for change from any planning perspective.

1.3 PURPOSE

1.3.1 Goal of this publication

This publication aims to provide practical guidance in evaluating and improving the quality of services, overall maturity of the ITSM service lifecycle and its underlying processes, at three levels within the organization:

- The overall health of ITSM as a discipline
- The continual alignment of the portfolio of IT services with the current and future business needs
- The maturity of the enabling IT processes required to support business processes in a continual service lifecycle model.

1.3.2 Scope of this publication

This publication focuses on CSI from both an IT service and an ITSM process perspective as part of an ongoing service management lifecycle. This publication also features the key inputs, outputs, activities and roles that are critical to successful CSI. It is one of a series of five core publications published by the Office of Government Commerce (OGC) as part of the ITIL Practices for Service Management. Although this publication can be applied in isolation, it is recommended that it be used in conjunction with the other four publications.

This volume covers the following major activities:

- Introduce the concepts of CSI at a high level
- Define the value of CSI
- Describe common methods and techniques for CSI
- Define how to use the common methods and techniques for service improvement.

1.3.3 Target audience

While this publication is relevant to any IT professional involved in the management of services throughout their lifecycle, it is particularly relevant to anyone who wants to review the current ITSM practices within an organization to identify, understand and measure their strengths and weaknesses. Roles such as process owner, process managers, service managers, service owners, business liaison managers, IT managers and anyone accountable and responsible for the delivery of IT services to the business will find it particularly pertinent.

There are several ways of delivering IT services to the business, such as in-house, outsourced and partnership (co-sourced). Even though this publication is written mainly from an in-house service provider perspective it is also relevant to all other methods of service provision. Those involved in outsourced service provision or working in partnerships will find that this publication is applicable to them as well. In some ways, the outsourced or co-sourced services require an increased focus on process integration between the client organization and service provider. Business managers as well as IT managers will find this publication helpful in understanding and establishing best practices for CSI.

1.4 USAGE

Whether an organization is looking for incremental improvements or a major overhaul, CSI activities should be woven into the fabric of the everyday life of IT services. CSI is not an emergency project kicked off when someone in authority yells that the service stinks, but rather, it is an ongoing way of life; continually reviewing, analysing and improving not only service management processes but the services themselves.

While analysing ways to improve services other opportunities the reader will learn techniques to improve their lifecycle practices of Service Strategy, Service Design and Service Transition as well as the day-to-day Service Operation more commonly associated with service improvement. The ITIL Practices for Service Management five core publications represent the entire service lifecycle and have intricate interrelationships. For example, if a Service Design is less than optimal, it makes it harder to transition that service into production and results in service issues in the Service Operation part of the lifecycle. These intricacies need to be addressed as part of CSI.

With CSI, it is important to remember the currently agreed service levels and perception customers have of the current services. CSI cannot be IT centric. Best practice is to be business oriented and customer centric while at the same time staying within the limits of the feasible.

There are many methods and techniques that can be used to improve service management processes and services in general. Don't rely upon only one but explore a number of them in an effort to provide the most effective and efficient results.

CSI needs to be treated just like any other service practice. There needs to be upfront planning, training and awareness, ongoing scheduling, roles created, ownership assigned and activities identified in order to be successful.

2 Service management as a practice

2 Service management as a practice

2.1 WHAT IS SERVICE MANAGEMENT?

Service management is a set of specialized organizational capabilities for providing value to customers in the form of services. The capabilities take the form of functions and processes for managing services over a lifecycle, with specializations in strategy, design, transition, operation and continual improvement. The capabilities represent a service organization's capacity, competency and confidence for action. The act of transforming resources into valuable services is at the core of service management. Without these capabilities, a service organization is merely a bundle of resources that by itself has relatively low intrinsic value for customers.

Definition of service management

Service management is a set of specialized organizational capabilities for providing value to customers in the form of services.

Organizational capabilities are shaped by the challenges they are expected to overcome.[1] Service management capabilities are similarly influenced by the following challenges that distinguish services from other systems of value-creation such as manufacturing, mining and agriculture:

- Intangible nature of the output and intermediate products of service processes – difficult to measure, control and validate (or prove).
- Demand is tightly coupled with customer's assets – users and other customer assets such as processes, applications, documents and transactions arrive with demand and stimulate service production.
- High level of contact for *producers* and *consumers* of services – little or no buffer between the customer, the front office and back office.
- The perishable nature of service output and service capacity – there is value for the customer from assurance on continued the supply of consistent quality. Providers need to secure a steady supply of demand from customers.

1 An example of this is how in the 1950s Toyota developed unique capabilities to overcome the challenge of smaller scale and financial capital compared to its American rivals. Toyota developed new capabilities in production engineering, operations management and managing suppliers to compensate for its inability to afford large inventories, make components, produce raw materials or own the companies that produced them (Magretta, Joan, 2002. What Management Is: How it works and why it's everyone's business. The Free Press.)

Service management, however, is more than just a set of capabilities. It is also a professional practice supported by an extensive body of knowledge, experience and skills. A global community of individuals and organizations in the public and private sectors fosters its growth and maturity. Formal schemes exist for the education, training and certification of practising organizations, and individuals influence its quality. Industry best practices, academic research and formal standards contribute to its intellectual capital and draw from it.

The origins of service management are in traditional service businesses such as airlines, banks, hotels and phone companies. Its practice has grown with the adoption by IT organizations of a service-oriented approach to managing IT applications, infrastructure and processes. Solutions to business problems and support for business models, strategies and operations are increasingly in the form of services. The popularity of shared services and outsourcing has contributed to the increase in the number of organizations who are service providers, including internal organizational units. This in turn has strengthened the practice of service management and at the same time imposing greater challenges upon it.

2.2 WHAT ARE SERVICES?

2.2.1 The value proposition

Definition of a service

A service is a means of delivering value to customers by facilitating outcomes customers want to achieve without the ownership of specific costs and risks.

Services are a means of delivering value to customers by facilitating outcomes customers want to achieve without the ownership of specific costs and risks. Services facilitate outcomes by enhancing the performance of associated tasks and reducing the effect of constraints. The result is an increase in the probability of desired outcomes (see Figure 2.1).

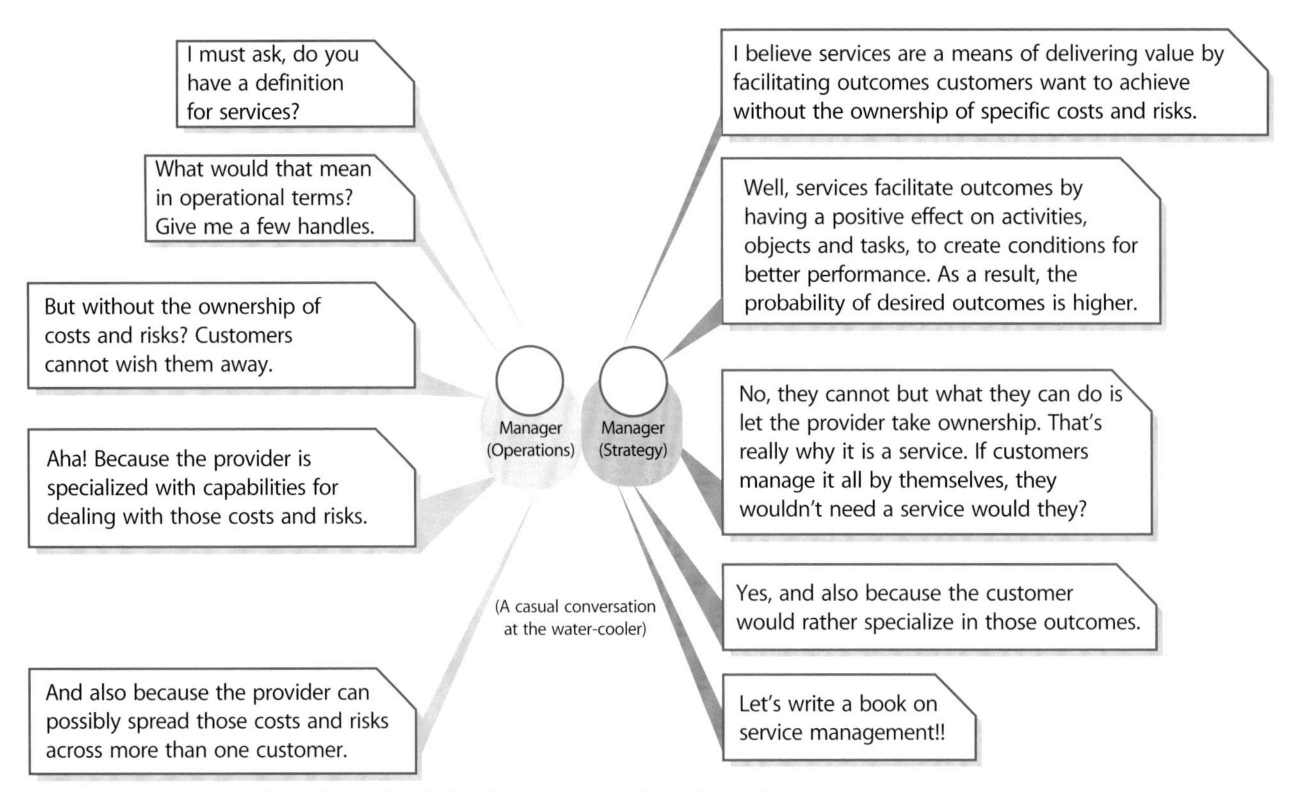

Figure 2.1 A conversation about the definition and meaning of services

2.3 FUNCTIONS AND PROCESSES ACROSS THE LIFECYCLE

2.3.1 Functions

Functions are units of organizations specialized to perform a certain type of work and responsible for specific outcomes. They are self-contained with capabilities and resources necessary for their performance and outcomes. Capabilities include work methods internal to the functions. Functions have their own body of knowledge, which accumulates from experience. They provide structure and stability to organizations.

Functions are means to structure organizations to implement the specialization principle. Functions typically define roles and the associated authority and responsibility for a specific performance and outcomes. Coordination between functions through shared processes is a common pattern in organization design. Functions tend to optimize their work methods locally to focus on assigned outcomes. Poor coordination between functions combined with an inward focus leads to functional silos that hinder alignment and feedback critical to the success of the organization as a whole. Process models help avoid this problem with functional hierarchies by improving cross-functional coordination and control. Well-defined processes can improve productivity within and across functions.

2.3.2 Processes

Processes are examples of closed-loop systems because they provide change and transformation towards a goal, and utilize feedback for self-reinforcing and self-corrective action (Figure 2.2). It is important to consider the entire process or how one process fits into another.

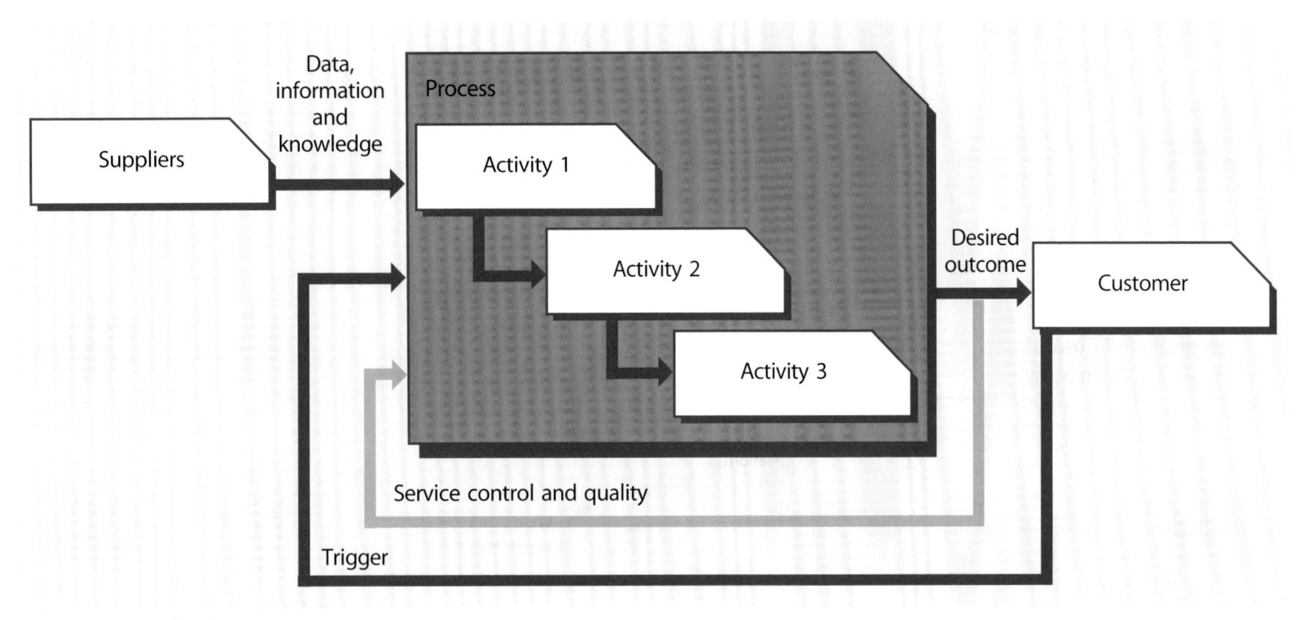

Figure 2.2 A basic process

Process definitions describe actions, dependencies and sequence. Processes have the following characteristics:

- **Measurable** – We are able to measure the process in a relevant manner. It is performance driven. Managers want to measure cost, quality and other variables while practitioners are concerned with duration and productivity.
- **Specific results** – The reason a process exists is to deliver a specific result. This result must be individually identifiable and countable. While we can count changes, it is impossible to count how many Service Desks were completed.
- **Customers** – Every process delivers its primary results to a customer or stakeholder. They may be internal or external to the organization but the process must meet their expectations.
- **Responds to a specific event** – While a process may be ongoing or iterative it should be traceable to a specific trigger.

Functions are often mistaken for processes. For example, there are misconceptions about Capacity Management being a service management process. First, Capacity Management is an organizational capability with specialized processes and work methods. Whether or not it is a function or a process depends entirely on organization design. It is a mistake to assume that Capacity Management can only be a process. It is possible to measure and control capacity and to determine whether it is adequate for a given purpose. Assuming that it is always a process with discrete countable outcomes can be an error.

2.3.3 Specialization and coordination across the lifecycle

Specialization and coordination are necessary in the lifecycle approach. Feedback and control between the functions and processes within and across the elements of the lifecycle make this possible. The dominant pattern in the lifecycle is the sequential progress starting from Service Strategy through Service Design, Service Transition, Service Operation and back to Service Strategy through CSI. That however is not the only pattern of action. Every element of the lifecycle provides points for feedback and control.

The combination of multiple perspectives allows greater flexibility and control across environments and situations. The lifecycle approach mimics the reality of most organizations where effective management requires the use of multiple control perspectives. Those responsible for the design, development and improvement of processes for service management can adopt a process-based control perspective. Those responsible for managing agreements, contracts and services may be better served by a lifecycle-based control perspective with distinct phases. Both these control perspectives benefit from systems thinking. Each control perspective can reveal patterns that may not be apparent from the other.

2.4 CONTINUAL SERVICE IMPROVEMENT FUNDAMENTALS

2.4.1 Purpose of CSI

The primary purpose of CSI is to continually align and re-align IT services to the changing business needs by identifying and implementing improvements to IT services that support business processes. These improvement activities support the lifecycle approach through Service Strategy, Service Design, Service Transition and Service Operation. In effect, CSI is about looking for ways to improve process effectiveness, efficiency as well as cost effectiveness.

Consider the following saying about measurements and management:

You cannot manage what you cannot control.

You cannot control what you cannot measure.

You cannot measure what you cannot define.

If ITSM processes are not implemented, managed and supported using clearly defined goals, objectives and relevant measurements that lead to actionable improvements, the business will suffer. Depending upon the criticality of a specific IT service to the business, the organization could lose productive hours, experience higher costs, loss of reputation or, perhaps, even a business failure. That is why it is critically important to understand what to measure, why it is being measured and carefully define the successful outcome.

2.4.2 CSI objectives

- Review, analyse and make recommendations on improvement opportunities in each lifecycle phase: Service Strategy, Service Design, Service Transition and Service Operation.
- Review and analyse Service Level Achievement results.
- Identify and implement individual activities to improve IT service quality and improve the efficiency and effectiveness of enabling ITSM processes.
- Improve cost effectiveness of delivering IT services without sacrificing customer satisfaction.
- Ensure applicable quality management methods are used to support continual improvement activities.

2.4.3 CSI scope

There are three main areas that CSI needs to address:

- The overall health of ITSM as a discipline
- The continual alignment of the portfolio of IT services with the current and future business needs
- The maturity of the enabling IT processes for each service in a continual service lifecycle model.

To implement CSI successfully it is important to understand the different activities that can be applied to CSI. The following activities support a continual process improvement plan:

- Reviewing management information and trends to ensure that services are meeting agreed service levels
- Reviewing management information and trends to ensure that the output of the enabling ITSM processes are achieving the desired results
- Periodically conducting maturity assessments against the process activities and roles associated with the process activities to demonstrate areas of improvement or, conversely, areas of concern
- Periodically conducting internal audits verifying employee and process compliance
- Reviewing existing deliverables for relevance
- Making ad-hoc recommendations for approval
- Conducting periodic customer satisfaction surveys
- Conducting external and internal service reviews to identify CSI opportunities.

These activities do not happen automatically. They must be owned within the IT organization which is capable of handling the responsibility and possesses the appropriate authority to make things happen. They must also be planned and scheduled on an ongoing basis. By default, 'improvement' becomes a process within IT with defined activities, inputs, outputs, roles and reporting. CSI must ensure that ITSM processes are developed and deployed in support of an end-to-end service management approach to business customers. It is essential to develop an ongoing continual improvement strategy for each of the processes as well as the services.

The deliverables of CSI must be reviewed on an ongoing basis to verify completeness, functionality and feasibility to ensure that they remain relevant and do not become stale and unusable. It is also important to ensure that monitoring of quality indicators and metrics will identify areas for process improvement.

Since any improvement initiative will more than likely necessitate changes, specific improvements will need to follow the defined ITIL Change Management process.

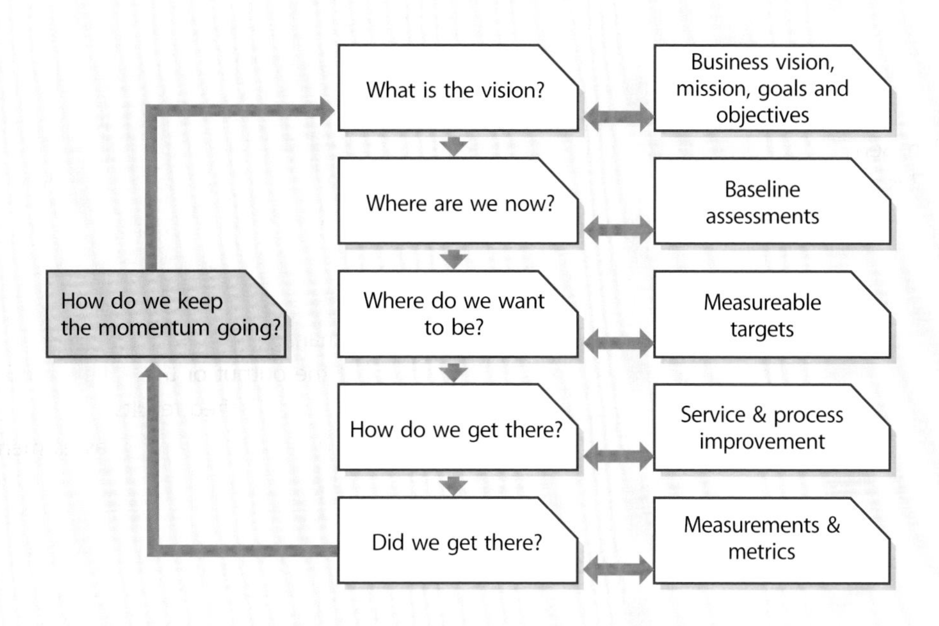

Figure 2.3 Continual Service Improvement model

2.4.4 CSI approach

As the above figure shows, there are many opportunities for CSI. The figure above also illustrates a constant cycle for improvement. The improvement process can be summarized in six steps:

- Embrace the vision by understanding the high-level business objectives. The vision should align the business and IT strategies.
- Assess the current situation to obtain an accurate, unbiased snapshot of where the organization is right now. This baseline assessment is an analysis of the current position in terms of the business, organization, people, process and technology.
- Understand and agree on the priorities for improvement based on a deeper development of the principles defined in the vision. The full vision may be years away but this step provides specific goals and a manageable timeframe.
- Detail the CSI plan to achieve higher quality service provision by implementing ITSM processes
- Verify that measurements and metrics are in place to ensure that milestones were achieved, processes compliance is high, and business objectives and priorities were met by the level of service.
- Finally, the process should ensure that the momentum for quality improvement is maintained by assuring that changes become embedded in the organization.

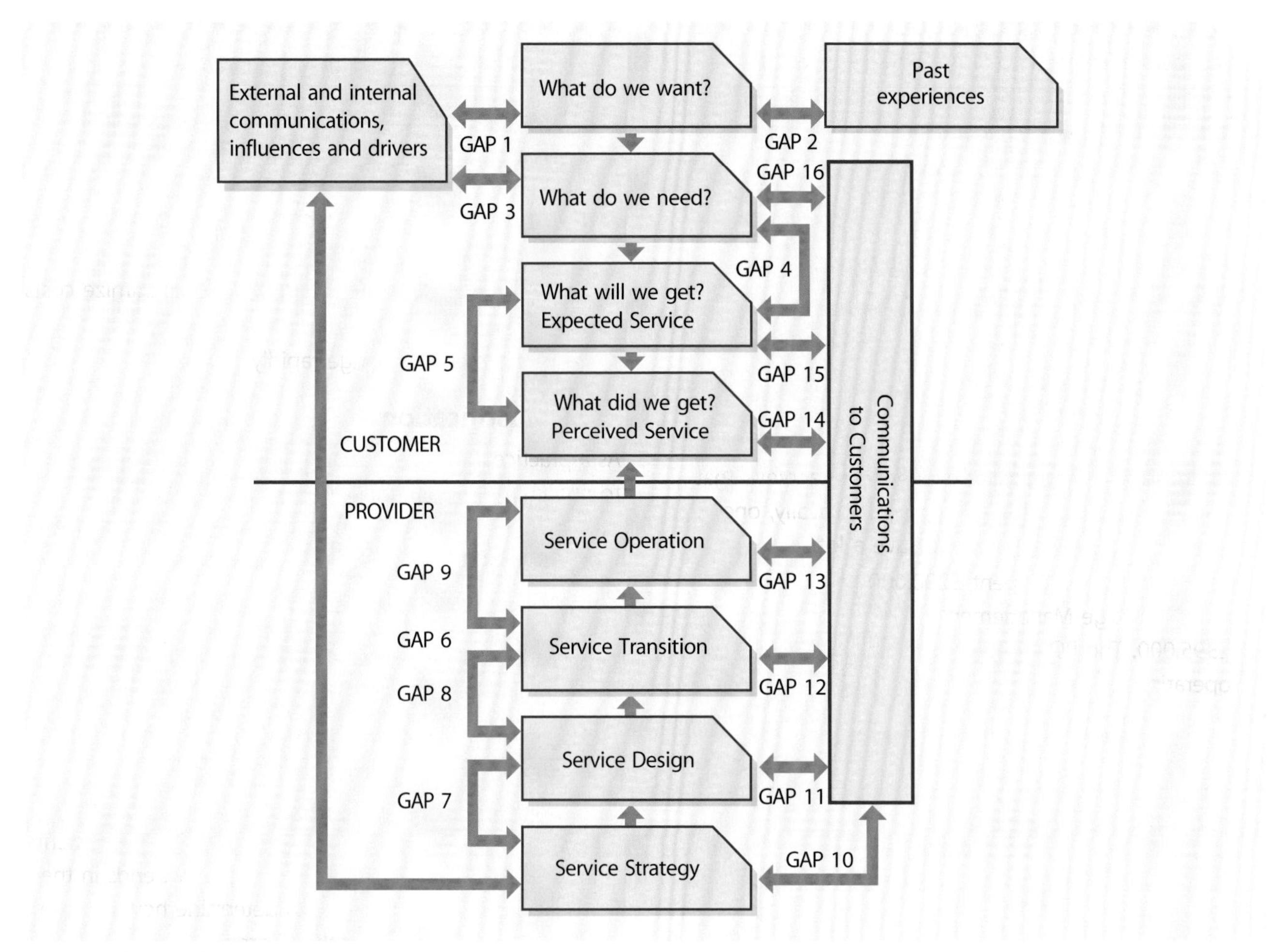

Figure 2.4 Service gap model

Service gap model

Since CSI involves ongoing change, it is important to develop an effective communication strategy to support CSI activities – ensuring people remain appropriately informed. This communication must include aspects of what the service implications are, what the impact on the personnel is and the approach or process used to reach the objective. In the absence of truth, people will fill in the gap with their own truth.

Perception will play a key role in determining the success of any CSI initiative. Proper reporting should assist in addressing the misconceptions about the improvements. It is important to understand why there are differences in perception between the customer and the service provider. Figure 2.4 identifies the most obvious potential gaps in the service lifecycle from both a business and an IT perspective:

Service Level Management has the task of ensuring that potential gaps are managed and that when there is a gap, to identify if there is a need for a Service Improvement Plan (SIP). Often a large gap exists between what the customer wants, what they actually need, and what they are willing to pay for. Add to this the fact that IT will often try to define and deliver what they 'think' the customer wants. As a result, it is not surprising that there is a perception and delivery gap between the Customer and IT.

2.4.5 Value to business

Perspectives on benefits

There are four commonly used terms when discussing service improvement outcomes:

- Improvements
- Benefits
- ROI (Return on Investment)
- VOI (Value on Investment).

Much of the angst and confusion surrounding IT process improvement initiatives can be traced to the misuse of these terms. Below is the proper use:

- **Improvements** – Outcomes that when compared to the 'before' state, show a measurable increase in a desirable metric or decrease in an undesirable metric

  Example: ABC Corp achieved a 15% reduction in failed changes through implementation of a formal Change Management process.
- **Benefits** – The gains achieved through realization of improvements, usually but not always expressed in monetary terms.

  Example: ABC Corp's 15% reduction in failed changes has saved the company £395,000 in productivity and re-works costs in the first year.
- **ROI** – The difference between the benefit (saving) achieved and the amount expended to achieve that benefit, expressed as a percentage. Logically, one would like to spend a little to save a lot.

  Example: ABC Corp spent £200,000 to establish the formal Change Management process that saved £395,000. The ROI at the end of the first year of operation was therefore £195,000 or 97.5%.
- **VOI** – The extra value created by establishment of benefits that include non-monetary or long-term outcomes. ROI is a subcomponent of VOI.

  Example: ABC Corp's establishment of a formal Change Management process (which reduced the number of failed changes) improved the ability of ABC Corp to respond quickly to changing market conditions and unexpected opportunities resulting in an enhanced market position. In addition, it promoted collaboration between business units and the IT organization and freed up resources to work on other projects that otherwise may not have been completed.

Intangible benefits

When used in Business Cases, soft benefits (intangibles) are IT investment payoff areas not expressed in monetary ways. 'Less frequent use of temporary workers makes hourly employees feel better' is intangible if no believable monetary impact is shown. Conversely, 'Less frequent use of temporary workers will save £100,000 annually in labour costs' is tangible when expressed in believable pound terms.

Traditionally, one of the most difficult Business Case problems is quantifying soft benefits such as increased brand image and customer satisfaction. When hard numbers are available to support an ROI argument, it may seem easier to leave the soft benefits out altogether. Instead, use the soft benefits to tell a story in the Business Case.

Attempt to capture value that lies beyond the reach of an ROI calculation such as:

- Increased organizational competency
- Integration between people and processes
- Reduction of redundancy increases business throughput
- Minimized lost opportunities
- Assured regulatory compliance that will minimize costs and reduce risk
- Ability to react to change rapidly.

2.4.6 Justification

As a practice, CSI must prove its worth to an organization to continue its existence. Like other practices, CSI must have a well-defined purpose within the organization with clear ongoing benefits that impact the entire organization. How CSI achieves this also needs to be easily understood, e.g. business efficiency, potential cost reduction when introducing services, increased customer satisfaction with the provision of existing services, more agility when responding to requests for new services, or more reliable IT services to support business critical services.

Organizations wishing to improve services also need to be aware of the impact of business and market developments on the IT area. Understanding these general trends in the context of the organization helps determine how ITIL can best be utilized for aligning the IT organization with ever-changing business demands.

To justify any improvement, the IT organization should compare the costs and revenue (savings). The difficulty in doing this, however, is that while the costs are relatively easy to measure (people, tools etc.) the increase in revenue as a direct result of the Service Improvement Plan (SIP) is more difficult to quantify.

Understanding the organization's target and current situation should form the basis of the Business Case for a SIP. A stakeholder assessment and a goal-setting exercise will help focus on the results and aims.

Business drivers

Businesses are becoming increasingly aware of the importance of IT as a service provider, to not only support but also enable business operations. As a result the business leaders of today ask much more pointed and direct questions regarding the quality of IT services and the competency and efficiency of their provider. This higher level of scrutiny buttresses the expanding need for CSI, meaning that:

- IT does more than enable existing business operations, IT enables business change and is, therefore, an integral component of the business change programme.
- There is additional focus on the quality of IT in terms of reliability, availability, stability, capacity, security and, especially, risk.
- IT and IT governance is an integral component in corporate governance.
- IT performance becomes even more visible – technical outages and customer dissatisfaction increasingly become boardroom issues.
- IT organizations increasingly find themselves in a position where they have to not only *realize* but *manage* business-enabling technology and services that deliver the capability and quality demanded by the business.
- IT must demonstrate value for money.
- IT within e-business is not only supporting the primary business processes, but is the core of those processes.

Technology drivers

The rapid pace of technology developments, within which IT provides solutions, becomes a core component of almost every area of business operations. As a result, IT services must:

- Understand business operations and advise about the short- and long-term opportunities (and limitations) of IT.
- Be designed for agility and nimbleness to allow for unpredictability in business needs.
- Accommodate more technological change, with a reduced cycle time, for realizing change to match a reduced window in the business cycle.
- Maintain or improve existing quality of services while adding or removing technology components.
- Ensure that quality of delivery and support matches the business use of new technology.
- Bring escalating costs under control.

2.4.7 Benefits

Benefits must be clearly identified to help justify the effort involved in gathering, analysing and acting on improvement data. Be sure to:

- Consider both direct and indirect benefits.
- Identify the benefits for each group of stakeholder at every level in the organization.
- Define the benefits in clear and measurable way.

The generic benefits described in the remainder of this section, are those that will be realized by implementing CSI within an organization.

Business/customer benefits

- Overall improved quality of business operations by ensuring that IT services underpin the business processes
- More reliable business support provided by Incident, Problem and Change Management processes
- Customers will know what to expect from IT and what is required of them to ensure this can be delivered
- Increased staff productivity because of increased reliability and availability of IT services
- IT Service Continuity procedures are increasingly focused on supporting business continuity and meeting the business needs through continued availability
- Better working relationships between customers and the IT service provider
- Enhanced customer satisfaction as service providers understand and deliver what is expected of them
- Improved quality of service and service availability, leading to improved business productivity and revenue
- Better planning for purchases, development and implementation
- Better management information regarding business processes and IT services
- Greater flexibility for the business through improved understanding of IT support
- Improved alignment between the business and IT
- Increased flexibility and adaptability will exist within the services
- Faster and improved quality of response to business needs
- Faster and better quality projects, deployments and changes (delivered on time, to cost and quality).

Financial benefits

- Cost-effective provision of IT services
- Cost-justified IT Infrastructure and services
- When implemented, CSI will have long-term financial benefits, for example:
  - Reduced costs for implementing changes
  - Reduced business impact due to IT changes
  - Services will not be over-engineered but rather they will be designed to meet the required service levels.

- Improved service reliability, stability and thus availability.
- Expenditures on IT service continuity are commensurate with the criticality of the business process they underpin
- Improved resource allocation and utilization.

Innovation benefits

- Clearer understanding of business requirements ensures that IT services successfully underpin business processes
- Better information about current services (and possibly about areas where changes would bring increased benefits)
- Greater flexibility for the business through improved understanding of IT support
- Increased flexibility and adaptability within the IT services
- Improved ability to recognize changing trends and more quickly adapt to new requirements and market developments
- Business confidence in their IT service provider allows them to have higher aspirations.

IT organization internal benefits

- Improved metrics and management reporting
- Alignment of cost structure with business needs
- Better information about current services and about where changes would bring the most benefit
- Improved communications, teamwork and interactivity (both IT and customer)
- Increased employee effectiveness – the impact on the employees can be seen through improvements in productivity, collaboration, communication (how we communicate and the meaning of what we say or do) and innovation
- Increased process effectiveness – ITIL framework investments will enable new business models or channels, real-time process management, integration flexibility, process simplification or scalability, and masking process complexity from users
- Defined roles and responsibilities
- Clearer view of current IT capability and future potential of IT services
- Process maturity benefits that are repeatable, consistent and self-improving
- CSI procedures provide more focus and confidence in the ability to provide incremental and major improvements to both services and service management processes
- Structured approach to gathering data, turning the data into information, generating knowledge of exactly what is happening within the organization and gaining wisdom on where to apply resources to improve services and make a greater impact to the business
- Improved resource utilization
- Business has greater clarity into current IT capability
- Knowledge on what tools and resources are required to support CSI activities
- Better information on current services (and possibly on where changes would bring most benefits)
- More motivated staff – improved job satisfaction through better understanding of capability and better management of expectations
- More proactive development and improvement of technology and services
- Services and systems designed to meet achievable business and operational targets and time-scales
- Better management of suppliers with improved supplier performance
- Reduced risk of failure in meeting commitments
- Improved working relationship with business.

2.4.8 Cost

A Service Improvement Plan (SIP), just like any other major plan, will have costs associated with executing its activities:

- Staff resources trained in the right skill sets to support ITSM processes
- Tools for monitoring, gathering, processing, analysing and presenting data
- Ongoing internal/external assessments or benchmarking studies
- Service improvements either to services or service management process
- Management time to review, recommend and monitor CSI progress
- Communication and awareness campaigns to change behaviours and ultimately culture
- Training and development on CSI activities.

Continual improvement benefits measurement

Once an improvement initiative is completed, that's not the end of the story. Benefits, ROI and VOI will be subject to change over time as processes become increasingly mature, or unravel due to neglect. Any continual process improvement programme should include periodic re-evaluation of benefits. KPIs may change as business drivers change, a new technology may revolutionize storage capacities, or a new web protocol creates entirely new business opportunities. In nearly every major improvement initiative the ROI and, perhaps, the VOI are intensely scrutinized and hotly debated in the steps leading up to project approval ... and then promptly forgotten and stuck in a drawer never to be seen or heard from again. If IT is serious and honest about the benefits of improvements beforehand then it is essential that IT quantify those benefits and report on them after the fact.

Benefits measurement considerations in this context may include:

- Checking year-by-year benefits/ROI/VOI realized by specific improvements
- Estimating benefits likely from competing initiatives arising out of the IT SIP, to identify the best-value investment, priorities and schedule of resources
- Analysing the impact on current benefits being estimated or realized, by a proposed organizational change either in the business or within the IT organization
- Analysing the impact on current benefits being estimated or realized, by a change in business strategic direction or regulatory legislation.

It is generally accepted that ITIL is the missing piece of the puzzle that enables better quality of service delivery. It facilitates saving money and time, and adds value to the organization. ITIL also spans the business and technology gap to create synergy with proven results.

Organizations adopt the ITIL framework because they want to establish a consistent, comprehensive service management foundation and better manage the cost of service delivery. ITIL emphasizes the importance of providing IT services to satisfy business needs in a cost effective manner. The most tangible benefit to organizations using ITIL is a marked improvement in resource utilization, eliminating redundant effort, decreasing errors and the amount of work that has to be redone, and increasing scalability with current resource levels. In addition, the ITIL framework helps improve the availability, reliability, stability and security of mission-critical IT services by providing demonstrable performance

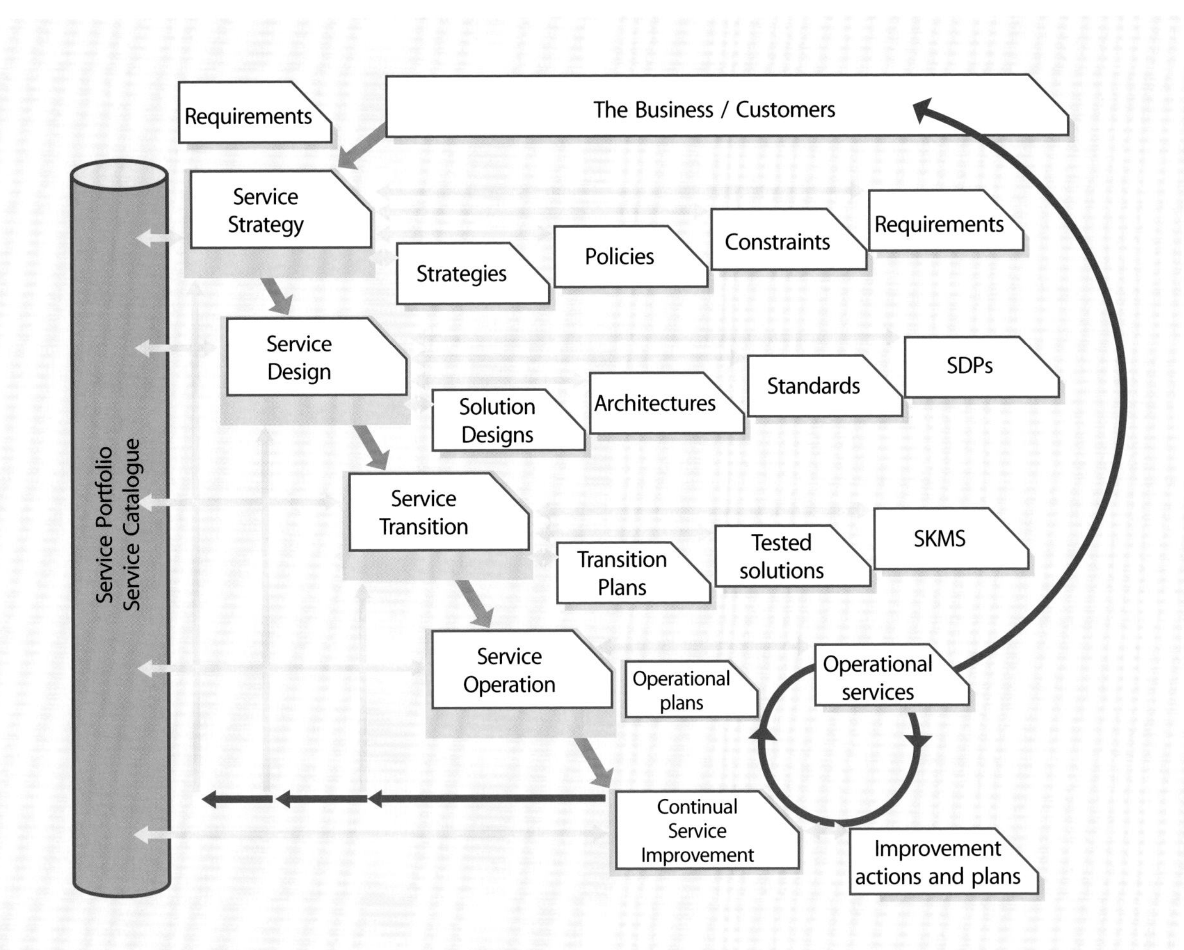

Figure 2.5 Service portfolio spine

indicators to measure and justify the cost of service quality. The provision of KPIs is essential to supporting CSI. These KPIs become the data inputs to analyse and identify improvement opportunities.

2.4.9 Interfaces to other service lifecycle practices

For CSI to be successful, it is important to provide improvement opportunities throughout the entire service lifecycle. If for example, CSI focuses only on the Service Operation phase of the lifecycle it will have limited success. This is like treating a symptom of a problem instead of treating the problem itself. Often the problem may actually start in the Service Strategy or Service Design stages of the service lifecycle. That is why implementing a service improvement process needs to take a wider view. There is much greater value to the business when service improvement takes a holistic approach throughout the entire lifecycle.

The connection point between each of the core volumes is the service portfolio. It is the 'spine' which connects the lifecycle stages to each other.

The remainder of this section covers the relationships between each of the publications and CSI.

Service Strategy

Service Strategy focuses on setting a strategic approach to service management as well as defining standards and policies that will be used to design IT services. It is at this phase of the lifecycle that standards and policies are determined around measuring and reporting for an enterprise-wide view of the organization, possibly utilizing a tool such as Kaplan and Norton's Balanced Scorecard.

Service improvement opportunities could be driven by external factors such as new security or regulatory requirements, new strategies due to mergers or acquisitions, changes in technology infrastructure or even new business services to be introduced. Feedback from the other core phases of the service lifecycle will also be important.

Service Design

Service Design is tasked with the creation or modification of services and infrastructure architecture that are aligned to the business needs. Design elements ensure that a customer-centric viewpoint is used in creating the capability, process specification and planning, and acceptance of service management practices. Service Design takes the strategy described in the first phase and transforms it through the design phase into deliverable IT services. Service Design is responsible for designing a management information framework that defines the need for critical success factors (CSF), key performance indicators (KPI), and activity metrics for both the services and the ITSM processes

New strategies, architecture, policies and business requirements will drive the need for continual improvement within Service Design.

Service Transition

Service Transition manages the transition of new or changed services into the production environment. Change and Configuration Management play major roles at this point in the lifecycle. This phase focuses on the best practices of creating support models, a knowledge base, workflow management, and developing communication and marketing for use in the transitioning of services to production. As new strategies and designs are introduced this provides an excellent opportunity for continual improvement. Service Transition is also responsible for defining the actual CSFs, KPIs and activity metrics, creating the reports and implementing the required automation to monitor and report on the services and ITSM processes.

Service Operation

Service Operation provides best practice advice and guidance on all aspects of managing the day-to-day operation of an organization's IT services. Service Operation is responsible for the monitoring and initial reporting related to the people, processes and infrastructure technology necessary to ensure a high-quality, cost-effective provision of IT services which meet the business needs. Every technology component and process activity should have defined inputs and outputs that can be monitored. The results of the monitoring can then be compared against the norms, targets or established Service Level Agreements. When there is a discrepancy between what was actually delivered and what was expected this becomes a service improvement opportunity. Within the Service Operation phase of the lifecycle, internal reviews would be performed to determine the results, what led to these results, and if necessary recommendations for some level of fine tuning. The integration of service improvement within the service lifecycle is represented in Figure 2.6. This is an approach that provides for Continual Service Improvement activities to be in place within each of the other core disciplines of the service lifecycle.

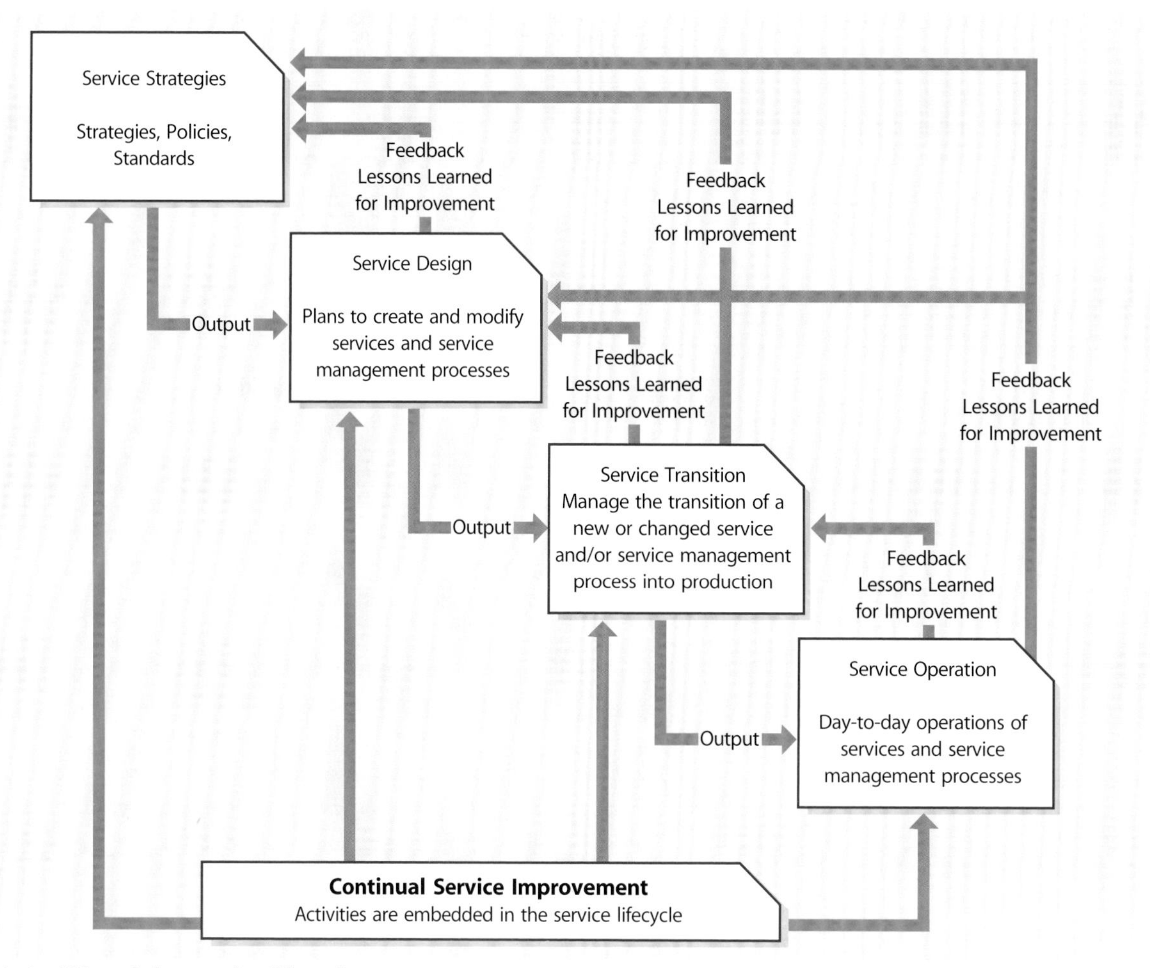

Figure 2.6 CSI and the service lifecycle

CSI throughout the lifecycle

An organization can find improvement opportunities throughout the entire service lifecycle. Figure 2.6 shows the interaction that should take place between each lifecycle phase. An IT organization does need to wait until a service or service management process is transitioned into the operations area to begin identifying improvement opportunities.

Each lifecycle phase will provide an output to the next lifecycle phase. This same concept applies to CSI.

As an example a new service is designed or modified and passed onto Service Transition. Service Transition can provide feedback to Service Design on any design issues or everything is looking good before the service moves into Service Operation. CSI does not have to wait for the service to be implemented and in operations before any improvement opportunities are identified and communicated. These CSI steps throughout the lifecycle should not be viewed as placing blame or pointing fingers, but as a learning tool on improvement.

To be effective, CSI requires open and honest feedback from IT staff. Debriefings, or activity reviews, work well for capturing information about lessons learned such as 'did we meet the timelines?' and 'did we provide quality?' Segmenting the debriefing or review into smaller, individual activities completed within each phase of the service lifecycle and capturing the lessons learned within that phase makes the plethora of data more manageable. Collecting this information is a positive beginning toward facilitating future improvements (see Figure 2.7).

CSI will make extensive use of methods and practices found in many ITIL processes such as Problem Management, Availability Management and Capacity Management used throughout the lifecycle of a service. The use of the outputs, in the form of flows, matrices, statistics or analysis reports, will provide valuable insight into the design and operation of services. This information,

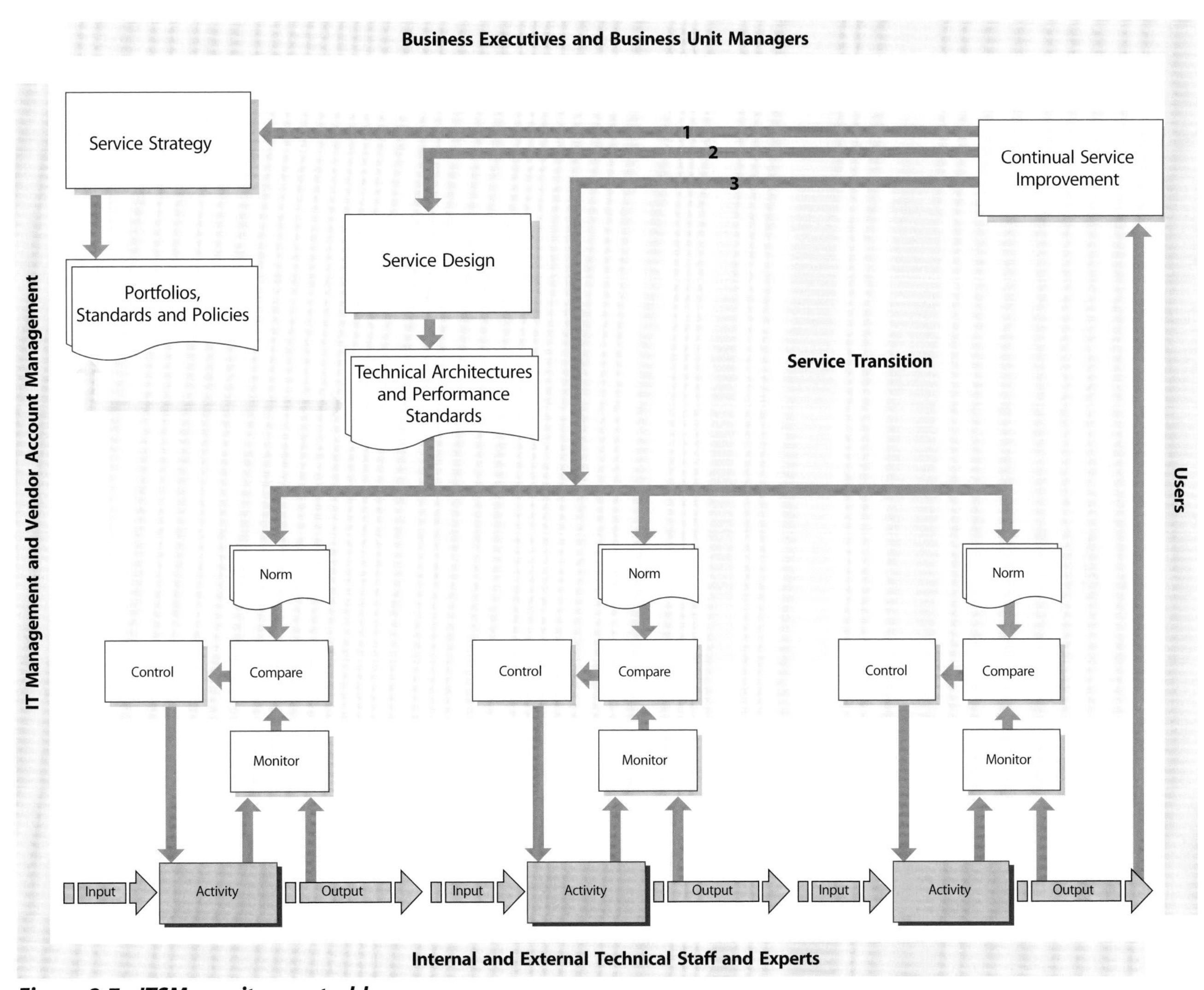

Figure 2.7 ITSM monitor control loop

combined with new business requirements, technology specifications, IT capabilities, budgets, trends and possibly external legislative and regulatory requirements will be vital to CSI to determine what needs to be improved, prioritize it and suggest improvements, if required.

It will be important to sift through large amounts of raw data before synthesizing the right information. This information must then be analysed and studied, but against what? This is where the different layers of management come in – strategic, tactical and operational – each with their own goals, objectives, CSFs and KPIs, all of which must be aligned and supportive of each other but, more importantly, aligned with the goals and objectives of the business. The ability to derive any meaningful information from the data collected depends not only on the maturity of the processes but also on the level of maturity of the services provided by IT.

Open and honest feedback is also needed from the staff responsible for hand-offs between the service lifecycles. Understanding the lessons learned, 'What went well?' and 'What could have been improved?' can influence future improvements in each stage of the lifecycle. Feedback from Service Operation to Service Transition and Service Transition to Service Design, and then from Service Design to Service Strategy is an effective way to integrate a holistic approach to CSI.

CSI on its own will not be able to achieve the desired results. It is therefore essential to leverage CSI activities and initiatives at each phase of the service lifecycle. Figure 2.8 illustrates the increased value to the organization when the sphere of influence of CSI is expanded to include each phase of the service lifecycle.

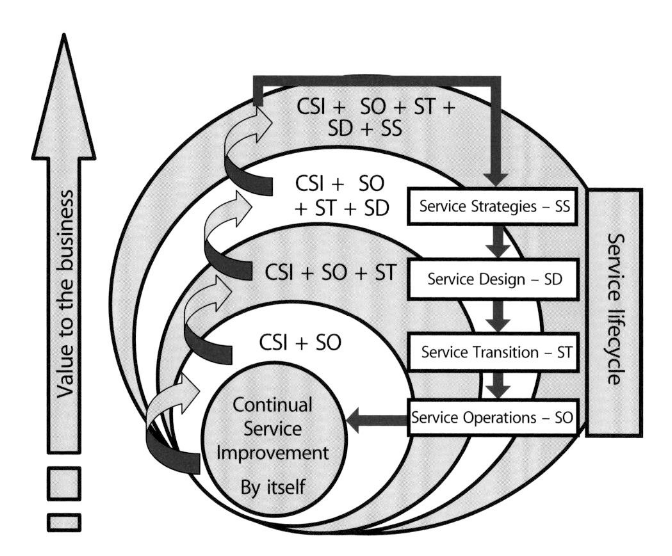

Figure 2.8 Bernard-Doppler service improvement levels of opportunity

At this point you may have concluded that all aspects of CSI must be in place before measurements and data gathering can begin. Nothing could be further from the truth. Measure now, gather data now, analyse now, begin reviews of lessons learned now, make incremental improvements now. Don't wait! Start improving now!

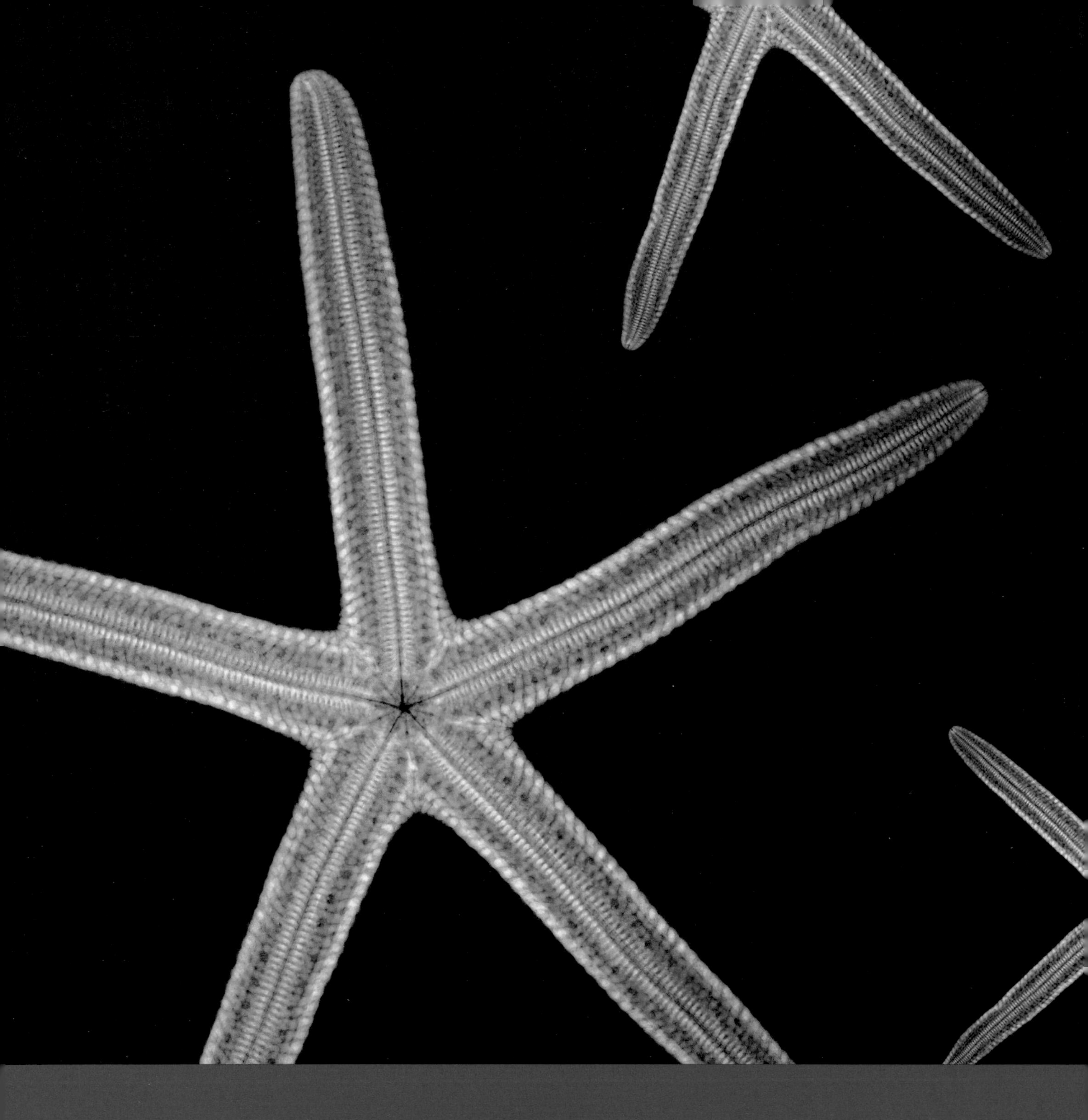

3 Continual Service Improvement principles

3 Continual Service Improvement principles

Service improvement must focus on increasing the efficiency, maximizing the effectiveness and optimizing the cost of services and the underlying ITSM processes. The only way to do this is to ensure that improvement opportunities are identified throughout the entire service lifecycle.

3.1 CSI AND ORGANIZATIONAL CHANGE

Improving service management is to embark upon an organizational change programme. Many organizational change programmes fail to achieve the desired results. Successful ITSM requires understanding the way in which work is done and putting in place a programme of change within the IT organization. This type of change is, by its very nature, prone to difficulties. It involves people and the way they work. People generally do not like to change; the benefits must be explained to everyone to gain their support and to ensure that they break out of old working practices.

Those responsible for managing and steering organizational change should consciously address these softer issues. Using an approach such as John P. Kotter's *Eight Steps To Transforming Your Organization*, coupled with formalized project management skills and practices, will significantly increase the chance of success.

Kotter, Professor of Leadership at Harvard Business School, investigated more than 100 companies involved in, or having attempted a complex organizational change programme and identified eight main reasons why transformation efforts fail. Organizational change and these eight steps are discussed in detail later in the publication.

3.2 OWNERSHIP

The principle of ownership is fundamental to any improvement strategy. CSI is a best practice and one of the keys to successful implementation is to ensure that a specific manager, a CSI manager, is responsible for ensuring the best practice is adopted and sustained throughout the organization. The CSI manager becomes the CSI owner and chief advocate. The CSI owner is accountable for the success of Continual Service Improvement in the organization. This ownership responsibility extends beyond ensuring the CSI practices are embedded in the organization but also to ensuring there are adequate resources (including people and technology) to support and enable CSI. Also included are ongoing CSI activities such as monitoring, analysing, evaluating trends and reporting as well as project-based service improvement activities – activities that are fundamental to the ITIL framework. Without clear and unambiguous accountability there will be no improvement.

3.3 ROLE DEFINITIONS

It is important to identify and differentiate between two basic role groupings within CSI: production vs. project. Production roles focus on CSI as a way of life within an organization. These are permanent roles that deal with ongoing service improvement efforts. Typical roles are CSI manager, service manager, service owner, process owner, operations analyst, measurement analyst, reporting analyst and quality assurance analyst among many others. These roles can range from having responsibility for the day-to-day operations of the IT infrastructure through to defining strategies, designing and transitioning new or changed services to the production environment. Project roles reflect the more traditional approach to improvement efforts based on formal programmes and projects. Taking a leadership position in the creation and adoption of processes and services, this group includes roles such as executive sponsor, process owners, process design/implementation/re-engineering team members, process adviser and project manager among others.

The following key activities require clearly defined roles and responsibilities:

Table 3.1 Key activities and roles assigned

Key activities	Key roles
Collect data and analyse trends compared to baselines, targets, SLAs and benchmarks. This would include output from services and service management processes	CSI Manager, Service Manager, Service Owner, IT Process Owner
Set targets for improvement in efficiency and cost effectiveness throughout the entire service lifecycle	CSI Manager, Service Manager
Set targets for improvements in service quality and resource utilization	CSI Manager, Service Manager, Service Owner, Business Process Owner
Consider new business and security requirements	CSI Manager, Service Manager, Business Process Owner
Consider new external drivers such as regulatory requirements	CSI Manager, Service Manager, Business Process Owner
Create a plan and implement improvements	CSI Manager, Service Manager, Service Owner, Process Owner
Provide a means for staff members to recommend improvement opportunities	CSI Manager, Service Manager
Measure, report and communicate on service improvement initiatives	CSI Manager, Service Manager
Revise policies, processes, procedures and plans where necessary	CSI Manager, Service Manager
Ensure that all approved actions are completed and that they achieve the desired results	CSI Manager, Service Manager, Business Manager, IT Process Owner, Business Process Owner

3.4 EXTERNAL AND INTERNAL DRIVERS

There are two major areas within every organization driving improvement: aspects which are external to the organization such as regulation, legislation, competition, external customer requirements, market pressures and economics; and, secondly, aspects which are internal to the organization such as organizational structures, culture, capacity to accept change, existing and projected staffing levels, unions rules, etc. In some cases these aspects may serve to hinder improvement rather than drive it forward. A SWOT analysis (Strengths, Weaknesses, Opportunities, Threats), discussed later in this publication, may be helpful in illuminating significant opportunities for improvement. The strengths and weaknesses focus on the internal aspects of the organization while the opportunities and threats focus on aspects external to the organization.

3.5 SERVICE LEVEL MANAGEMENT

Adopting the Service Level Management (SLM) process is a key principle of CSI. While in the past many IT organizations viewed SLM as merely a smattering of isolated agreements around system availability or help desk calls this is no longer true. SLM is no longer optional. Today's business demands that IT be driven by the service model. This service orientation of IT toward the business becomes the foundation for the trusted partnership that IT must endeavour to create. Today IT is a core enabler of every critical business process. IT can no longer afford to operate as the 'geeks in the basement' but rather must strive to be included in every channel of communication and level of decision making all the way to the boardroom.

SLM involves a number of steps:

- Fully accepting that the IT organization must become a service provider to the business or cease to be relevant
- Involving the business and determining their service level requirements
- Defining the internal portfolio of services: services that are planned, in development, in production. This service portfolio also contains modular or component services which will make up a finished service package
- Defining a customer-facing Service Catalogue which details every service and service package offered by IT with options, parameters and pricing
- Identifying internal IT departmental relationships, negotiating the terms and responsibilities of the internal relationships, and codifying them with Operational Level Agreements (OLAs)
- Identifying existing contractual relationships with external vendors. Verifying that these Underpinning

Contracts (UCs) meet the revised business requirements. Renegotiating them, if necessary
- Utilizing the Service Catalogue as the baseline, negotiate Service Level Agreements (SLAs) with the business
- Create a Service Improvement Plan (SIP) to continually monitor and improve the levels of service.

Once the IT organization and the business begin working together through Service Level Management, IT management soon realizes that the old definitions of 'successful IT' are beginning to fall by the wayside. A high network availability percentage or great ratings in a customer satisfaction survey are no longer the end goal but merely positive metrics rolling towards the achievement of a service level. IT management understands that with the adoption of Service Level Management a fundamental shift has taken place. The definition of success in IT is now crystal clear. It has become the service level – a set of expectations mutually agreed to by IT and the business. IT is then structured, managed, staffed, funded, and operated to meet or exceed the service levels. The service level rules and everything else is just details. A complete SLM process is defined in the ITIL Service Design publication.

3.6 THE DEMING CYCLE

W. Edwards Deming is best known for his management philosophy leading to higher quality, increased productivity, and a more competitive position. As part of this philosophy he formulated 14 points of attention for managers. Some of these points are more appropriate to service management than others. For quality improvement he proposed the Deming Cycle or Circle. This cycle is particularly applicable in CSI. The four key stages of the cycle are Plan, Do, Check and Act, after which a phase of consolidation prevents the circle from rolling back down the hill. Our goal in using the Deming Cycle is steady, ongoing improvement. It is a fundamental tenet of Continual Service Improvement.

The Deming Cycle is critical at two points in CSI: implementation of CSIs, and for the application of CSI to services and service management processes. At implementation, all four stages of the Deming Cycle are used. With ongoing improvement, CSI draws on the check and act stages to monitor, measure, review and implement initiatives.

The cycle is underpinned by a process-led approach to management where defined processes are in place, the activities are measured for compliance to expected values and outputs are audited to validate and improve the process.

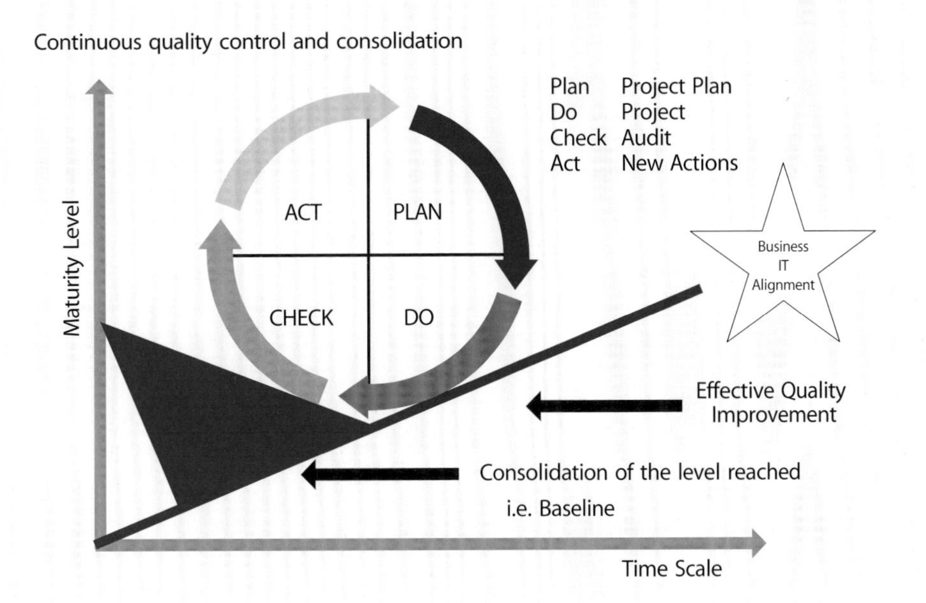

Figure 3.1 The Deming Cycle

3.7 SERVICE MEASUREMENT

3.7.1 Baselines

An important beginning point for highlighting improvement is to establish baselines as markers or starting points for later comparison. Baselines are also used to establish an initial data point to determine if a service or process needs to be improved. As a result, it is important that baselines are documented, recognized and accepted throughout the organization. Baselines must be established at each level: strategic goals and objectives, tactical process maturity, and operational metrics and KPIs.

If a baseline is not initially established the first measurement efforts will become the baseline. That is why it is essential to collect data at the outset, even if the integrity of the data is in question. It is better to have data to question than to have no data at all. Figure 3.2 defines the improvement model.

3.7.2 Value to business

Basically, there are four reasons to monitor and measure:

- **To validate** – monitoring and measuring to validate previous decisions
- **To direct** – monitoring and measuring to set direction for activities in order to meet set targets. It is the most prevalent reason for monitoring and measuring
- **To justify** – monitoring and measuring to justify, with factual evidence or proof, that a course of action is required
- **To intervene** – monitoring and measuring to identify a point of intervention including subsequent changes and corrective actions.

The four basic reasons to monitor and measure lead to three key questions: 'Why are we monitoring and measuring?', 'When do we stop?' and 'Is anyone using the data?' To answer these questions, it is important to identify

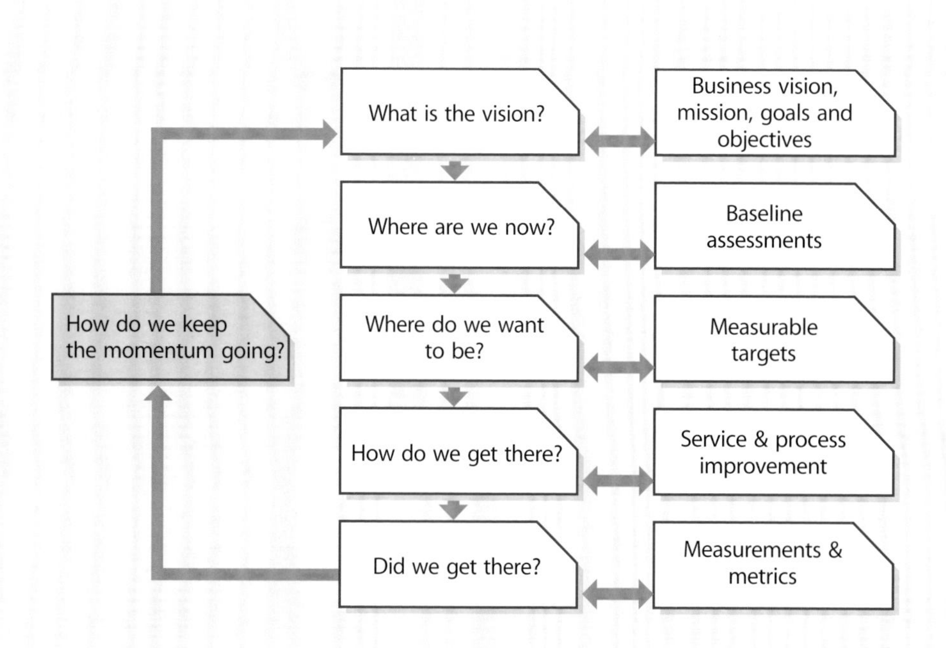

Figure 3.2 Continual Service Improvement model

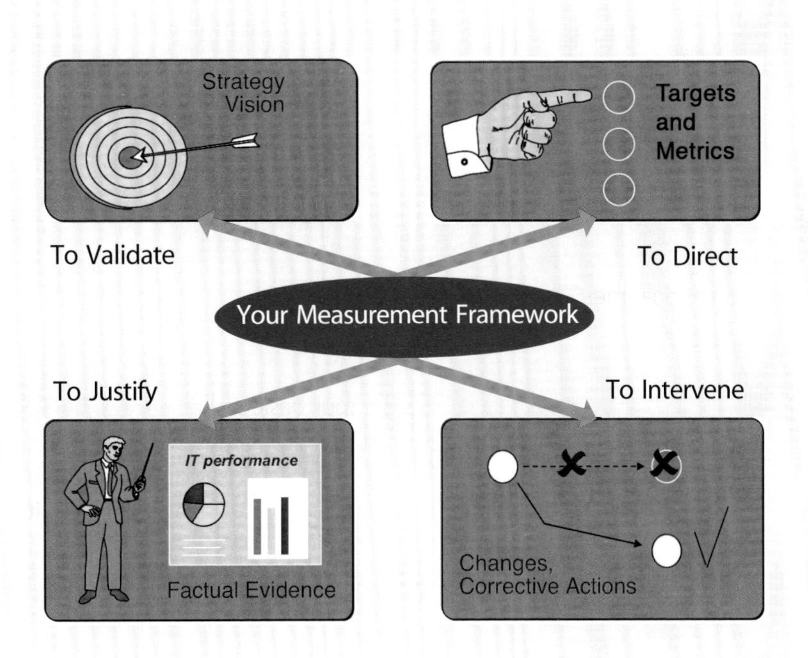

Figure 3.3 Why do we measure?

which of the above reasons is driving the measurement effort. Too often, we continue to measure long after the need has passed. Every time you produce a report you should ask: 'Do we still need this?'

3.7.3 The 7-Step Improvement Process

Fundamental to CSI is the concept of measurement. CSI uses the 7-Step Improvement Process shown in Figure 3.4.

Which steps support CSI?

It is obvious that all the activities of the improvement process will assist CSI in some way. It is relatively simple to identify what takes places but the difficulty lies in understanding exactly how this will happen. The improvement process spans not only the management organization but the entire service lifecycle. This is a cornerstone of CSI.

1 Define what you should measure

   At the onset of the service lifecycle, Service Strategy and Service Design should have identified this information. CSI can then start its cycle all over again at 'Where are we now?' This identifies the ideal situation for both the Business and IT.

2 Define what you can measure

   This activity related to the CSI activities of 'Where do we want to be?' By identifying the new service level requirements of the business, the IT capabilities (identified through Service Design and implemented via Service Transition) and the available budgets, CSI can conduct a gap analysis to identify the opportunities for improvement as well as answering the question 'How will we get there?'

3 Gathering the data

   In order to properly answer the 'Did we get there?' question, data must first be gathered (usually through Service Operations). Data is gathered based on goals and objectives identified. At this point the data is raw and no conclusions are drawn.

4 Processing the data

   Here the data is processed in alignment with the CSFs and KPIs specified. This means that timeframes are coordinated, unaligned data is rationalized and made consistent, and gaps in data are identified. The simple

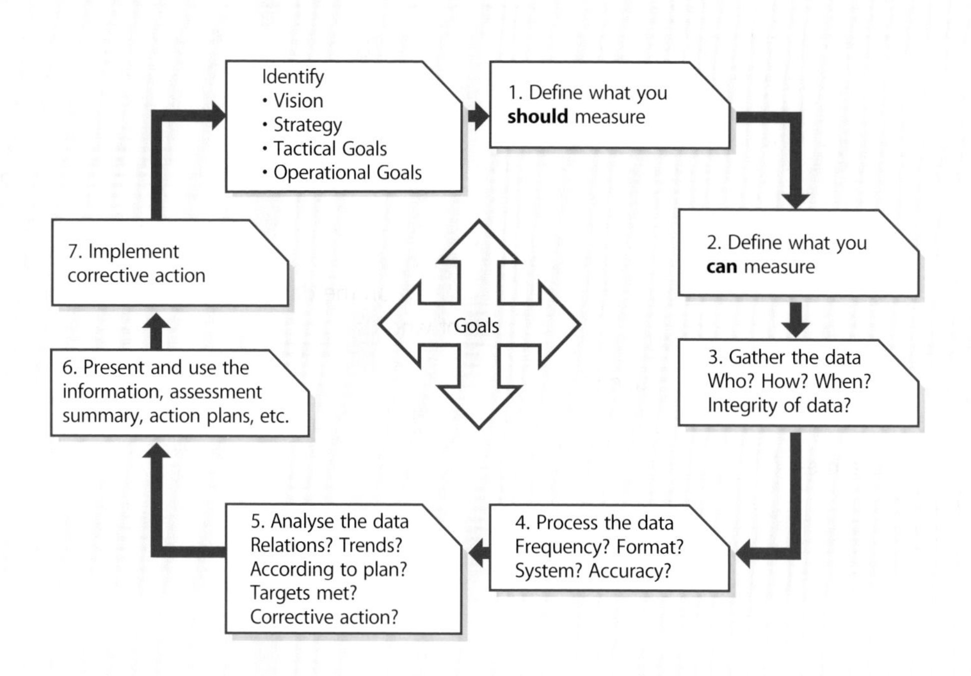

Figure 3.4 The 7-Step Improvement Process

goal of this step is to process data from multiple disparate sources into an 'apples to apples' comparison. Once we have rationalized the data we can then begin analysis.

5 Analysing the data

Here the data becomes information as it is analysed to identify service gaps, trends and the impact on business. It is the analysing step that is most often overlooked or forgotten in the rush to present data to management.

6 Presenting and using the information

Here the answer to 'Did we get there?' is formatted and communicated in whatever way necessary to present to the various stakeholders an accurate picture of the results of the improvement efforts. Knowledge is presented to the business in a form and manner that reflects their needs and assists them in determining the next steps.

7 Implementing corrective action

The knowledge gained is used to optimize, improve and correct services. Managers identify issues and present solutions. The corrective actions that need to be taken to improve the service are communicated and explained to the organization. Following this step the organization establishes a new baseline and the cycle begins anew.

While these seven steps of measurement appear to form a circular set of activities, in fact, they constitute a knowledge spiral (see Figure 3.5). In actual practice, knowledge gathered and wisdom derived from that knowledge at one level of the organization becomes a data input to the next.

People often believe data, information, knowledge and wisdom to be synonymous or at least broadly similar in meaning. This view is incorrect. There is a significant difference between each of the four items.

Data is quantitative. Data is defined as numbers, characters, images or other outputs from devices to convert physical quantities into symbols, in a very broad sense. Essentially it can be defined as a collection of facts, whereas information is the result of processing and organizing data in a way that adds to the knowledge of the person receiving it. Raw data is a relative term; data processing commonly occurs by stages, and the 'processed data' from one stage may be considered the 'raw data' of the next. Example: The Service Desk and Incident Management collect data on an average of 12,000 incident tickets per month.

Information is defined as a message received and understood. In terms of data, it can be defined as a collection of facts from which conclusions may be drawn. Information is the result of processing and organizing data in a way that adds to the knowledge of the person receiving it. Data can also be qualitative such as comments in a customer satisfaction survey.

By processing data into information it is possible to know the breakdown of which customers are using the Service Desk and the specific issues that are incidents or Service Requests. Example: Further processing of the data into information shows that 32% of all contacts to the Service Desk are 'How to' questions, and that 18% of all contacts are true incidents with the organization's e-mail system.

Knowledge can be defined as information combined with experience, context, interpretation and reflection. Example: based on the data and information, and an understanding of who uses the service, and their reasons for using the service, the impact to the business can be determined.

Wisdom is defined as the ability to make correct judgements and decisions. It consists of making the best

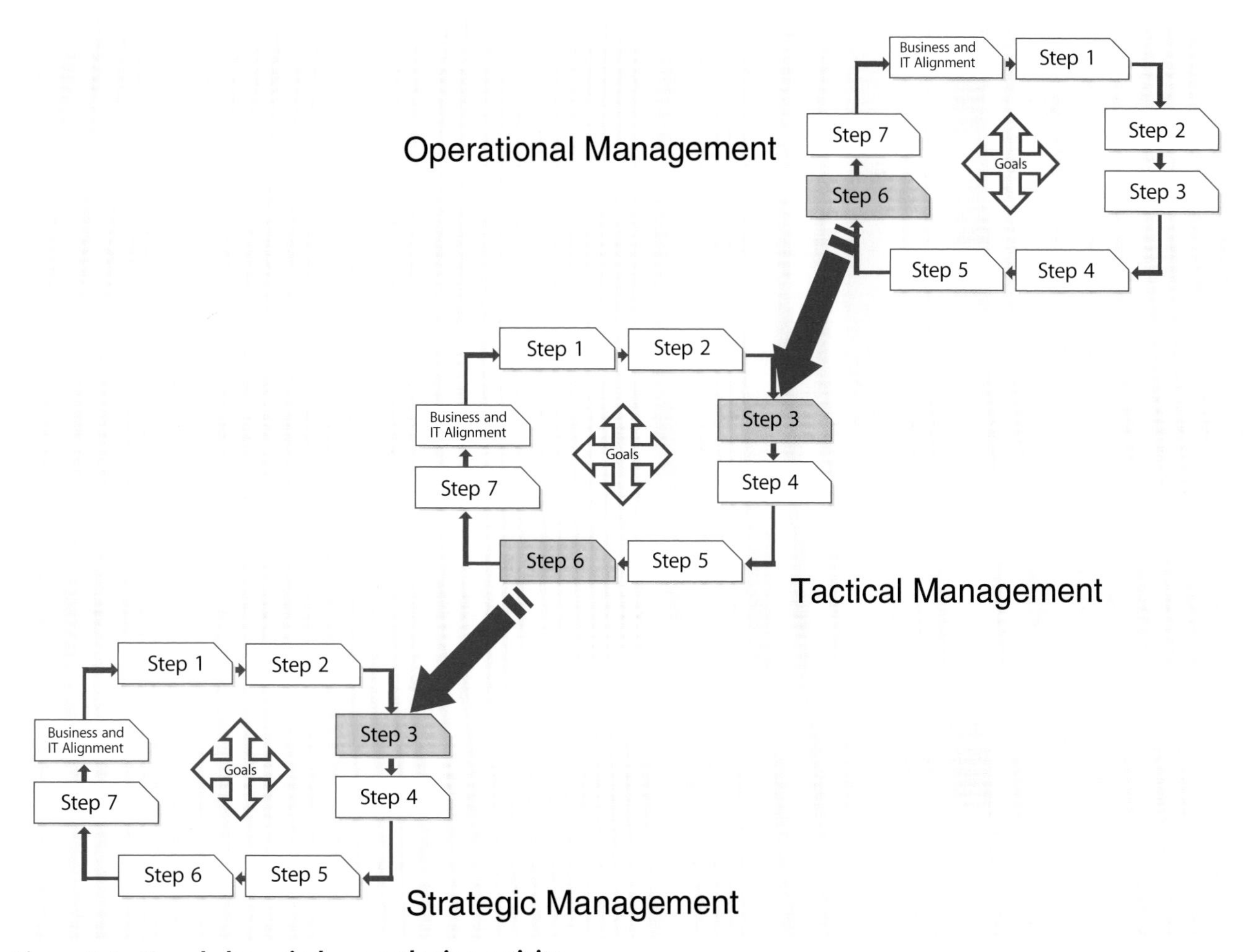

Figure 3.5 Knowledge spiral – a gathering activity

use of available knowledge. Example: knowledge about the customer impact of incidents can lead to identifying improvement opportunities such as training programmes or initiating a SIP for improving the e-mail service.

3.8 KNOWLEDGE MANAGEMENT

> Those who do not learn from history are condemned to repeat it.

Knowledge Management plays a key role in CSI. Within each service lifecycle phase, data should be captured to enable knowledge gain and an understanding of what is actually happening, thus enabling wisdom. This is often referred to as the DIKW (Data, Information, Knowledge and Wisdom) model. See Figure 3.6. All too often an organization will capture the appropriate data but fail to process the data into information, synthesize the information into knowledge and then combine that knowledge with others to bring us wisdom. Wisdom will lead us to better decisions around improvement.

This applies both when looking at the IT services themselves and when drilling down into each individual IT process. Knowledge Management is a mainstay of any improvement process.

3.9 BENCHMARKS

Benchmarking (also known as 'best practice benchmarking' or 'process benchmarking') is a process used in management, particularly strategic management, in which organizations evaluate various aspects of their processes in relation to best practice, usually within their own sector. This then allows organizations to develop plans on how to adopt such best practice, usually with the aim of increasing some aspect of performance. Benchmarking may be a one-time event, but is often treated as a continual process in which organizations continually seek to challenge their practices.

Organizations have a growing need to get a clear view on their own level of quality and performance with regard to their competitors and in the eye of their customers. It isn't sufficient any more to have internal self-assessment reports on the status of IT performance; it is equally important to test and compare it with the view the market has on the performance of the organization. A positive result of this test and comparison can give a competitive edge to the organization in the marketplace and generates trust with its customers. The results of benchmarking and self-assessments lead to identification of gaps in terms of people, process and technology.

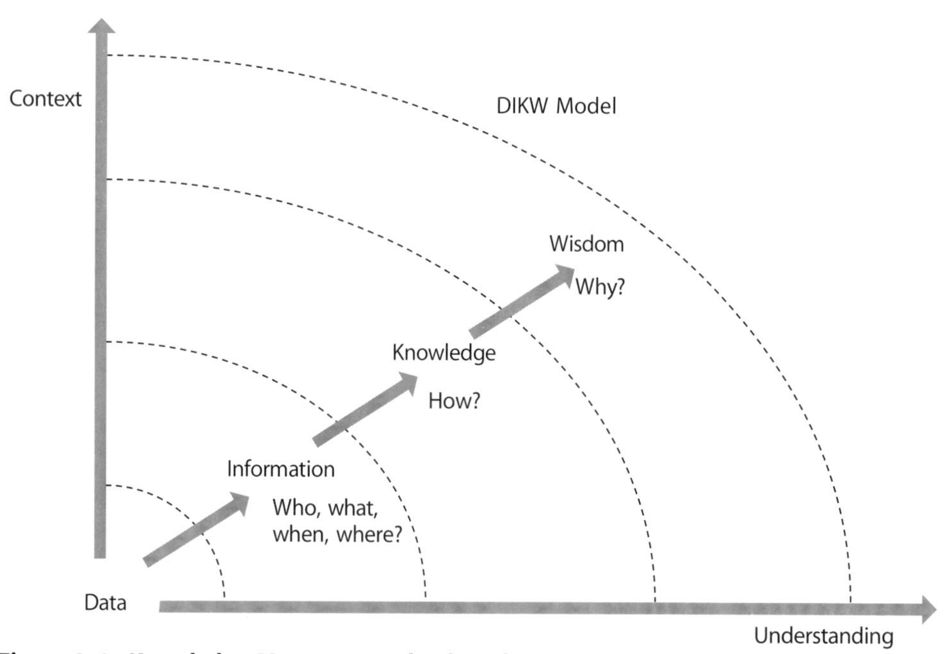

Figure 3.6 Knowledge Management leads to better IT decisions

A benchmark can be the catalyst to initiating prioritization of where to begin formal process improvement. The results of benchmarking must clearly display the gaps, identify the risks of not closing the gaps, facilitate prioritization of development activities and facilitate communication of this information.

3.9.1 Benchmarking as a lever

Consider the following 'paradigm blindness': 'The way we do it is the best because this is the way we've always done it.'

Benchmarking is sometimes the only way to open an organization to new methods, ideas and tools to improve their effectiveness. It helps crack through resistance to change by demonstrating other methods of solving problems than the one currently employed, and demonstrating that they are irrefutably better, because they are being used successfully by others.

3.9.2 Benchmarking as a steering instrument

Benchmarking is a management technique to improve performance. It is used to compare performance between different organizations – or different units within a single organization – undertaking similar processes. Benchmarking is an ongoing method of measuring and improving products, services and practices against the best that can be identified in any industry anywhere. It has been defined as 'the search for industry best practices which lead to superior performance'.

3.9.3 Benchmarking categories

Benchmarking is a great tool to identify improvement opportunities as well as to verify the outcome of improvement activities. Organizations can conduct internal or external benchmark studies. Improving service management can be as simple as: 'Are we better today than we were yesterday?' These are incremental improvements.

- An internal benchmark is where an organization sets a baseline at a certain point in time for the same system or department and they measure how they are doing today compared to the baseline originally set. This type of benchmark is often overlooked by organizations (service targets are a form of benchmark)
- Comparison to industry norms provided by external organizations
- Direct comparisons with similar organizations
- Comparison with other systems or departments within the same company.

3.9.4 Benefits

Benchmarking often reveals quick wins – opportunities for improvement that are relatively easy and inexpensive to implement while providing substantial benefits in terms of process effectiveness, cost reduction, or staff synergy. The costs are clearly repaid through the improvements realized when organizations use benchmarking successfully.

3.10 GOVERNANCE

Governance has been around the IT arena for decades. The mainframe had significant controls built around its day-to-day operations. With the advent of distributed processing in the early 90s, then n-tier processing, the internet, and increasing virtualization, governance and controls simply went out of fashion; just when they were the most desperately needed. With the exposure of high-level corporate fraud in the early years of this century, IT was thrust, without warning, into a completely unfamiliar game with incredibly high stakes. Governance is back with a vengeance. IT is now forced to comply with sweeping legislation and an ever-increasing number of external regulations. External auditors are commonplace in large IT shops. IT can no longer mask their operations behind a veil of secrecy or a cloud of obfuscation but rather they must run an organization which prides itself on its transparency.

Before specifically discussing IT governance, there is a need to understand what governance, in general, is. See Figure 3.7 for a depiction of enterprise governance.

3.10.1 Enterprise governance

> Enterprise governance is an emerging term ... to describe a framework that covers both the corporate governance and the business management aspects of the organization. Achieving a panacea of good corporate governance that is linked strategically with performance metrics will enable companies to focus all their energies on the key drivers that move their business forward.
>
> This is a huge challenge as well as a huge opportunity. Much work has been carried out recently on corporate governance. But the performance aspects of governance have not received so much attention. Enterprise governance considers the whole picture to ensure that strategic goals are aligned and good management is achieved.
> (Chartered Institute of Management Accountants – CIMA.)

3.10.2 Corporate governance

> Corporate governance is about promoting corporate fairness, transparency and accountability. (J. Wolfensohn, President, World Bank, *Financial Times*, 21 June 1999.)

The most recent and highly visible example of a renewed emphasis on corporate governance is the Sarbanes-Oxley Act (SOX) of 2002 in the United States. Created in the aftermath of fraudulent behaviour by corporate giants, SOX demands corporate fairness mandates complete transparency of transactions and holds executives accountable for any material deficiencies. The accountability provisions in SOX include criminal charges and incarceration for non-compliance.

3.10.3 IT governance

> IT governance is the responsibility of the board of directors and executive management. It is an integral part of enterprise governance and consists of the leadership, organizational structures and processes that ensure that the organization's IT sustains and extends the organization's strategies and objectives. (*Board Briefing on IT Governance*, 2nd Edition, 2003, IT Governance Institute – ITGI)

IT governance touches nearly every area detailed in the figure above. On one hand, IT must now comply with new rules and legislation and continually demonstrate their compliance through successful independent audits by external organizations. On the other hand, IT is increasingly being called upon to do more with less and create additional value while maximizing the use of existing resources.

These increasing pressures dovetail perfectly with the basic premise of ITIL: IT is a service business. Existing internal IT organizations must transform themselves into effective and efficient IT service providers or they will cease to be relevant to the business and, soon after, cease to exist. This continual and unceasing drive toward greater business value with greater internal efficiency is at the heart of CSI.

3.11 FRAMEWORKS, MODELS, STANDARDS AND QUALITY SYSTEMS

At this point a discussion is warranted to increase our understanding of where CSI fits into the larger ITSM landscape. Each of the following frameworks, models, standards and quality systems fully supports the concepts embodied in CSI.

3.11.1 Frameworks

ITIL, created in 1989, provides detailed guidance on the structure, integration and improvement of IT services and processes. It has been updated and revised and is governed by the Office of Government Commerce, UK. It is the most widely adopted set of principles for IT Service Management worldwide.

COBIT (Control OBjectives for Information and related Technology), originally created in 1995 as an information systems audit framework, has matured to become an overall IT management framework. COBIT processes and principles are often used by IT and SOX auditors. COBIT is governed by the IT Governance Institute.

PMBOK (Project Management Body of Knowledge) is owned and authored by the Project Management Institute (PMI).

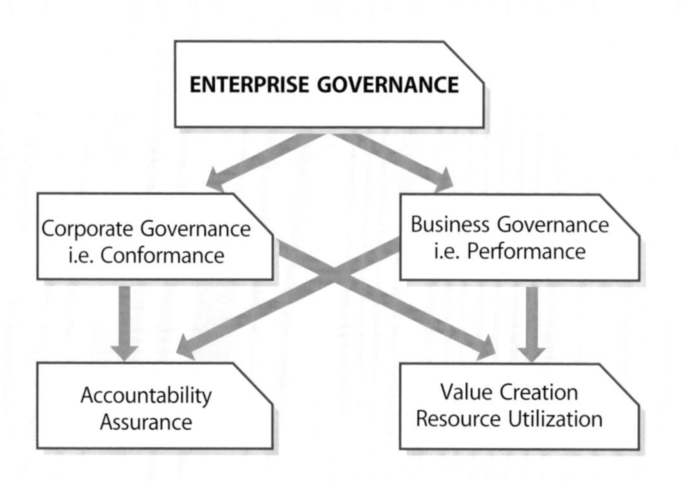

Figure 3.7 Enterprise governance (source: CIMA)

> The Project Management Body of Knowledge is the sum of knowledge within the profession of project management. As with other professions such as law, medicine and accounting, the body of knowledge rests with the practitioners and academics who apply and advance it. The complete Project Management Body of Knowledge includes proven traditional practices that are widely applied, as well as innovative practices that are emerging in the profession, including published and unpublished material. As a result, the Project Management Body of Knowledge is constantly evolving.
> (Introduction to PMBOK – 2004)

PRINCE2 (PRojects IN Controlled Environments, v2) is a structured project management method owned by the OGC. Structured project management means managing the project in a logical, organized way following defined steps. A structured project management method is the written description of this logical, organized approach.

Individuals can receive certifications verifying their knowledge of each framework. Organizations may be assessed against a framework. In many cases the Capability Maturity Model (CMM) scale is used for these organizational assessments.

3.11.2 Models

CMMI (Capability Maturity Model Integration): Created by SEI (Software Engineering Institute) at Carnegie Mellon University in 1991. In the beginning CMM was a model for demonstrating the maturity of software development processes in the belief that more mature development processes led to better software. The basic software CMM model has grown and been revised. CMMI is now the de facto standard for measuring the maturity of any process. Organizations can be assessed against the CMMI model using SCAMPI (Standard CMMI Appraisal Method for Process Improvement).

3.11.3 Standards

Standards exist because a widely recognized governing body, in most cases a governing body with worldwide scope, has agreed on a specific set of principles or protocols and published them for everyone to use. Standards are usually set by committees working under various trade and international organizations.

Some standards govern technical specifications that profoundly impact our daily lives. Without standards we would be unable to plug in appliances, make phone calls, send faxes, connect computers together, or even buy groceries in most developed countries. Examples of these international technical governing bodies are the ITU (International Telecommunications Union) and the IEEE (Institute of Electrical and Electronics Engineers). Other less technical standards define what activities should be implemented and often add a code of practice to determine what level these activities should achieve. The most prevalent and highly visible international standards body in this area is the ISO (International Standards Organization) which boasts member organizations in every developed country in the world. In the world of ITSM it is the ISO that creates the standards. The ISO operates in Europe in conjunction with the IEC (International Electrotechnical Commission), therefore, the correct nomenclature for the international standards is: ISO/IEC xxxxx. This standard number is often followed by the year it was issued. This serves as the version of the standard. The most important standards applying to the world of ITSM are:

- ISO/IEC 20000:2005 promotes the adoption of an integrated process approach to effectively deliver managed services to meet business and customer requirements. For an organization to function effectively it has to identify and manage numerous linked activities. Coordinated integration and implementation of the service management processes provides the ongoing control, greater efficiency and opportunities for continual improvement. (ISO). ISO/IEC 20000 is based on the ITIL service management processes.
- ISO/IEC 27001:2005 covers all types of organizations and specifies the requirements for establishing, implementing, operating, monitoring, reviewing, maintaining and improving a documented Information Security Management System within the context of the organization's overall business risks. It specifies requirements for the implementation of security controls customized to the needs of individual organizations or parts thereof. It is designed to ensure the selection of adequate and proportionate security controls that protect information assets and give confidence to interested parties.
- ISO/IEC 17799:2005 establishes guidelines and general principles for initiating, implementing, maintaining and improving Information Security Management in an organization. The objectives outlined provide general guidance on the commonly accepted goals of Information Security Management. The control objectives and controls in ISO/IEC 17799:2005 are intended to be implemented to meet the requirements identified by a risk assessment. ISO/IEC 17799:2005 is intended as a common basis and

practical guideline for developing organizational security standards and effective Security Management practices, and to help build confidence in inter-organizational activities.

- ISO/IEC 15504 (also known as SPICE – Software Process Improvement and Capability dEtermination) provides a framework for the assessment of process capability. This framework can be used by organizations involved in planning, managing, monitoring, controlling and improving the acquisition, supply, development, operation, evolution and support of products and services. It is also intended for use by assessors in the performance of process assessment, and by organizations involved in the development of process reference models, process assessment models or process assessment processes.
- ISO/IEC 19770:2006 has been developed to enable an organization to prove that it is performing software asset management (SAM) to a standard sufficient to satisfy corporate governance requirements and ensure effective support for IT service management overall. ISO/IEC 19770:2006 is intended to align closely to, and to support, ISO/IEC 20000. Good practice in SAM should result in several benefits, and certifiable good practice should allow management and other organizations to place reliance on the adequacy of these processes. The expected benefits should be achieved with a high degree of confidence.

An individual can be accredited as an ISO auditor. Organizations can be audited against an ISO standard. If the audit is passed successfully, that organization is 'ISO xxxxx Certified'.

3.11.4 Quality systems

'Six Sigma' was pioneered at Motorola in 1986 and was originally defined as a metric for measuring defects and improving quality, and a methodology to reduce defect levels below six standard deviations or six sigma. In 1995 it was implemented at GE and has since become the most widely recognized and accepted quality system in the world.

From a process perspective the statistical representation of Six Sigma describes quantitatively how a process is performing. To achieve Six Sigma, a process must not produce more than 3.4 defects per million opportunities or, looking at it another way, a process would need to be 99.99966% error-free. A Six Sigma defect is defined as anything outside of customer specifications. A Six Sigma opportunity is then the total quantity of chances for a defect.

The fundamental objective of the Six Sigma methodology is the implementation of a measurement-based strategy that focuses on process improvement and variation reduction through the application of Six Sigma improvement projects. This is accomplished through the use of two Six Sigma sub-methodologies: DMAIC and DMADV. The Six Sigma DMAIC process (define, measure, analyse, improve, control) is an improvement system for existing processes falling below specification and looking for incremental improvement. The Six Sigma DMADV process (define, measure, analyse, design, verify) is an improvement system used to develop new processes or products at Six Sigma quality levels. It can also be employed if a current process requires more than just incremental improvement. Both Six Sigma processes are executed by individuals who are certified as Six Sigma Green Belts and Six Sigma Black Belts, and are overseen by Six Sigma Master Black Belts. The CSI model described in this publication is very close to the DMAIC methodology in Six Sigma.

'Lean manufacturing' or 'lean production' was pioneered by Toyota in the mid-1980s. It is a quality systems built around these five principles:

- Specify value from the standpoint of the end customer.
- Identify all the steps in the value stream for each product family, eliminating every step and every action and every practice that does not create value.
- Make the remaining value-creating steps occur in a tight and integrated sequence so the product will flow smoothly toward the customer.
- As flow is introduced, let customers pull value from the next upstream activity.
- As these steps lead to greater transparency, enabling managers and teams to eliminate further waste, pursue perfection through continual improvement. (Lean Enterprise Institute)

Which one of these should I choose?

Field experience has shown that while each may be complete unto itself, none provides a total answer for IT management. Indeed, there is a good deal of overlap between them but, for the most part, they are not competitive or exclusive. In fact, many organizations use a combination to more effectively manage and improve IT.

IBM Global Business Services recommends a combination of ITIL, CMMI, Lean and Six Sigma as the best approach to transform organizations. The Information Systems Audit and Control Association (ISACA), in conjunction with OGC, created a briefing paper entitled 'Aligning COBIT, ITIL and ISO17799 for Business Benefit'. Other organizations have combined ITIL, CMMI and Six Sigma as their formula for success. Confusion reigns.

Many organizations become paralysed when faced with this basic decision. After all, no one wants to go down the wrong path. Experience tells us that the best way to break the 'which framework' logjam is the bottom-up approach. While the arguments continue in the conference room, IT management can implement and mature Change Management, Service Desk, Incident Management and Problem Management all the while continue to align with every framework or standard mentioned above and prepare for their corporate governance audit to boot. The decision is not 'Which one should I choose?' but rather 'What should I improve first?'

An effective CSI practice will be integrated within all phases of the service lifecycle. The greatest value to the business and IT will be realized by having a continuous monitoring and feedback loop as the service and ITSM processes move through the service lifecycle. Look for improvement opportunities within Service Strategy, Service Design, Service Transition as well as Service Operation. It is imperative that the concept of continual improvement be woven into the day-to-day fabric of the organization.

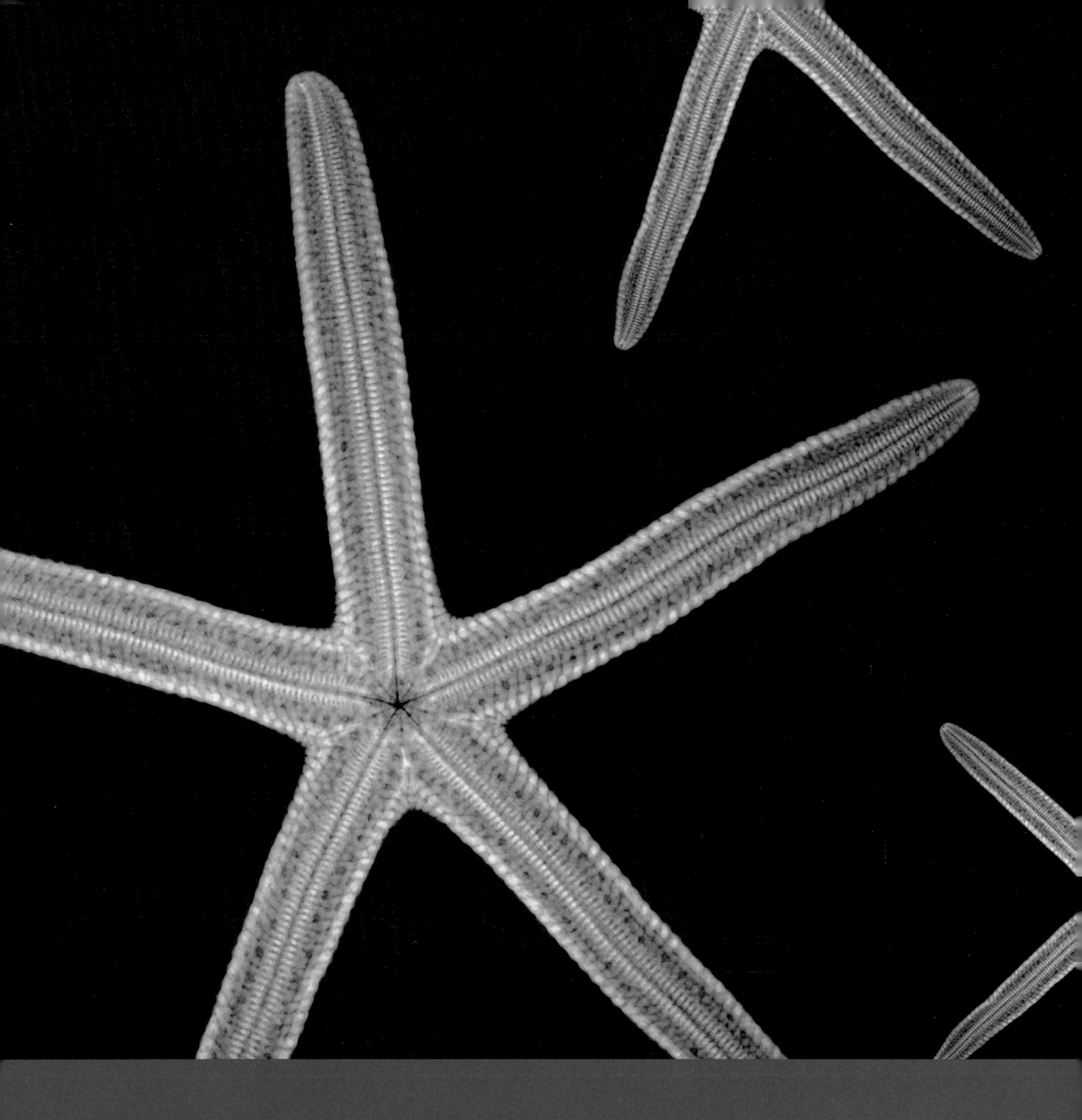

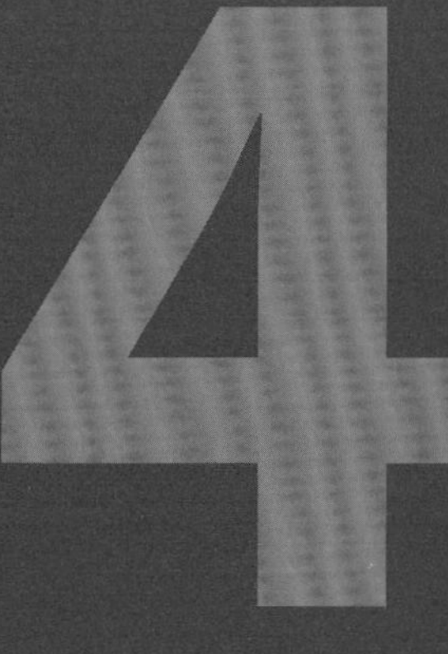

Continual Service Improvement processes

4 Continual Service Improvement processes

4.1 THE 7-STEP IMPROVEMENT PROCESS

Chapter 3 introduced the 7-Step Improvement Process shown in Figure 4.1. This chapter will go into more detail on this. What do you actually measure and where do you find the information? These are two very important questions and should not be ignored or taken lightly.

Steps 1 and 2 are directly related to the strategic, tactical and operational goals that have been defined for measuring services and service management processes as well as the existing technology and capability to support measuring and CSI activities.

Steps 1 and 2 are iterative during the rest of the activities. Depending on the goals and objectives to support service improvement activities, an organization may have to purchase and install new technology to support the gathering and processing of the data and/or hire staff with the required skills sets.

These two steps are too often ignored because:

- The process does not include this step. Too often people start gathering information without asking what should be collected in the first place or what they are going to do to with it later. This is common but poor practice.
- IT knows better. When it comes to data, IT believes, incorrectly, that they know the needs of their customers. The reality is that neither the customer nor the IT organization sit down together to discuss what should be measured or to identify the purpose of the data in the first place. Even in organizations where SLAs have been signed, they often will include measurement and reporting requirements that cannot be met. This always makes for significant customer dissatisfaction issues.

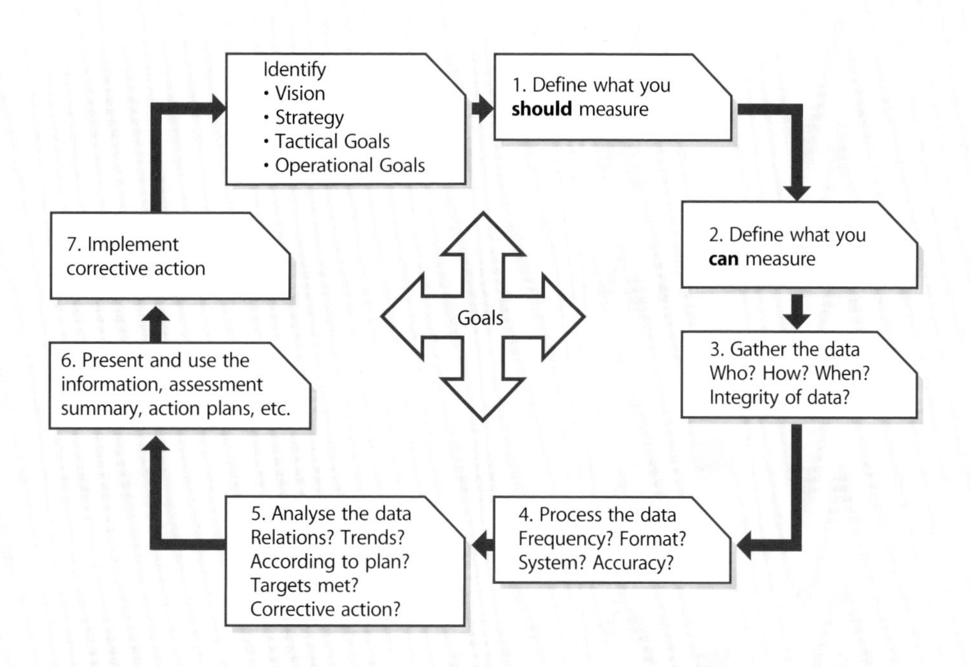

Figure 4.1 7-Step Improvement Process

- Tools are very sophisticated and can gather myriads of data points. IT organizations get lulled into a false sense of security in the knowledge that the data will be there when they need it. Too often the tool is too powerful for the needs of the organization. It is like hammering a small finishing nail using a sledgehammer.

When the data is finally presented (Step 6) without going through the rest of the steps, the results appear incorrect or incomplete. People blame each other, the vendor, the tools, anyone but themselves. Step 1 is crucial. A dialogue must take place between IT and the customer. Goals and objectives must be identified in order to properly identify what should be measured.

Based on the goals of the target audience (operational, tactical, or strategic) the service owners need to define what they should measure in a perfect world. To do this:

- Map the activities of the service or service management processes that need to be measured.
- Consider what measurements would indicate that each service and service management activity is being performed consistently and can determine the health of the process.

Identify the measurements that can be provided based on existing tool sets, organizational culture and process maturity. Note there may be a gap in what can be measured vs. what should be measured. Quantify the cost and business risk of this gap to validate any expenditures for tools.

When initially implementing service management processes don't try to measure everything, rather be selective of what measures will help to understand the health of a process. Further chapters will discuss the use of CSFs, KPIs and activity metrics. A major mistake many organizations make is trying to do too much in the beginning. Be smart about what you choose to measure.

Step One – Define what you should measure

Question: Where do you actually find the information?

Answer: Talk to the business, the customers and to IT management. Utilize the service catalogue as your starting point as well as the service level requirements of the different customers. This is the place where you start with the end in mind. In a perfect world, what should you measure? What is important to the business?

Compile a list of what you should measure. This will often be driven by business requirements. Don't try to cover every single eventuality or possible metric in the world. Make it simple. The number of what you should measure can grow quite rapidly. So too can the number of metrics and measurements.

Identify and link the following items:

- Corporate vision, mission, goals and objectives
- IT vision, mission, goals and objectives
- Critical success factors
- Service level targets
- Job description for IT staffs.

Inputs:

- Service level requirements and targets
- Service Catalogue
- Vision and mission statements
- Corporate, divisional and departmental goals and objectives
- Legislative requirements
- Governance requirements
- Budget cycle
- Balanced Scorecard.

Step Two – Define what you can measure

Every organization may find that they have limitations on what can actually be measured. If you cannot measure something then it should not appear in an SLA.

Question: What do you actually measure?

Answer: Start by listing the tools you currently have in place. These tools will include service management tools, monitoring tools, reporting tools, investigation tools and others. Compile a list of what each tool can currently measure without any configuration or customization. Stay away from customizing the tools as much as possible; configuring them is acceptable

Question: Where do you actually find the information?

Answer: The information is found within each process, procedure and work instruction. The tools are merely a way to collect and provide the data. Look at existing reports and databases. What data is currently being collected and reported on?

Perform a gap analysis between the two lists. Report this information back to the business, the customers and IT management. It is possible that new tools are required or that configuration or customization is required to be able to measure what is required.

Inputs:

- List of what you should measure
- Process flows
- Procedures
- Work instructions
- Technical and user manuals from existing tools
- Existing reports.

Step Three – Gathering the data

Gathering data requires having some form of monitoring in place. Monitoring could be executed using technology such as application, system and component monitoring tools or even be a manual process for certain tasks.

Quality is the key objective of monitoring for Continual Service Improvement. Monitoring will therefore focus on the effectiveness of a service, process, tool, organization or Configuration Item (CI). The emphasis is not on assuring real-time service performance, rather it is on identifying where improvements can be made to the existing level of service, or IT performance. Monitoring for CSI will therefore tend to focus on detecting exceptions and resolutions. For example, CSI is not as interested in whether an incident was resolved, but whether it was resolved within the agreed time, and whether future incidents can be prevented.

CSI is not only interested in exceptions, though. If a Service Level Agreement is consistently met over time, CSI will also be interested in determining whether that level of performance can be sustained at a lower cost or whether it needs to be upgraded to an even better level of performance. CSI may therefore also need access to regular performance reports.

However since CSI is unlikely to need, or be able to cope with, the vast quantities of data that are produced by all monitoring activity, they will most likely focus on a specific subset of monitoring at any given time. This could be determined by input from the business or improvements to technology.

When a new service is being designed or an existing one changed, this is a perfect opportunity to ensure that what CSI needs to monitor is designed into the service requirements (see Service Design publication).

This has two main implications:

- Monitoring for CSI will change over time. They may be interested in monitoring the e-mail service one quarter, and then move on to look at HR systems in the next quarter.
- This means that Service Operation and CSI need to build a process which will help them to agree on what areas need to be monitored and for what purpose.

It is important to remember that there are three types of metrics that an organization will need to collect to support CSI activities as well as other process activities. The types of metrics are:

- Technology metrics – these metrics are often associated with component and application based metrics such as performance, availability etc.
- Process metrics – these metrics are captured in the form of CSFs, KPIs and activity metrics for the service management processes. These metrics can help determine the overall health of a process. Four key questions that KPIs can help answer are around quality, performance, value and compliance of following the process. CSI would use these metrics as input in identifying improvement opportunities for each process.
- Service metrics – these metrics are the results of the end-to-end service. Component/technology metrics are used to compute the service metrics. .

Question: What do you actually measure?

Answer: You gather whatever data has been identified as both needed and measurable. Please remember that not all data is gathered automatically. A lot of data is entered manually by people. It is important to ensure that policies are in place to drive the right behaviour to ensure that this manual data entry follows the SMART (Specific-Measurable-Achievable-Relevant-Timely) principle.

As much as possible, you need to standardize the data structure through policies and published standards. For example, how do you enter names in your tools – John Smith; Smith, John or J. Smith? These can be the same or different individuals. Having three different ways of entering the same name would slow down trend analysis and will severely impede any CSI initiative.

Question: Where do you actually find the information?

Answer: IT service management tools, monitoring tools, reporting tools, investigation tools, existing reports and other sources.

Gathering data is defined as the act of monitoring and data collection. This activity needs to clearly define the following:

- Who is responsible for monitoring and gathering the data?
- How the data will be gathered?
- When and how often is the data gathered?
- Criteria to evaluate the integrity of the data

The answers will be different for every organization.

Service monitoring allows weak areas to be identified, so that remedial action can be taken (if there is a justifiable Business Case), thus improving future service quality. Service monitoring also can show where customer actions are causing the fault and thus lead to identifying where working efficiency and/or training can be improved.

Service monitoring should also address both internal and external suppliers since their performance must be evaluated and managed as well.

Service management monitoring helps determine the health and welfare of service management processes in the following manner:

- Process compliance – Are the processes being followed? Process compliance seeks to monitor the compliance of the IT organization to the new or modified service management processes and also the use of the authorized service management tool that was implemented.
- Quality – How well are the processes working? Monitor the individual or key activities as they relate to the objectives of the end-to-end process.
- Performance – How fast or slow? Monitor the process efficiency such as throughput or cycle times.
- Value – Is this making a difference? Monitor the effectiveness and perceived value of the process to the stakeholders and the IT staff executing the process activities.

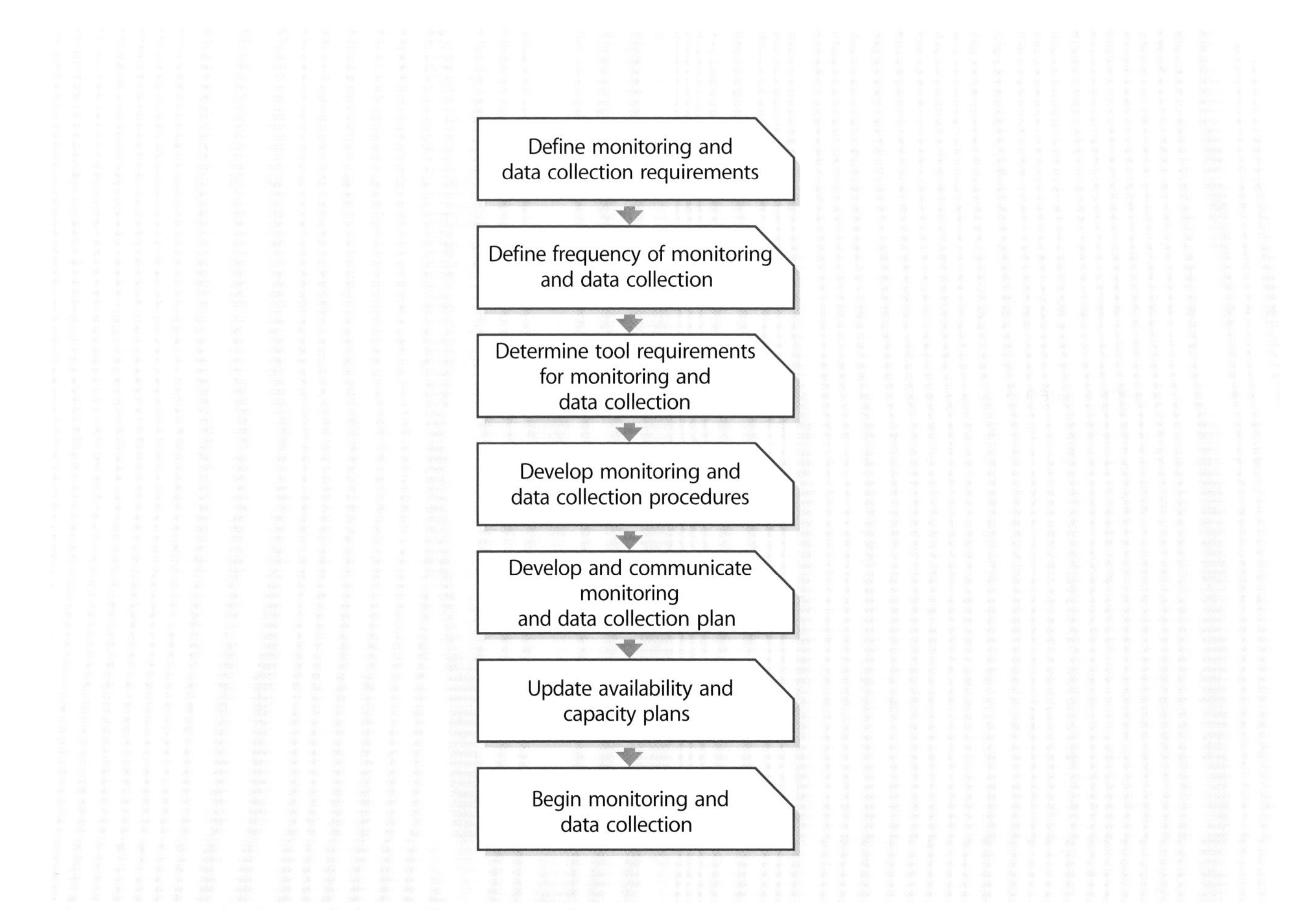

Figure 4.2 Monitoring and data collection procedures

Monitoring is often associated with automated monitoring of infrastructure components for performance such as availability or capacity, but monitoring should also be used for monitoring staff behaviour such as adherence to process activities, use of authorized tools as well as project schedules and budgets.

Exceptions and alerts need to be considered during the monitoring activity as they can serve as early warning indicators that services are breaking down. Sometimes the exceptions and alerts will come from tools, but they will often come from those who are using the service or service management processes. We don't want to ignore these alerts.

Inputs to gather-the-data activity:

- New business requirements
- Existing SLAs
- Existing monitoring and data capture capability
- Availability and Capacity Plans
- Service improvement plans
- Previous trend analysis reports
- List of what you should measure
- List of what you can measure
- Gap analysis report
- List of what to measure
- Customer satisfaction surveys.

Figure 4.2 and Table 4.1 show the common procedures to follow in monitoring.

Outputs from gather-the-data activity:

- Updated Availability and Capacity Plans
- Monitoring procedures
- Identified tools to use
- Monitoring plan
- Input on IT capability
- Collection of data
- Agreement on the integrity of the data.

It is also important in this activity to look at the data that was collected and ask – does this make any sense?

Table 4.1 Monitoring and data collection procedure

Tasks	Procedures
Task 1	Based on service improvement strategies, goals and objectives plus the business requirements determine what services, systems, applications and/or components as well as service management process activities will require monitoring
	Specify monitoring requirements
	Define data collection requirements, changes in budgets
	Document the outcome
	Get agreement with internal IT
Task 2	Determine frequency of monitoring and data gathering
	Determine method of monitoring and data gathering
Task 3	Define tools required for monitoring and data gathering
	Build, purchase, or modify tools for monitoring and data gathering
	Test the tool
	Install the tool
Task 4	Write monitoring procedures and work instructions when required for monitoring and data collection
Task 5	Produce and communicate monitoring and data collection plan
	Get approval from internal IT and external vendors who may be impacted
Task 6	Update Availability and Capacity Plans if required
Task 7	Begin monitoring and data collection
	Process data into a logical grouping and report format
	Review data to ensure the data make sense

Example

An organization that was developing some management information activities asked a consultant to review the data they had collected. The data was for Incident Management and the Service Desk. It was provided in a spreadsheet format and when the consultant opened the spreadsheet it showed that for the month the organization had opened approximately 42,000 new incident tickets and 65,000 incidents tickets were closed on the first contact. It is hard to close more incident tickets than were opened – in other words the data did not make sense.

However, all is not lost. Even if the data did not make any sense, it provides insight into the ability to monitor and gather data, the tools that are used to support monitoring and data gathering and the procedures for processing the raw data into a report that can be used for analysis. When investigating the example above, it was discovered that it was a combination on how data was pulled from the tool plus human error in inputting the data into a spreadsheet. There was no check and balance before the data was actually processed and presented to key people in the organization.

Step Four – Processing the data

Question: What do you actually do here?

Answer: Convert the data in the required format and for the required audience. Follow the trail from metric to KPI to CSF, all the way back to the vision if necessary. See Figure 4.3.

Question: Where do you actually find the information?

Answer: IT service management tools, monitoring tools, reporting tools, investigation tools, existing reports and other sources.

Once data is gathered, the next step is to process the data into the required format. Report-generating technologies are typically used at this stage as various amounts of data are condensed into information for use in the analysis activity. The data is also typically put into a format that provides an end-to-end perspective on the overall performance of a service. This activity begins the transformation of raw data into packaged information. Use the information to develop insight into the performance of the service and/or processes. Process the data into information (i.e. create logical groupings) which provides a better means to analyse the data – the next activity step in CSI.

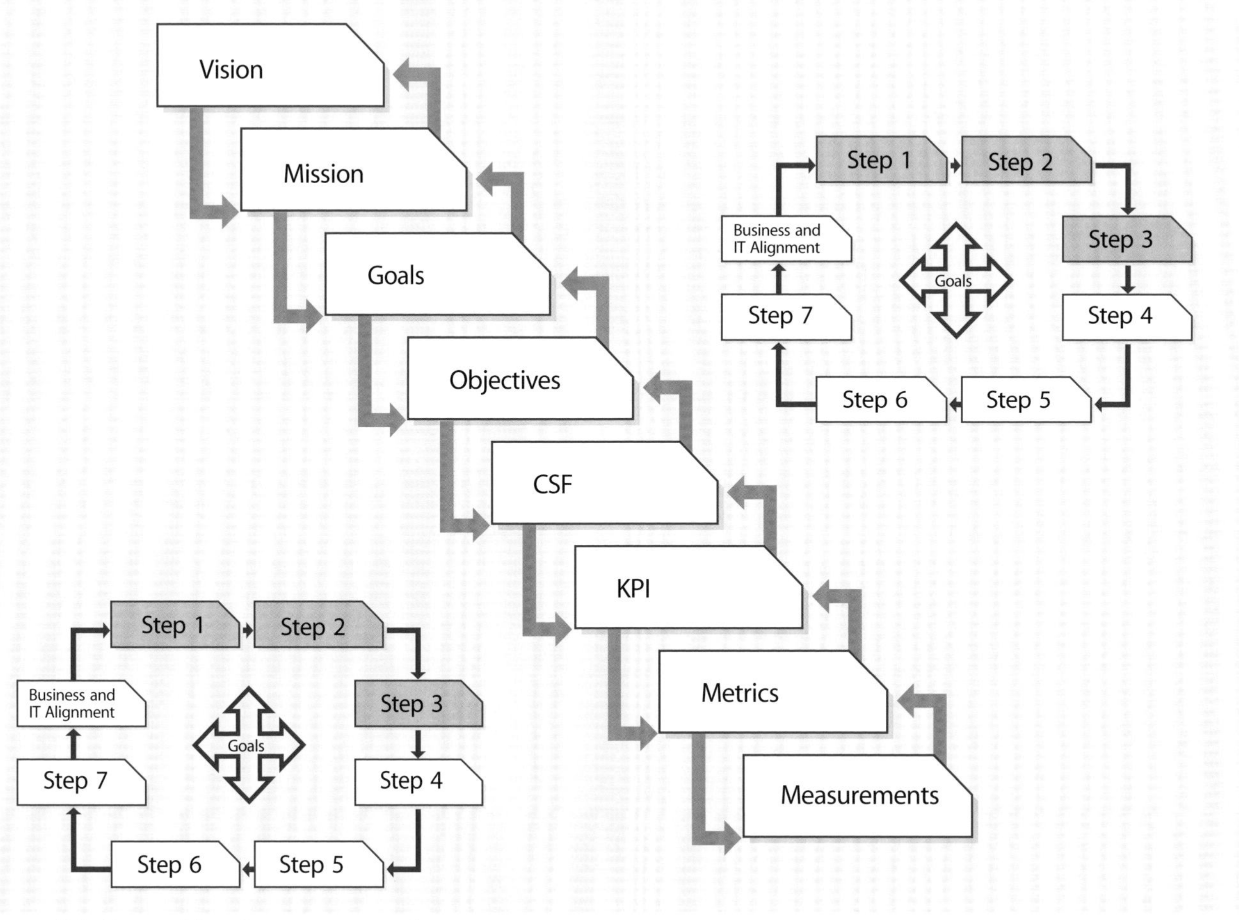

Figure 4.3 From vision to measurements

The output of logical groupings could be in spreadsheets, reports generated directly from the service management tool suite, system monitoring and reporting tools, or telephony tools such as an automatic call distribution tool.

Processing the data is an important CSI activity that is often overlooked. While monitoring and collecting data on a single infrastructure component is important, it is also important to understand that component's impact on the larger infrastructure and IT service. Knowing that a server was up 99.99% of the time is one thing, knowing that no one could access the server is another. An example of processing the data is taking the data from monitoring of the individual components such as the mainframe, applications, WAN, LAN, servers etc and process this into a structure of an end-to-end service from the customer's perspective.

Key questions that need to be addressed in the processing activity are:

- What is the frequency of processing the data? This could be hourly, daily, weekly or monthly. When introducing a new service or service management process it is a good idea to monitor and process in shorter intervals than longer intervals. How often analysis and trend investigation activities take place will drive how often the data is processed.
- What format is required for the output? This is also driven by how analysis is done and ultimately how the information is used.
- What tools and systems can be used for processing the data?
- How do we evaluate the accuracy of the processed data?

There are two aspects to data gathering. One is automated and the other is manual. While both are important and contribute greatly to the measuring process, accuracy is a major differentiator between the two types. The accuracy of the automated data gathering and processing is not the issue here. The vast majority of CSI-related data will be gathered by automated means. Human data gathering and processing is the issue. It is important for staff to properly document their compliance activities, to update logs and records. Common excuses are that people are too busy, that this is not important or that it is not their job. On-going communication about the benefits of performing administrative tasks is of utmost importance. Tying these administrative tasks to job performance is one way to alleviate this issue.

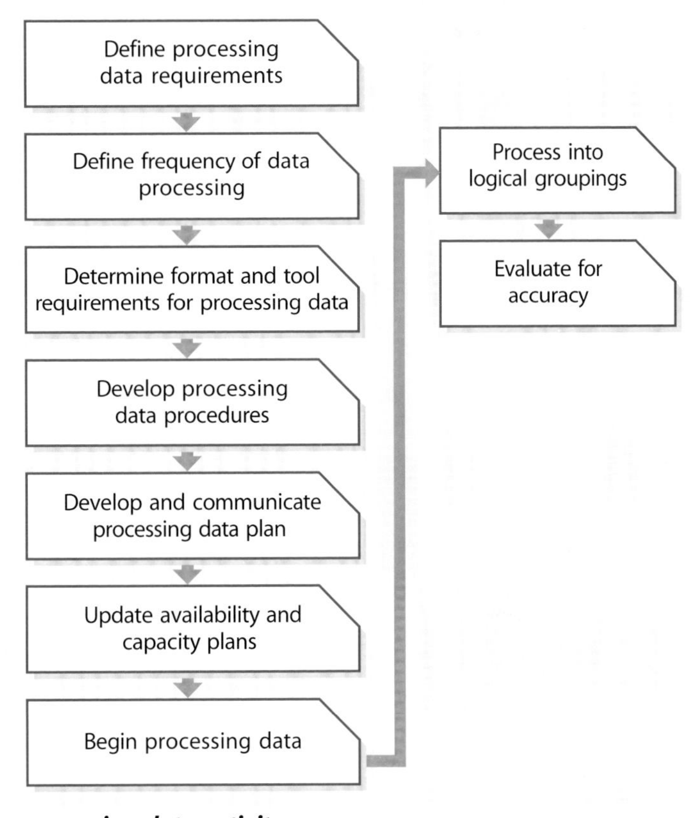

Figure 4.4 Common procedure for processing data activity

Inputs to processing-the-data activity:

- Data collected through monitoring
- Reporting requirements
- SLAs
- OLAs
- Service Catalogue
- List of metrics, KPI, CSF, objectives and goals
- Report frequency
- Report template.

Figure 4.4 and Table 4.2 show common procedures for processing data activity

A flow diagram is nice to look at and it gracefully summarizes the procedure but it does not contain all the required information. It is important to translate the flow diagram into a more meaningful way for people to understand the procedure with the appropriate level of detail including roles and responsibilities, timeframes, input and outputs, and more.

- Outputs of processing-the-data activity:
  While it is important to identify the outputs of each activity such as data and decisions it is even more important to determine the output of the procedure, the level of detail, the quality, the format etc.

Examples of outputs from procedures:

- Updated Availability and Capacity Plans
- Reports
- Logical groupings of data ready for analysis.

Step Five – Analysing the data

Your organization's Service Desk has a trend of reduced call volumes consistently over the last four months. Even though this is a trend, you need to ask yourself the question: 'Is this a good trend or a bad trend?' You don't know if the call reduction is because you have reduced the number of recurring errors in the infrastructure by good problem management activities or if the customers feel that the Service Desk doesn't provide any value and they have started bypassing the Service Desk and going directly to second-level support groups.

Data analysis transforms the information into knowledge of the events that are affecting the organization. More skill and experience is required to perform data analysis than data gathering and processing. Verification against goals and objectives is expected during this activity. This verification validates that objectives are being supported and value is being added. It is not sufficient to simply produce graphs of various types but to document the observations and conclusions.

Table 4.2 Procedure for processing data activity

Tasks	Procedures
Task 1	Based on strategy, goals and SLAs, define the data processing requirements
Task 2	Determine frequency of processing the data
	Determine method of processing the data
Task 3	Identify and document the format of logical grouping of data elements
	Define tools required for processing data
	Build, purchase or modify tools for measuring
	Test tool
	Install tool
Task 4	Develop processing data procedures
	Train people on procedures
Task 5	Develop and communicate monitoring plan
	Get approval from internal IT and external vendors who may be impacted
Task 6	Update Availability and Capacity Plans if required
Task 7	Begin the data processing
Task 8	Process into logical groupings
Task 9	Evaluate processed data for accuracy

Question: What do you actually analyse?

Answer: Once the data is processed into information, you can then analyse the results, looking for answers to questions such as:

- Are there any clear trends?
- Are they positive or negative trends?
- Are changes required?
- Are we operating according to plan?
- Are we meeting targets?
- Are corrective actions required?
- Are there underlying structural problems?
- What is the cost of the service gap?

Question: Where do you actually find the information?

Answer: Here you apply knowledge to your information. Without this, you have nothing more than sets of numbers showing metrics that are meaningless. It is not enough to simply look at this month's figures and accept them without question, even if they meet SLA targets. You should analyse the figures to stay ahead of the game. Without analysis you merely have information. With analysis you have knowledge. If you find anomalies or poor results, then look for ways to improve.

It is interesting to note the number of job titles for IT professionals that contain the word 'analyst' and even more surprising to discover that few of them actually analyse anything. This step takes time. It requires concentration, knowledge, skills, experience etc. One of the major assumptions is that the automated processing, reporting, monitoring tool has actually done the analysis. Too often people simply point at a trend and say 'Look, numbers have gone up over the last quarter.' However, key questions need to be asked, such as:

- Is this good?
- Is this bad?
- Is this expected?
- Is this in line with targets?

Combining multiple data points on a graph may look nice but the real question is what does it actually mean. 'A picture is worth a thousand words' goes the saying. In analysing the data an accurate question would be 'Which thousand words?' To transform this data into knowledge, compare the information from step 3 against both the requirements from step 1 and what could realistically be measured from step 2.

Be sure to also compare against the clearly defined objectives with measurable targets that were set in the Service Design, Transition and Operations lifecycle stages. Confirmation needs to be sought that these objectives and the milestones were reached. If not, have improvement initiatives been implemented? If so, then the CSI activities start again from the gathering data, processing data and analysing data to identify if the desired improvement in service quality has been achieved. At the completion of each significant stage or milestone, a review should be conducted to ensure the objectives have been met. It is possible here to use the Post-Implementation Review (PIR) from the Change Management process. The PIR will include a review of supporting documentation and the general awareness amongst staff of the refined processes or service. A comparison is required of what has been achieved against the original goals.

During the analysis activity, but after the results are compiled and analysis and trend evaluation have occurred, it is recommended that internal meetings be held within IT to review the results and collectively identify improvement opportunities. It is important to have these internal meetings before you begin presenting and using the information which is the next activity of Continual Service Improvement. The result is that IT is a key player in determining how the results and any actions items are presented to the business.

This puts IT in a better position to formulate a plan of presenting the results and any action items to the business and to senior IT management. Throughout this publication the terms 'service' and 'service management' have been used extensively. IT is too often focused on managing the various systems used by the business, often (but incorrectly) equating service and system. A service is actually made up of systems. Therefore if IT wants to be perceived as a key player, then IT must move from a systems-based organization to a service-based organization. This transition will force the improvement of communication between the different IT silos that exist in many IT organizations.

Performing proper analysis on the data also places the business in a position to make strategic, tactical and operational decisions about whether there is a need for service improvement. Unfortunately, the analysis activity is often not done. Whether it is due to a lack of resources with the right skills and/or simply a lack of time is unclear. What is clear is that without proper analysis, errors will continue to occur and mistakes will continue to be repeated. There will be little improvement.

Data analysis transforms the information into knowledge of the events that are affecting the organization. As an example, a sub-activity of Capacity Management is workload management. This can be viewed as analysing the data to determine which customers use what resource, how they use the resource, when they use the resource and how this impacts the overall performance of the resource. You will also be able to see if there is a trend on the usage of the resource over a period of time. From an incremental improvement process this could lead to some focus on Demand Management, or influencing the behaviour of customers.

Consideration must be given to the skills required to analyse from both a technical viewpoint and from an interpretation viewpoint.

When analysing data, it is important to seek answers to questions such as:

- Are operations running according to plan? This could be a project plan, financial plan, availability, capacity or even IT Service Continuity Management plan.
- Are targets defined in SLAs or the Service Catalogue being met?
- Are there underlying structural problems that can be identified?
- Are corrective actions required?
- Are there any trends? If so then what are the trends showing? Are they positive trends or negative trends?
- What is leading to or causing the trends?

Reviewing trends over a period of time is another important task. It is not good enough to see a 'snapshot' of a data point at a specific moment in time, but to look at the data points over a period of time. How did we do this month compared to last month, this quarter compared to last quarter, this year compared to last year?

It is not enough to only look at the results but also to look at what led to the results for the current period. If we had a bad month, did we have an anomaly that took place? Is this a demonstrable trend or simply a one-off?

Example

When one organization started performing trend analysis activities around Incident Management, they discovered that their number of incidents increased for a one month period every three months. When they investigated the cause, they found it was tied directly to a quarterly release of an application change. This provided statistical data for them to review the effectiveness of their Change and Release Management processes as well as understand the impact each release would have on the Service Desk with the number of increased call volumes. The Service Desk was also able to begin identifying key skill sets needed to support this specific application.

Trends are an indicator that more analysis is needed to understand what is causing it. When a trend goes up or down it is a signal that further investigation is needed to determine if it is positive or negative.

Another example

A Change Manager communicates that the Change Management process is doing well because the volume of requests for changes has steadily decreased. Is this positive or negative? If Problem Management is working well, it could be positive as recurring incidents are removed therefore fewer changes are required as the infrastructure is more stable. However, if users have stopped submitting requests for changes because the process is not meeting expectations, the trend is negative.

Without analysis the data is merely information. With analysis comes improvement opportunities.

Throughout CSI, assessment should identify whether targets were achieved and, if so, whether new targets (and therefore new KPIs) need to be defined. If targets were achieved but the perception has not improved, then new targets may need to be set and new measures put in place to ensure that these new targets are being met.

When analysing the results from process metrics keep in mind that a process will only be as efficient as its limited bottleneck activity. So if the analysis shows that a process activity is not efficient and continually creates a bottleneck then this would be a logical place to begin looking for a process improvement opportunity.

Step Six – Presenting and using the information

The sixth step is to take our knowledge and present it, that is, turn it into wisdom by utilizing reports, monitors, action plans, reviews, evaluations and opportunities. Consider the target audience; make sure that you identify exceptions to the service, benefits that have been revealed, or can be expected. Data gathering occurs at the operational level of an organization. Format this data into knowledge that all levels can appreciate and gain insight into their needs and expectations.

Question: What do you actually measure?

Answer: There are no measurements in this step.

Question: Where do you actually find the information?

Answer: From all previous steps.

Historical/previous presentations

This stage involves presenting the information in a format that is understandable, at the right level, provides value, notes exceptions to service, identifies benefits that were revealed during the time period, and allows those receiving the information to make strategic, tactical and operational decisions. In other words, presenting the information in the manner that makes it the most useful for the target audience.

Creating reports and presenting information is an activity that is done in most organizations to some extent or another; however it often is not done well. For many organizations this activity is simply taking the gathered raw data (often straight from the tool) and reporting this same data to everyone. There has been no processing and analysis of the data.

The other issue often associated with presenting and using information it that it is overdone. Managers at all levels are bombarded with too many e-mails, too many meetings, too many reports. Too often they are copied and presented to as part of an I-am-covering-my-you-know-what exercise. The reality is that the managers often don't need this information or at the very least, not in that format. There often is a lack of what role the manager has in making decisions and providing guidance on improvement programmes.

As we have discussed, Continual Service Improvement is an ongoing activity of monitoring and gathering data, processing the data into logical groupings, analysing the data for meeting targets, identifying trends and identifying improvement opportunities. There is no value in all the work done to this point if we don't do a good job of presenting our findings and then using those findings to make improvement decisions.

Begin with the end in mind is habit number 2 in Stephen Covey's publication *Seven Habits of Highly Effective People* (Simon & Schuster, 1989). Even though the publication is about personal leadership, the habit holds true with presenting and using information. In addition to understanding the target audience, it is also important to understand the report's purpose. If the purpose and value cannot be articulated, then it is important to question if it is needed at all.

There are usually three distinct audiences:

- **The business** – Their real need is to understand whether IT delivered the service they promised at the levels they promised and if not, what corrective actions are being implemented to improve the situation.
- **Senior (IT) management** – This group is often focused on the results surrounding CSFs and KPIs such as, customer satisfaction, actual vs. plan, costing and revenue targets. Information provided at this level helps determine strategic and tactical improvements on a larger scale. Senior (IT) management often wants this type of information provided in the form of a Balanced Scorecard or IT scorecard format to see the big picture at one glance.
- **Internal IT** – This group is often interested in KPIs and activity metrics that help them plan, coordinate, schedule and identify incremental improvement opportunities.

Often there is a gap between what IT reports and what is of interest to the business. IT is famous for reporting availability in percentages such as 99.85% available. In most cases this is not calculated from an end-to-end perspective but only mainframe availability or application availability and often doesn't take into consideration LAN/WAN, server or desktop downtime. In reality, most people in IT don't know the difference between 99.95% and 99.99% availability let alone the business. Yet reports continue to show availability achievements in percentages. What the business really wants to understand is the number of outages that occurred and the duration of the outages with analysis describing the impact on the business processes, in essence, unavailability expressed in a commonly understood measure – time.

Now more than ever, IT must invest the time to understand specific business goals and translate IT metrics to reflect an impact against these goals. Businesses invest in tools and services that affect productivity, and support should be one of those services. The major challenge, and one that can be met, is to effectively communicate the business benefits of a well-run IT support group. The starting point is a new perspective on goals, measures, and reporting, and how IT actions affect business results. You will then be prepared to answer the question: 'How does IT help to generate value for your company?'

Although most reports tend to concentrate on areas where things are not going as well as hoped for, do not forget to report on the good news as well. A report showing improvement trends is IT services' best marketing vehicle. It is vitally important that reports show whether CSI has actually improved the overall service provision and if it has not, the actions taken to rectify the situation.

The figure below is an example of a SLA monitoring chart that provides a visual representation of an organization's ability to meet defined targets over a period of months.

Some of the common problems associated with the presenting and reporting activity:

- Everyone gets the same report (business, senior management and IT managers).
- The format is not what people want. It is important to understand the audience and how they like to receive information. Some like the information in text format, some in graphs, pie charts etc. It is hard to please everyone, but getting agreement on the report format is a step in the right direction.

This is why many organizations are moving to a Balanced Scorecard or IT scorecard concept. This concept can start at the business level, then the IT level, and then functional groups and/or services within IT.

- Lack of an executive summary – the executive summary should discuss the current results, what led to the results and what actions have or will be taken to address any issues.
- Reports are not linked to any baseline, IT scorecard or Balanced Scorecard.
- Too much supporting data provided.
- Reports are presented in terms that are not understandable. For example, availability is reported in percentages when the business often is interested in knowing the number, duration and impact of outages.

The resources required to produce, verify and distribute reports should not be under-estimated. Even with automation, this can be a time-consuming activity.

Step Seven – Implementing corrective action

Use the knowledge gained to optimize, improve and correct services. Managers need to identify issues and present solutions. Explain how the corrective actions to be taken will improve the service.

Example

An organization hired an expensive consulting firm to assess the maturity of the processes against the ITIL framework. The report from the consulting organization had the following observation and recommendation about the Incident Management process:

The help desk is not doing Incident Management the way ITIL does. Our recommendation is that you must implement Incident Management.

The reaction from the customer was simple. They fired the consulting organization.

What would happen to you if you presented a similar observation and recommendation to your CIO?

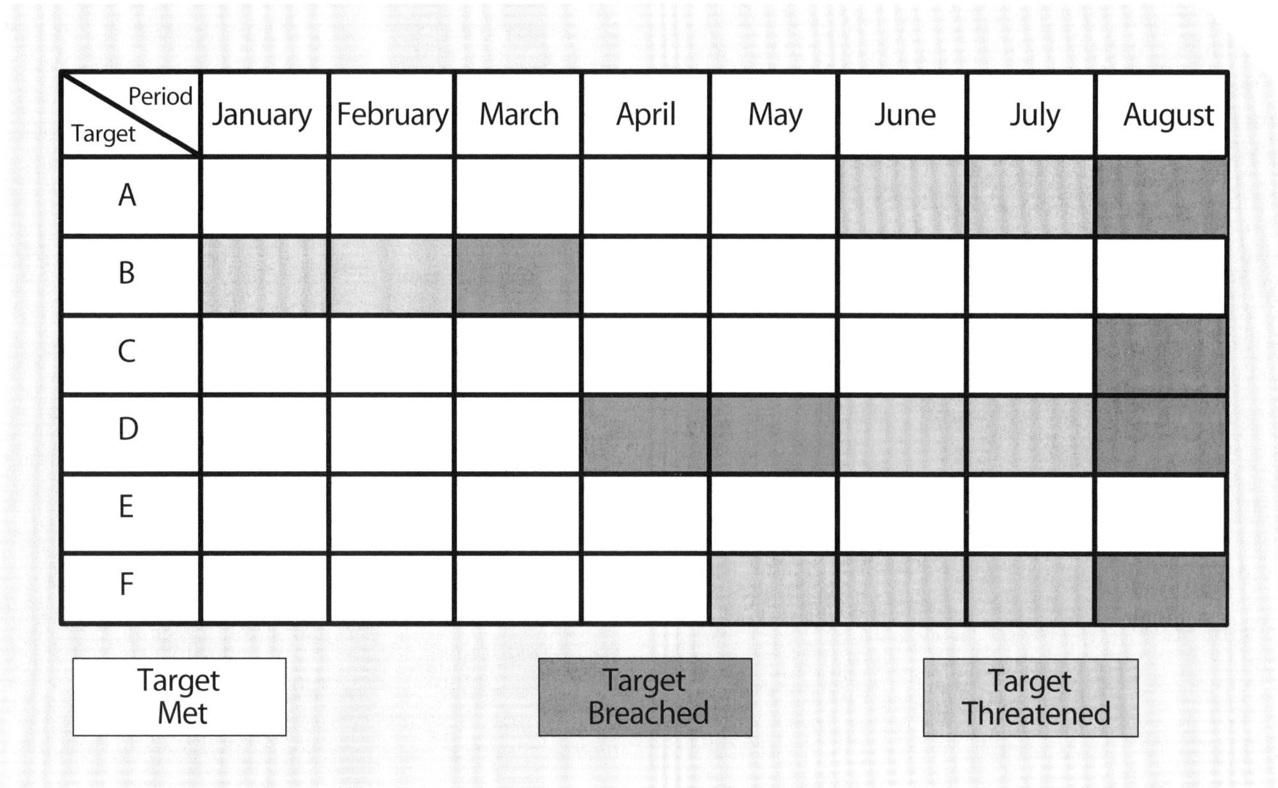

Target \ Period	January	February	March	April	May	June	July	August
A								
B								
C								
D								
E								
F								

Target Met

Target Breached

Target Threatened

Figure 4.5 Service level achievement chart

CSI identifies many opportunities for improvement however organizations cannot afford to implement all of them. Based on goals, objectives and types of service breaches, an organization needs to prioritize improvement activities. Improvement initiatives can also be externally driven by regulatory requirements, changes in competition, or even political decisions.

If organizations were implementing corrective action according to CSI, there would be no need for this publication. Corrective action is often done in reaction to a single event that caused a (severe) outage to part or all of the organization. Other times, the squeaky wheel will get noticed and specific corrective action will be implemented in no relation to the priorities of the organization, thus taking valuable resources away from real emergencies. This is common practice but obviously not best practice.

After a decision to improve a service and/or service management process is made, then the service lifecycle continues. A new Service Strategy may be defined, Service Design builds the changes, Service Transition implements the changes into production and then Service Operation manages the day-to-day operations of the service and/or service management processes. Keep in mind that CSI activities continue through each phase of the service lifecycle.

Each service lifecycle phase requires resources to build or modify the services and/or service management processes, potential new technology or modifications to existing technology, potential changes to KPIs and other metrics and possibly even new or modified OLAs/UCs to support SLAs. Communication, training and documentation is required to transition a new/improved service, tool or service management process into production.

Often steps are forgotten or are taken for granted or someone assumes that someone else has completed the step. This indicates a breakdown in the process and a lack of understanding of roles and responsibilities. The harsh reality is that some steps are overdone while others are incomplete or overlooked.

Example of corrective action being implemented

A financial organization with a strategically important website continually failed to meet its operational targets, especially with regard to the quality of service delivered by the site. The prime reason for this was their lack of focus on the monitoring of operational events, service availability and response. This situation was allowed to develop until senior business managers demanded action from the senior IT management. There were major repercussions, and reviews were undertaken to determine the underlying cause. After considerable pain and disruption, an operations group was identified to monitor this particular service. A part of the requirement was the establishment of weekly internal reviews and weekly reports on operational performance. Operational events were immediately investigated whenever they occurred and were individually reviewed after resolution. An improvement team was established, with representation from all areas, to implement the recommendations from the reviews and the feedback from the monitoring group. This eventually resulted in considerable improvement in the quality of service delivered to the business and its customers.

There are various levels or orders of management in an organization. Individuals need to know where to focus their activities. Line managers need to show overall performance and improvement. Directors need to show that quality and performance targets are being met, while risk is being minimized. Overall, senior management need to know what is going on so that they can make informed choices and exercise judgement. Each order has its own perspective. Understanding these perspectives is where maximum value of information is leveraged.

Understanding the order your intended audience occupies and their drivers helps you present the issues and benefits of your process. At the highest level of the organization are the strategic thinkers. Reports need to be short, quick to read and aligned to their drivers. Discussions about risk avoidance, protecting the image or brand of the organization, profitability and cost savings are compelling reasons to support your improvement efforts.

The second order consists of vice presidents and directors. Reports can be more detailed, but need to summarize findings over time. Identifying how processes support the business objectives, early warning around issues that place the business at risk, and alignment to existing measurement frameworks that they use are strong methods you can use to sell the process benefits to them.

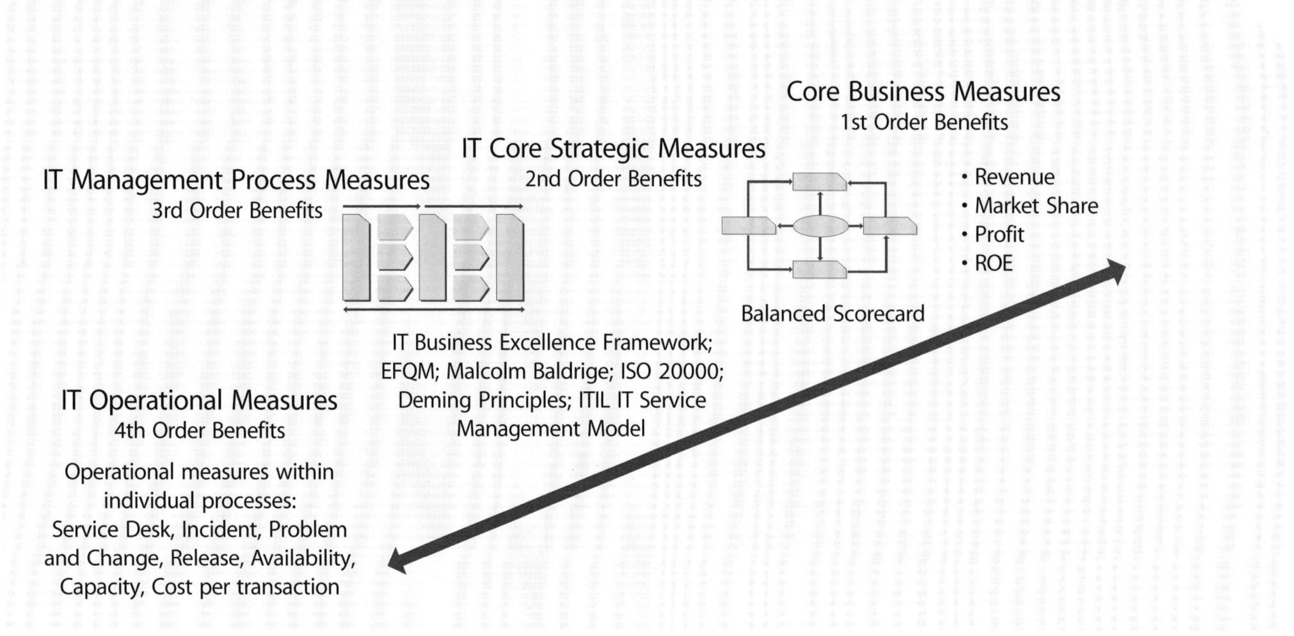

Figure 4.6 First- to fourth-order drivers

The third order consists of managers and high level supervisors. Compliance to stated objectives, overall team and process performance, insight into resource constraints and continual improvement initiatives are their drivers. Measurements and reports need to market how these are being supported by the process outputs.

Lastly at the fourth level of the hierarchy are the staff members and team leaders. At a personal level, the personal benefits need to be emphasized. Therefore metrics that show their individual performance, provide recognition of their skills (and gaps in skills) and identify training opportunities are essential in getting these people to participate in the processes willingly.

CSI is often viewed as an ad hoc activity within IT services. The activity usually kicks in when someone in IT management yells loud enough. This is not the right way to address CSI. Often these reactionary events are not even providing continual improvement, but simply stopping a single failure from occurring again.

CSI takes a commitment from everyone in IT working throughout the service lifecycle to be successful at improving services and service management processes. It requires ongoing attention, a well-thought-out plan, consistent attention to monitoring, analysing and reporting results with an eye toward improvement. Improvements can be incremental in nature but also require a huge commitment to implement a new service or meet new business requirements.

This section spelled out the seven steps of CSI activities. All seven steps need attention. There is no reward for taking a short cut or not addressing each step in a sequential nature. If any step is missed, there is a risk of not being efficient and effective in meeting the goals of CSI.

IT services must ensure that proper staffing and tools are identified and implemented to support CSI activities. It is also important to understand the difference between what should be measured and what can be measured. Start small – don't expect to measure everything at once. Understand the organizational capability to gather data and process the data. Be sure to spend time analysing data as this is where the real value comes in. Without analysis of the data, there is no real opportunity to truly improve services or service management processes. Think through the strategy and plan for reporting and using the data. Reporting is partly a marketing activity. It is important that IT focus on the value added to the organization as well as reporting on issues and achievements. In order for steps 5 to 7 to be carried out correctly, it is imperative that the target audience is considered when packaging the information.

An organization can find improvement opportunities throughout the entire service lifecycle. An IT organization does not need to wait until a service or service management process is transitioned into the operations area to begin identifying improvement opportunities.

4.1.1 Integration with the rest of the lifecycle stages and service management processes

In order to support improvement activities it is important to have CSI integrated within each lifecycle stage including the underlying processes residing in each lifecycle phase.

Monitoring and data collection throughout the service lifecycle

Service Strategy is responsible for monitoring the progress of strategies, standards, policies and architectural decisions that have been made and implemented.

Service Design monitors and gathers data associated with creating and modifying (design efforts) of services and service management processes. This part of the service lifecycle also measures against the effectiveness and ability to measure CSFs and KPIs that were defined through gathering business requirements. Service Design also defines what should be measured. This would include monitoring project schedules, progress to project milestones, and project results against goals and objectives.

Service Transition develops the monitoring procedures and criteria to be used during and after implementation. Service Transition monitors and gathers data on the actual release into production of services and service management processes. It is the responsibility of Service Transition to ensure that the services and service management processes are embedded in a way that can be managed and maintained according to the strategies and design efforts. Service transition develops the monitoring procedures and criteria to be used during and after implementation.

Service Operation is responsible for the actual monitoring of services in the production environment. Service Operation plays a large part in the processing activity. Service Operation provides input into what can be measured and processed into logical groupings as well as doing the actual processing of the data. Service Operation would also be responsible for taking the component data and processing it in the format to provide a better end-to-end perspective of the service achievements.

CSI receives the collected data as input in the remainder of CSI activities.

Role of other processes in monitoring and data collection

Service Level Management

SLM plays a key role in the data gathering activity as SLM is responsible for not only defining business requirements but also IT's capabilities to achieve them.

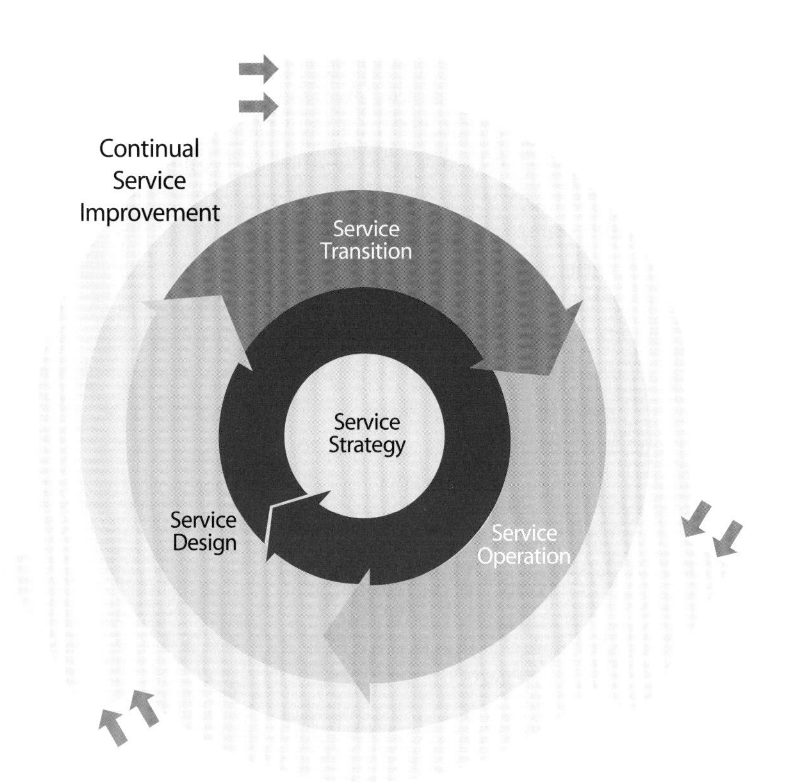

Figure 4.7 Lifecycle integration diagram

- One of the first items in defining IT's capabilities is to identify what monitoring and data collection activities are currently taking place
- SLM then needs to look at what is happening with the monitoring data. Is the monitoring taking place only at a component level and, if so, is anyone looking at multiple components to provide an end-to-end service performance perspective?
- SLM should also identify who gets the data, whether any analysis takes place on the data before it is presented, and if any trend evaluation is undertaken to understand the performance over a period of time. This information will be helpful in following CSI activities
- Through the negotiation process with the business, SLM would define what to measure and which aspects to report. This would in turn drive the monitoring and data collection requirements. If there is no capability to monitor and/or collect data on an item then it should not appear in the SLA. SLM should be a part of the review process to monitor results
- SLM is responsible for developing and getting agreement on OLAs and UCs that require internal or external monitoring.

Availability and Capacity Management

- Provide significant input into existing monitoring and data collection capabilities, tool requirements to meet new data collection requirements and ensuring the Availability and Capacity Plans are updated to reflect new or modified monitoring and data collection requirements
- Are accountable for the actual infrastructure monitoring and data collection activities that take place. Therefore roles and responsibilities need to be defined and the roles filled with properly skilled and trained staff
- Are accountable for ensuring tools are in place to gather data
- Are accountable for ensuring that the actual monitoring and data collection activities are consistently performed.

Incident Management and Service Desk

- Incident Management can define monitoring requirements to support event and incident detection through automation and also has the ability to automatically open incident tickets and/or auto-escalate incident tickets
- Event and incident monitoring can identify abnormal situations and conditions which helps with predicting and pre-empting situations and conditions thereby avoiding possible service and component failures
- Monitoring the response times, repair times, resolution times and incident escalations
- As a single point of contact it is important for the Service Desk to monitor telephony items such as call volumes, average speed of answer, call abandonment rates etc. so that immediate action can be taken when there is an increase in contacts to the Service Desk. This would also apply to those Service Desks who provide support via e-mail and via the web.

Security Management

Security Management contributes to monitoring and data collection in the following manner:

- Define security monitoring and data collection requirements
- Monitor, verify and track the levels of security according to the organizational security policies and guidelines
- Assist in determining effects of security measures on the data monitoring and collection from the confidentiality (accessible only to those who should), integrity (data is accurate and not corrupted or not corruptible) and availability (data is available when needed) perspectives.

Financial Management

Financial Management is responsible for monitoring and collecting data associated with the actual expenditures vs. budget and is able to provide input on questions such as: are costing or revenue targets on track? Financial Management should also monitor the ongoing cost per service etc.

In addition Financial Management will provide the necessary templates to assist CSI to create the budget and expenditure reports for the various improvement initiatives as well as providing the means to compute the ROI of the improvements.

Role of other processes in measuring the data

Service Level Management

SLM supports the CSI processing data activity in the following manner:

- Define requirements to support any default levels of service that are described in the Service Catalogue
- Ensure that the SLAs only incorporate measurements that truly can be measured and reported on
- Negotiate and document OLAs and UCs that define the required measurements

- Review the results of the processed data from an end-to-end approach
- Help define the reporting frequency of processing and reporting formats.

Availability and Capacity Management

- Availability and Capacity Management would be responsible for processing the data at a component level and then working with SLM providing the data in an end-to-end perspective
- Process data on KPIs such as availability or performance measures
- Utilize the agreed upon reporting formats
- Analyse processed data for accuracy.

Incident Management and Service Desk

- Process data on incidents and Service Requests such as who is using the Service Desk and what is the nature of the incidents
- Collect and processing data on KPIs such as mean time to restore service and percentage of incidents resolved within service targets
- Process data for telephony statistics such as number of inbound/outbound calls, average talk time, average speed of answer, abandoned calls etc.
- Utilize the agreed upon reporting format
- Analyse processed data for accuracy.

Security Management

- Process response and resolution data on security incidents
- Create trend analyses on security breaches
- Validate success of risk mitigation strategies
- Utilize the agreed upon reporting format
- Analyse processed data for accuracy.

Analysing the data throughout the service lifecycle

Service Strategy analyses results associated with implemented strategies, policies and standards. This would include identifying any trends, comparing results against goals and also identifying any improvement opportunities.

Service Design analyses current results of design and project activities. Trends are also noted with results compared against the design goals. Service Design also identifies improvement opportunities and analyses the effectiveness and ability to measure CSFs and KPIs that were defined when gathering business requirements.

Service Operation analyses current results as well as trends over a period of time. Service Operation also identifies both incremental and large-scale improvement opportunities, providing input into what can be measured and processed into logical groupings. This area also performs the actual data processing. Service Operation would also be responsible for taking the component data and processing it in the format to provide a better end-to-end perspective of service achievements.

If there is a CSI functional group within an organization, this group can be the single point for combining all analysis, trend data and comparison of results to targets. This group could then review all proposed improvement opportunities and help prioritize the opportunities and finally make a consolidated recommendation to senior management. For smaller organizations, this may fall to an individual or smaller group acting as a coordinating point and owning CSI. This is a key point. Too often data is gathered in the various technical domains … never to be heard from again. Designating a CSI group provides a single place in the organization for all the data to reside and be analysed.

Role of other processes in analysing the data

Service Level Management

SLM supports the CSI process data activity in the following manner:

- Analyse the Service Level Achievements compared to SLAs and service level targets that may be associated with the Service Catalogue
- Document and review trends over a period of time to identify any consistent patterns
- Identify the need for service improvement plans
- Identify the need to modify existing OLAs or UCs.

Availability and Capacity Management

- Analyse and identify trends on component and service data
- Compare results with prior months, quarters or annual reports
- Identify the need for updating the need for improvement in gathering and processing data
- Analyse the performance of components against defined technical specifications
- Document and review trends over a period of time to identify any consistent patterns
- Identify the need for service improvement plans or corrective actions
- Analyse processed data for accuracy.

Incident Management and Service Desk

- Document and review incident trends on incidents, Service Requests and telephony statistics over a period of time to identify any consistent patterns
- Compare results with prior months, quarters or annual reports
- Compare results with agreed-to levels of service
- Identify the need for service improvement plans or corrective actions
- Analyse processed data for accuracy.

Problem Management

Problem Management plays a key role in the analysis activity as this process supports all the other processes with regards to trend identification and performing root cause analysis. Problem Management is usually associated with reducing incidents, but a good Problem Management process is also involved in helping define process-related problems as well as those associated with services.

Overall, Problem Management seeks to:

- Perform root cause investigation as to what is leading identified trends
- Recommend improvement opportunities
- Compare results with prior results
- Compare results to agreed to service levels.

Security Management

Security Management as a function relies on the activities of all other processes to help determine the cause of security related incidents and problems. The Security Management function will submit requests for changes to implement corrections or for new updates to, say, the anti-virus software. Other processes such as Availability (confidentiality, integrity, availability and recoverability), Capacity (capacity and performance) and Service Continuity Management (planning on how to handle crisis) will lend a hand in planning longer term. In turn Security Management will play a key role in assisting CSI regarding all security aspects of improvement initiatives or for security-related improvements.

- Document and review security incidents for the current time period
- Compare results with prior results
- Identify the need for SIP or corrective actions
- Analyse processed data for accuracy.

Presenting and using the information throughout the service lifecycle

Service Strategy presents current results, trends and recommendations for improvement associated with implemented strategies, policies and standards.

Service Design presents current results, trends and recommendations for improvement of design and project activities.

Service Transition presents current results, trends and recommendations for moving services and service management processes into production.

Service Operation presents current results, trends and recommendations on improvement initiatives for both services and service management processes.

Role of other processes in presenting and using the information

Service Level Management

SLM presents information to the business and discusses the service achievements for the current time period as well as any longer trends that were identified. These discussions should also include information about what led to the results and any incremental or fine-tuning actions required.

Overall, SLM:

- Conducts consistent service review meetings (internal and external)
- Supports the preparation of reports
- Updates the SLA monitoring chart (SLAM) (see Chapter 9 for more details on the SLAM chart)
- Provides input into prioritizing improvement activities.

Availability and Capacity Management

- Supports preparation of the reports
- Provides input into prioritizing SIP or corrective actions
- Implements incremental or fine-tuning activities that do not require business approval.

Incident Management and Service Desk

- Supports preparation of the reports
- Provides input into prioritizing SIPs or corrective actions
- Implements incremental or fine-tuning activities that do not require business approval.

Problem Management

- Provides input into service improvement initiatives and prioritizes improvement initiatives

- Security Management
- Supports preparation of the reports
- Provides input into prioritizing SIP or corrective actions
- Implements incremental or fine-tuning activities that do not require business approval.

Role of other processes in implementing corrective action

Change Management

When CSI determines that an improvement to a service is warranted, an RFC must be submitted to Change Management. In turn Change Management treats the RFC like any other RFC. The RFC is prioritized and categorized according to policies and procedures defined in the Change Management process. Release Management, as a part of Service Transition, is responsible for moving this change to the production environment. Once the change is implemented, CSI is part of the PIR to assess the success or failure of the change.

Representatives from CSI should be part of the CAB and the CAB/EC. Changes have an effect on service provision and may also affect other CSI initiatives. As part of the CAB and CAB/EC, CSI is in a better position to provide feedback and react to upcoming changes.

Service Level Management

The SLM process often generates a good starting point for a service improvement plan (SIP) – and the service review process may drive this. Where an underlying difficulty that is adversely impacting service quality is identified, SLM must, in conjunction with Problem Management and Availability Management, instigate a SIP to identify and implement whatever actions are necessary to overcome the difficulties and restore service quality. SIP initiatives may also focus on such issues as training, system testing and documentation. In these cases, the relevant people need to be involved and adequate feedback given to make improvements for the future. At any time, a number of separate initiatives that form part of the SIP may be running in parallel to address difficulties with a number of services.

Some organizations have established an up-front annual budget held by SLM from which SIP initiatives can be funded.

If an organization is outsourcing Service Delivery to a third party, the issue of service improvement should be discussed at the outset and covered (and budgeted for) in the contract, otherwise there is no incentive during the lifetime of the contract for the supplier to improve service targets.

There may be incremental improvement or large-scale improvement activities within each stage of the service lifecycle. As already mentioned, one of the activities IT management have to address is prioritization of service improvement opportunities.

4.1.2 Metrics and measurement

It is important to remember that there are three types of metrics that an organization will need to collect to support CSI activities as well as other process activities. The types of metrics are:

- **Technology metrics** – These metrics are often associated with component and application-based metrics such as performance, availability etc.
- **Process metrics** – These metrics are captured in the form of CSFs, KPIs and activity metrics for the service management processes. These metrics can help determine the overall health of a process. Four key questions that KPIs can help answer are around quality, performance, value and compliance of following the process. CSI would use these metrics as input in identifying improvement opportunities for each process.
- **Service metrics** – These metrics are the results of the end-to-end service. Component metrics are used to compute the service metrics.

In general, a metric is a scale of measurement defined in terms of a standard, i.e. in terms of a well-defined unit. The quantification of an event through the process of measurement relies on the existence of an explicit or implicit metric, which is the standard to which measurements are referenced.

Metrics are a system of parameters or ways of quantitative assessment of a process that is to be measured, along with the processes to carry out such measurement. Metrics define what is to be measured. Metrics are usually specialized by the subject area, in which case they are valid only within a certain domain and cannot be directly benchmarked or interpreted outside it. Generic metrics, however, can be aggregated across subject areas or business units of an enterprise.

Metrics are used in several business models including CMMI They are used in Knowledge Management (KM). These measurements or metrics can be used to track trends, productivity, resources and much more. Typically, the metrics tracked are KPIs.

How many CSFs and KPIs?

The opinions on this are varied. Some recommended that no more than two to three KPIs are defined per CSF at any given time and that a service or process has no more that two to three CSFs associated with it at any given time while others recommend upwards of four to five. This may not sound much but when considering the number of services, processes or when using the Balanced Scorecard approach, the upper limit can be staggering!

It is recommended that in the early stages of a CSI programme only two to three KPIs for each CSF are defined, monitored and reported on. As the maturity of a service and service management processes increase, additional KPIs can be added. Based on what is important to the business and IT management the KPIs may change over a period of time. Also keep in mind that as service management processes are implemented this will often change the KPIs of other processes. As an example, increasing first-contact resolution is a common KPI for Incident Management. This is a good KPI to begin with, but when you implement Problem Management this should change. One of Problem Management's objectives is to reduce the number of recurring incidents. When these types of recurring incidents are reduced this will reduce the number of first-contact resolutions. In this case a reduction in first-contact resolution is a positive trend.

The next step is to identify the metrics and measurements required to compute the KPI. There are two basic kinds of KPI, qualitative and quantitative.

Here is a qualitative example:

CSF: Improving IT service quality

KPI: 10 percent increase in customer satisfaction rating for handling incidents over the next 6 months.

Metrics required:

- Original customer satisfaction score for handling incidents
- Ending customer satisfaction score for handling incidents.

Measurements:

- Incident handling survey score
- Number of survey scores.

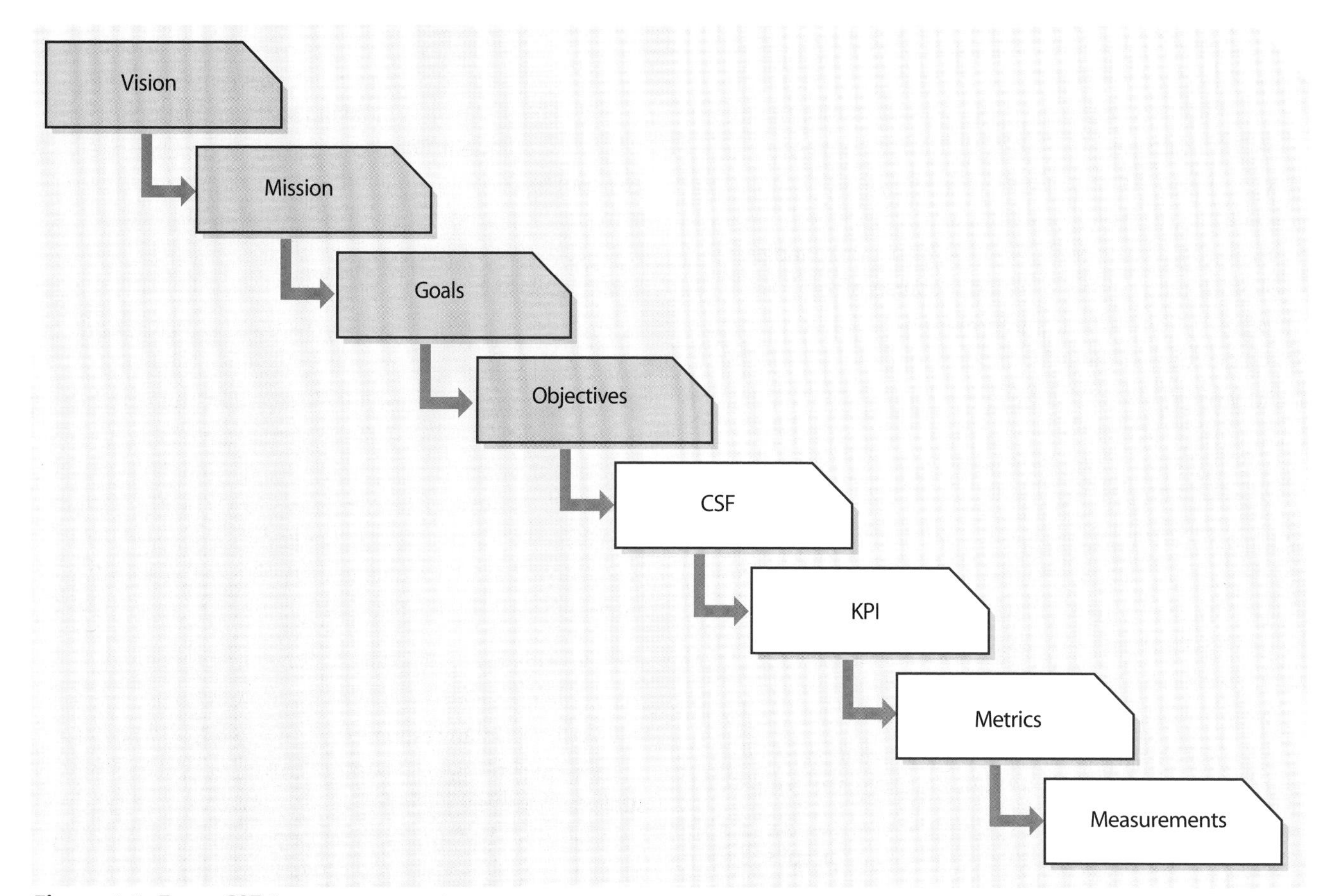

Figure 4.8 From CSF to measurement

Here is a quantitative example:

CSF: Reducing IT costs

KPI: 10 percent reduction in the costs of handling printer incidents.

Metrics required:

- Original cost of handling a printer incidents
- Final cost of handling a printer incidents
- Cost of the improvement effort.

Measurements:

- Time spent on the incident by first-level operative and their average salary
- Time spent on the incident by second-level operative and their average salary
- Time spent on Problem Management activities by second-level operative and their average salary
- Time spent on the training first-level operative on the workaround
- Cost of a service call to third-party vendor
- Time and material from third-party vendor.

An important aspect to consider is whether a KPI is fit for use. Key questions are:

- What does the performance indicator really tell us about goal achievement? If we fail to meet the target set for a performance indicator, does that mean we fail to achieve some of our goals? And if we succeed in meeting certain targets, does this mean we will achieve our goals?
- How easy is it to interpret the performance indicator? Does it help us to decide on a course of action?
- When do we need the information? How often? How rapidly should the information be available?
- To what extent is the performance indicator stable and accurate? Is it sensitive to external, uncontrollable influences? What amount of effort is needed for a change in result that is not marginal?
- How easy is it to change the performance indicator itself? How easy is it to adapt the measurement system to changing circumstances or changes in our goals with respect to IT service provision?
- To what extent can the performance indicator be measured now? Under which conditions can measurement continue? Which conditions impede measurement? Which conditions render the result meaningless?
- Who owns this KPI? Who is responsible for collecting and analysing the data? Who is accountable for improvements based on the information?

To become acquainted with the possibilities and limitations of your measurement framework, critically review your performance indicators with the above questions in mind before you implement them.

Tension metrics

The effort from any support team is a balancing act of three elements:

- Resources – people and money
- Features – the product or service and its quality
- The schedule.

The delivered product or service therefore represents a balanced trade-off between these three elements. Tension metrics can help create that balance by preventing teams from focusing on just one element – for example, on delivering the product or service on time. If an initiative is being driven primarily towards satisfying a business driver of on-time delivery to the exclusion of other factors, the manager will achieve this aim by flexing the resources and service features in order to meet the delivery schedule. This unbalanced focus will therefore either lead to budget increases or lower product quality. Tension metrics help create a delicate balance between shared goals and delivering a product or service according to business requirements within time and budget. Tension metrics do not, however, conflict with shared goals and values, but rather prevent teams from taking shortcuts and shirking on their assignment. Tension metrics can therefore be seen as a tool to create shared responsibilities between team members with different roles in the service lifecycle.

Goals and metrics

Each phase of the service lifecycle requires very specific contributions from the key roles identified in Service Design, Service Transition and Service Operation, each of which has very specific goals to meet. Ultimately, the quality of the service will be determined by how well each role meets its goals, and by how well those sometimes conflicting goals are managed along the way. That makes it crucial that organizations find some way of measuring performance – by applying a set of metrics to each goal.

Breaking down goals and metrics

It is really outside the scope of this publication to dig too deeply into human resources management, and besides, there is no shortage of literature already available on the subject. However, there are some specific things that can be said about best practices for goals and metrics as they apply to managing services in their lifecycle.

Many IT service organizations measure their IT professionals on an abstract and high-level basis. During appraisal and counselling, most managers discuss such things as 'taking part in one or more projects/performing activities of a certain kind', or 'fulfilling certain roles in projects/activities' and 'following certain courses'. Although accomplishing such goals might be important for the professional growth of an individual, it does not facilitate the service lifecycle or any specific process in it. In reality, most IT service organizations do not use more detailed performance measures that are in line with key business drivers, because it is difficult to do, and do correctly.

But there is a way. In the design phase of a service, key business drivers were translated into service level requirements (SLRs) and operations level requirements, the latter consisting of process, skills and technology requirements. What this constitutes is a translation from a business requirement into requirements for IT services and IT components. There is also the question, of the strategic position of IT. In essence, the question is whether IT is an enabler or a cost centre, the answer to which determines the requirements for the IT services and IT components. The answer also determines how the processes in the service lifecycle are executed, and how the people in the organization should behave. If IT is a cost centre, services might be developed to be used centrally in order to reduce Total cost of ownership (TCO). Services will have those characteristics that will reduce total costs of ownership throughout the lifecycle. On the other hand, if IT is an enabler, services will be designed to flexibly adjust to changing business requirements and meet early time-to-market objectives.

Either way, the important point is that those requirements for IT services and IT components would determine how processes in the lifecycle are measured and managed, and thus how the performance and growth of professionals should be measured.

Best practice shows that goals and metrics can be classified into three categories: financial metrics, learning and growth metrics, and organizational or process effectiveness metrics. An example of financial metrics might be the expenses and total percentage of hours spent on projects or maintenance, while an example of learning and growth might be the percentage of education pursued in a target skill area, certification in a professional area, and contribution to Knowledge Management. These metrics will not be discussed in this publication.

The last type of metrics, organizational or process effectiveness metrics, can be further broken down into product quality metrics and process quality metrics. Product quality metrics are the metrics supporting the contribution to the delivery of quality products. Examples of product quality metrics are shown in the following table. Process quality metrics are the quality metrics related to efficient and effective process management.

Using organizational metrics

To be effective, measurements and metrics should be woven through the complete organization, touching the strategic as well as the tactical level. To successfully

Table 4.3 Examples of service quality metrics

Measure	Metric	Quality goal	Lower limit	Upper limit
Schedule	% variation against revised plan	Within 7.5% of estimate	Not to be less than 7.5% of estimate	Not to exceed 7.5% of estimate
Effort	% variation against revised plan	Within 10% of estimate	Not to be less than 10% of estimate	Not to exceed 10% of estimate
Cost	% variation against revised plan	Within 10% of estimate	Not to be less than 10% of estimate	Not to exceed 10% of estimate
Defects	% variation against planned defect	Within 10% of estimate	Not to be less than 10% of estimate	Not to exceed 10% of estimate
Productivity	% variation against productivity goal	Within 10% of estimate	Not to be less than 10% of estimate	Not to exceed 10% of estimate
Customer satisfaction	Customer satisfaction survey result	Greater than 8.9 on the range of 1 to 10	Not to be less than 8.9 on the range of 1 to 10	

support the key business drivers, the IT services manager needs to know what and how well each part of the organization contributes to the final success.

It is also important, when defining measurements for goals that support the IT services strategy, to remember that measurements must focus on results and not on efforts. Focus on the organizational output and try to get clear what the contribution is. Each stage in the service lifecycle has its processes and contribution to the service. Each stage of the lifecycle also has its roles, which contribute to the development or management of the service. Based on the process goals and the quality attributes of the service, goals and metrics can be defined for each role in the processes of the lifecycle.

4.2 SERVICE REPORTING

This section will look into the various aspects of reporting such as identifying the purpose, the target audience and what the report will be used for.

A significant amount of data is collated and monitored by IT in the daily delivery of quality service to the business; however, only a small subset is of real interest and importance to the business. The majority of data and its meaning are more suited to the internal management needs of IT.

The business likes to see a historical representation of the past period's performance that portrays their experience; however, it is more concerned with those historical events that continue to be a threat going forward, and how IT intend to militate against such threats.

Cross-referenced data must still be presented which align precisely to any contracted, chargeable elements of the delivery; which may or may not be technical depending upon the business focus and language used within contracts and SLAs.

It is not satisfactory simply to present reports which depict adherence (or otherwise) to SLAs, which in themselves are prone to statistical ambiguity. IT needs to build an actionable approach to reporting. i.e. this is what happened, this is what we did, this is how we will ensure it doesn't impact you again, and this is how we are working to improve the delivery of IT services generally.

A reporting ethos which focuses on the future as strongly as it focuses on the past also provides the means for IT to market its wares directly aligned to the positive or negative experiences of the business.

4.2.1 Reporting policy and rules

An ideal approach to building a business-focused service-reporting framework is to take the time to define and agree the policy and rules with the business and Service Design about how reporting will be implemented and managed.

This includes:

- Targeted audience(s) and the related business views on what the service delivered is
- Agreement on what to measure and what to report on
- Agreed definitions of all terms and boundaries
- Basis of all calculations
- Reporting schedules
- Access to reports and medium to be used
- Meetings scheduled to review and discuss reports.

Right content for the right audience

Numerous policies and rules can exist as long as it is clear for each report which policies and rules have been applied, e.g. one policy may be applied to manufacturing whereas a variant may be more suited to the sales team. However all policies and rules form part of the single reporting framework.

Once the framework, policies and rules are in place, targeting suitably styled reports becomes simply a task of translating flat historical data into meaningful business views (which can be automated). These need to be annotated around the key questions, threats, mitigations and improvements such data provoke. Reports can then be presented via the medium of choice, e.g. paper-based hard copies, online soft copies, web-enabled dynamic HTML, current snapshot whiteboards, or real-time portal/dashboards.

Simple and effective customizable and automated reporting is crucial to a successful, ongoing reporting system that is seen as adding value to the business. Over time, many of the initial standard reports may become obsolete in favour of the regular production of custom reports which have been shaped to meet changing business needs and become the standard.

The end result is the targeted recipient having clear, unambiguous and relevant information in a language and style they understand and like, accessible in the medium of their choice, and detailing the delivery of IT into their environment within their boundaries, without such information being clouded by the data related to the delivery of IT into other areas of the business. Figure 4.9 depicts the service-reporting process.

4.3 SERVICE MEASUREMENT

4.3.1 Objective

For all sizes of businesses, private and public organizations, educational institutions, consumers and the individuals working within these organizations, IT services have become an integral means for conducting business. Without IT services many organizations would not be able to deliver the products and services in today's market. As reliance on these IT services increase so do the expectations for availability, reliability and stability. This is why having the business and IT integrated is so important. No longer can they be thought of separately. The same holds true when measuring IT services. It is no longer sufficient to measure and report against the performance of an individual component such as a server or application. IT must now be able to measure and report against an end-to-end service.

For services there are three basic measurements that most organizations utilize. The Service Design publication covers these measures in more detail.

- Availability of the service
- Reliability of the service
- Performance of the service

In many cases when an organization is monitoring, measuring and reporting on component levels they are doing so to protect themselves and possibly to point the blame elsewhere -'My server or my application was up 100% of the time.' Service measurement is not about placing blame or protecting oneself but is really about providing a meaningful view of the IT service as the customer experiences the service. The server may be up, but because the network is down, the customer is not able to connect to the server. Therefore the IT service was not available even though one or more of the components used to provide the service was available the whole time. Being able to measure against a service is directly linked to the components, systems and applications that are being monitored and reported on.

Measuring at the component level is necessary and valuable, but service measurement must go further than the component level. Service measurement will require someone to take the individual measurements and combine them to provide a view of the true customer experience. Too often we provide a report against a component, system or application but don't provide the true service level as experienced by the customer. Figure 4.10 shows how it is possible to measure and report against different levels of systems and components to provide a true service measurement. Even though the

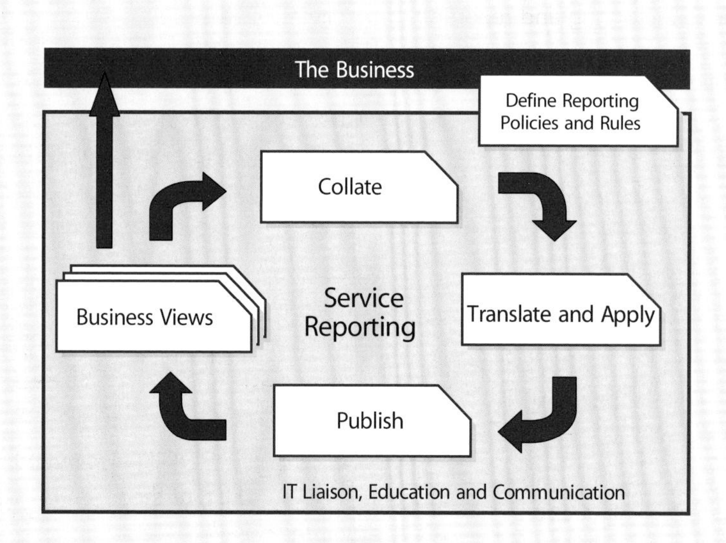

Figure 4.9 Service reporting process

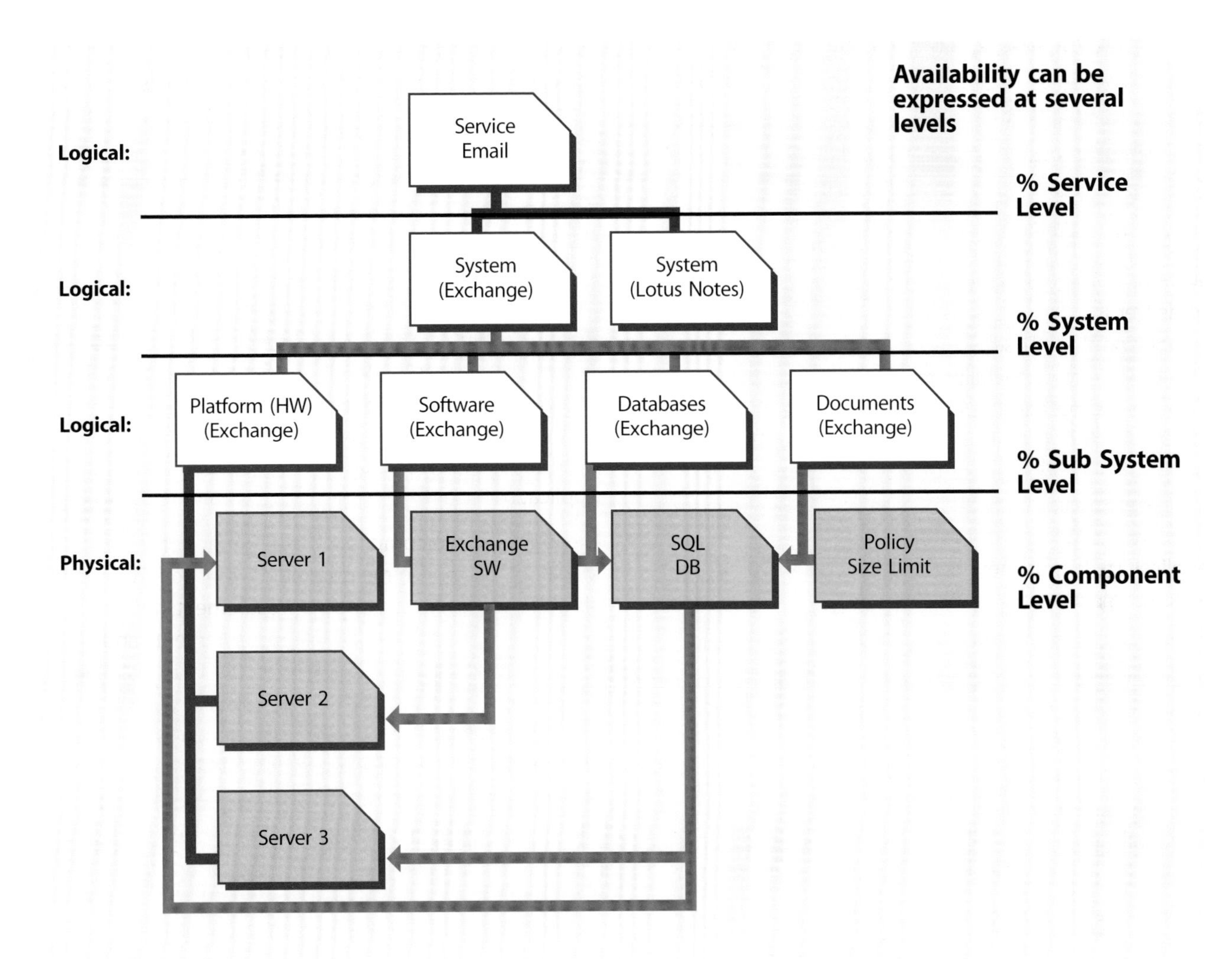

Figure 4.10 Availability reporting

figure references availability measuring and reporting the same can apply for performance measuring and reporting.

4.3.2 Developing a Service Measurement Framework

A challenge many organizations face is the creation of a Service Measurement Framework that leads to value-added reporting.

Setting up a framework is as much an art as a science. It may prove difficult at first but the results over time are worth the effort. An organization may go through some trial and error in the beginning so it should not be afraid to admit mistakes on particular measures or targets and make adjustments to the framework.

Keep in mind that service measurement is not an end in itself. The end result should be to improve services and also improve accountability.

One of the first steps in developing a Service Measurement Framework is to understand the business processes and to identify those that are most critical to the delivery of value to the business. The IT goals and objectives must support the business goals and objectives. There also needs to be a strong link between the operational, tactical and strategic level goals and objectives, otherwise an organization will find itself measuring and reporting on performance that may not add any value.

Service measurement is not only looking at the past but also the future – what do we need to be able to do and how can we do things better? The output of any Service Measurement Framework should allow individuals to make operational, tactical or strategic decisions.

Building a Service Measurement Framework means deciding which of the following need to be monitored and measured:

- Services
- Components

- Service Management processes that support the services
- Activities within the process
- Outputs.

Selecting a combination of measures is important to provide an accurate and balanced perspective. The measurement framework as a whole should be balanced and unbiased, and able to withstand change, i.e. the measures are still applicable (or available) after a change has been made.

Whether measuring one or multiple services the following steps are key to service measurement.

Origins

- Defining what success looks like. What are we trying to achieve and how will we know when we've achieved it?

Building the framework and choosing measures

- What do we need to measure that will provide us with useful information that allows us to make strategic, tactical and/or operational decisions?
- What measures will provide us with the data and information we need?
- Setting targets for all measures. This may be set by Service Level Agreements or service level targets/objectives that have been agreed internally within IT.

Defining the procedures and policies

- Define the procedures for making the measurements and determine the tools to be used to support gathering of the data and other measurement activities defined at the beginning of Chapter 4.
- Identify the roles and responsibilities for service measurement – who will do what?
- Define any policies necessary to support service measurement.
- Decide the criteria for continual improvement initiatives.
- Consider when targets should be raised?

Critical elements of a Service Measurement Framework

For a successful Service Measurement Framework the following critical elements are required.

A Performance Framework that is:

- Integrated into business planning
- Focused on business and IT goals and objectives
- Cost-effective
- Balanced in its approach on what is measured
- Able to withstand change.

Performance measures that:

- Are accurate and reliable
- Are well defined, specific and clear
- Are relevant to meeting the objectives
- Do not create a negative behaviour
- Lead to improvement opportunities.

Performance targets that:

- Are SMART.

Defined roles and responsibilities

- Who defines the measures and targets?
- Who monitors and measures?
- Who gathers the data?
- Who processes and analyses the data?
- Who prepares the reports?
- Who presents the reports?

4.3.3 Different levels of measurement and reporting

Creating a Service Measurement Framework will require the ability to build upon different metrics and measurements. The end result is a view of the way individual component measurements feed the end-to-end service measurement which should be in support of key performance indicators defined for the service. This will then be the basis for creating a service scorecard and dashboard. The service scorecard will then be used to populate an overall Balanced Scorecard or IT scorecard. As shown in Figure 4.11 there are multiple levels that need to be considered when developing a Service Measurement Framework.

What gets reported at each level is dependent on the measures that are selected.

Starting at the bottom, the technology domain areas will be monitoring and reporting on a component basis. This is

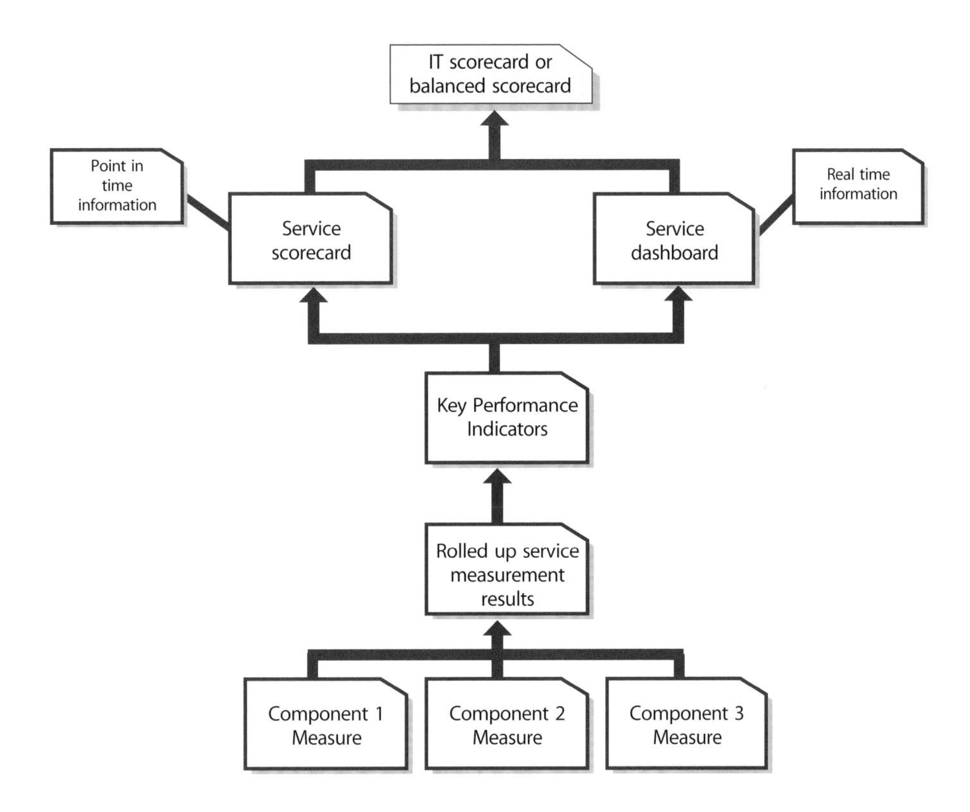

Figure 4.11 Service measurement model

valuable as each domain area is responsible for ensuring the servers are operating within defined guidelines and objectives. At this level, measurements will be on component availability, reliability and performance. The output of these measurements will feed into the overall end-to-end service measurement as well as the Capacity and Availability Plans. These measurements will also feed into any incremental operations improvements and into a more formal CSI initiative.

A part of service measurement is then taking the individual component measurements and using these to determine the true service measurement for an end-to-end service derived from availability, reliability and performance measurements.

As an example let's use e-mail as a service that is provided. As Figure 4.12 shows, we have four technology domains that often are monitored and reported on. The availability numbers are examples provided only for illustrative purposes.

- Mainframe availability 99.96%
- WAN availability 98%
- LAN availability 97.5%
- Desktop availability 96%

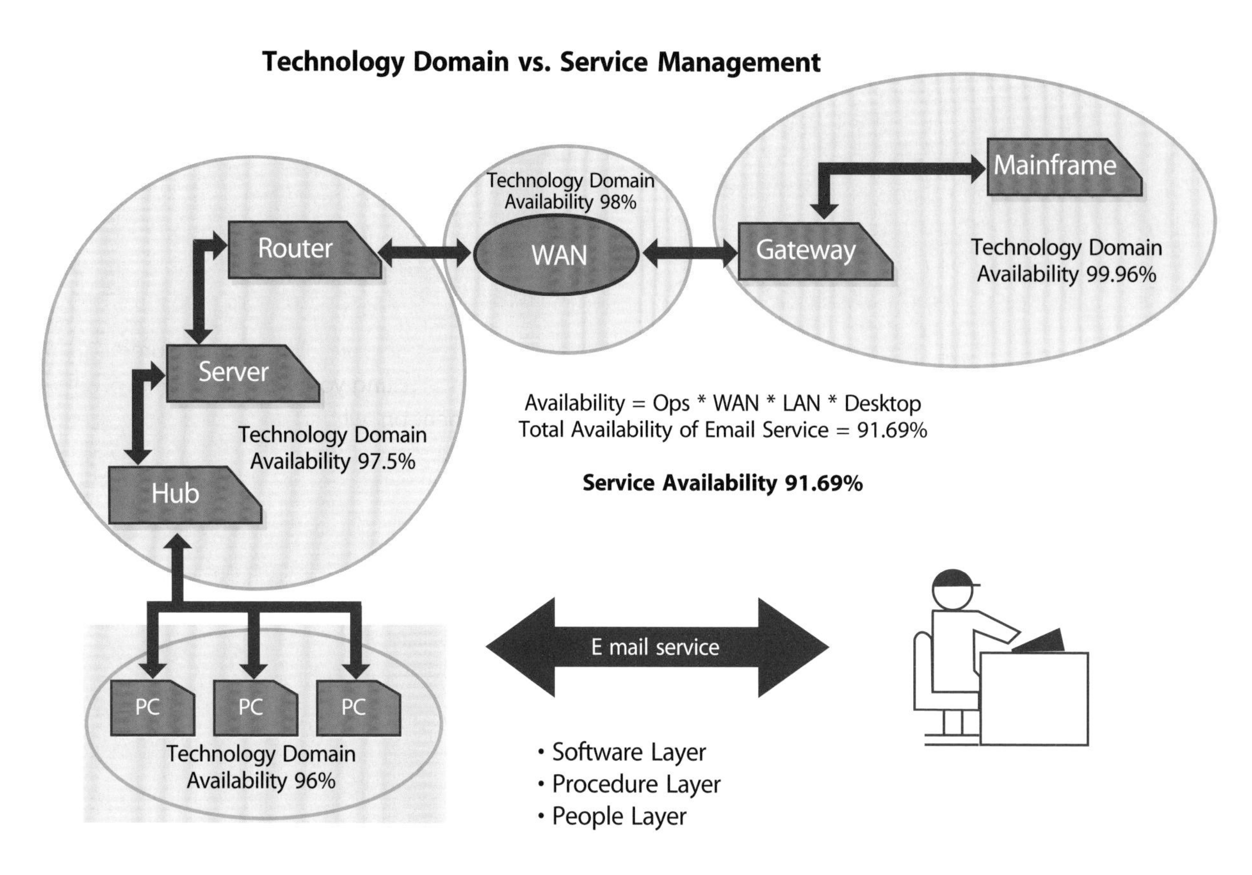

Figure 4.12 Technology domain vs. service management

Many people think the end-to-end service availability in this example is 96% because it is the lowest availability number. However, since all the failures which led to decreased availability did not occur at the same time within each technology domain the availability numbers have to be multiplied together. So the simple calculation is 99.96% x 98% x 97.5% x 96%. This provides an availability of the e-mail service at 91.69% which is what the customer experiences.

Service scorecard

This provides a snapshot view of a particular service. The timing is usually monthly but could be weekly or quarterly. It is recommended to report at least on a monthly basis.

Service dashboard

This can include the same measures as those reported on the service scorecard but these are real-time measures that can be made available to IT and the business through the intranet or some other portal mechanism.

At the highest level is a Balanced Scorecard or some form of IT scorecard that provides a comprehensive view of the measured aspects of the service. What should be measured should reflect strategic and tactical goals and objectives.

When developing a Service Management Framework it is important to understand which are the most suitable types of report to create, who they are being prepared for, and how they will be used.

4.3.4 Defining what to measure

Effective service measures concentrate on a few vital, meaningful indicators that are economical, quantitative and usable for the desired results. If there are too many measures, organizations may become too intent on measurement and lose focus on improving results. A guiding principle is to measure that which matters most.

IT has never lacked in the measuring area. In fact, many IT organizations measure far too many things that have little or no value. There is often no thought or effort given to alignment measures to the business and IT goals and objectives. There is often no measurement framework to guide the organization in the area of service measurement. Defining what to measure is important to ensure that the proper measures are in place to support the following:

- Service performance against the strategic business and IT plans – this would be a part of a Balanced Scorecard or IT scorecard.
- Risk and compliance with regulations and security requirements for the service – monitoring of security incidents and embedding security requirements in the Service Design and Transition practices.
- Business contribution including but not limited to financials – how does IT support the business in delivering services. As an example if your organization is an insurance company the major business services are writing policies and paying claims. Does IT make it easier to write policies and process claims for their agents especially when agents work remotely, such as during times of natural disaster?
- Key IT processes that support the service – how do availability, capacity and IT service continuity support the service?
- Internal and external customer satisfaction – measuring customer satisfaction to ensure that the customer's needs are being met.

To assess the business performance of IT, organizations may want to consider the categories in Table 4.4.

When measuring and reporting, IT needs to shift from their normal way of reporting to a more business view that the business can really understand. As an example, the traditional IT approach on measuring and reporting availability is to present the results in percentages but these are often at a component level and not at the service level. Availability when measured and reported should reflect the experience of the customer. Below are the common measurements that are meaningful to a customer.

- Number of outages on each service – there were two outages this month on Service 1.
- Duration of outages for each service – Service 1 outages lasted 179 minutes.
- Impact of the outages to each business – Business 1 uses five services and the total of all outages was 11 and the total duration was 1,749 minutes which prevented the business from being able to generate revenue during this time period.

Following on from this are common measurements to consider when selecting your measures. Remember this will be contingent on 'what you can measure'. If you cannot measure some of your choices at this time, then you will need to identify what tools, people etc. that will be required to effect those particular measurements.

Don't forget that you can use Incident Management data to help determine availability.

Service levels

This measure will include service, system, component availability, transaction and response time on components as well as the service, delivery of the service/application on time and on budget, quality of the service and compliance with any regulatory or security requirements. Many SLAs also require monitoring and reporting on Incident Management measures such as mean time to repair (MTTR) and mean time to restore a service (MTRS). Other normal measurements will be mean time between system incidents (MTBSI) and mean time between failures (MTBF). Many of the operational metrics and measures defined in the Service Design publication address the above measures in more detail.

Table 4.4 Categories for assessing business performance

Category	Definition
Productivity	Productivity of customers and IT resources
Customer satisfaction	Customer satisfaction and perceived value of IT services
Value chain	Impact of IT on functional goals
Comparative performance	Comparison against internal and external results with respect to business measures or infrastructure components
Business alignment	Criticality of the organization's services, systems and portfolio of applications to business strategy
Investment targeting	Impact of IT investment on business cost structure, revenue structure or investment base
Management vision	Senior management's understanding of the strategic value of IT and ability to provide direction for future action

Customer satisfaction

Surveys are conducted on a continual basis to measure and track customer satisfaction. It is common for the Service Desk and Incident Management to conduct a random sampling of customer satisfaction on incident tickets.

Business impact

Measure what actions are invoked for any disruption in service that adversely affects the customer's business operation, processes or its own customers.

Supplier performance

Whenever an organization has entered into a supplier relationship where some services or parts of services have been outsourced or co-sourced it is important to measure the performance of the supplier. Any supplier relationship should have defined, quantifiable measures and targets and measurement and reporting should be against the delivery of these measures and targets. Besides those discussed above, service measurements should also include any process metrics and KPIs that have been defined.

One of CSI's key sets of activities is to measure, analyse and report on IT services and ITSM results. Measurements will, of course, produce data. This data should be analysed over time to produce a trend. The trend will tell a story that may be good or bad. It is essential that measurements of this kind have ongoing relevance. What was important to know last year may no longer be pertinent this year.

As part of the measuring process it is important to confirm regularly that the data being collected and collated is still required and that measurements are being adjusted where necessary. This responsibility falls on the owner of each report or dashboard. They are the individuals designated to keep the reports useful and to make sure that effective use is being made of the results.

4.3.5 Setting targets

Targets set by management are quantified objectives to be attained. They express the aims of the service or process at any level and provide the basis for the identification of problems and early progress towards solutions and improvement opportunities.

Service measurement targets are often defined in response to business requirements or they may result from new policy or regulatory requirements. Service Level Management through Service Level Agreements will often drive the target that is required. Unfortunately, many organizations have had targets set with no clear understanding of the IT organization's capability to meet the target. That is why it is important that Service Level Management not only looks at the business requirements but also IT capability to meet business requirements.

When first setting targets against a new service it may be advisable to consider a phased target approach. In the other words, the target in the first quarter may be lower than the second quarter. With a new service it would be unwise to enter into a Service Level Agreement until overall capabilities are clearly identified. Even with the best Service Design and Transition, no one ever knows how a service will perform until it is actually in production.

Setting targets is just as important as selecting the right measures. It is important that targets are realistic but challenging. Good targets will be SMART (specific, measurable, achievable, relevant and timely). Targets should be clear, unambiguous and easy to understand by those who will be working toward them.

Remember that the choice of measures and their targets can affect the behaviour of those who are doing the work that is being measured. That is why it is always important to have a balanced approach.

Let's look at an example of common measures that are captured for the Service Desk. It is common for the Service Desk to measure the Average Speed of Answer (ASA), number of calls answered and call duration. These measures are often collected through telephony systems. If a Service Desk manager emphasizes the above measures more than others such as quality incident tickets, first contact resolution, customer satisfaction etc., it may be that the Service Desk analysts are focused on how many calls they can answer in a day and how quickly they can complete one call and start the next. When this happens with no thought about the quality of service being provided to restore service, or how the customer is treated, it will result in negative behaviour that is counter-productive to the goal of providing good service. The focus is only on volume and not quality.

When setting targets it is important to determine the baseline: this is the starting point from which you will measure improvement.

4.3.6 Service management process measurement

The same principles apply when measuring the efficiency and effectiveness of a service management process. As the figure below shows you will need to define what to measure at the process activity level. These activity

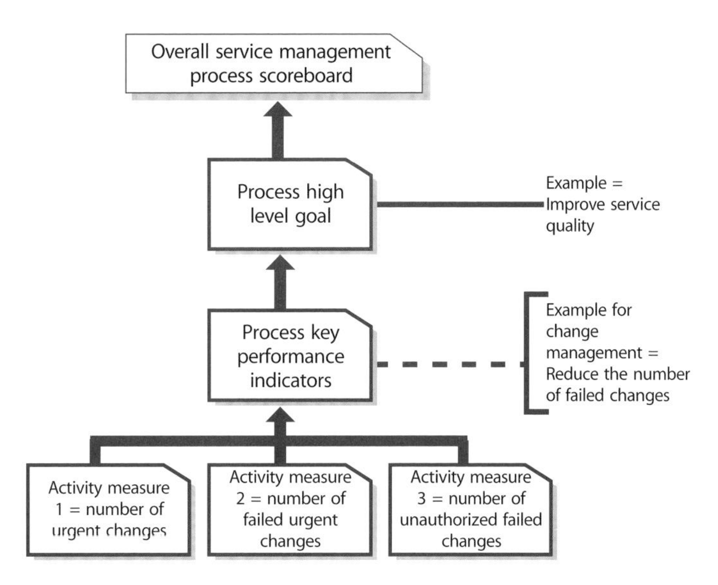

Figure 4.13 Service management model

measures should be in support of process key performance indicators (KPIs). The KPIs need to support higher-level goals. In the example below for Change Management, the higher level goal is to improve the service quality. One of the major reasons for service quality issues is the downtime caused by failed changes. And one of the major reasons for failed changes is often the number of urgent changes an organization implements with no formal process. Given that, then some key activity metrics it would be advisable to capture are:

- Number of urgent changes
- Number of failed urgent changes
- Unauthorized changes that failed.

There are four major levels to report on. The bottom level contains the activity metrics for a process and these are often volume type metrics such as number of Request for Changes (RFC) submitted, number of RFCs accepted into the process, number of RFCs by type, number approved, number successfully implemented, etc. The next level contains the KPIs associated with each process. The activity metrics should feed into and support the KPIs. The KPIs will support the next level which is the high-level goals such as improving service quality, reducing IT costs or improving customer satisfaction, etc. Finally, these will feed into the organization's Balanced Scorecard or IT scorecard. When first starting out, be careful to not pick too many KPIs to support the high-level goals. Additional KPIs can always be added at a later time.

Table 4.5 identifies some KPIs that reflect the value of service management. The KPIs are also linked to the service management process or processes that directly support the KPI. This table is not inclusive of all KPIs but simply an example of how KPIs may be mapped to processes.

4.3.7 Creating a measurement framework grid

It is recommended to create a framework grid that will lay out the high-level goals and define which KPIs will support the goal and also which category the KPI addresses.

KPI categories can be classified as the following:

- Compliance – are we doing it?
- Quality – how well are we doing it?
- Performance – how fast or slow are we doing it?
- Value – is what we are doing making a difference?

4.3.8 Interpreting and using metrics

Results must be examined in context of the objectives, environment and any external factors. Therefore after collecting the results, organizations will conduct measurement reviews to determine how well the indicators worked and how the results contribute to objectives.

Before starting to interpret the metrics and measures it is important to identify if the results that are being shown even make sense. If they do not, then instead of interpreting the results, action should be taken to identify the reasons the results appear the way they do. An example was an organization that provided data for the Service Desk and the data showed there were more first-contact resolutions at the Service Desk than there were incident tickets opened by the Service Desk. This is impossible and yet this organization was ready to

Table 4.5 Key performance indicators of the value of service management

Key performance indicator	Service management process	Comment
Improved availability (by service/systems/applications)	Availability Capacity Incident Management Problem Management Change Management Service Level Management	Improved monitoring and reporting on service availability. Expanded incident lifecycle, removing errors from the infrastructure, and reduction of failed changes; improved understanding of business requirements and IT capability – proactive planning
Reduction of service level breaches (by service/systems/applications)	Availability Capacity Incident Management Problem Management Change Management Service Level Management	Improved monitoring of services. Priority model, incident ownership, monitoring and tracking; removal of errors from the infrastructure. Reduction of failed changes; explicit Service Level Agreements
Reduction of mean time to repair (this should be measured by priority level, and not on a cumulative basis)	Incident Management Event Management Problem Management	Improved escalations, improved knowledge, improved prioritization. Priority model and Operational Level Agreements
Reduce percentage of urgent and emergency changes (by business unit)	Change Management Service Level Management	Creating lead time policies. Improved planning and scheduling reduces the need for urgent and emergency changes. Communicating change lead times to the business
Reduction of major incidents	Problem Management Change Management Service Level Management	Removing errors from the infrastructure, and reduction of failed changes; improved understanding of business requirements and IT capability – proactive planning

Table 4.6 High-level goals and key performance indicators

High-level goal	KPI	KPI category	Measurement	Target	How and who
Manage availability and reliability of a service	Percentage improvement in overall end-to-end availability of services	Value Quality	End-to-end service availability based on the component availability that makes up the service AS 400 availability Network availability Application availability	99.995%	Technical Managers Technical Analyst Service Level Manager

distribute this report. When this kind of thing happens than some questions need to be asked, such as:

- How did we collect this data?
- Who collected the data?
- What tools were used to collect the data?
- Who processed the data?
- What could have led to the incorrect information?

4.3.9 Interpreting metrics

When beginning to interpret the results it is important to know the data elements that make up the results, the purpose of producing the results and the expected normal ranges of the results.

Simply looking at some results and declaring a trend is dangerous. Figure 4.14 shows a trend that the Service Desk is opening fewer incident tickets over the last few months. One could believe that this is because there are fewer incidents or perhaps it is because the customers are not happy with the service that is being provided, so they go elsewhere for their support needs. Perhaps the organization has implemented a self help knowledge base and some customers are now using this service instead of contacting the Service Desk. Some investigation is required to understand what is driving these metrics.

One of the keys to proper interpretation is to understand whether there have been any changes to the service or if there were any issues that could have created the current results.

The chart can be interpreted in many ways so it would not be wise to share this chart without some discussion of the meaning of the results.

Figure 4.15 is another example of a Service Desk measurement. Using the same number of incident tickets we have now also provided the results of first contact resolution. The figure shows that not only are fewer incident tickets being opened, but the ability to restore service on first contact is also going down. Before jumping to all kinds of conclusions, some questions need to be asked.

- What has happened that could drive down the number of incidents?
- What would impact our ability to restore service on the first contact?
- Did we hire new Service Desk analysts?
- Did we remove some services?
- Have we provided other means to access our services?
- Have other processes been implemented that could impact incident volume and first contact resolution?

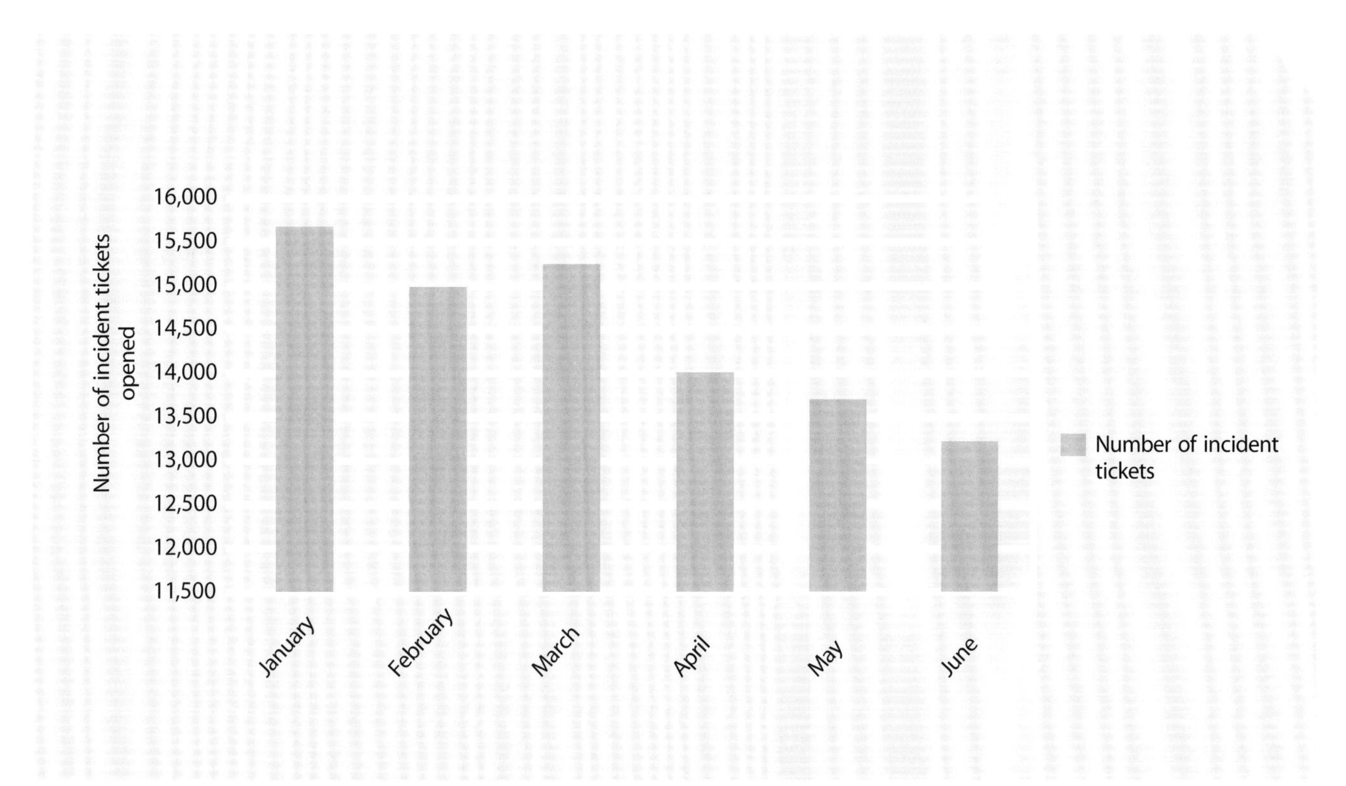

Figure 4.14 Number of incident tickets opened by Service Desk over time

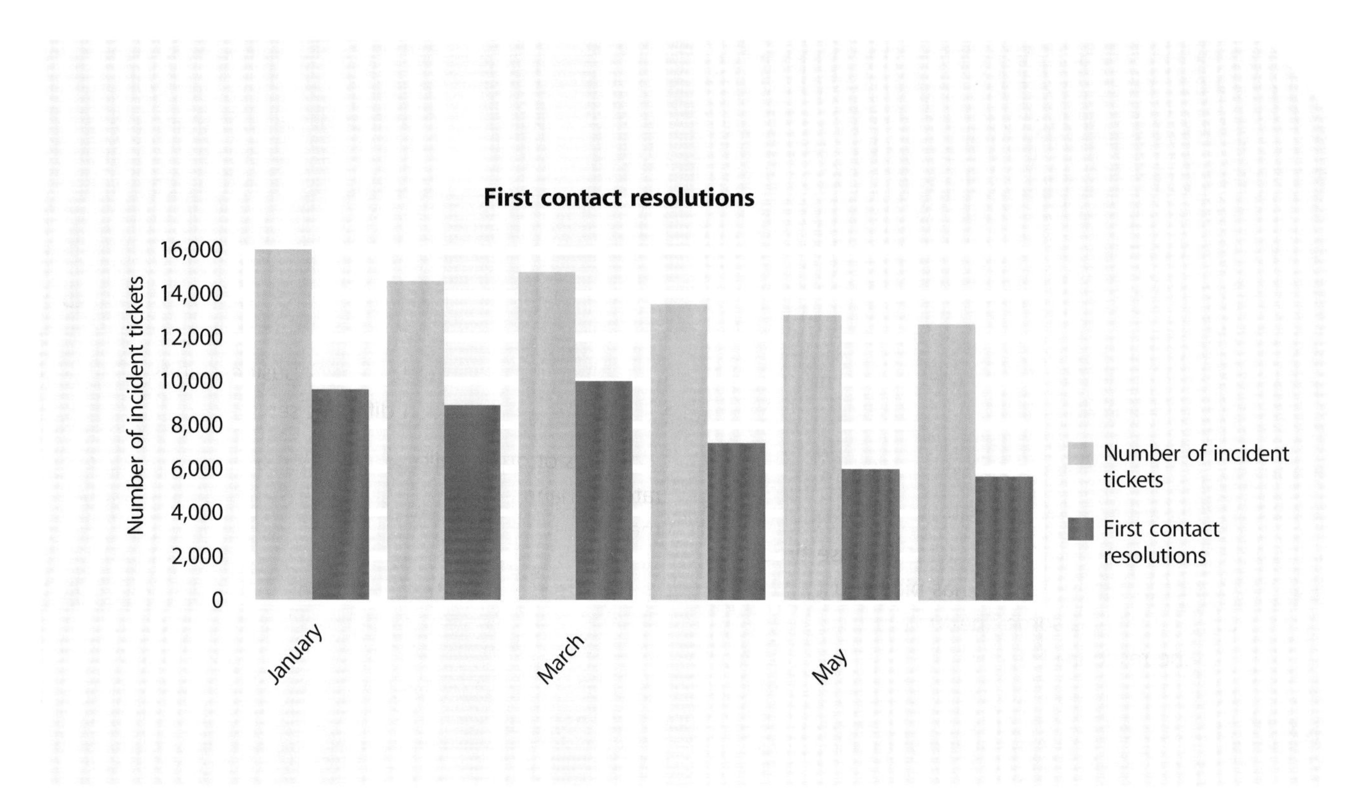

Figure 4.15 Comparison between incident tickets opened and resolved on first contact by the Service Desk

In this particular case, the organization had implemented Problem Management. As the process matured and through the use of incident trend analysis, Problem Management was able to identify a couple of recurring incidents that created a lot of incident activity each month. Through root cause analysis and submitting a request for change, a permanent fix was implemented, thus getting rid of the recurring incidents. Through further analysis it was found that these few recurring incidents were able to be resolved on the first contact. By removing these incidents the opportunity to increase first contact resolution was also removed. During this time period the Service Desk also had some new hires.

Table 4.7 provides a current view and year-to-date (YTD) view for response times for three services. The table provides a transaction count for each service, the minimum response time measured in seconds, the maximum response time measured in seconds and the average for the month. The table also provided the YTD average for each service. In order to understand if these

Table 4.7 Response times for three Service Desks

Service measurement response time							
Service	Response times in seconds						
	Current month				YTD	Percent within SLA 99.5% is the target	
	Count	Min	Max	Avg		Monthly	YTD %
Service 1 Target = 1.5 seconds	1,003,919	1.20	66.25	3.43	1.53	99.54%	98.76%
Service 2 Target = 1.25 seconds	815,339	0.85	21.23	1.03	1.07	98.44%	99.23%
Service 3 Target = 2.5 seconds	899,400	1.13	40.21	2.12	2.75	96.50%	94.67%

numbers are good or not it is important to define the target for each service as well as the target for meeting the Service Level Agreement.

When looking at the results for the three services it may appear that Service 2 is the best and this might be because it handles fewer transactions on a monthly basis than the other two services. Interpreting that Service 2 is the best by only looking at the numbers is dangerous. Investigations will find that Service 2 is a global service that is accessed 7 x 24 and the other two services have peak time utilization between 8 am and 7 pm Eastern Time. This is no excuse because the services are not hitting targets so further investigation needs to be conducted at the system and component levels to identify any issues that are creating the current response time results. It could be that the usage has picked up and this was not planned for and some fine tuning on components can improve the response time.

4.3.10 Using measurement and metrics

Metrics can be used for multiple purposes such as to:

- Validate – are we supporting the strategy and vision?
- Justify – do we have the right targets and metrics?
- Direct – based on factual data, people can be guided to change behaviour
- Intervene – take corrective actions such as identifying improvement opportunities.

Service measurements and metrics should be used to drive decisions. Depending on what is being measured the decision could be a strategic, tactical or operational decision. This is the case for CSI. There are many improvement opportunities but there is often only a limited budget to address the improvement opportunities, so decisions must be made. Which improvement opportunities will support the business strategy and goals, and which ones will support the IT goals and objectives? What are the Return on Investment and Value on Investment opportunities? These two items are discussed in more detail in section 4.4.

Another key use of measurement and metrics is for comparison purposes. Measures by themselves may tell the organization very little unless there is a standard or baseline against which to assess the data. Measuring only one particular characteristic of performance in isolation is meaningless unless it is compared with something else that is relevant. The following comparisons are useful:

- Comparison against the baseline
- Comparison against a target or goal
- Comparison with other organizations – be sure to understand that the strategy, goals and objectives of other organizations may not be in alignment with yours so there may be driving factors in the other organization that you don't have or it could be the other way around
- Comparison over time such as day to day, week to week, month to month, quarter to quarter, or year to year
- Comparison between different business units
- Comparison between different services.

Measures of quality allow for measuring trends and the rate of change over a period of time. Examples could be measuring trends against standards that are set up either internally or externally and could include benchmarks, or it could be measuring trends with standards and targets to be established. This is often done when first setting up baselines.

A minor or short-term deviation from targets should not necessarily lead to an improvement initiative. It is important to set the criteria for the deviations before an improvement programme is initiated.

Comparing and analysing trends against service level targets or an actual Service Level Agreement is important as it allows for early identification of fluctuations in service delivery or quality. This is important not only for internal service providers but also when services have been outsourced. It is important to identify any deviations and discuss them with the external service provider in order to avoid any supplier relationship problems. Speed and efficiency of communication when there are missed targets is essential to the continuation of a strong relationship.

Using the measurements and metrics can also help define any external factors that may exist outside the control of the internal or external service provider. The real world needs to be taken into consideration. External factors could include anything from language barriers to governmental decisions.

Individual metrics and measures by themselves may tell an organization very little from a strategic or tactical point of view. Some types of metrics and measures are often more activity based than volume based, but are valuable from an operational perspective. Examples could be:

- The services used
- The mapping of customers to services
- Frequency of use of each service
- Times of day each service is used

- The way each service is used (internally or externally through the web)
- The performance of each component used to provide the service
- The availability of each component used to provide the service.

Each of these measures by themselves will provide some information that is important to IT staff including the technical managers who are responsible for Availability and Capacity Management as well as those who may be responsible for a technology domain such as a server farm, an application or the network, but it is the examination and use of all the measurements and metrics together that delivers the real value. It is important for someone to own the responsibility to not only look at these measurements as a whole but also to analyse trends and provide interpretation of the meaning of the metrics and measures.

4.3.11 Creating scorecards and reports

Service measurement information will be used for three main purposes: to report on the service to interested parties; to compare against targets; and also to identify improvement opportunities. Reports must be appropriate and useful for all those who use them.

There are typically three distinct audiences for reporting purposes.

- The business – is it really focused on delivery to time and budget?
- IT management – management will be interested in the tactical and strategic results that support the business.
- IT operational/technical managers – these people will be concerned with the tactical and operational metrics which support better planning, coordination and scheduling of resources. The operational managers will be interested in their technology domain measurements such as component availability and performance.

Many organizations make the mistake of creating and distributing the same report to everyone. This does not provide value for everyone.

Creating scorecards that align to strategies

Reports and scorecards should be linked to overall strategy and goals. Using a Balanced Scorecard approach is one way to manage this alignment.

Figure 4.16 illustrates how the overall goals and objectives can be used to derive the measurements and metrics required to support the overall goals and objectives. The arrows point both ways because the strategy, goals and objectives will drive the identification of required KPIs and measurements, but it is also important to remember that the measures are input in KPIs and the KPIs support the goals in the Balanced Scorecard.

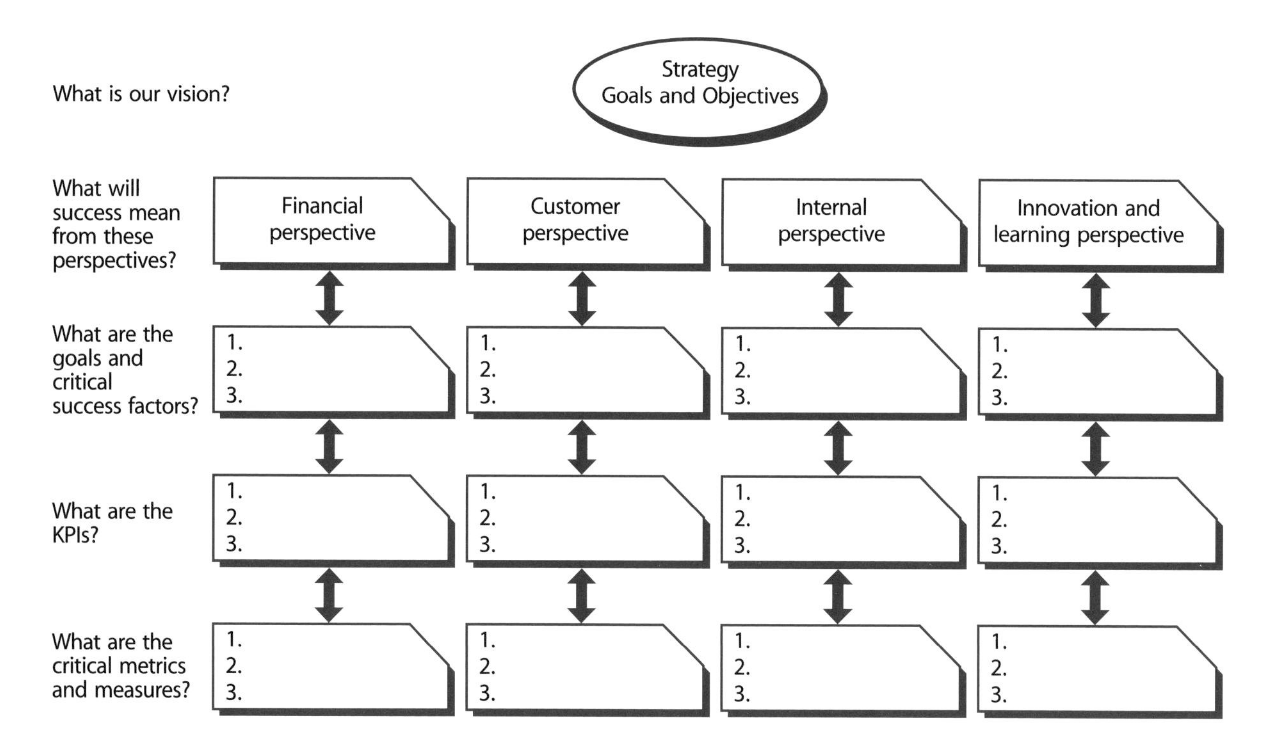

Figure 4.16 Deriving measurements and metrics from goals and objectives

Table 4.8 An example of a summary report format

Report for the month of:	
Monthly overview	This is a summary of the service measurement for the month and discusses any trends over the past few months. This section can also provide input into ...
Results	This section outlines the key results for the month.
What led to the results	Are there any issues/activities that contributed to the results for this month?
Actions to take	What action have you taken or would like to take to correct any undesirable results? Major deficiencies may require CSI involvement and the creation of a service improvement plan.
Predicting the future	Define what you think the future results will be.

It is important to select the right measures and targets to be able to answer the ultimate question of whether the goals are being achieved and the overall strategy supported.

The Balanced Scorecard is discussed in more detail in Chapter 5. A sample Balanced Scorecard is also provided in Chapter 5.

Creating reports

When creating reports it is important to know their purpose and the details that are required. Reports can be used to provide information for a single month, or a comparison of the current month with other months to provide a trend for a certain time period. Reports can show whether service levels are being met or breached.

Before starting the design of any report it is also important to know the following:

- Who is the target audience of the report?
- What will the report be used for?
- Who is responsible for creating the report?
- How will the report be created?
- How frequently is the report to be created?
- What information will be produced, shared or exchanged?

One of the first items to consider is who is the target audience. Most senior managers don't want a report that is 50 pages long. They like to have a short summary report and access to supporting details if they are interested. Table 4.8 provides a suitable overview that will fit the needs of most senior managers. This report should be no longer than two pages but ideally a single page if that is achievable without sacrificing readability.

It is also important to know what report format the audience prefers. Some people like text reports, some like charts and graphs with lots of colour, and some like a combination. Be careful about the type of charts and graphs that are used. They must be understandable and not open to different interpretations.

Many reporting tools today produce canned reports but these may not meet everyone's business requirements for reporting purposes. It is wise to ensure that a selected reporting tool has flexibility for creating different reports, that it will be linked or support the goals and objectives, that its purpose is clearly defined, and that its target audience is identified.

Reports can be set up to show the following:

- Results for a service – supporting reports would be the individual measurements on components
- Health of a service management process – this report will have certain process KPI results
- Functional reports – such as telephony reports for the Service Desk.

Figure 4.17 shows the amount of outage minutes for a service. However, through analysis of the results, a direct relationship was discovered between failed changes and the amount of outage minutes. Seeing this information together convinced an organization that it really needed to improve its Change Management process.

Table 4.9 is another example of a service measurement report. The report clearly states an objective and also provides a YTD status. The report compares this year's outage to last year's outage. The report also addresses the actual customer impact. Depending on needs, this report format can be used for many reporting purposes such as performance, Service Level Agreements, etc.

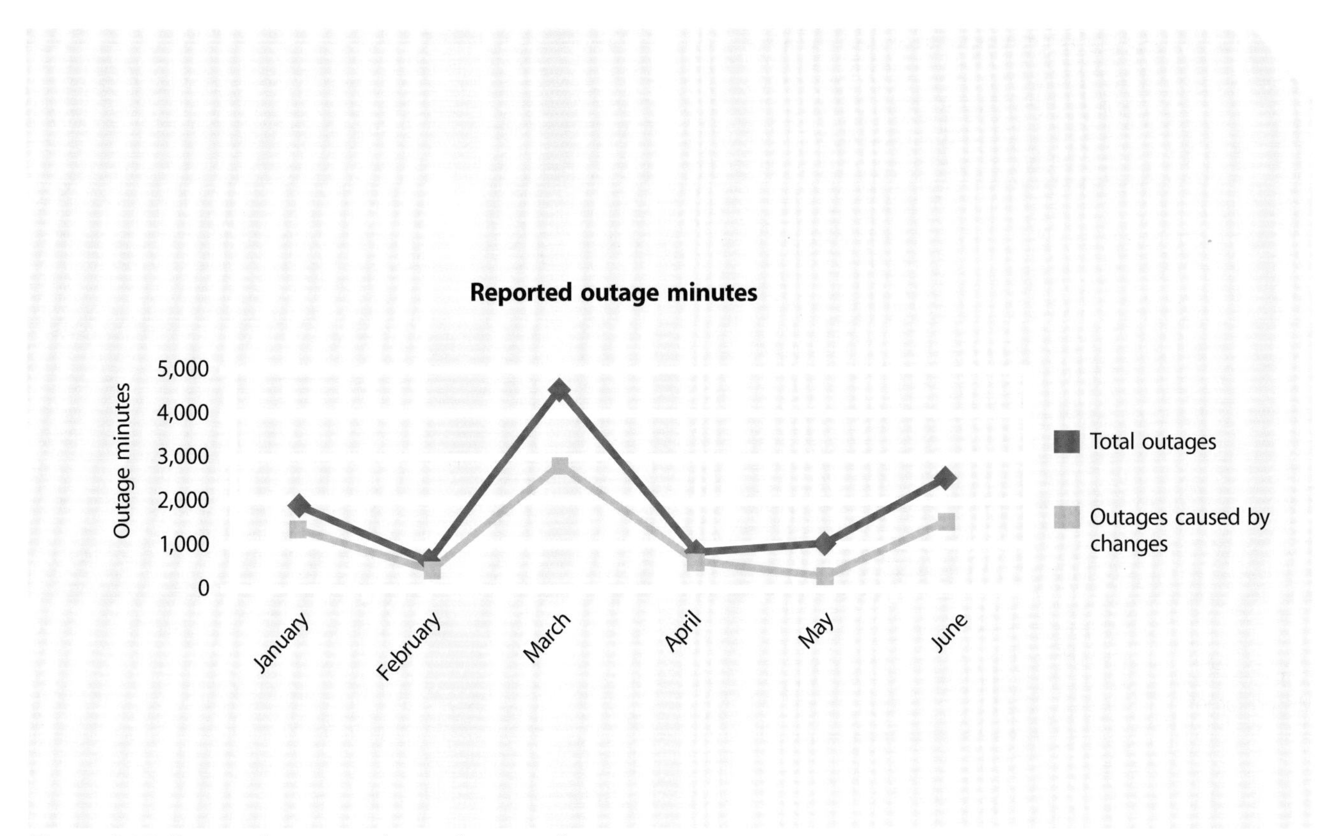

Figure 4.17 Reported outage minutes for a service

Table 4.9 Service report of outage minutes compared to goal

Actual outage minutes compared to goal						
Objective	20% decrease in outages					
Status	18% decrease year to date					
Monthly report	Month 1	Month 2	Month 3	Month 4	Month 5	Month 6
Previous year's outage minutes						
This year's outage minutes						
Running year to date reduction						
Monthly indicator	Positive	Negative	Positive	Positive	Negative	Positive
Reduction in customer impact						
Objective	% decrease in number of customers impacted					
Status						
Next steps						

Table 4.10 Percentage of incidents meeting target time for service restoration

	Target	Month 1		Month 2	
		Number of tickets	%	Number of tickets	%
All incidents					
Within target		7,540	97.15	6,339	95.12
Missed target		221	2.85	325	4.88
Grand total		7,761		6,664	
Priority 1					
Within target	95% within 1 hour	24	77.42	17	77.28
Missed target		7	22.58	5	22.72
Grand total		39		24	
Priority 2					
Within target	90% within 4 hours	127	78.40	153	92.73
Missed target		35	21.60	12	7.27
Grand total		164		83	
Priority 3					
Within target	80% within 1 business day	2,532	89.66	2,176	88.92
Missed target		292	10.34	241	11.08
Grand total		1,064		1,081	
Priority 4					
Within target	70% within 2 business days	4,683	98.09	4,301	98.44
Missed target		61	1.91	67	1.56
Grand total		7,761		6,664	

Table 4.10 shows Incident Management data in reference to number of incident tickets by priority and the success of meeting the Service Level Agreement for service restoration.

Table 4.11 Sample key performance indicators

Process	KPI/Description	Type	Progress indicator
Incident	Tickets resolved within target time	Value	Meets/exceeds target times
Incident	% of incidents closed – first call	Performance	Service Desk only – target is 80%
Incident	Abandon rate		Service Desk with ACD. 5% or less goal (after 24 seconds)
Incident	Count of incidents submitted by support group	Compliance	Consistency in number of incidents – investigation is warranted for (1) rapid increase which may indicate infrastructure investigation, and (2) rapid decrease which may indicate compliance issues
Problem	% of repeated problems over time	Quality	Problems that have been removed from the infrastructure and have re-occurred. Target: less than 1% over a 12-month rolling timeframe
Problem	% root cause with permanent fix	Quality	Calculated from problem ticket start date to permanent fix found. This may not include implementation of permanent fix. Internal target: 90% of problems – within 40 days. External target: 80% of problems – within 30 days. Internal = BMO internal; External = 3rd party/vendor
Problem	% and number of incidents raised to Problem Management	Compliance	Sorted by infrastructure (internal and external) and development (internal and external)
Change	% of RFCs successfully implemented without backout or issues	Quality	Grouped by infrastructure/development
Change	% of RFCs that are emergencies	Performance	Sort by infrastructure or development – and by emergency quick fix (service down) or business requirement
Config	Number of CI additions or updates	Compliance	Configuration item additions or updates broken down by group – CMDB/change modules
Config	Number of records related to CI	Performance	Number of associations grouped by process
Release	% of releases using exceptions	Value	Exceptions are criteria deemed mandatory – identify by groups
Release	% of releases bypassing process	Compliance	Identify groups by passing release process
Capacity	Action required	Value	Number of services that require action vs. total number of systems
Capacity	Capacity-related problems	Quality	Number of problems caused by capacity issues sorted by group

Table 4.11 provides some sample KPIs for different processes. This is not an all-inclusive list but simply an example. Each organization will need to define what KPIs to report on.

4.3.12 CSI policies

As mentioned in Chapter 3, use of CSI policies is a key principle that needs to be defined and communicated throughout the IT organization. Many of the policies that support CSI activities are often found as a part of Service Level Management, Availability Management and Capacity Management. Examples of some of these policies are:

- Monitoring requirements must be defined and implemented
- Data must be gathered and analysed on a consistent basis
- Trend reporting must be provided on a consistent basis
- Service Level Achievement reports must be provided on a consistent basis
- Internal and external service reviews must be completed on a consistent basis (internal is within IT and external is with the business)
- Services must have either clearly defined service levels or service targets that can be used to determine if there are gaps in the services provided
- Service management processes must have critical success factors and key performance indicators to determine if there are gaps between the expected outcome and the real outcome.

On a consistent basis means that the activity is not done ad hoc but on scheduled dates such as monthly or quarterly. Most organizations review service achievement and service management process results on a monthly basis.

If a new service is being introduced, it is recommended to monitor, report and review much sooner than after a month. You may want to review the new service daily for a period of time, before going to weekly and then finally monthly.

Additional CSI polices that an IT organization should implement:

- All improvement initiatives must use the formal Change Management process
- All functional groups within IT have a responsibility for CSI activities. This might be only one person in the group, but the intent here is that CSI is not usually a functional group within an organization but that everyone has a hand in supporting CSI activities
- Roles and responsibilities will be documented, communicated and filled within IT.

When defining the CSI policies you may want to use a consistent template. The template in Table 4.12 is an example that documents the policy statement, reason for the policy and a definition of the benefits of the policy. If an organization has difficulty defining the reason for and benefits of a policy it should consider whether the policy is needed. If compliance to a policy cannot be monitored then the value of the policy must be in doubt.

Table 4.12 Example policy template

Title	Monitoring services, systems and components
Policy statement	IT and the business must agree on what to monitor and collect data for each service. This data should reflect the Service Level Agreements.
Reason for policy	Provides input into CSI activities to identify gaps and improvement opportunities.
Benefits	Ensure agreement on defining what to monitor (work with SLM).
	Define monitoring requirements for new services and/or existing services to support CSI activities.
	Identification of trends and gaps.
	Supports prioritization of improvement projects.

4.4 RETURN ON INVESTMENT FOR CSI

Few organizations are willing to underwrite the cost and effort associated with process improvement without some quantification of costs and evidence of benefits and outcomes. Unfortunately, going beyond the 'sounds like a good idea' point into measurable outcomes presents several challenges. These may include the following:

- There is no true understanding of current IT capabilities or costs.
- There is limited knowledge of the business drivers, and their link with IT.
- Viable data is difficult to find in a low-process maturity, data-poor environment.
- Frequently there is limited knowledge of the cost of IT downtime to the business and IT.
- There is limited knowledge of the support at a unit level (e.g. cost of an incident, cost of a Level 2 support visit).
- There is limited experience in establishing measurement frameworks beyond simple component/system measurement.
- There is limited experience in identifying measurable benefits.
- There is a lack of understanding of the difference between benefits and ROI.
- Tangible and intangible benefits are difficult to distinguish.
- Compiling a clear and persuasive case for process improvement is difficult.
- Success criteria are inadequately identified, or a way to measure them is not clear.
- A failure to progressively measure and monitor benefits/returns.

4.4.1 Creating a Return on Investment

The Return on Investment challenge needs to take into consideration many factors. On one side is the investment cost. This is the money an organization pays to improve services and service management processes. These costs will be internal resource costs, tool costs, consulting costs, etc. It is often easy to come up with these costs.

On the other side is what an organization can gain in a return. These returns are often hard to define. In order to be able to compute these items it is important to know the following:

- What is the cost of downtime? This would include both lost productivity of the customers and the loss of revenue.
- What is the cost of doing rework? How many failed changes have to be backed out and reworked?
- What is the cost of doing redundant work? Many organizations who don't have clear processes in place and good communication often find that redundant work is being done.
- What is the cost of non-value added projects? Many projects have been fully funded and resourced but due to changing requirements no longer add value but the project moves forward instead of being stopped.
- What is the cost of late delivery of an application? Does this impact on the ability to deliver a new service or possibly an additional way to deliver an existing service?
- What is the cost of escalating incidents to second and third level support groups instead of resolving incidents at the first level? There is often a difference in utilization staff in second level and third level support groups. The more we escalate incidents to these groups the less time they have to work on projects that they may also be assigned to.
- What is the fully allocated hourly cost for different employee levels?

These are only some of the things that have to be considered when creating a ROI statement.

There are different approaches to measuring and reporting on the availability. Availability is a good measure to understand the cost of lost productivity, the cost of not being able to complete a business transaction, or the true cost of downtime.

- Impact by minutes lost – this is a calculation on the duration of downtime multiplied by the number of customers impacted. This can be used to report on lost customer productivity (see Table 4.13).
- Impact by business transaction – this calculation is based on the number of business transactions that could not be processed during the downtime. This measurement provides a better indication of business impact.
- The true cost of downtime that has been agreed on.

A good way to look at the impact by lost minutes is to create a component failure impact analysis table that identifies the number of users impacted when a component fails. Understanding the number of users impacted allows you to calculate the cost of their non-productivity. Table 4.13 is an example only.

Table 4.13 Component Failure Impact Analysis

Component Description	Number of users impacted
Main frame	28,547
Core Router	17,433
Mid range	10,442
XYZ application	7,354
ABC database	1,819
Single desktop	1

When you have a failure you can determine the duration of the failure, how many people were impacted and using an allocated cost model for employees, define the cost of their non-productivity. Granted not all of them will try to access the application during the failure but remember you are creating a scenario that is based on what could happen. As an example, let's say there is an application failure that impacts 7,364 employees. The application was down for 39 minutes.

Calculation: number of users multiplied by 39 minutes divided by 60 (to convert to hours) multiplied by £45 equals £215,397.

The next question is what is the investment cost to improve availability of the overall service?

The method chosen should be influenced by the nature of the business operations and business processes.

One of the keys for measuring and reporting is to be able to define improvement opportunities that will create a Return on Investment for the business. If your business is insurance and you cannot write policies than this can translate into lost revenue. This is especially true for those companies who sell their products and services via the internet. An organization's competition is only a couple of clicks away when a service is not available.

That is why it is so important to understand the cost of downtime. Defining the cost to downtime is an exercise that IT and the business should conduct. It is important to have agreement on what the financial impact is to the business when a service is not available for whatever reason.

Let's say that your organization truly knows the cost of downtime. This is often measured based on the type of service being provided. In Table 4.14 we have defined three different levels of service. The mission-critical services have a higher downtime cost than the other services. Based on the hourly cost of downtime and with an investment of £300,000 to improve services you can see that the return is quick on the first two services.

Another option if the business and IT cannot agree to the cost of downtime or the cost of non-productive employees, is to take the annual cost of a service that the business pays and divide by the number of service hours for the year. This will provide a monetary cost the business is paying for each hour of service.

4.4.2 Establishing the Business Case

The Business Case should articulate the reason for undertaking a service or process improvement initiative. As far as possible, data and evidence should be provided relating to the costs and expected benefits of undertaking process improvement, noting that:

- Process redesign activities are more complex and therefore more costly than initially expected
- Organizational change impact is often underestimated

Table 4.14 Downtime costs of different services and investment information

Type of service	Cost per hour of downtime
Mission-critical service	£200,000
Critical service	£90,000
Non-critical service	£11,500
Investment information	Financial investment
Investment to make improvements to reduce the amount of downtime	£300,000
Number of minutes of downtime avoided needed to cover the investment	Return in minutes/hours
Mission-critical service	90 minutes
Critical service	200 minutes or 3.33 hours
Non-critical service	1,556 minutes or 26 hours

- Changed process usually requires changed competencies and tools, adding further to the expense.

In developing a Business Case, the focus should not be limited to ROI but also on the business value that service improvement brings to the organization and its customers (VOI). That's because ROI alone does not capture the real value of service improvement. Should an organization choose to focus solely on ROI, much of the potential benefit achievable will not be disclosed nor reviewed after the fact. This could in turn result in worthwhile initiatives not being approved, or a review of the initiative revealing apparent failure, when it was actually successful.

Not surprisingly, most business and IT executives expect a return on their investment. It is important to recognize that an investment in CSI, and realizing its benefits, can vary depending on the customer base, size of IT and the maturity of the ITIL process implemented. Also benefits will cross existing organizational boundaries and true benefits can only be captured in collaboration with the users/customers and ITIL process owners. The focus is therefore to work with the stakeholders to develop business and IT specific indicators that link business value measures with IT's contributions. In other words, how does ITIL process improvement add value to the organization?

Examples of business value measures are:

- Time to market
- Customer retention
- Inventory carrying cost
- Market share.

IT's contribution can be captured as follows:

- Gaining agility
- Managing knowledge
- Enhancing knowledge
- Reducing costs
- Reducing risk.

IT should begin by defining the types of business values that each improvement will contribute to.

As an example, the US Sarbanes-Oxley legislation as well as other international laws require that the business processes be certified to produce financial reports in addition to certifying the reports themselves. Sarbanes-Oxley is about improving transparency and accountability in business processes and corporate accounting to restore confidence in public markets. It regulates processes and business practices. Therefore having a higher level of ITIL maturity will enable regulatory compliance.

Without a mature process framework it is natural for organizations to take an ad hoc approach to compliance. They address requirements as they emerge, through a series of one-offs, just-in-time projects. Since compliance affects a lot of ongoing business activity, this is disruptive, increases the required effort and becomes time-consuming and very expensive.

If an investment is well conceived, solid and delivers results, it can lead to cost savings in the long run. Therefore it is important to choose the right investment and make sure they deliver. When presenting a Business Case for an ITIL process improvement project, it is important to help executives understand the business value of the ITIL process framework. The tendency for most IT executives is to over-emphasize technology and tools. Technology is a means to an end. The benefits are realized from the business changes. It is really important to address how people and processes will change: i.e. 'as is' to the 'to be' state.

The 'as is' stage can be defined as a baseline. Capturing the baseline of the performance measurements affected by the proposed implementation is paramount to the Business Case. The careful preparation of the baseline will facilitate meaningful business information and level setting about relevant business issues; allowing strategic alignment to take place. Focus should be to develop cause-and-effect metrics to link the benefits against the measurements selected along with the impact on other areas of the enterprise. The metrics should be monitored before, during and after the ITIL implementation to determine how the projected values are being delivered.

Another aspect to consider in Business Case development is situations where value will be lost by *not* undertaking

Table 4.15 A balanced focus – people, process and technology

	As is	To be
People	Operating in silos, no common language, focus and no seamless handoffs between groups.	Common language, integrated matrix approach and common focus.
Process	Lacks common processes, not consistent and repeatable.	Seamless process framework, end-to-end service delivery, consistent and repeatable.
Technology	Multiple redundant tools, no tools, domain-based tools, not integrated with people and processes.	Integrated suite of tools which enable IT service modelling, process integration and shared data access.

process improvement activities. There will be situations where failure to take action will severely impact the business and IT – the value of process improvement may, in fact, not be value added, but value retained.

As a final note, care should be taken in developing the Business Case to ensure that the success criteria are clearly defined, how they are to be measured, and also when they are going to be measured.

Expectations – What's in it for me?

Business executives:

- What are the benefits of ITIL process improvements?
- How does it impact my business?
  - Revenue increase
  - Cost reduction
  - Value on Investment.

CFO:

- What is the ROI?
- Payback time?

IT:

- How do ITIL benefits translate to business benefits? Find one or two compelling reasons why the organization should spend so much time and money.

Determine the current or anticipated concern of the organization with respect to IT. Estimate the cost if the status quo were to remain and subsequently estimate the savings that could be realized if the ITSM processes were put in place or improved upon. Examples include new lines of business overseas, poor response time or time taken to handle incidents/problems, or number of incidents in the organization.

Business cases in a data-poor environment

Organizations intending to undertake service improvement activities may find themselves in a situation where the lack of process means that there is no viable body of data or evidence to quantify expected benefits, ROI or VOI. How, then, does such an organization justify process improvement, or recognize how much expenditure is appropriate to achieve cost-effective improvements?

An approach that circumvents this situation is to gain approval to establish basic measurement capabilities, as a means of gathering consistent data. This may be as simple as ensuring that all IT staff record data in a consistent fashion, or start measuring activities or outcomes that are not currently captured. After an agreed period of data capture, some evidence will exist to support (or perhaps not support) a process improvement initiative.

Another approach is to undertake a process maturity assessment of current processes, to identify which processes are most divergent from ITIL practices. It should, however, be noted that this activity will only identify the absence of process and/or data. A process maturity assessment will not in itself provide the data to justify how much to spend on improving process.

Example

XYZ Limited has grown rapidly from a single site to a multi-site environment and now employs 1,500 people, up from 250 people two years ago. The IT group has struggled to match the business growth with growth in process consistency and service delivery. The business is demanding that the IT group do things better as the shortcomings in IT service are now impacting the business bottom-line.

The IT manager identifies that lack of consistent process and business focus are the roadblock to delivering better service to the business. She realizes that the staff are working very hard, but are often doing re-work or repairing self-inflicted errors. While good technicians, they are averse to documenting activities or outcomes.

Data and measurement are currently inconsistent. While she knows average business and IT staff salary costs, the costs of service outage etc. are not known nor can they be calculated using current data.

Rather than requesting funding to undertake process improvements, the IT manager requests funding for a pilot project to establish a rudimentary measurement framework to start capturing data in a standard fashion, using more-or-less existing processes. This pilot initiative after three months provides clear evidence that the true failure rate of changes is much higher than previously expected, and is a key contributor to business and IT loss of productivity.

Armed with this evidence, the IT manager prepares a Business Case detailing some of the current deficiencies and expected benefits/returns to be delivered from properly quantifying process gaps and undertaking appropriate process improvement.

Where organizations do establish a basic measurement and monitoring capability, some caution should be exercised regarding the quality of this data: be aware of limitations of new data. Even if the data doesn't make any sense, this is reason enough to explore the opportunity for improvements.

It is important that once the decision to start capturing and reporting on data is made, that an initial baseline is created so that improvements can be measured against it.

4.4.3 Measuring benefits achieved

While the initial identification of benefits is an estimate of those likely to be realized by the proposed process improvement initiative, there is also a need to subsequently measure the benefits actually achieved. These measurements attest to whether the improvement activity achieved the intended outcomes and should consider:

- Whether the envisaged improvements were realized
- Whether the benefits arising from the improvements were achieved
- Whether the target ROI was achieved
- Whether the intended value-added was actually achieved (VOI)
- Whether the outcomes of the preceding points lead to further process improvement actions being re-evaluated
- Whether enough time has passed before measuring the benefits. Some benefits will not be immediately apparent; and it is likely that benefits will continue to change over time, as both ongoing costs and ongoing benefits continue to move.

A further consideration in the measurement of benefits is that data quality and measurement precision pre- and post-improvement could be different, thus giving rise to the direct comparison not being valid. If this is the case, the data will need to be normalized before validating benefits.

In 2006, the state of North Carolina implemented some improvements based on the ITIL framework. The improvements took place in a span of less than three months. ITS is the name of their IT department. These are the results of tactical quick-win efforts targeted in tandem with the training programme and the state's awareness campaign. This information is reproduced with permission:

- ITS improved its ability to resolve incidents within their target timeframe by 32%.
- ITS improved its ability to resolve Service Requests within its target timeframe by 20%.
- Change Management process compliance increased more than two-fold resulting in fewer incidents and reduced downtime.

The first two processes to be developed and implemented were Incident and Change Management. As with most organizations they already had an existing change and incident process. This organization started showing immediate improvement before any formal improvement programme was implemented simply by identifying and communicating the key metrics that were going to be reviewed by senior management. Staff began following their existing process simply because they knew reporting against certain performance measures had started and that

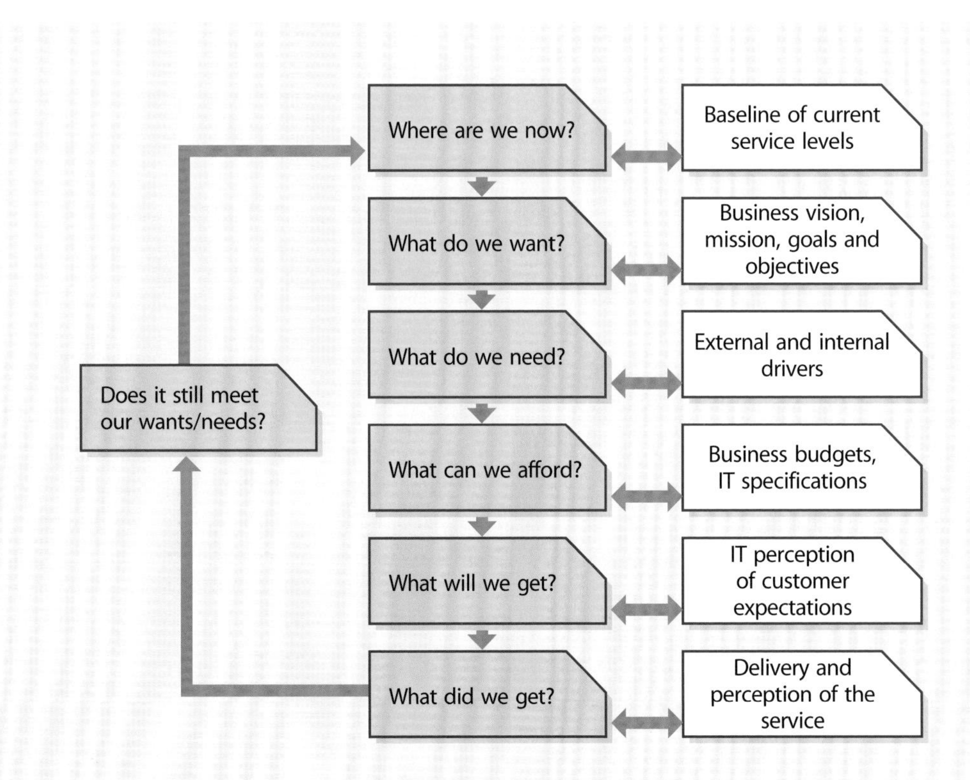

Figure 4.18 Business perspective improvement model

these performance measures were discussed among senior managers. Not only were these discussions held but there was clear guidance that the performance measures had to improve.

4.5 BUSINESS QUESTIONS FOR CSI

The business needs to be involved with CSI in decision making on what improvement initiatives make sense and add the greatest value back to the business. There are some key questions that will assist the business in making decisions about whether a CSI initiative is warranted or not.

The following questions are often asked from a business and IT perspective. Not understanding some of these questions can lead to challenges, perceived poor service or in some cases actual poor service:

- Where are we now? This is a question every business should start out asking as this creates a baseline of data for services currently being delivered.
- What do we want? This is often expressed in terms of business requirements such as 100% availability.
- What do we actually need? When Service Level Management starts talking with the business they may realize they don't really need 100% availability 24X7.
- Service Level Management plays a key role in working with the business to provide answers to the business questions.
- What can we afford? This question often moves the business from looking at what they want to what they actually need. As an example a large financial organization wanted to move from 99.9999% availability to 99.99999% availability and found the cost was going to be £900,000.
- What will we get? This is often defined in a SLA. Defining the service as well as service levels.
- What did we get? This is documented through monitoring, reporting and reviewing of service level achievements.

Before starting, it is important to remember that CSI activities cannot take place for a service that does not exist yet; the service has to be operational to identify improvement opportunities. However, don't overlook the fact that CSI can be actively engaged in identifying improvement opportunities on the elements that were involved in building or modifying a service. CSI activities can be executed within Service Strategy, Service Design, Service Transition as well as Service Operation.

Where are we now?

A baseline must be established for all future measurements to be meaningful. Measurements may often reflect a single snapshot or a point in time but analysing these snapshots over time will give us the trends we need to identify areas of improvement. The first snapshot is the baseline, the starting point. It is essential that the same measurements be used consistently to establish trend patterns.

What do we want?

This question provides the best answers when the business and IT work in partnership to identify what the business wants from IT services. The compiled list can be akin to a wish-list of all the nice things that the business would love to have. Here are a few samples:

- One hundred percent availability guaranteed
- Unlimited capacity
- Sub-second transactional responses
- Polite and courteous technicians
- IT staff that understand the business
- Inexpensive provision of IT services
- Stable, fault-free infrastructure.

It is important to also identify the reasons behind what the business wants. These reasons must be valid and failure to address them may result in difficult times ahead for the business. Here are a few sample valid reasons:

- Compliance to new/upcoming legislation, can be legislation from other countries as well
- Satisfying business customer demands
- Strong competition
- Financial or fiscal constraints
- Age and/or state of the IT infrastructure
- Eroding or lack of confidence by investors
- Supply-chain management
- Global events.

This question will require a few iterations to complete. It is important to identify long- and short-term goals and objectives for the business as a whole as well as for each major business units. Table 4.16 maps the goals and objectives and the reasons for the 'want' to help ease the process.

Table 4.16 Mapping wants, goals and reasons

Department	We want ...	To support our goal or objective of ...	The reason is to address ...
Sales	Improved availability for web services	Improve web service availability by 25%	Lost sales opportunities Increased competition Cost of working incidents and problems
Marketing	Improved availability for web services	Improve use of web for marketing initiatives by 40%	Reach a larger potential customer base Gain knowledge of customer perception of our business Current web marketing surveys are always breaking down
...	...	...	...
Department N	<...>	Goal Objective Objective	<...>

What do we need?

This question is similar to the 'what do we want' question and is actually a fine-tuning activity of the outputs identified in Table 4.16. The first step is for the business and CSI to prioritize the 'wants'. This exercise can be emotionally charged as people might be reluctant to let go of any 'wants'. Deciding on the priority must be based on rational, well-defined criteria. That is why goals and objectives are also identified – to give the business the opportunity to really address the most important goals and objectives based on the vision and mission of the organization and of the departments.

It is therefore important to start at the top and understand the priorities of the organization's senior executives (CEO, CFO, COO, CIO etc.). Once they have established the priorities in terms of goals and objectives for the long and short term, their subordinates will, in turn, prioritize their goals and objectives based on that list.

A recommendation is to ensure that a detailed analysis of services has been conducted and that the business and IT clearly understand what the mission-critical services are. This doesn't mean that only mission-critical services are reviewed as a part of CSI, but we don't want to lose focus on these. Incident Management, Problem Management and Change Management talk about assessing the impact on the business and the urgency to get it done when determining the priority. CSI should be no different and should use a similar rating scheme albeit with different parameters.

There are many factors that can go into choosing what improvement projects to work on in what order. Below are some of the driving factors.

- Support of business strategy and goals
- Support of IT strategy and goals
- External drivers such as regulatory requirements
- Cost to implement improvement
- Quick wins that can be realized
- Ease of implementation.

Policies must be established for such cases to determine the answers to such questions as:

- Who decides which is first?
- Should an escalation path be identified?
- Which (vital) business function is more important than the other?
- What happens during critical business periods?

What can we afford?

Most business and IT organizations have a budget they need to work within. If an organization is working from a zero-based budget, i.e. every project has to go through a review for ROI or other standards to obtain funding, there are still questions that have to be answered. So a part of the determining what improvement projects to work on first will have to do with the cost of the improvement project. Is the business going to fund the improvement or is IT going to fund the improvement?

From a service management perspective, it is imperative that Service Level Management and Financial Management work together to understand the ability to fund from IT or work with the business to define what the priority is for funding of improvement projects.

What will we get?

It is important that CSI ensures that IT works with the business to clearly define what the requirements and output are of any improvement project. It doesn't do any good for IT to guess what the business needs. This leads to perception problems for both the business and IT.

What did we get?

Service Operation will do the actual monitoring and reporting on the achieved service levels. Based on the results and any gaps to the desired results, CSI working with the business will identify improvement opportunities.

4.6 SERVICE LEVEL MANAGEMENT

Service Level Management (SLM) is critical for CSI. SLM activities support The 7-Step Improvement Process in that the SLM should drive what to measure, defining monitoring requirements, reporting Service Level Achievements and working with the business to understand new service requirements or changes to existing services. This provides input into CSI activities and helps prioritize improvement projects. Even though SLM is critical for many organizations it is often one of the least mature processes.

Service Level Management can be described in two words: building relationships. That is building relations with IT customers, building relationships between functional groups within IT, and building relationships with the vendor community who provide services to IT. Service Level Management is so much more than simply a SLA.

Many people have worked in organizations where management and/or the business refuse to sign any document that will commit anyone to a level of service. This leads many organizations to think that they cannot implement Service Level Management, but they are wrong. You can still build relationships with your customers by meeting with them on a consistent basis. Share with them your Service Level Achievements, and discuss any future new services or requirements. Having knowledge about what they need doesn't necessarily mean they get it, but it is surely better than not knowing what they need at all.

Even without any formal SLAs or OLAs, an organization can still strive to improve the services they provide to its customers.

Every organization already has three types of SLAs in place whether they know it or not. The first is an explicit SLA and this is one of the goals of SLM, to get a formal document that clearly defines the service provided, levels of service, quality of service and cost of the service. Everyone understands their responsibilities. The second type of SLA is the implicit SLA. This is based on how you have provided service in the past. If you provide good service the customers expect good service. If you improve on your service, then this becomes the new minimal level expected. Also if you have provided poor service in the past then your customers will actually expect poor service. Implicit SLAs are difficult to manage. The third type is psychological SLAs. They are often associated with the Service Desk where we publish information to the end users often by putting a sticker on their monitor or other piece of equipment that basically says: 'If you need help, please call xxxxxx'. In the mind of the end user this creates a psychological agreement in that all the end user has to do is call the Service Desk and they will get help. We all know how there are still some Service Desks and help desks that provide less than ideal help.

CSI plays a part in all three types of SLAs. If they are formal, then it will take a more formal approach to service improvement. If they fall in the other areas it may be less formal, but still very important and improvement opportunities have to be reviewed.

Service Level Management is essential in any organization so that the levels of IT service needed to support the business can be determined, and monitoring can be initiated to identify whether the required service levels are being achieved – and if not, why not. SLM is a cornerstone of CSI. Why embark on any service improvement initiative if the customers and the business are satisfied with the levels of service received? Because business requirements change!

4.6.1 Goal for SLM

The goal for SLM is to maintain and improve the IT service quality through a constant cycle of agreeing, monitoring and reporting upon IT service achievements and instigation of actions to eradicate poor service – in line with business or cost justification. Through these methods, a better relationship between IT and its customers can be developed and maintained.

First, what is quality? Is a Rolex™ watch costing thousands of pounds necessarily a better product than a Timex™ watch costing less than fifty pounds? Both products are leaders in their market segments and both are very good products in their own rights. The major difference is the price. The answer to the above question lies in the goal of the customer. If the customer wants to impress their friends, then a Rolex™ is probably a better choice but if the customer wants to keep track of time to keep up with their busy schedule of picking up the kids, appointments etc. then a Timex™ is probably more appropriate. A good enough definition of quality is 'fitness for purpose' and fits very well with the above example.

The SLM process is created in the Service Design stage of the lifecycle and is fully documented in that publication. It is important the CSI is involved in the design of SLM to ensure that measurable targets are created from which to identify potential service improvements.

4.6.2 Service improvement plan

The SLM process is one of the triggers for a service improvement plan (SIP) as part of CSI and can be the result of the service review activity. A SIP is a formal plan to implement improvements to a process or IT service. A SIP is managed as part of the Continual Service Improvement process.

Where an underlying difficulty has been identified which is adversely impacting upon service quality, Service Level Management must, in conjunction with CSI (and possibly using Problem Management (see Service Operation publication) and Availability Management (see Service Design publication), instigate a SIP to identify and implement whatever actions are necessary to overcome the difficulties and restore service quality. Further guidance on this and the specific techniques that might be used can be found throughout this publication. SIP initiatives may also focus on such issues as user training, system testing and documentation. In these cases the relevant people need to be involved and adequate feedback given to make improvements for the future. At any time, a number of separate initiatives that form part of the SIP may be running in parallel to address difficulties with a number of services.

Some organizations have established an upfront annual budget held by SLM from which SIP initiatives can be funded. This means that action can be undertaken quickly and that SLM is demonstratively effective. This practice should be encouraged and expanded to enable SLM to become increasingly proactive and predictive.

If an organization is outsourcing its service provision to a third party, the issue of service improvement should be discussed at the outset and covered (and budgeted for) in the contract, otherwise there is no incentive during the lifetime of the contract for the supplier to improve service targets if they are already meeting contractual obligations and additional expenditure is needed to make the improvements.

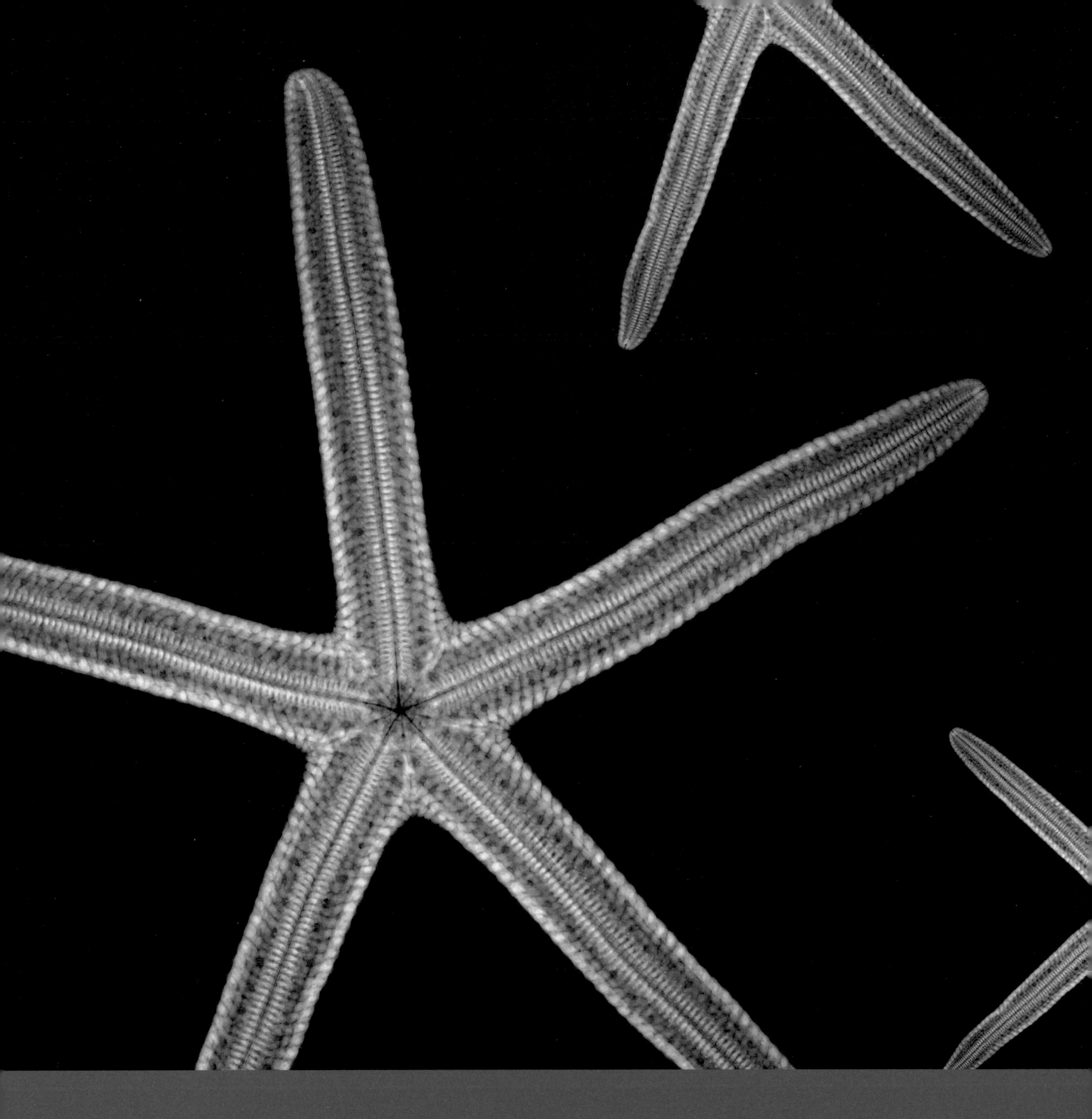

5 Continual Service Improvement methods and techniques

5 Continual Service Improvement methods and techniques

5.1 METHODS AND TECHNIQUES

A wide variety of methods and techniques can be used in the CSI activities ranging from 'soft and vague' to 'factual and scientific' often providing either both or a mixture of qualitative and quantitative measurement results. To ensure consistency of execution and effective measurement, especially for the activities of gathering and processing data, the techniques and methods that are used should be clearly documented in advance and communicated to the staff that will be responsible for their execution. To increase the trustworthiness of the factual data delivered to these processes it may be required for these processes to be audited for compliance to the agreed and prescribed methods and techniques.

An effective choice of methods and techniques for the analysis, presentation and use of the measurement information is highly dependant on the particular circumstances in which these tasks are performed and can generally not be documented in advance. A goal-oriented attitude and professional expertise and education of the individuals are required.

5.1.1 Effort and cost

CSI improvement activities can require a considerable amount of effort and money for larger-scale improvement projects to minimal time and effort for some incremental improvements. If the effort is going to be costly then the organization, both IT and the business has to ask is it worth it?

Let's first look at the costs of implementing and operating a measurement framework with respect to IT service provision. Possible major cost topics are:

- **Labour cost** – Salaries of the organization's staff who are involved in implementing the measurement framework or who spend effort on performing one of the activities in operating or maintaining the measurement framework; including costs associated with managing it. If (part of) IT is outsourced, the external provider costs should be included here too.
- **Tooling cost** – Purchase, licenses, installation and configuration (remember – no customization!), maintenance costs of hardware, software and other equipment specifically used for the measurement activities. Tools could be a cost on the provider which they will pass on back to you.
- **Training cost** – Cost of training and coaching staff in the use of measurement methods, techniques, tools and procedures.
- **Expertise cost** – Payments to hired experts and consulting firms, typically for the planning, implementation and maintenance activities pertaining to the measurement framework. Also includes the out-of-pocket costs of acquiring information used in the measurement framework that is not in the possession of the organization itself such as benchmarking data.

When deciding whether the measurement framework is worth the effort, consider the amounts to spend on:

- **Implementation of the measurement framework, initially and if it changes** – In practice these types of costs can be reliably estimated and controlled by using a project-oriented approach.
- **Operation** – The level of costs associated with the operation of the measurement framework is largely fixed as a result of the way it is designed and equipped.
- **Maintenance** – The level of these types of costs depends mainly on the expected rate at which the measurement framework will require adaptation to changing circumstances and on the quality of its implementation.

5.1.2 Implementation review and evaluation

Implementation review and evaluation is key to determining the effectiveness of a CSI improvement programme. Some common areas for review include:

- Were we correct in our assessment of the current situation and in defining the problem statement?
- When defining the goals for improving IT services did we commit to the right goals?
- When developing our strategy for improving the use and management of IT services, did we make the right choices and take the right decisions?
- When implementing our strategy, did we do it right?
- In the new situation, have we improved the provision of IT services?
- And finally, what are the lessons learned and ... where are we now?

Review and evaluation of a CSI initiative fall within two broad categories:

- Issues closely tied to the original problem situation with respect to the IT service provision to the business and ensuing business aims and strategy for the improvement thereof
- Issues in relation to the planning, implementation and proceedings of the IT improvement programme itself and associated projects such as measurements, problems, actions and changes.

The issues in the first category are closely related to the characteristics of the original problem situation which instigated the actions for understanding and improvements and will therefore include:

- Ability of IT services to meet business needs
- Business satisfaction with the service provision
- Business benefits in the area of productivity, effectiveness, efficiency and economy
- Financial issues such as understanding the costs of IT service provision control of IT costs to the business, accountability of IT costs to the business
- Quality of IT service provision and support of IT use
- Communication between the business and IT service provider and the degree of mutual understanding
- Degree of understanding and control of the management of the IT infrastructure and IT service provision on the part of the business.

For the second category the following issues should be reviewed and evaluated:

- Costs of staff involved in the improvement programme and costs of implementing and maintaining the measurement framework
- Project management such as planning, performance, timeliness of achieving results and milestones, amount of re-planning
- Adequacy of methods and techniques used
- Problems, bottlenecks, causes of progress performance problems, corrective actions and changes
- Communication, information gathering, reporting.

5.2 ASSESSMENTS

Assessments are the formal mechanisms for comparing the operational process environment to the performance standards for the purpose of measuring improved process capability and/or to identify potential shortcomings that could be addressed. The advantage of assessments is they provide an approach to sample particular elements of a process or the process organization which impact the efficiency and the effectiveness of the process.

Just by conducting a formal assessment an organization is demonstrating their significant level of commitment to improvement. Assessments involve real costs, staff time and management promotion. Organizations need to be

Table 5.1 Assessment resources

Using external resources for assessments	
Pro:	**Con:**
Objectivity	Cost
Expert ITIL knowledge	Risk of acceptance
Broad exposure to multiple IT organizations	Limited knowledge of existing environments
Analytical skills	Improper preparation affects effectiveness
Credibility	
Minimal impact to operations	
Performing self-assessments	
Pro:	**Con:**
No expensive consultants	Lack of objectivity (internal agendas)
Self-assessments available for free	Little acceptance of findings
Promotes internal cooperation and communication	Internal politics
Good place to get started	Limited knowledge or skills
Internal knowledge of environment	Resource intensive

more than just involved in an assessment, they need to be committed to improvement.

Comparison of the operational environment to industry norms is a relatively straightforward process. The metrics associated with industry norms are typically designed into the process control structure. Sampling and comparison then can be considered an operational exercise. Dealing with gaps apparent from such monitoring and reporting are addressed as an element of the check stage of the improvement lifecycle. An assessment based on comparison to a maturity model has been common over the last several years.

A well-designed maturity-assessment framework evaluates the viability of all aspects of the process environment including the people, process and technology as well as factors effecting overall process effectiveness within the business – culture of acceptance, process strategy and vision, process organization, process governance, business/IT alignment, process reporting/metrics and decision making. The balance of this section focuses on this form of assessment. However the principles of maturity assessment can easily be extended to assessments based on industry norms.

The initial step in the assessment process is to choose (or define) the maturity model and in turn the maturity attributes to be measured at each level. A suggested approach is to turn to the best practice frameworks such as CMMI, COBIT, ISO/IEC 20000 or the process maturity framework. These frameworks define maturity models directly or a model can be inferred. The frameworks are also useful in the definition of process maturity attributes.

When to assess

Assessments can be conducted at any time. A way to think about assessment timing is in line with the improvement lifecycle:

- **Plan (project initiation)** – Assess the targeted processes at the inception of process introduction to form the basis for a process improvement project. Processes can be of many configurations and design which increases the complexity of assessment data collection.
- **Plan (project midstream)** – A check during process implementation or improvement activities serves as validation that process project objectives are being met and, most importantly, provide tangible evidence that benefits are being achieved from the investment of time, talent and resources to process initiatives.
- **Do/Check (process in place)** – Upon the conclusion of a process project, it is important to validate the maturation of process and the process organization through the efforts of the project team. In addition to serving as a decisive conclusion for a project, scheduling periodic reassessments can support overall organizational integration and quality efforts.

What to assess and how

The assessment's scope is one of the key decisions. Scope should be based on the assessment's objective and the expected future use of process assessments and assessment reports. Assessments can be targeted broadly at those processes currently implemented or focused specifically where known problems exist within the current process environment. There are three potential scope levels:

- **Process only** – Assessment only of process attributes based on the general principles and guidelines of the process framework which defines the subject process.
- **People, process and technology** – Extend the process assessment to include assessment of the skills, roles and talents of the managers and practitioners of the process as well as the ability of the process-enabling technology deployed to support the objectives and transaction state of the process.
- **Full assessment** – Extend the people, process and technology assessment to include an assessment of the culture of acceptance within the organization, the ability of the organization to articulate a process strategy, the definition of a vision for the process environment as an 'end state', the structure and function of the process organization, the ability of process governance to assure that process objectives and goals are met, the business/IT alignment via a process framework, the effectiveness of process reporting/metrics, and the capability and capacity of decision-making practices to improve processes over time.

All these factors are compared to the maturity attributes of the selected maturity model.

Assessments can be conducted by the sponsoring organization or with the aid of a third party. The advantages of conducting a self-assessment is the reduced cost and the intellectual lift associated with learning how to objectively gauge the relative performance and progress of an organization's processes. Of course the downside is the difficulty associated with remaining objective and impartial during the assessment.

The pitfall of a lack of objectivity can be eliminated by using a third party to conduct the assessment. There are a number of public 'mini-assessments' that are available on various websites which provide a general perspective of maturity. However a more detailed assessment and resulting report can be contracted through a firm specializing in an assessment practice. Balancing against the obvious increased cost of a third-party assessment is the objectivity and experience of an organization that performs assessments on a regular basis.

Whether conducted internally or externally, the assessment should be reported using the levels of the maturity model. A best-practice reporting method is to communicate assessment results in a graphical fashion. Graphs are an excellent tool as they can fulfil multiple communication objectives. For instance, graphs can reflect changes or trends of process maturity over time or reflect comparison of the current assessment to standards or norms.

Advantages and disadvantages of assessments

The advantages include:

- They can provide an objective perspective of the current operational process state compared to a standard maturity model and a process framework. Through a thorough assessment, an accurate determination of any process gaps can be quickly completed, recommendations put forward and action steps planned.
- A well-planned and well-conducted assessment is a repeatable process. Thus the assessment is a useful management process in measuring progress over time and in establishing improvement targets or objectives.
- Using a common or universally accepted maturity framework, applied to a standard process framework, can serve to support comparing company process maturity to industry benchmarks.

The disadvantages include:

- An assessment provides only a snapshot in time of the process environment. As such it does not reflect current business or cultural dynamics and process operational issues.
- If the decision is to outsource the assessment process, the assessment and maturity framework can be vendor or framework dependent. The proprietary nature of vendor-generated models may make it difficult to compare to industry standards.
- The assessment can become an end in itself rather than the means to an end. Rather than focusing on improving the efficiency and effectiveness of processes through process improvement, organizations can

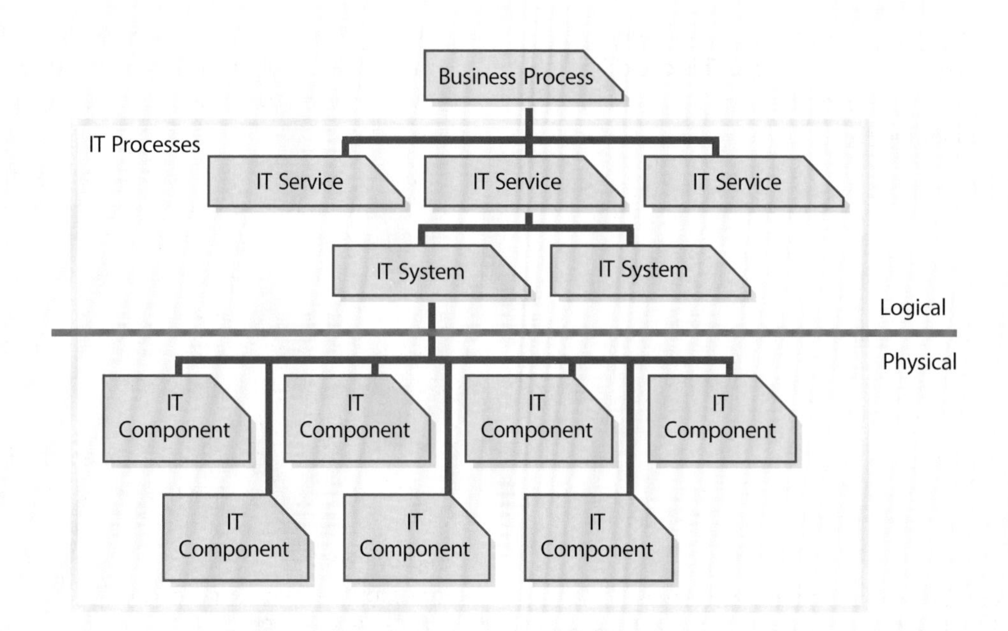

Figure 5.1 Relationship of services, processes and systems

adopt a mindset of improving process for the sake of achieving maturity targets.

- Assessments are labour-intensive efforts. Resources are needed to conduct the assessments in addition to those responding such as process or tool practitioners, management and others. When preparing for an assessment, an honest estimate of time required from all parties is in order.
- Assessments attempt to be as objective as possible in terms of measurements and assessment factors, but when all is said and done assessment results are still subject to opinion of assessors. Thus assessments themselves are subjective and the results can have a bias based on the attitudes, experience and approach of the assessors themselves.

Assessments are an effective method of answering the question 'Where are we now?' Understanding how an existing service is performing or how effective and efficient service management processes are, is important for identifying the gap between where we are and where we want to be. As we begin our discussion of assessments, we need to look at the relationship between business processes, IT services, IT systems and components that make up an IT system. IT service management processes support the IT services, IT systems and components. CSI will need to review the results of each one of these areas for effectiveness and efficiency. This will help identify the areas for improvement.

In the CSI journey the decisions as to what to improve are critical to the overall results that can be achieved. Any discussion on improvements has to begin with the services being provided to the business. This could lead to improvements on the service itself or lead to process improvements supporting the business service.

Improvement activities require the investment of human, financial and technological resources in the quest of continual improvement. These resources are allocated from other uses (e.g. customer support initiatives, new product development) to the improvement work. The business rationalizes decisions to allocate resources on the basis of the greatest ROI. An important consideration then becomes understanding and articulating improvement needs and the benefits of improvement.

The goal of service improvement for an organization is two-fold:

- First the organization seeks to achieve service objectives in cost-efficient manner. The objectives can (and should) be linked to the overall strategy of the business. The efficiency issue for an organization is determining that the process is achieving its objectives with the most cost-efficient use of resources. There is potential for cost savings through elimination of unnecessary, redundant, overlapping or manual process activities and procedures, which in turn can be a significant benefit driver for justifying a process improvement.
- Second, the organization identifies those elements of process that detract from meeting service objectives effectively. Effectiveness relates to the ability of the process to achieve or exceed its principles and goals. In other words, a process would be considered effective if, through the implementation of the process, the organization meets, sustains and potentially exceeds the strategic goals and tactical objectives of the organization. Thus service improvements focus on addressing perceived or measurable process deficiencies, impacting specific organizational objectives, and can be quantified as delivered improvement benefits.

Service improvements are governed by the improvement lifecycle. The improvement lifecycle is modelled upon the Deming Model (see Figure 5.6) of Plan-Do-Check-Act. The model establishes a clear pattern for continual improvement efforts.

- **Plan** – Establishes goals for improvement including gap analysis, definition of action steps to close the gap and establishing and implementing measures to assure that the gap has been closed and benefits achieved.
- **Do** – Development and implementation of a project to close the gap. Implementation or improvement of processes and establishing the smooth operation of the process.
- **Check** – Comparison of the implemented environment to the measures of success established in Plan phase. The comparison determines if a gap still exists between the improvement objectives of the process and the operational process state. Gaps don't necessarily require closure. A gap may be considered tolerable if the actual performance is within allowable limits of performance.
- **Act** – The decision process to determine if further work is required to close remaining gaps, allocation of resources necessary to support another round of improvement. Project decisions at this stage are the input for the next round of the lifecycle, closing the loop as input in Plan.

Value of processes vs. maturity of processes

Figure 5.2 below illustrates the value of a process in comparison to its maturity. For service management process improvement projects one of the questions asked should be around how mature we need our processes to be. The answer to this is tied directly back to the business. In other words how important is a process to the business.

Let's say that a particular organization has gone through an assessment and have found that three key processes; SLM, Availability and Capacity Management shown on the below table are not very mature. This particular organization is changing their strategy around how they sell and deliver their products and services to a web-based strategy. Because of the importance of Capacity and Availability Management to any organization that provides their products and services over the web, this company has to implement an improvement programme for increasing the maturity of both processes. Without any improvement initiatives this particular organization is putting itself at risk. We have all read about companies who have experienced larger-than-planned-for usage and how these often create catastrophic results for organizations. The lack of proper capacity planning has in many cases created availability issues that have shut down an organization's ability to sell its products.

Having a low SLM process maturity also will create some issues for CSI activities. How do we know the new business requirements? What is currently being monitored and how well are we doing against targets? Do we have roles identified for reporting and analysis of data?

The maturity of a process should ideally fall in the 'safe' areas. If a process is immature but the business heavily depends on it there is a significant danger to the organization. If a process is very mature yet provides very little to the business, then an organization may be over-investing resources and money. When CSI is looking at improving processes in support of IT services, understanding the value of processes to a business is critical.

5.2.1 Gap analysis

Gap analysis is a business assessment tool enabling an organization to compare where it is currently and where it wants to go in the future. This provides the organization with insight to areas which have room for improvement. This can be used to determine the gap between 'What do we want?' and 'What do we need?' for example.

The process involves determining, documenting and approving the variance between business requirements and current capabilities. Gap analysis naturally flows from benchmarking or other assessments such as service or process maturity assessments. Once the general expectation of performance is understood then it is possible to compare that expectation with the level of performance at which the company currently functions. This comparison becomes the gap analysis. Such analysis

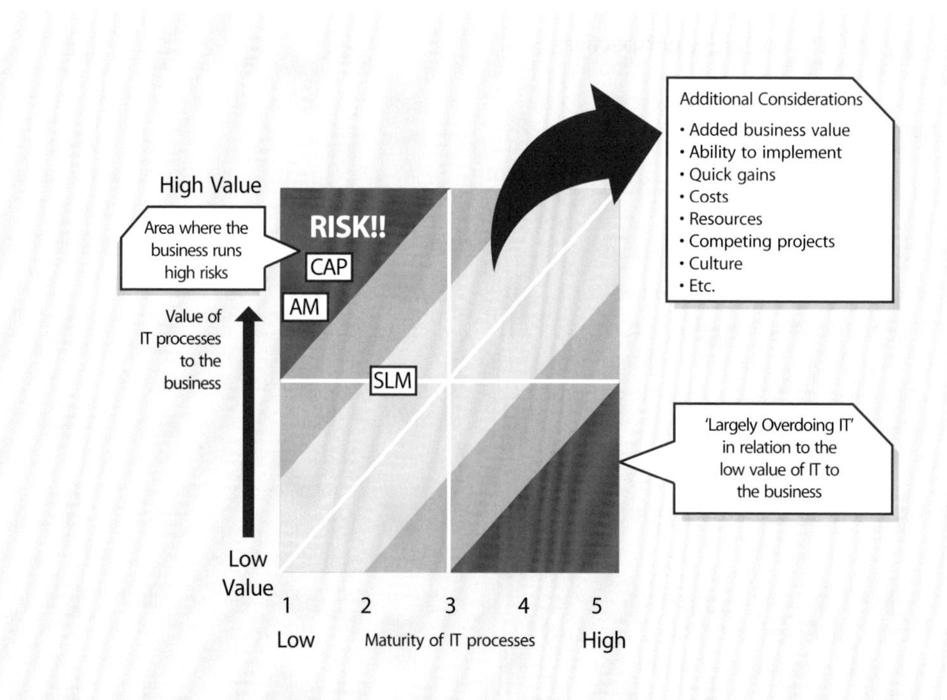

Figure 5.2 Value of a process vs. maturity of a process

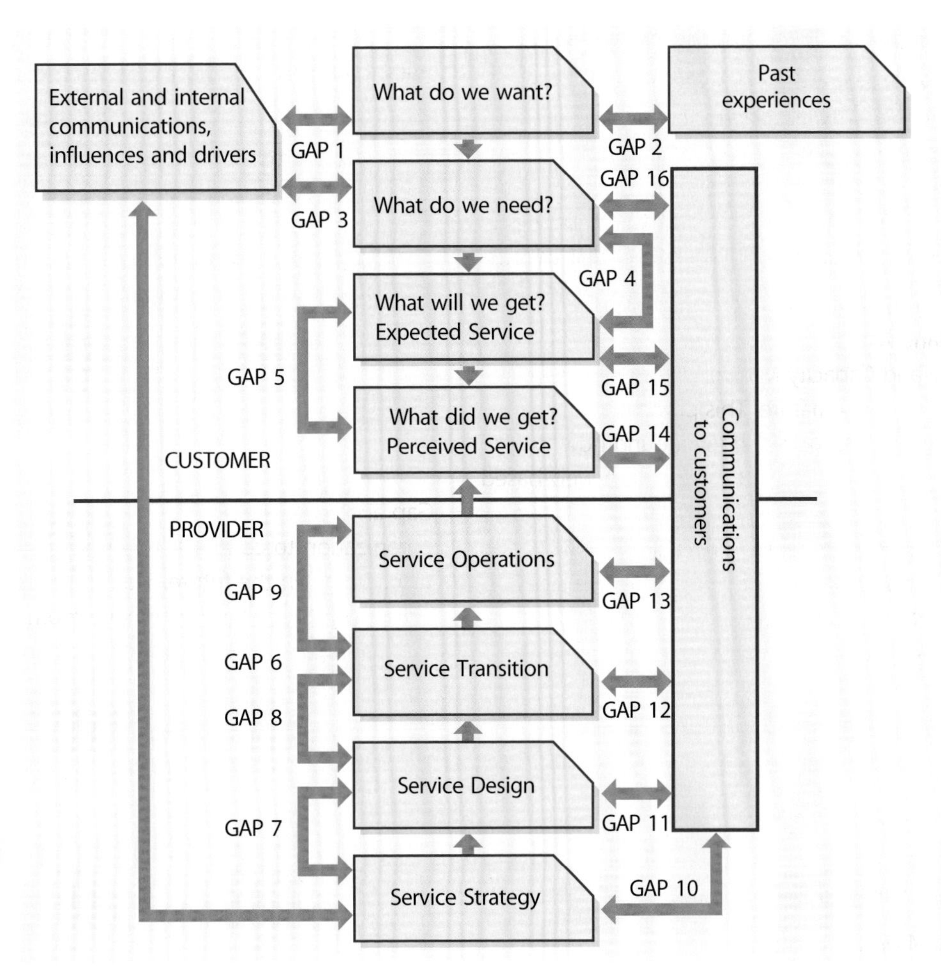

Figure 5.3 Service gap model

can be performed at the strategic, tactical or operational level of an organization.

Gap analysis can be conducted from different perspectives such as:

- Organization (e.g. human resources)
- Business direction
- Business processes
- Information technology.

Gap analysis provides a foundation for how much effort, in terms of time, money and human resources, is required to have a particular goal achieved (e.g. how to bring a service from a maturity level of 2 to 3).

Figure 5.3 illustrates the many gaps that can exist between the CSI model and the service lifecycle. Table 5.2 provides further explanation on the gaps.

Table 5.2 Explanations of the gaps in above figure

Gap	Description
1	This gap comes from the interpretation of the information coming from the outside and how it influences or directs the question 'what do we want?'
2	This gap comes from the interpretation of past experiences or the lack of data, information and knowledge to properly reduce this gap and how it influences or directs the question 'what do we want?'
3	This gap comes from the interpretation of the information coming from the outside and the organization's incorrect assessments of what it really needs.
4	This gap comes from the translation of the information into requirements.
5	This gap comes from either a lack communication or from unclear communication. Often expectations are not set properly or are unrealistic.
6	This gap comes from the interpretation of the information coming from the outside and how it influences or directs the service strategy.
7	This gap comes from the interpretation of Service Strategy into design specifications and from the limitation of the tools used to translate requirements and specifications into a plan.
8	This gap comes from the interpretation of Service Strategy and design specifications and from the limitation of the tools used to create and transition the service into existence.
9	This gap comes from the interpretation of what the provider perceives the deliverables to be and from either a lack of communication or from unclear communication. Often expectations are not set properly or are unrealistic even from the perspective of the provider.
10	This gap comes from the interpretation of what the message should be, what the message is and the frequency of the message.
11	This gap comes from the interpretation of what the message should be, what the message is and the frequency of the message.
12	This gap comes from the interpretation of what the message should be, what the message is and the frequency of the message.
13	This gap comes from the interpretation of what the message should be, what the message is and the frequency of the message.
14	This gap comes from the interpretation of what the message should be, what the message is and the frequency of the message.
15	This gap comes from the interpretation of what the message should be, what the message is and the frequency of the message.
16	This gap comes from the interpretation of what the message should be, what the message is and the frequency of the message.

5.3 BENCHMARKING

Benchmarking is a process used in management, particularly strategic management, in which organizations evaluate various aspects of their processes in relation to best practice, usually within their own sector. This then allows organizations to develop plans on how to adopt such best practice, usually with the aim of increasing some aspect of performance. Benchmarking may be a one-time occurrence event, but is often treated as a continuous process in which organizations continually seek to challenge their practices.

Benchmarking is actually a logical sequence of stages that an organization goes through to achieve continual improvement in its key processes. It involves cooperation with others as benchmarking partners learn from each other where improvements can be made. It will be necessary to:

- Ensure senior management support.
- Take an external view – Bring together business intelligence and internal performance to draw conclusions about the way internal resources and

processes must be improved to achieve and surpass the performance of others.

- Compare processes, not outputs – Comparisons with organizations in the same sector are unlikely to identify the significant improvements that have been made elsewhere or overturn the conventions of the sector.
- Involve process owners – Their involvement encourages acceptance and buy-in by those who will be affected immediately by the changes which will be required to improve performance.
- Set up benchmarking teams – As a benchmarking culture develops, people will apply the method as part of the normal way in which they manage their work.
- Acquire the skills – People who undertake benchmarking require a small amount of training and guidance; an experienced in-house facilitator or external consultant will probably be required to provide technical assurance and encouragement in the application of the method.

Organizations should plan their benchmarking process based on their improvement needs, and should understand that this may require measurement of other companies. Some cross-industry figures may be published by the international research organizations, but will not necessarily include the assumptions and measurements a given organization needs. A research organization may, however, be a valuable benchmarking partner, for example, if target companies are competitors.

There is a general expectation that benchmarking is a process of comparing an organization's performance to industry-standard figures. By extension, having such benchmark figures available is often seen as the first hurdle in a benchmarking exercise. However, as this section will show, benchmarks are only relevant when the comparison is of the same performance measures or indicators, and is with similar organizations in terms of size, industry and geography.

5.3.1 Benchmarking procedure

Identify your problem areas. Because benchmarking can be applied to any business process or function, a range of research techniques may be required. They include:

- Informal conversations with customers, employees, or suppliers
- Focus groups
- In-depth marketing research
- Quantitative research
- Surveys
- Questionnaires
- Re-engineering analysis
- Process mapping
- Quality control variance reports
- Financial ratio analysis.

5.3.2 Benchmarking costs

Benchmarking is a moderately expensive process, but most organizations find that it more than pays for itself. The three main types of costs are:

- **Visit costs** – This includes travel- and accommodation-related expenses for team members who need to travel to the site.
- **Time costs** – Members of the benchmarking team will be investing time in researching problems, finding exceptional companies to study, visits and implementation. This will take them away from their regular tasks for part of each day so additional staff might be required.
- **Benchmarking database costs** – Organizations that institutionalize benchmarking into their daily procedures find it is useful to create and maintain a database of best practices and the companies associated with each best practice.

5.3.3 Value of benchmarking

Organizations have a growing need to get a clear view on their own qualities and performances with regard to their competitors and in the eye of their customers. It isn't sufficient any more to have self-assessment reports on the status of the IT performance; it is important to test and compare it with the view the market has on the performance of the organization. A positive result of this test and comparison can give a competitive edge to the organization in the market and gives trust to its customers. The results of benchmarking and self-assessments lead to identification of gaps in terms of people, process and technology. A benchmark can be the catalyst to initiating prioritization of where to begin formal process improvement. The results of benchmarking must clearly display the gaps, identify the risks of not closing the gaps, facilitate prioritization of development activities and facilitate communication of this information.

To summarize, a benchmark is the basis for:

- Profiling quality in the market
- Boosting self-confidence and pride in employees as well as motivating and tying employees to an organization. This is relevant with today's staff

shortages in the IT industry – IT personnel want to work in a highly efficient, cutting-edge environment
- Trust from customers that the organization is a good IT service management provider.

Optimizing service quality is key to all IT organizations to maximize performance and customer satisfaction and provide value for money. Organizations will be required to focus on end results and service quality, rather than simply on their business activities and processes.

5.3.4 Benefits

Using benchmark results will help deliver major benefits in:

- Achieving economy in the form of lower prices and higher productivity on the part of the service provider
- Achieving efficiency by comparing the costs of providing IT services and the contribution these services make to the business with what is achieved in other organizations. This helps the organization to identify areas for improvement
- Achieving effectiveness in terms of actual business objectives realized compared with what was planned.

Benchmarking helps the organization to focus on strategic planning by identifying the relative effectiveness of IT support for the business. Economy is the easiest area to investigate although efficiency and effectiveness may deliver the most benefit to the business. To obtain the maximum benefit, it is necessary to look at all of these three areas, rather than focusing on one to the exclusion of the others.

5.3.5 Who is involved?

Within an organization there will be three parties involved in benchmarking:

- **The customer** – that is, the business manager responsible for acquiring IT services to meet business objectives. The customer's interest in benchmarking would be: 'How can I improve my performance in procuring services and managing service providers, and in supporting the business through IT services?'
- **The user or consumer** – that is, anyone who uses IT services to support his or her work. The user's interest in benchmarking would be: 'How can I improve my performance by exploiting IT?'
- **The internal service provider** – providing IT services to users under Service Level Agreements negotiated with and managed by the customer. The provider's interest in benchmarking would be: 'How can we improve our performance in the delivery of IT services which meet the requirements of our customers and which are cost-effective and timely?'

There will also be participation from external parties:

- **External service providers** – providing IT services to users under contracts and Service Level Agreements negotiated with and managed by the customer
- **Members of the public** – are increasingly becoming direct users of IT services
- **Benchmarking partners** – that is, other organizations with whom comparisons are made in order to identify the best practices to be adopted for improvements.

5.3.6 What to benchmark?

Differences in benchmarks between organizations are normal. All organizations and service-provider infrastructures are unique, and most are continually changing. There are also intangible but influential factors that cannot be measured, such as growth, goodwill, image and culture.

Direct comparison with similar organizations is most effective if there is a sufficiently large group of organizations with similar characteristics. It is important to understand the size and nature of the business area, including the geographical distribution and the extent to which the service is used for business or time-critical activities.

Comparison with other groups in the same organization normally allows a detailed examination of the features being compared, so that it can be established whether or not the comparison is of like with like.

Tip

When benchmarking one or more services or service management processes, the IT organization has to ascertain which of these the organization should focus on first, if all cannot be implemented simultaneously. Determine which services and supporting processes to compare. Benchmarking of a service management process is used to find out if a process is cost-effective, responsive to the customer's needs and effective in comparison with other organizations. Some organizations use benchmarking to decide whether they should change their service provider.

It is essential in planning for service management to start with an assessment or review of the relevant service management processes. The results of this can provide a baseline for future comparison.

Example

One large company started with the implementation of all service management processes. Senior management never answered the question *why* all these processes should be implemented. It sounded like a good thing to do: 'Everybody else is doing service management so why don't we?'. After two years the whole project had to be stopped because customers were complaining about poor service. It was decided to restart the service management project. This time senior management decided to implement only a part of service management (the processes where the pain was most felt) and there was an assessment conducted to provide a baseline of results for future comparison.

Benchmarking techniques can be applied at various levels from relatively straightforward in-house comparisons through to an industry-wide search for best practice. It comprises four basic stages: planning, analysis, action and review. Or better yet, let's apply the improvement process to benchmarking.

- What should we measure?
  - Select the broad service or service management process or function to benchmark (such as Service Desk) in relation to stakeholder needs.
  - Draw up a preliminary list of potential benchmarking partners (these may be within the organization or outside).
  - Identify possible sources of information and methods of collection to confirm the suitability of potential partners.
- What can we measure?
  - Within that process, define the activities to be benchmarked (such as incident lifecycle).
  - Identify the resources required for the study.
  - Confirm the key performance measures or indicators to measure the performance in carrying out the activity.
  - Document the way the activities are currently completed.
  - Agree the plan and its implementation.
- Gathering:
  - Collect information to identify the most likely potential benchmarking partner to contact.
- Processing
- Analysing:
  - Confirm the best potential benchmarking partner and make a preliminary assessment of the performance gap.
  - Establish contacts and visits, if appropriate, to validate and substantiate the information.
  - Compare the existing process with that of the benchmarking partner to identify differences and innovations.
  - Agree targets for improvement that are expected as a result of adopting the benchmarking partner's ways of doing things.
- Presenting and using:
  - Communicate the results of the study throughout the relevant parts of the organization and to the benchmarking partner.
  - Plan how to achieve the improvements.
- Taking corrective action:
  - Review performance when the changes have been embedded in the organization.
  - Identify and rectify anything which may have caused the organization to fall short of its target.
  - Communicate the results of the changes implemented to the organization and the benchmarking partner.
  - Consider benchmarking again to continue the improvement process.

Ideally, benchmark reviews should be built into an ongoing service management lifecycle so that regularly scheduled reviews or benchmarks are conducted. The formality and rigour with which they are conducted will vary depending on the environment, the rate of business change, the complexity of the environment and the elapsed time since the last review. Conducting these reviews regularly provides valuable metrics and trend analysis with which to judge improvements (or lack thereof) and take corrective action as early as possible to maximize performance gains.

5.3.7 Comparison with industry norms

ITIL is itself an industry-recognized best practice, which is a growing standard for service management worldwide. The ITIL core publications provide documented guidance on detailed process assessment and service benchmarking that can be used as checklists and templates for organizations doing their own service reviews and benchmarks. Additionally, many IT service organizations around the world provide consulting and professional expertise in the process of conducting service management benchmarks and assessments to compare the current processes with published best practices and the ITIL recommendations. It may be worthwhile to investigate using these services if the scope of an assessment is very large or complex.

Process maturity comparison

Conducting a process maturity assessment is one way to identify service management improvement opportunities. Often when an organization conducts a maturity assessment they want to know how they compare to the other organizations. Figure 5.4 reflects average maturity scores for over 100 separate organizations that went through a maturity assessment.

Finance	2.67
Incident/SD	2.49
Continuity	2.42
Release	2.36
Change	2.26
Capacity	2.02
Availability	1.97
Service Level	1.96
Problem	1.83
Configuration	1.66

Figure 5.4 Cumulative results of over 100 process assessments before improvement

Table 5.3 CMMI maturity model

0. Non-Existent	Nothing present
1. Initial	Concrete evidence of development
2. Repeatable	Some process documentation but some errors likely
3. Defined	Standardized and documented
4. Managed	Monitored for compliance
5. Optimized	Processes are considered best practices through improvement

As you can see Service Level Management which is a key process in support of CSI is at a fairly low maturity level in the organizations used in the above example. The lack of a mature SLM process that provides for identification of new business requirements, monitoring and reporting of results can make it difficult to identify service improvement opportunities. A prime target for improvements in this example would be first to mature the SLM practice to help achieve measurable targets to improve services going forward.

Total cost of ownership

The total cost of ownership (TCO), developed by Gartner, has become a key measurement of the effectiveness and the efficiency of services. TCO is defined as all the costs involved in the design, introduction, operation and improvement of services within an organization from its inception until retirement. Often, TCO is measured relating to hardware components. The TCO of an IT service is even more meaningful. CSI needs to take the TCO into perspective when looking at service improvement plans.

TCO is often used to benchmark specific services in IT against other organizations, i.e. managed service providers.

5.3.8 Benchmark approach

Benchmarking will establish the extent of an organization's existing maturity with best practice and will help in understanding how that organization compares with industry norms. Deciding what the KPIs are going to be and then measuring against them will give solid management information for future improvement and targets.

A benchmark exercise would be used as the first stage in this approach. This could be either one or other of:

- **An internal benchmark** – completed internally using resources from within the organization to assess the maturity of the service management processes against a reference framework
- **An external benchmark** – this would be completed by an external third-party company. Most of these have their own proprietary models for the assessment of service management process maturity.

The results and recommendations contained within the benchmarking review can then be used to identify and rectify areas of weakness within the IT service management processes.

Viewed from a business perspective, benchmark measurements can help the organization to assess IT services, performance and spend against peer or competitor organizations and best practice, both across the whole of IT and by appropriate business areas, answering questions such as:

- How does IT spend compare to other similar organizations – overall, as a percentage of revenue, or per employee?
- How does IT spend compare for similar functions, e.g. payroll functions either within an organization or with other organizations?
- How does IT spend compare across business units or business processes?
- How does IT spend compare across locations or technologies?
- How effective is IT service delivery (and identify opportunities and measures for improvement)?

- Which is the most appropriate sourcing option?
- Is the value of a long-term sourcing contract being maintained year on year?

Benchmarking activities need to be business-aligned. They can be expensive exercises whether undertaken internally or externally, and therefore they need to be focused on where they can deliver most value. For internal service providers, cost benchmarking can assess the efficiency and effectiveness of the IT unit. For external service providers, especially outsourced services, they can help to ensure the right IT services for the right price. Results of benchmarking not only provide a statement of performance, but can also be used to identify, recommend and plan improvements. They can also demonstrate value to the business and set targets for improvement levels, with subsequent benchmarking to assess achievement.

Comparisons of service performance and workload characteristics between peer organizations, the effectiveness of business process and the IT contribution to IT are also of value as part of a TCO assessment. Third-party specialists are available to conduct benchmarking and assessments, giving the business an external perspective and helping to lend credibility to the results and recommendations for improvements.

There is a variety of IT benchmarking types available separately or in combination, including:

- Cost and performance for internal service providers
- Price and performance for external service providers
- Process performance against industry best practice
- Financial performance of high-level IT costs against industry or peers
- Effectiveness considering satisfaction ratings and business alignment at all levels.

The context for benchmarking requires information about the organization's profile, complexity and relative comparators. An effective and meaningful profile contains four key components:

- **Company information profile** – The company profile defines the landscape of an organization, i.e. basic information on the company size, industry type, geographic location and types of user are typical of data gathered to establish this profile.
- **Current assets** – The IT assets mix within the organization may include production IT, desktop and mobile clients, peripherals, network and server assets.
- **Current best practices** – These include policies, procedures and/or tools that improve returns, and their maturity and degree of usage.
- **Complexity** – Complexity includes information about the end-user community, the types and quantities of varied technologies in use and how IT is managed.

5.4 MEASURING AND REPORTING FRAMEWORKS

There are many techniques used today to measure the effectiveness and efficiency of IT and the services it provides. Often organizations use a combination of methods rather than just one individual technique. CSI should assume responsibility for ensuring that the quality of service required by the business is provided within the imposed cost constraints. CSI is also instrumental in determining if IT is still on course with the achievement of planned implementation targets and, if not, plotting course corrections to bring it back into alignment.

However, it must be remembered that although the measurement of progress is vital it is not the end product; rather, it is a means to an end. Often people gather measurements and produce reports as a full-time occupation. It is essential that the production of statistics is not seen as the sole objective of the strategy implementation but rather an indicator of its progress and success.

5.4.1 Balanced Scorecard

This is a technique developed by Kaplan and Norton in the mid-1990s and involves the definition and implementation of a measurement framework covering four different perspectives: customer, internal business, learning and growth, and lastly financial. The four linked perspectives provide a Balanced Scorecard to support strategic activities and objectives, and can be used to measure overall IT performance.

The Balanced Scorecard is complementary to ITIL. Some of the links to IT include the following:

- **Client perspective** – IT as a service provider, primarily documented in Service Level Agreements (SLAs)
- **Internal processes** – Operational excellence utilizing Incident, Problem, Change, Configuration and Release Management as well as other IT processes; successful delivery of IT projects
- **Learning and growth** – Business productivity, flexibility of IT, investments in software, professional learning and development
- **Financial** – Align IT with the business objectives, manage costs, manage risks, deliver value; IT Financial Management is the process used to allocate costs and calculate ROI.

Kaplan and Norton first introduced the idea of a Balanced Scorecard in the early 1992 *Harvard Business Review*. The need for such a method emerged out of a growing recognition that financial measures alone were insufficient to manage the modern organization. Much of the emphasis in today's work environment is preparation to achieve financial goals, achieve process innovations, training workers and creating and maintaining new kinds of relationship with customers.

The Balanced Scorecard is not simply a measurement system but a management system that enables organizations to clarify their vision, mission, goals, objectives and strategies and to translate them into action. When fully deployed, the Balanced Scorecard transforms strategic planning from an academic exercise into the nerve centre of an enterprise. It provides feedback around both the internal business processes and external outcomes in order to continually improve strategic performance and results.

The Balanced Scorecard, as an aid to organizational Performance Management, is a common method of tracking metrics and performing trend analysis. It helps to focus, not only on the financial targets but also on the internal processes, Customers and learning and growth issues. The balance should be found between four perspectives. The four perspectives are focused around the following questions:

- **Customers** – What do customers expect of IT provision?
- **Internal processes** – What must IT excel at?
- **Learning and growth** – How does IT guarantee that the business will keep generating added value in the future?
- **Financial** – What is the cost of IT?

Cascading the Balanced Scorecard

Many organizations are structured around strategic business units (SBUs) with each business unit focusing on a specific group of products or services offered by the business. The structure of IT may match the SBU organization or may offer services to the SBU from a common, shared services IT organization or both. This last hybrid approach tends to put the central infrastructure group in the shared services world and the business solutions or application development group in the SBU itself. This often results in non-productive finger-pointing when things go wrong. The business itself is not interested in this blame-storming exercise but rather in the quality of IT service provision. Therefore, the Balanced Scorecard is best deployed at the SBU level (see Figure 5.5).

Once a Balanced Scorecard has been defined at the SBU level, it can then be cascaded down through the organization. For each strategic business level measure and related target, business units can define additional

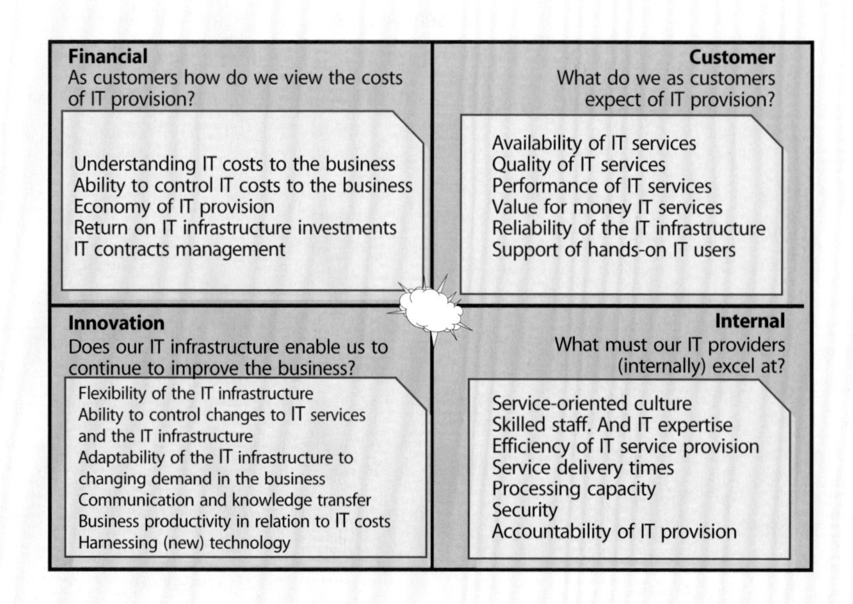

Figure 5.5 IT Balanced Scorecard

measures and targets that support the strategic goal and target. In addition, action plans and resource allocation decisions can be made with reference to how they contribute to the strategic Balanced Scorecard. As with any measurement system it is important to link the reward systems to the Balanced Scorecard objectives. The following is an example of a Balanced Scorecard for a Service Desk.

The Balanced Scorecard is not an exclusive IT feature. On the contrary, many organizations use scorecards in other departments – even at the board level.

Start very conservatively when implementing the Balanced Scorecard. Start with two to three, maybe four, goals and metrics for each perspective. Organizations have to make choices; for many, this will be extremely difficult and time consuming.

Implementation is not the most difficult part of using the Balanced Scorecard – consolidation is. Usually, consultants are employed to assist in the introduction of the Balanced Scorecard. The challenge is to keep measuring once they are gone. The danger is in the temptation to fall back on prior measuring techniques or not measuring at all.

The Balanced Scorecard and measurement-based management

The Balanced Scorecard approach focuses on including customer-defined quality, continual improvement, employee empowerment, and measurement-based management and feedback.

The Balanced Scorecard incorporates feedback around internal business process outputs, as in Total Quality Management (TQM), but also adds a feedback loop around the outcomes of business strategies. This creates a double-loop feedback process in the Balanced Scorecard.

An old saying goes: 'You can't improve what you can't measure.' Metrics must be developed based on the priorities of the strategic plan, which provides the key business drivers and criteria for metrics that managers most desire to watch. Services and processes are then designed to collect information relevant to these metrics. Strategic management can then examine the outcomes of various measured services, processes and strategies and track the results to guide the company and provide feedback. The value of metrics is in their ability to provide a factual basis for defining:

- Strategic feedback to show the present status of the organization from many perspectives for decision makers

Table 5.4 Service Desk Balanced Scorecard example

Financial Goal	Performance Indicator	Customer Goal	Performance Indicator
Ability to control Service Desk costs Economy of Service Desk Value of Service Desk	Accuracy of Service Desk cost forecasts Competitiveness of service Costs of Service Desk	Quality of Service Desk services Reliability of Service Desk Performance of Service Desk Support of hands-on users	Availability of Service Desk (in IT users' perception) Compliance to SLAs Restoration of service On-time service delivery Number of registered user complaints about IT
Innovation Goal	**Performance Indicator**	**Internal goal**	**Performance Indicator**
Business productivity Service culture Flexibility	Minimize MTRS Improvements in business turnover Reduction in business costs ascribable to the Service Desk New ways to improve service	Incident resolution Elapsed time for incidents Meetings SLAs Professionalism	Percentage of first-time-right incident resolution Time spent on resolution Incidents resolved within SLAs Treating customers with respect

- Diagnostic feedback into various services and processes to guide improvements on a continual basis
- Trends in performance over time as the metrics are tracked
- Feedback around the measurement methods themselves, and which metrics should be tracked
- Quantitative inputs to forecasting methods and models for decision-support systems.

5.4.2 SWOT analysis

SWOT stands for strengths, weaknesses, opportunities and threats. This section provides guidance on properly conducting and using the result of a SWOT analysis, how to select the scope and range of this common assessment tool, as well as the common mistakes people make when using a SWOT analysis.

This technique involves the review and analysis of four specific areas of an organization: the internal strengths and weaknesses, and the external opportunities and threats. Once analysed, actions should be taken to:

- Develop, exploit and capitalize on the organization's *strengths*
- Reduce, minimize or remove *weaknesses*
- Take maximum advantage of *opportunities*
- Manage, mitigate and eliminate *threats*.

SWOT analyses can be performed quickly and can be used to target a specific area rather than looking at the entire enterprise.

Purpose

A SWOT analysis is a strategic planning tool used to evaluate the strengths, weaknesses, opportunities and threats involved in a project, business venture or in any other situation requiring a decision. Sizing up a firm's internal strengths and weaknesses and its external opportunities and threats provides a quick overview of a firm's strategic situation.

How to use

The first step is to define the desired end state or objective. This objective definition must be explicit and approved by all participants in the process.

Once the objective is identified, SWOT are discovered and listed:

- **Strengths** are internal attributes of the organization that are helpful to the achievement of the objective.
- **Weaknesses** are internal attributes of the organization that are harmful to the achievement of the objective.
- **Opportunities** are external conditions that are helpful to the achievement of the objective.
- **Threats** are external conditions that are harmful to the achievement of the objective.

Correct identification of the SWOT is essential because subsequent steps in the process are all derived from the SWOT. To ensure a successful SWOT, it is a good idea to ensure that the objective follows the SMART principle which stands for specific, measurable, achievable, realistic and timely.

SWOTs are used as inputs to the creative generation of possible strategies, by asking and answering the following four questions many times:

- How can we *use* each *strength*?
- How can we *stop* each *weakness*?
- How can we *exploit* each *opportunity*?
- How can we *defend* against each *threat*?

Scope/reach and range

SWOT analyses can be done at various levels, from an individual perspective, to a departmental, divisional or even corporate perspective. It is important to consolidate the lower hierarchical management levels before proceeding to the next level.

For example, all the members of a functional team perform an individual SWOT analysis. Then a SWOT for the functional team is performed. Each functional team within the department does the same and a departmental SWOT is conducted and so on until a corporate SWOT is completed.

It is also possible to conduct a SWOT analysis for a service or a process.

Table 5.5 SWOT analysis

Things to consider for *strengths*	Things to consider for *weaknesses*
Core competencies	No clear strategic direction
Financial resources	Obsolete facilities
Reputable buyers	Low profitability
Acknowledged as market-leader	Lack of managerial depth and talent
Well-conceived functional-area strategies	Missing some key competencies
Access to economies of scale	Poor track record for performance
Little competitive pressure	Falling behind R&D
Proprietary technology	Too narrow product line
Cost advantages	Weak market image
Strong campaigns	Weak distribution network
Product innovation	Below-average marketing skills
Proven management	Unable to finance needed changes
Ahead on experience curve	Higher overall unit costs
Better development/production capability	
Superior technology	
Things to consider for *opportunities*	**Things to consider for *threats***
Ability to serve additional customer groups or expand into new market or segments	Entry of lower-cost foreign competitors
Ways to expand product line to meet broader range of customer needs	Rising sales of substitute products
Ability to transfer skills or technological know-how to new products or businesses	Slower market growth
Integrating forward or backward	Adverse shifts in foreign exchange rates and trade policies of foreign governments
Falling trade barriers in attractive foreign markets	Costly regulatory requirements
Complacency among rival firms	Potentially sudden deregulation
Ability to grow rapidly because of strong increases in market demand	Vulnerability to recession and business cycle
Emerging new technologies	Growing bargaining power of customers or suppliers
	Adverse demographic changes

Table 5.6 Sample CSI SWOT analysis

Strengths	*Weaknesses*
■ People with the right attitude, values and commitment ■ Management commitment to CSI ■ CSI manager in place	■ Reactive organization ■ Immature processes ■ Lack of monitoring and reporting tools ■ Insufficient data
Opportunities	*Threats*
■ Increased market share of current services ■ Become a third-party service provider ■ Efficiencies through more integrated operations ■ Be quicker to market with new products	■ Competition ■ New regulatory requirements ■ New technology ■ Lack of trained staff ■ Lack of Knowledge Management

Common pitfalls of a SWOT analysis

The failure to correctly identify the end state will result in wasted resources and possibly failure. It is therefore important to align the SWOT analysis with the organization's vision, mission, goals and objectives. The following errors have been observed in published accounts of SWOT analysis. Making these errors can result in serious losses:

- Conducting a SWOT analysis before defining and agreeing upon the desired end state.
- Opportunities (external to the company) are often confused with strengths (internal to the company). Keep them separate.
- Do not confuse opportunities with possible strategies. It may also be useful to keep in mind that SWOT is a description of conditions, while possible strategies define actions.

5.5 THE DEMING CYCLE

The Deming Cycle was introduced in Chapter 3. Below we expand the methods and techniques involved.

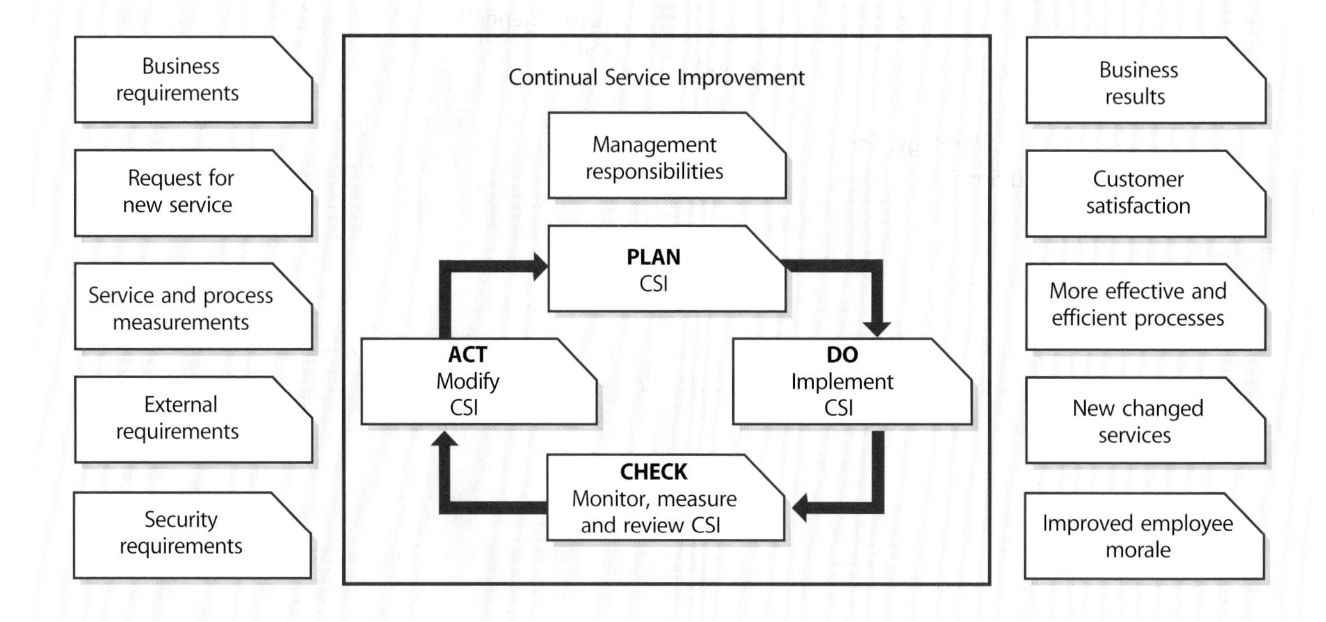

Figure 5.6 Deming Cycle – adapted for CSI

- Planning for CSI (Plan) – the planning process should address the following items:
  - Scope of CSI
  - Establishing goals for improvement including gap analysis, definition of action steps to close any gaps and establishing and implementing measures to assure that the gaps have been closed and benefits achieved
  - Objectives and requirements for CSI
  - Interfaces between CSI and the rest of the service lifecycle
  - Process activities to be developed
  - Framework of management roles and responsibilities
  - Tools as appropriate to support the processes
  - Methods and techniques to measure, assess, analyse and report on the quality, effectiveness and efficiency of services and service management processes.
- Implement CSI (Do) – implementing CSI includes the following:
  - Funding and budgets required to support CSI
  - Documenting roles and responsibilities
  - Allocation of roles and responsibilities to work on CSI initiatives
  - Documenting and maintaining CSI policies, plans and procedures
  - Communicating and training on documented policies, plans and procedures
  - Ensuring monitoring, analysis, trend evaluating and reporting tools are in place
  - Integrating with Service Strategy, Service Design, Service Transition and Service Operation.
- Monitor, measure and review CSI activities (Check)

  The objective of this stage is to monitor, measure and review that the CSI objectives and plans are being achieved. As with other processes, this includes reporting against plans, documentation review, conducting process assessments and audits. The key is to identify and recommend CSI process improvement opportunities.
- Continual improvement (Act)

  This stage requires implementing the actual CSI enhancements. For example, this could involve updating CSI policies, procedures, roles and responsibilities.

5.5.1 Deming Cycle used for improving services and service management processes

When applying CSI against services and service management process the last two stages of Check and Act play a significant role, however, there are still activities that take pace in the Plan and Do stages of the Deming Cycle.

- **Planning for improvement initiatives (Plan)** – At this stage goals and measures for success are established, a gap analysis is performed, action steps to close the gap are defined, and measures to ensure the gap was closed are established and implemented.
- **Implementation of improvement initiative (Do)** – This includes development and implementation of a project to close the identified gaps, implementation of the improvement to service management processes, and establishing the smooth operation of the process.
- **Monitor, measure and review services and service management processes (Check)** – During this stage the implemented improvements are compared to the measures of success established in the Plan phase. The comparison determines if a gap still exists between the improvement objectives and the operational process state. Gaps don't necessarily require closure. A gap may be considered tolerable if the actual performance is within allowable limits of performance. At the Check stage, the expected output is recommendations for improvement. For example, recommendations to update or modify the Service Catalogue, measurements to be tracked in SLAs, Operating Level Agreements (OLAs) and Underpinning Contracts (UCs) could also come out of this stage.
- **Continual service and service management process improvement (Act)** – This stage requires implementing the actual service and service management process improvements. A decision to keep the status quo, close the gap or add necessary resources needs to be made to determine if further work is required to close remaining gaps and to allocate resources necessary to support another round of improvement. Project decisions at this stage are the input for the next round of the Plan-Do-Check-Act cycle, closing the loop as input to the next Plan stage.

Too many people and too many organizations are looking for the big-bang approach to improvements. It is important to understand that a succession or series of small, planned increments of improvements will not stress the infrastructure as much and will eventually amount to a large amount of improvement over time.

5.6 CSI AND OTHER SERVICE MANAGEMENT PROCESSES

The CSI process makes extensive use of methods and practices found in many ITIL processes throughout the lifecycle of a service. Far from being redundant, the use of the outputs in the form of flows, matrices, statistics or analysis reports provide valuable insight into the service's design and operation. This information, combined with new business requirements, technology specifications, IT capabilities, budgets, trends and possibly legislation is vital to CSI to determine what needs to be improved – prioritize it and suggest improvements if required.

5.6.1 Availability Management

Availability Management's (AM) methods are part of the measuring process explained in Chapter 4. They are part of the measuring process – gathering, processing and analysing activities. When the information is provided to CSI in the form of a report or a presentation, it then becomes part of CSI's gathering activity. For more details on each method, please consult the Service Design publication.

With regards to AM, it provides IT with the business and user perspective about how deficiencies in the infrastructure and underpinning process and procedures impact the business operation. The use of business-driven metrics can demonstrate this impact in real terms and help quantify the benefits of improvement opportunities.

AM plays an important role in helping the IT support organization recognize where they can add value by exploiting technical skills and competencies in an availability context. The continual improvement technique can be used by AM to harness this technical capability. This can be used with either small groups of technical staff or a wider group within a workshop environment. The information provided by AM is made available to CSI through the Availability Management Information System (AMIS).

This section provides practical usage and details on how each AM method mentioned below can be used in various activities of CSI.

Component Failure Impact Analysis

Component Failure Impact Analysis (CFIA) identifies single points of failure, IT services at risk from failure of various Configuration Items (CI) and the alternatives that are available should a CI fail. It should also be used to assess the existence and validity of recovery procedures for the selected CIs. The same approach can be used for a single IT service by mapping the component CIs against the vital business functions and users supported by each component.

When a single point of failure is identified, the information is provided to CSI. This information, combined with business requirements, enable CSI to make recommendations on how to address the failure.

Fault Tree Analysis

Fault Tree Analysis (FTA) is a technique that is used to determine the chain of events that cause a disruption of IT services. This technique offers detailed models of availability. It makes a representation of a chain of events using Boolean algebra and notation. Essentially FTA distinguishes between four events: basic events, resulting events, conditional events and trigger events.

When provided to CSI, FTA information indicates which part of the infrastructure, process or service was responsible in the service disruptions. This information, combined with business requirements, enables CSI to make recommendations about how to address the fault.

Service Failure Analysis

Service Failure Analysis (SFA) is a technique designed to provide a structured approach to identify end-to-end availability improvement opportunities that deliver benefits to the user. Many of the activities involved in SFA are closely aligned with those of Problem Management. In a number of organizations these activities are performed jointly by Problem and Availability Management. SFA should attempt to identify improvement opportunities that benefit the end user. It is therefore important to take an end-to-end view of the service requirements.

CSI and SFA work hand in hand. SFA identifies the business impact of an outage on a service, system or process. This information, combined with business requirements, enables CSI to make recommendations about how to address improvement opportunities.

Technical Observation

A Technical Observation (TO) is a prearranged gathering of specialist technical support staff from within IT support. They are brought together to focus on specific aspects of IT availability. The TO's purpose is to monitor events, real-time as they occur, with the specific aim of identifying improvement opportunities within the current IT infrastructure. The TO is best suited to delivering proactive business and end-user benefits from within the real-time IT environment. Bringing together specialist technical staff to observe specific activities and events within the IT infrastructure and operational processes creates an environment to identify improvement opportunities.

The TO gathers, processes and analyses information about the situation. Too often the TO is reactive by nature and is assembled hastily to deal with an emergency. Why wait? If the TO is included as part of the launch of a new service, system or process for example, a lot of the issues inherent to any new component would be identified and dealt with more quickly.

One of the best examples for a TO is the mission control room for a space agency. All the specialists from all aspects of the mission are gathered in one room. Space agencies don't wait for the rocket to be launched and experience a problem before gathering specialists to monitor, observe and provide feedback. They set it up well before the actual launch and they practise the monitoring, observing and providing feedback.

Certainly, launching a rocket is very costly, but so is launching a new service, system or process. Can the business afford a catastrophic failure of a new ERP application, for example? Oh, by the way, rocket launches are often aborted seconds before the launch. Shouldn't organizations (including yours) do the same when someone discovers a major potential flaw in a service or system? CSI starts from the beginning and includes preventing things from failing in the first place. Let's fix the flaw before it goes into production instead of fixing the fixes (what a concept!). This information, combined with business requirements, enables CSI to make recommendations about how to address the TO's findings.

Expanded incident lifecycle

First, let's define a few items:

- **Availability Management** – To optimize the capability of the IT infrastructure, services and supporting organization to deliver a cost-effective and sustained level of availability enabling the business to meet their objectives. The AM process has both a reactive and proactive nature.
- **Expanded Incident lifecycle** – A technique to help with the technical analysis of Incidents affecting the availability of components and IT services. The Expanded Incident lifecycle is further made up of two parts: time to restore service (aka downtime) and time between failures (aka uptime). There is a diagnosis part to the Incident lifecycle as well as repair, restoration and recovery of the service.

Let's assume that CSI has decided to improve the incident lifecycle by reducing the mean time to restore service (MTRS) and expanding the mean time between failures (MTBF).

Here is an example of how AM can assist in reducing downtime in the expanded Incident lifecycle by using many techniques:

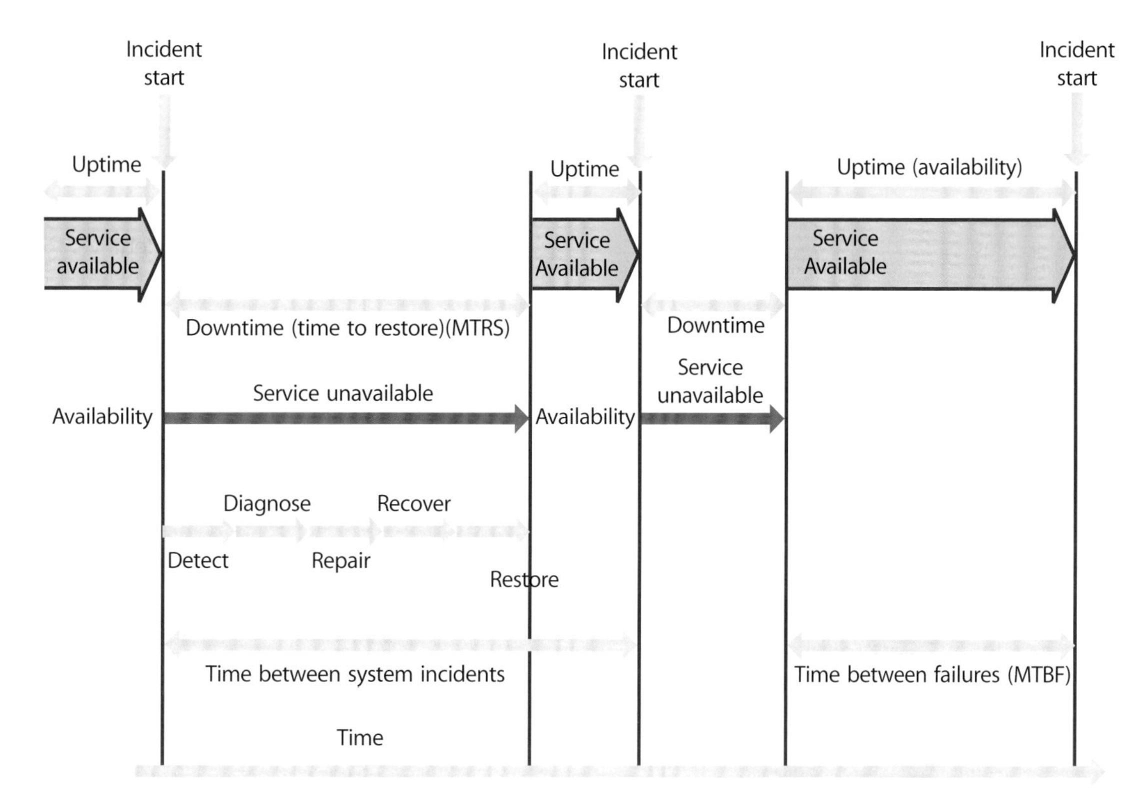

Figure 5.7 Expanded incident lifecycle

- **Monitoring (detection of Incident)** – By adequately monitoring for availability of vital business functions through automated monitoring tools (set at the right threshold) that record and escalate incidents, the time it takes to detect and record incidents is reduced.
- **Incident recording** – Since one of AM's goal is to 'optimize the ... support organization', educating and training first-line staff as well as simplifying and/or automating Incident recording helps reduce the time it takes to record Incidents.
- **Investigation** – Using the FTA method, AM assists in reducing the time to investigate by creating proper investigation procedures for Incident management staff. The same logic applies to the diagnosis of the Incident cause, resolution and recovery.

Here is an example of how AM can assist in increasing up-time in the expanded Incident lifecycle by using many techniques:

- Using SFA, AM can make recommendations to increase the reliability of components thus reducing the likelihood of an Incident occurring in the first place.
- Scheduling and performing adequate and required internal maintenance of components (maintainability), AM can help to increase the resilience of components, thus reducing the likelihood of an Incident causing an outage.
- Ensuring that external maintenance of components (serviceability) is properly scheduling and performed by external vendors, AM can help to increase the resilience of components, thus reducing the likelihood of an incident causing an outage.
- Conducting a CFIA to predict and evaluate the impact on IT service availability arising from component failures assists in identifying single points of failure. AM will either submit recommendations for enhancements to the resilience and reliability of such components or provide better troubleshooting procedures to the support groups.
- Implementing security recommendations coming from Security Management regarding the confidentiality, integrity and availability of associated data helps reduce malicious or unauthorized access to data, ensuring data integrity, and thus reducing the likelihood of an Incident occurring or decreasing the time it takes to respond or resolving an Incident.

5.6.2 Capacity Management

This section provides practical usage and details about how each Capacity Management method mentioned below can be used in various activities of CSI.

The Capacity Management process must be responsive to changing requirements for processing capacity. New services are required to underpin the changing business. Existing services will require modification to provide extra functionality. Old services will become obsolete, freeing up capacity. Capacity Management must ensure sufficient hardware, software and personnel resources are in place to support existing and future business capacity and performance requirements.

Similarly to AM, Capacity Management can play an important role in helping the IT support organization recognize where they can add value by exploiting their technical skills and competencies in a capacity context. The continual improvement technique can be used by Capacity Management to harness this technical capability. This can be used with either small groups of technical staff or a wider group within a workshop environment.

The information provided by Capacity Management is made available to CSI through the Capacity Management Information System (CMIS).

Business Capacity Management

A prime objective of the Business Capacity Management sub-process is to ensure that future business requirements for IT services are considered and understood, and that sufficient capacity to support the services is planned and implemented in an appropriate timescale.

As a result, the ability to satisfy the customers' SLRs will be affected. It is the responsibility of Capacity Management to predict and cater to these changes. These new requirements may come to the attention of Capacity Management from many different sources and for many different reasons. They may be generated by the business or may originate from the Capacity Management process itself. Such examples could be a recommendation to upgrade to take advantage of new technology, or the implementation of a tuning activity to resolve a performance problem.

Information gathered here enables CSI to answer the 'What do we need?' question.

Service Capacity Management

A prime objective of the Service Capacity Management sub-process is to identify and understand the IT services, their use of resource, working patterns, peaks and troughs, as well as to ensure that the services can and do meet their SLA targets. In this sub-process, the focus is on managing service performance, as determined by the targets contained in the SLAs or SLRs.

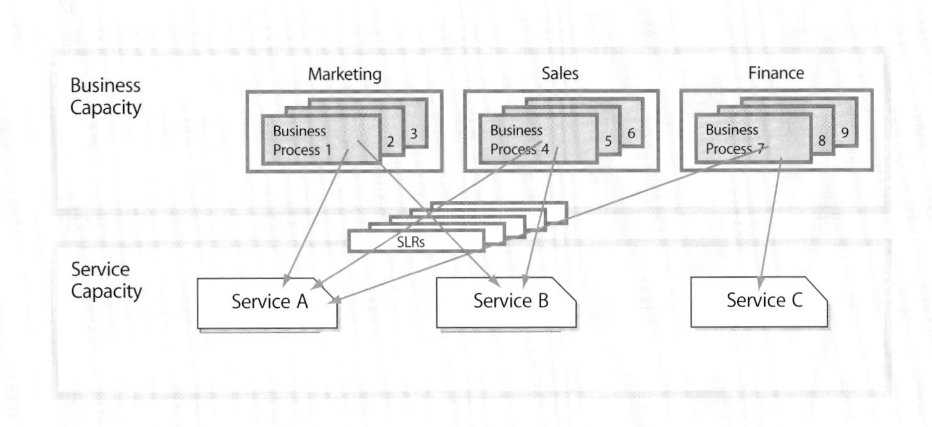

Figure 5.8 Connecting Business and Service Capacity Management

The key to successful Service Capacity Management is to pre-empt difficulties, wherever possible. This is another sub-process that has to be proactive and anticipatory rather than reactive. However there are times when it has to react to specific performance problems. Based on the knowledge and understanding of the performance requirements for each service, the effects of changes in the use of services can be estimated, and actions taken to ensure that the required service performance can be achieved. Information gathered here enables CSI to answer the 'What do we need?' question.

Component Capacity Management

A prime objective of Component Capacity Management sub-process is to identify and understand the capacity and utilization of each of the components of the IT infrastructure. This ensures the optimum use of the current hardware and software resources in order to achieve and maintain the agreed service levels. All hardware components and many software components in the IT infrastructure have a finite capacity, which, when exceeded, have the potential to cause performance problems.

As in Service Capacity Management, the key to successful Component Capacity Management is to pre-empt difficulties wherever possible. Therefore this sub-process has to be proactive and anticipatory rather than reactive. However there are times when it has to react to specific problems that are caused by a lack or inefficient use of resources.

It is important to understand how the three sub-processes tie together. Let's look at the example above (Figure 5.8):

There are three services: A, B and C

There are three departments: Marketing, Sales and Finance

Service A is used by all three departments.

Service B is used only by Marketing and Sales.

Service C is used only by Finance.

The requirements for each service from each department are:

Table 5.7 Departmental requirements

	Marketing	Sales	Finance
Employees	15	40	5
Number of e-mails per day	100	200	50
Size of attachment	10 Mb	5 Mb	10 Mb
Frequency of large attachment	infrequent	very (contracts)	often
Requires remote access	No	Yes	Yes
Requires PDA	No	Yes	No

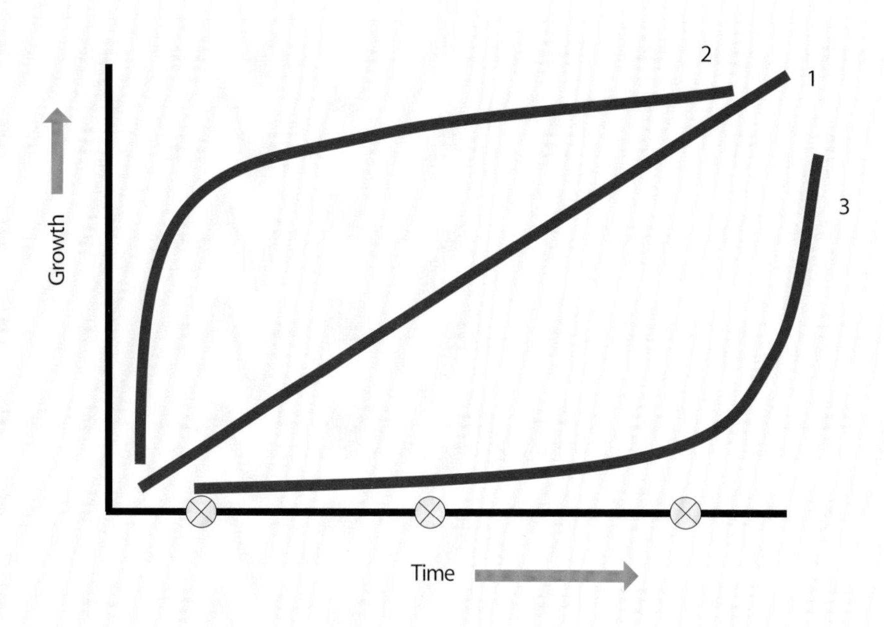

Figure 5.9 Business capacity growth model

From Table 5.7 the overall size of the e-mail service can be computed. If e-mail was the only service, it would be relatively simple. There are other services offered and each service makes use of four major components: hardware, software, documentation and people. Using the CFIA report from AM it is possible to identify all the components of each service and which component is used by which service. From there optimizing the capacity of each component can be reviewed. This, in turn, enables the optimization of the service based on the usage and performance requirements from each customer.

This however, only focuses on the current utilization. Future business requirements for this service also need to be reviewed. Basically growth can happen in one of three ways as shown in Figure 5.9.

- Curve 1 indicates a steady growth or deployment of the service over time.
- Curve 2 indicates a big-bang approach where everyone starts using the new service at the same time and usage stabilizes over time.
- Curve 3 indicates a small number of people using the new service before it is eventually deployed to everyone.

Predicting which growth curve is the correct one is just as accurate as predicting the weather a year from now. Looking at curve 2, it is important to ensure sufficient initial capacity for all components – hardware, software, documentation and people. Looking at curve 1 additional capacity is required but can wait if curve 3 is considered. Now what would happen if the business scenario predicts curve 2 and curve 3 is what actually happens? The result is over-capacity and IT is blamed for poor planning and for overspending. Consider the opposite scenario where the business predicts curve 3 and curve 2 is what actually happens. The result is under-capacity and IT gets blamed for poor planning.

Remember that only one service was reviewed so far. There are three services in the example. You need to understand the service and business along with the component capacity requirements to be able to truly identify the true capacity requirements. More importantly business capacity can be computed since how much a business unit consumes a service is known. This is when the infrastructure required to deliver and support the services can be properly put in place (see Figures 5.10 and 5.11).

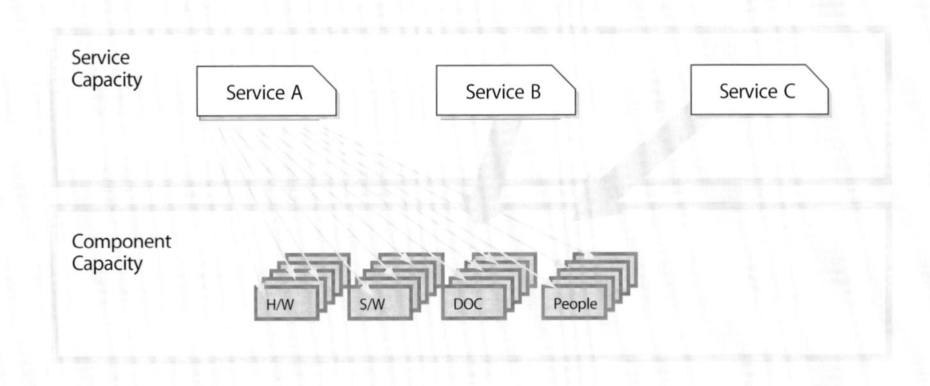

Figure 5.10 Connecting Service and Component Capacity Management

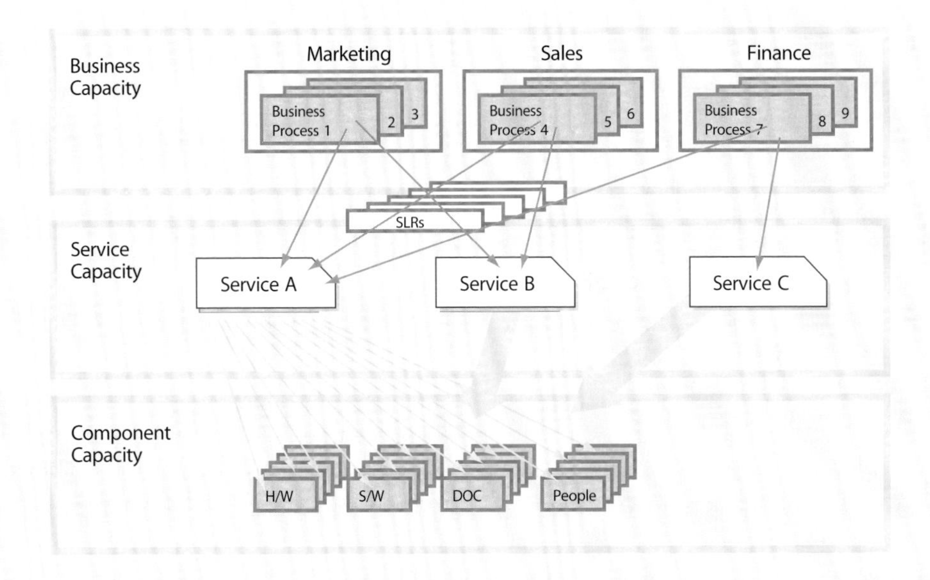

Figure 5.11 Connecting Business, Service and Component Capacity Management

From this point, IT is in a better position to improve the service provision. In order to do this IT must not only start to measure but also to influence the business. Influencing the business is part of Demand Management.

Workload Management and Demand Management

Workload Management can be defined as understanding which customers use what service, when they use the service, how they use the service and finally how using the service impacts the performance of a single or multiple systems and/or components that make up a service.

Demand Management is often associated with influencing the end users' behaviour. By influencing the end users' behaviour an organization can change the workload thus improving the performance of components that support IT services. Using Demand Management can be an effective way of improving services without investing a lot of money. A full discussion of Demand Management can be found in the ITIL Service Strategy and Service Design publications.

There are different ways to influence customer behaviour. Charging for services is an obvious way. However charging is not always effective. People still need to use the service and will use it regardless of the price. Putting in place policies regarding proper usage of the service is another way to influence customer behaviour; communicating expectations for both IT and the business, educating people on how to use the service and negotiating maintenance windows are just as effective in influencing customers. Also putting in place restrictions such as amount of space allocated for e-mail storage is another way to influence behaviour.

Consider carefully how you try to influence a customer's behaviour and it may become a negative influence rather than a positive influence. As an example, if an organization chooses to charge for every contact to the Service Desk, this could create a negative behaviour in that end users no longer call or e-mail the Service Desk, but call second-level support directly, or turn to peer-to-peer support which ultimately makes the cost of support go up, not down. However if the goal is to move end users to using a new self-service web-based knowledge system, then with a proper communication and education plan on using the new self-service system this could be a positive influencing experience.

CSI needs to review Demand Management policies to ensure that they are still effective. A policy that was good a couple of years ago, may not be workable or useful today. A few years ago, large e-mail attachments were uncommon. It made sense to limit attachments to 2 Mb. Today's reality is different.

Iterative activities of Capacity Management

Trend analysis

Trend analysis can be done on the resource utilization and service performance information that was collected by the Service and Component Capacity Management sub-processes. The data can be held in a spreadsheet and the graphical, trend analysis and forecasting facilities used to show the utilization of a particular resource over a previous period of time, and how it can be expected to change in the future. Typically trend analysis only provides estimates of future resource utilization. Trend analysis is less effective in producing an accurate estimate of response times in which case either analytical or simulation modelling should be used.

This activity provides insight into resource utilization and is used by both CSI and Problem Management (and later back to CSI) to identify opportunities for improvements. Trend analysis is rooted in the data analysis activity of the measuring process.

It is important to recognize that trend analysis is also an activity of proactive Problem Management. However, the focus is different. Whereas Problem Management focuses on trends in errors and faults (i.e. the past), Capacity Management is forward looking. It might be looking for innovation in storage management. It might be looking at expected growth versus real growth and recommend adjustments.

Modelling

Modelling types range from making estimates based on experience and current resource utilization information, to pilot studies, prototypes and full-scale benchmarks. The former are cheaper and more reasonable for day-to-day small decisions, while the latter are expensive but may be advisable when implementing a large new project.

Since it is impossible to have an exact duplicate of the infrastructure for testing purposes, CSI makes use of the information provided by the Capacity Management modelling activity to predict the behaviour of service improvements before the improvement is actually done. This may prevent costly implementations or problems down the road. Modelling results can be used by Change Management to assess the impact of a change on the infrastructure or may be used as part of release testing. Whether it is used by another process before the information makes its way to CSI, modelling is a valuable tool.

Modelling can also be used in conjunction with Demand Management to predict the possible effects of Demand Management efforts and initiatives. This allows IT to answer questions like 'what happens if we fail?' and 'What happens if we are successful?'.

Analytical Modelling

Analytical models are representations of computer system's behaviour using mathematical techniques such as multi-class network queuing theory. When the model is run, the queuing theory is used to calculate computer system response times. If the response times predicted by the model are sufficiently close to the response times recorded in real life, the model can be regarded as an accurate representation of the computer system. The technique of analytical modelling requires less time and effort than simulation modelling, but typically gives less accurate results. Also the model must be kept up-to-date.

Simulation modelling

Simulation involves the modelling of discrete events, such as transaction arrival rates, against a given hardware configuration. This type of modelling can be very accurate in sizing new applications or predicting the effects of changes on existing applications. It can also be very time-consuming and therefore costly.

When simulating transaction arrival rates, have a number of staff enter a series of transactions from prepared scripts, or use software to input the same scripted transactions with a random arrival rate. Either of these approaches takes time and effort to prepare and run. However it can be cost-justified for organizations with very large systems where the cost, and associated performance implications, assume great importance.

Baseline models

Improvements are gradual and incremental by nature. How can one claim to have improved if a baseline is not established before the improvement takes place?

The first stage in modelling is to create a baseline model that accurately reflects the performance that is being achieved. When this baseline model is created, predictive modelling can be done. If the baseline model is accurate, then the accuracy of the result of the predicted changes can be trusted.

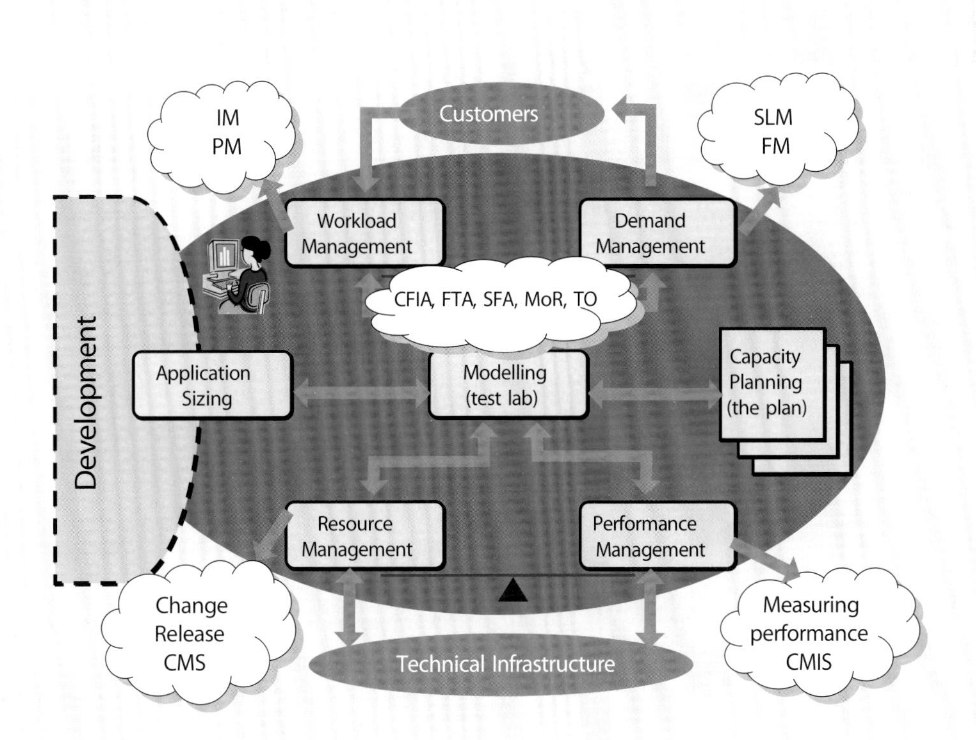

Figure 5.12 Capacity Management activities

Effective Service and Component Capacity Management together with modelling techniques enable Capacity Management to answer the 'What if?' questions: 'What if the throughput of service A doubles?' 'What if service B is moved from the current processor onto a new processor – how will the response times in the two services be altered?'

Figure 5.12 illustrates how CSI can make use of the intricate relationships between Capacity Management and the other service management processes.

At first glance the diagram seems very busy. However it illustrates the inputs and outputs from the other service management processes into and out of the various sub-activities of Capacity Management. CSI will then use this information to assist Capacity Management in planning for future capacity and performance as well as identifying improvement opportunities.

5.6.3 IT Service Continuity Management

This section provides practical usage and details about how each IT Service Continuity Management (ITSCM) method can be used in various activities of CSI.

Business Continuity Management, ITSCM and CSI

Any CSI initiative to improve services needs to also have integration with ITSCM as any changes to the service requirements, infrastructure etc. need to be taken into account for any changes that may be required for the Continuity Plan. That is why it is important for all service improvement plans to go through Change Management.

Business Continuity Management (BCM) is concerned with managing risks to ensure that an organization can continue operating to a predetermined minimum level. The BCM process involves reducing the risk to an acceptable level and planning for the recovery of business processes should a risk materialize and a disruption to the business occur.

ITSCM allows an IT organization to identify, assess and take responsibility for managing its risks, thus enabling it to better understand the environment in which it operates, decide which risks it wishes to counteract, and act positively to protect the interests of all stakeholders (including staff, customers, shareholders, third parties and creditors). CSI can complement this activity and help to deliver business benefit.

Risk Management

Every organization manages its risk, but not always in a way that is visible, repeatable and consistently applied to support decision making. The task of Risk Management is to ensure that the organization makes cost-effective use of a risk process that has a series of well-defined steps. The aim is to support better decision making through a good understanding of risks and their likely impact.

There are two distinct phases: risk analysis and risk management. Risk analysis is concerned with gathering information about exposure to risk so that the organization can make appropriate decisions and manage risk appropriately. Risk analysis involves the identification and assessment of the level (measure) of the risks calculated from the assessed values of assets and the assessed levels of threats to, and vulnerabilities of, those assets.

Risk Management involves having processes in place to monitor risks, access to reliable and up-to-date information about risks, the right balance of control in place to deal with those risks, and decision-making processes supported by a framework of risk analysis and evaluation. Risk Management also involves the identification, selection and adoption of countermeasures justified by the identified risks to assets in terms of their potential impact upon services if failure occurs, and the reduction of those risks to an acceptable level.

Risk Management covers a wide range of topics, including business continuity management, security, programme/project risk management and operational service management. These topics need to be placed in the context of an organizational framework for the management of risk. Some risk-related topics, such as security, are highly specialized and this guidance provides only an overview of such aspects.

A certain amount of risk taking is inevitable if an organization is to achieve its objectives. Effective management of risk helps to improve performance by contributing to:

- Increased certainty and fewer surprises
- Better service delivery
- More effective management of change
- More efficient use of resources
- Better management at all levels through improved decision making
- Reduced waste and fraud, and better value for money
- Innovation
- Management of contingent and maintenance activities.

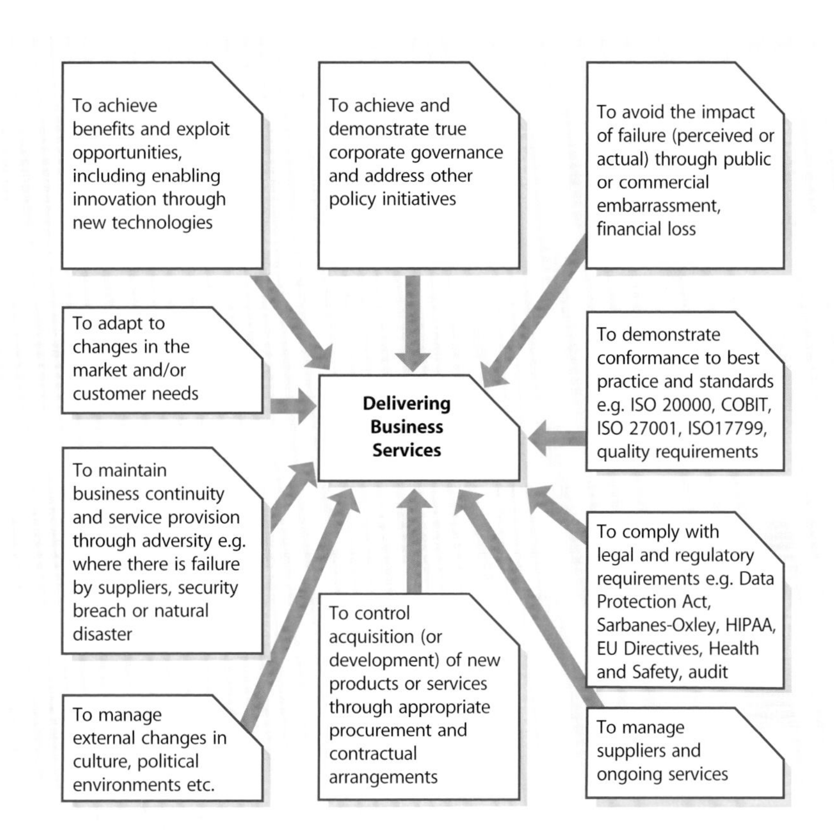

Figure 5.13 Reasons for a Risk Management process

Relating management of risk to safety, security and business continuity

Management of risk should be carried out in the wider context of safety concerns, security and business continuity:

- **Health and safety** policy and practice is concerned with ensuring that the workplace is a safe environment.
- **Security** is concerned with protecting the organization's assets, including information, buildings and so on.
- **Business continuity** is concerned with ensuring that the organization could continue to operate in the event of a disaster, such as loss of a service, flood or fire damage.

Business perspective on Risk Management

Risk Management from the business perspective, in the context of working with suppliers, centres on assessing vulnerabilities in supplier arrangements which pose threats to any aspect of the business including:

- Customer satisfaction
- Brand image
- Market share
- Share price
- Profitability
- Regulatory impacts or penalties (in some industries).

The nature of the relationship affects the degree of risk to the business.

Risks associated with an outsourced supplier are likely to be greater in number, and more complex to manage, than with an internal supply. It is rarely possible to outsource risk. Blaming a supplier does not impress customers or internal users affected by a security incident or a lengthy system failure. New risks arising from the relationship need to be identified and managed, with communication and escalation as appropriate.

A substantial risk assessment should have been undertaken pre-contract, but this needs to be maintained in the light of changing business needs, changes to the contract scope or changes in the operational environment.

Risk profiles and responsibilities

The organization and the supplier must consider the threats posed by the relationship to their own assets, and have their own risk profile. Each must identify their respective risk owners. In a well-functioning relationship it is possible for much or all of the assessment to be openly shared with the other party. By involving supplier experts

Table 5.8 Risk register

Ref.	Description	Weighted priority			Proposed actions or controls and costs	Owner
		Prob. HML	Impact HML	Prob. x Impact = Exposure		
R1		H	H	9		
R2		H	M	6		
R3		M	L	3		
R4		L	L	1		

in risk assessments, the organization may gain valuable insights into how best to mitigate risks, as well as improving the coverage of the assessment.

Risk assessments typically consider threats which may exploit vulnerabilities to impact the confidentiality, integrity or availability of one or more assets.

Scope of risk assessments:

- Identification of risks (threats and vulnerabilities)
- Target, i.e. the assets under threat
- Impact of risks, qualitative and quantitative
- Probability of occurrence
- Possible mitigating actions or controls
- Identification of stakeholders who are accountable for the risk, and responsible for selecting an appropriate action (including possibly accepting the risk with no control)
- Responsibility for implementing selected actions or controls
- Choice of actions or controls, based on evaluation of impact vs. cost of action or control.

For outsourced operations, particular care needs to be taken when considering the ownership of the assets at risk. These will be different for each party.

Risk Management processes need to be considered as cyclical, reviewing the suitability of previous actions, and reassessing risks in the light of changing circumstances. Risks are likely to be managed through a Risk Register such as the example provided in Table 5.8.

For further information on risk management, consult the ITIL Service Design and Service Transition publications.

While Risk Management is primarily conducted during design and transition stages of the service lifecycle, a good CSI programme will assess the results of Risk Management activities to identify service improvements through risk mitigation, elimination and management.

5.6.4 Problem Management

CSI and Problem Management are closely related as one of the goals of Problem Management is to identify and remove errors permanently that impact services from the infrastructure. This directly supports CSI activities of identifying and implementing service improvements.

Problem Management also supports CSI activities through trend analysis and the targeting of preventive action.

Problem Management activities are generally conducted within the scope of Service Operation and CSI must take an active role in the proactive aspects of Problem Management to identify and recommend changes that will result in service improvements.

Further information on the Problem Management process can be found in the ITIL Service Operation publication.

Post-Implementation Review

As a part of Change Management a Post-Implementation Review (PIR) is done on certain changes. CSI working with Change Management can require a PIR for all changes that CSI was a part of for improving a service (see Service Transition publication). CSI needs to participate in any PIR on changes that are implemented to improve a service. As part of a PIR it is important for CSI to identify if the change actually improved the service or if there are still some issues. If a change, once implemented, fails to improve the service as desired then CSI activities need to continue working with Service Design, Service Transition and Service Operation.

5.6.5 Change, Release and Deployment Management

All CSI activities will fall under the scope of Change, Release and Deployment Management. CSI's goal is to identify and implement improvement activities on IT services that support the business processes as well as identify and implement improvements to ITSM processes. The improvement activities support the lifecycle approach through Service Strategy, Service Design, Service Transition and Service Operation.

CSI is an ongoing process constantly monitoring and analysing and researching improvement opportunities whereas Release and Deployment Management depends on the Change Management process for its marching orders.

There are many activities of the Release and Deployment Management process that can be utilized by CSI. Once CSI has come up with a recommendation for improvement, a change request is submitted. The proposed change is then scheduled as part of a release.

5.6.6 Knowledge Management

One of the key domains in support of CSI is Knowledge Management. Capturing, organizing, assessing for quality and using knowledge is great input in CSI activities. An organization has to gather knowledge and analyse what the results are in order to look for trends in Service Level Achievements and/or results and output of service management processes. This input is used for determining what service improvement plans to be working on.

Knowledge Management in today's market is vastly different from what it was 10 years ago. Just in that short amount of time there has been:

- An increase in the **rate of change** in industry and market landscapes, as barriers to entry have decreased and new opportunities opened up
- An increase in **employee turnover**, as it has become more socially acceptable and often beneficial to change companies during a career to develop and share new experiences and perspectives
- An increase in **access to information** via the internet and a more open global economy
- Greater **market competition** forcing company employees to share knowledge between departments and subsidiaries.

Knowledge Management concepts

Effective Knowledge Management enables a company to optimize the benefits of these changes, while at the same time:

- Enhancing the **organization's effectiveness** through better decision making enabled by having the right information at the right time, and facilitating enterprise learning through the exchange and development of ideas and individuals
- Enhancing **customer-supplier relationships** through sharing information and services to expand capabilities through collaborative efforts
- Improving **business processes** through sharing lessons learned, results and best practices across the organization.

Knowledge Management is key to the overall viability of the enterprise, from capturing the competitive advantage in an industry to decreasing cycle time and cost of an IT implementation. The approach to cultivating knowledge depends heavily on the make-up of the existing knowledge base, and Knowledge Management norms for cultural interaction.

There are two main components to successful Knowledge Management:

- An **open culture** where knowledge, both best practices and lessons learned is shared across the organization and individuals are rewarded for it. Many cultures foster an environment where 'knowledge is power' (the more you know that others do not, the more valuable you are to the company). This type of knowledge hoarding is a dangerous behaviour for a company to reward since that knowledge may leave the company at any time. Another tenet of an open culture is a willingness to learn. This is an environment where growing an individual's knowledge base is rewarded and facilitated through open support and opportunities.
- The **infrastructure** – a culture may be open to knowledge sharing, but without the means or infrastructure to support it, even the best intentions can be impaired, and over time this serves as a demotivator, quelling the behaviour. This infrastructure can be defined in various ways, it may be a technical application or system which allows individuals to conduct online, self-paced training, or it may be a process such as post-mortems or knowledge sharing activities designed to bring people together to discuss best practices or lessons learned.

The identification of knowledge gaps and resulting sharing and development of that knowledge must be built into CSI throughout the IT lifecycle. This also raises the issues of dependencies and priorities. The IT lifecycle itself drives a natural priority of knowledge development and sharing. But, regardless of the IT project's lifecycle stage, it is important to identify and develop the necessary knowledge base prior to the moment where the knowledge may be applied. This may seem obvious and yet the majority of organizations fail to recognize the need to train the individuals until the process is halted due to a skills shortage. Knowledge sharing is an activity that should be fostered prior to, during and after the application of knowledge to the task.

Knowledge Management could be seen at the opposite end of a spectrum from fully automated processes that have all the required knowledge built into the process itself. Service management processes fall somewhere between these two extremes, with the operational processes nearer to the automation of processes than the tactical or strategic processes. This should be taken into account when designing the ITSM processes. Knowledge Management may very well enable quick wins on the more Knowledge Management intensive processes. This is not to imply that there would be a difference of levels of knowledge required for the people participating to the processes – rather that, in order to further develop SLM and vendor-management processes, the tactical knowledge needs to be harvested. It is easier to automate the operational level processes than the tactical or strategic processes, which require a greater breadth and depth of knowledge.

Throughout a CSI initiative, a lot of experience and information is acquired. It is important that this knowledge be gathered, organized and accessible. To ensure the ongoing success of the programme, Knowledge Management techniques must be applied.

So, where does all this knowledge come from? From the Service Knowledge Management System (SKMS). The ITIL Service Transition publication explains the principles and structure of the SKMS.

5.7 SUMMARY

There are many methods and techniques used to support CSI activities. Each organization can choose what works best for them. However, you should never adopt only one as it takes a blend of different methods to have an effective CSI programme.

CSI relies on the activities of all other service management processes. Don't overlook the value Incident, Problem, Availability, Capacity Management can provide to CSI. Of course Service Level Management plays a key role and most organizations will be hard pressed to have an effective CSI programme without some form of SLM in place.

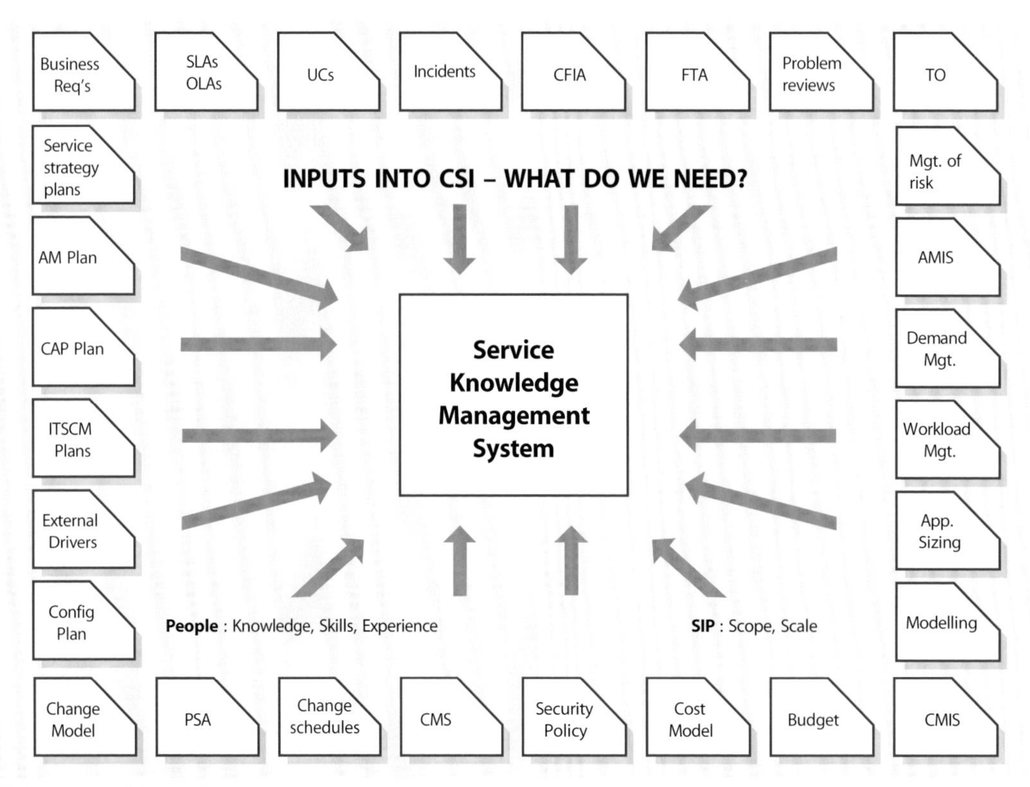

Figure 5.14 Sources of knowledge

6 Organizing for Continual Service Improvement

6 Organizing for Continual Service Improvement

6.1 ROLES AND RESPONSIBILITIES THAT SUPPORT CSI

CSI activities will be successful if specific roles and responsibilities are properly identified. As with many roles, these may or may not be a full-time position, however, it is important that roles are identified at the outset of any CSI initiative. If things change along the way the roles can be redefined and responsibilities reallocated.

6.1.1 CSI activities and skills required

Figure 6.1 describes the nature of many of these activities and the skills required to perform them.

The following section expands upon Figure 6.1 by detailing each of the seven steps in the improvement process and its related activities.

Define what you should measure

Roles: Individuals involved with decision making from IT and the business who understand the internal and external factors that influence the necessary elements that should be measured to support the business, governance and, possibly, regulatory legislation.

Example titles: Service Manager, Service Owner, Service Level Manager, CSI Manager, Process Owner, process managers, customers, business/IT analysts and senior IT managers.

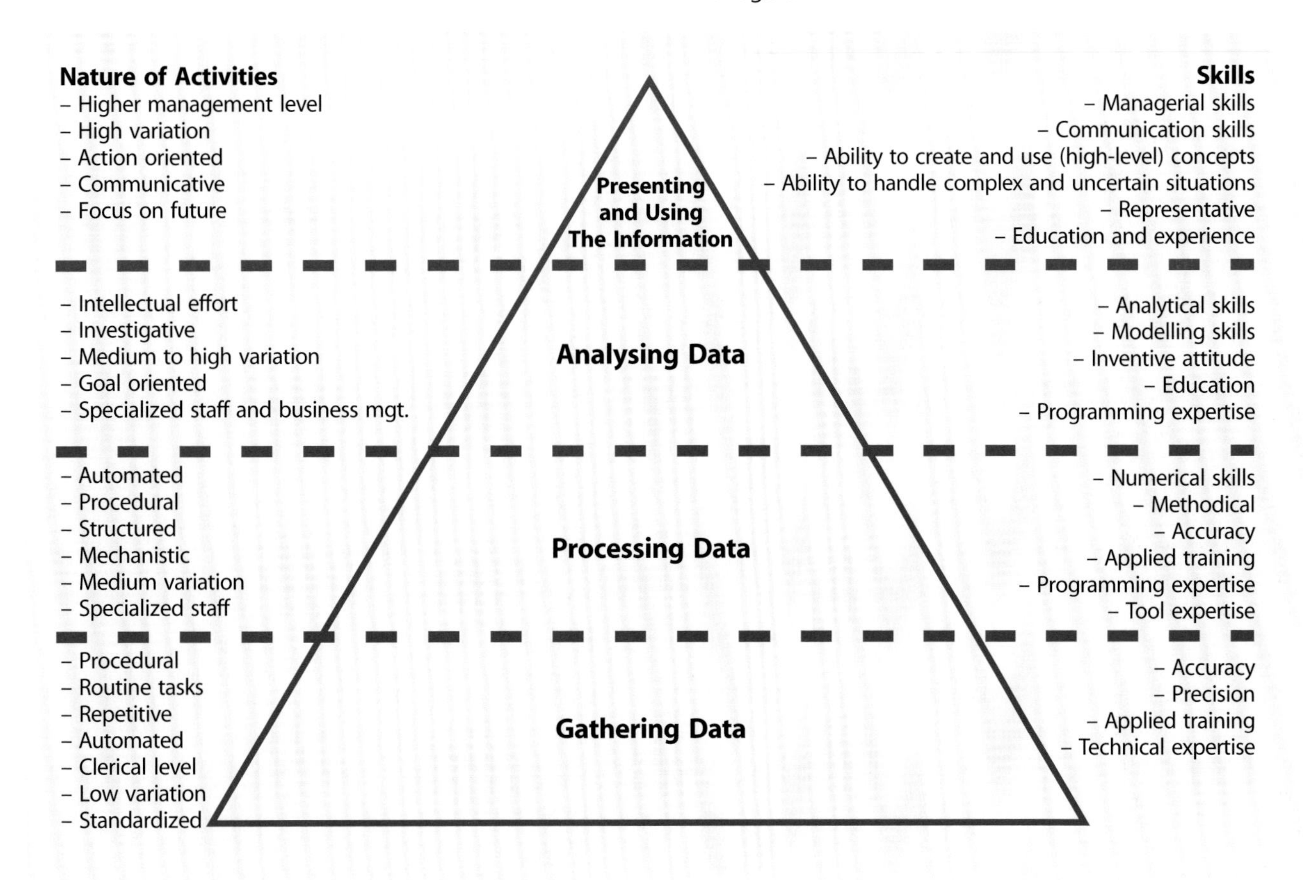

Figure 6.1 Activities and skill levels needed for CSI

Table 6.1 Roles involved in the 'define what you should measure' activity

Nature of activities	Skills
Higher management level	Managerial skills
High variation	Communication skills
Action-oriented	Ability to create, use (high-level) concepts
Communicative	Ability to handle complex/uncertain situations
Focused on future	Education and experience

Define what you can measure

Roles: Individuals involved with providing the service (internal and external providers) who understand the capabilities of the measuring processes, procedures, tools and staff.

Example titles: Service Manager, Service Owner, Process Owner, process managers, internal and external providers.

Gathering the data

Roles: Individuals involved in day-to-day process activities within the Service Transition and Service Operation lifecycle phases.

Example titles: Service desk staff, technical management staff, application management staff, IT security staff.

Table 6.2 Roles involved in the 'define what you can measure' activity

Nature of activities	Skills
Intellectual effort	Analytical skills
Investigative	Modelling
Medium to high variation	Inventive attitude
Goal-oriented	Education
Specialized staff and business management	Programming experience

Table 6.3 Roles involved in the 'gathering the data' activity

Nature of activities	Skills
Procedural	Accuracy
Routine tasks	Precision
Repetitive	Applied training
Automated	Technical experience
Clerical level	
Low variation	
Standardized	

Processing the data

Roles: Individuals involved in day-to-day process activities within the Service Transition and Service Operation lifecycle phases.

Example titles: Service desk staff, technical management staff, application management staff, IT security staff.

Analysing the data

Roles: Individuals involved with providing the service (internal and external providers) who understand the capabilities of the measuring processes, procedures, tools and staff.

Example titles: Service Owner, Process Owner, process managers, business/IT analysts, senior IT analysts, supervisors and team leaders.

Table 6.4 Roles involved in the 'processing the data' activity

Nature of activities	Skills
Automated	Numerical skills
Procedural	Methodical
Structures	Accurate
Mechanistic	Applied training
Medium variation	Programming experience
Specialized staff	Tool experience

Table 6.5 Roles involved in the 'analysing the data' activity

Nature of activities	Skills
Intellectual effort	Analytical skills
Investigative	Modelling
Medium to high variation	Inventive attitude
Goal-oriented	Education
Specialized staff and business management	Programming experience

Table 6.6 Roles involved in the 'presenting and using the information' activity

Nature of activities	Skills
Higher management level	Managerial skills
High variation	Communication skills
Action-oriented	Ability to create, use (high-level) concepts
Communicative	Ability to handle complex/uncertain situations
Focused on future	Education and experience

Table 6.7 Roles involved in the 'implementing corrective action' activity

Nature of activities	Skills
Intellectual effort	Analytical skills
Investigative	Modelling
Medium to high variation	Inventive attitude
Goal-oriented	Education
Specialized staff and business management	Programming experience

Presenting and using the information

Roles: Individuals involved with providing the service (internal and external providers) who understand the capabilities of the service and the underpinning processes and possess good communication skills. Key personnel involved with decision making from both IT and the business.

Example titles: CSI Manager, Service Owner, Service Manager, Service Level Manager, Process Owner, process managers, customers, business/IT analysts, senior IT managers, internal and external providers.

Implementing corrective action

Roles: Individuals involved with providing the service (internal and external providers).

Example titles: CSI Manager, Service Owner, Service Manager, Service Level Manager, Process Owner, process managers, customers, business/IT analysts, senior IT managers, internal and external providers.

6.1.2 Service Manager

Service Manager is an important role that manages the development, implementation, evaluation and on-going management of new and existing products and services. Responsibilities include business strategy development, competitive market assessment/benchmarking, financial and internal customer analysis, vendor management, inventory management, internal supplier management, cost management, delivery and full lifecycle management of products and/or services. Service Managers are responsible for managing very complex projects in order to achieve objectives and strategies and strive for global leadership in the marketplace. In order to attain this goal, they must evaluate new market opportunities, operating models, technologies and the emerging needs of customers in a company with international scope.

At this level, Service Managers are recognized as global product/service experts. They drive the decision-making processes, manage product/service objectives and strategies, hold internal and external suppliers accountable via formal agreements, and provide the integration of individual product plans and new technologies into a seamless customer-focused services. Service Managers may also be required to coach other managers (Service Owners, Process Owners) with differing levels of expertise for managing a business function or a particular product/service, within a specified product/service family.

Key responsibilities

- Provide leadership on the development of the Business Case and product line strategy and architecture, new service deployment and lifecycle management schedules.
- Perform service cost management activities in close partnership with other organizations such as operations, engineering and finance. Many of these organizations are held to strict internal supplier agreements.
- Manage various and sometimes conflicting objectives in order to achieve the organization's goals and financial commitments.
- Instil a market focus.
- Create an imaginative organization which encourages high performance and innovative contributions from its members within a rapidly changing environment.

Service Managers are able to effectively communicate product/service line strategies to corporate business leaders, and develop partnerships with other organizations within the company with both similar and dissimilar objectives and also with suppliers in order to satisfy internal and external customer needs. This is most often achieved via formalized agreement for both internal and external suppliers.

They must be able to formulate development programmes in response to new market opportunities, assess the impact of new technologies and guide creation of innovative solutions in order to bring best-in-breed solutions to our internal and external customers. They market the development and implementation of products/services that incorporate new technologies or system development. This requires extensive cross-organization communications. They also are able to identify, develop and implement financial improvement opportunities in order to meet the firm's commitments.

Key skills and competencies

- Previous product/market management experience
- Working knowledge of market analysis techniques and marketing programmes
- Advanced degree or equivalent experience
- Working knowledge of the domestic and international marketplace including industry applications, needs/trends, competitive vendor offerings, outsourcing, licensing, vendor management and customer relationships
- Product knowledge must include complex engineering, telecommunications and data protocols, as well as data processing applications and the ability to analyse the impact of new technologies
- Demonstrated sustained performance in previous assignments
- Sound business judgment
- Negotiating skills
- Human resource management skills
- Excellent communications skills
- Accept challenges and manage risk effectively and innovatively
- Produce solutions on time within cost objectives.

6.1.3 CSI Manager

This new role is essential for a successful improvement programme. The CSI owner is ultimately responsible for the success of all improvement activities. This single point of accountability coupled with competence and authority virtually guarantees a successful improvement programme.

Key responsibilities

- Responsible for development of the CSI domain

- Responsible for communicating the vision of CSI across the IT organization
- Ensures that CSI roles have been filled
- Works with the Service Owner to identify and prioritize improvement opportunities
- Works with the Service Level Manager to ensure that monitoring requirements are defined
- Works with the Service Level Manager to identity service improvement plans
- Ensures that monitoring tools are in place to gather data
- Ensures that baseline data is captured to measure improvement against it
- Defines and reports on CSI CSFs, KPIs and CSI activity metrics
- Identifies other frameworks, models and standards that will support CSI activities
- Ensures that Knowledge Management is an integral part of the day-to-day operations
- Ensures that CSI activities are coordinated throughout the service lifecycle
- Reviews analysed data
- Presents recommendations to senior management for improvement
- Helps prioritize improvement opportunities
- Lead, manage and deliver cross-functional and cross-divisional improvement projects
- Build effective relationships with the business and IT senior managers
- Identify and deliver process improvements in critical business areas across manufacturing and relevant divisions
- Set direction and provide framework through which improvement objectives can be delivered
- Coach, mentor and support fellow service improvement professionals
- Possess the ability to positively influence all levels of management to ensure that service improvement activities are receiving the necessary support and are resourced sufficiently to implement solutions.

6.1.4 Service Owner

The Service Owner is accountable for a specific service within an organization regardless of where the underpinning technology components, processes or professional capabilities reside. Service ownership is as critical to service management as establishing ownership for processes which cross multiple vertical silos or departments.

Key responsibilities

- Service Owner for a specified service
- Provides input in service attributes such as performance, availability etc.
- Represents the service across the organization
- Understands the service (components etc.)
- Point of escalation (notification) for major Incidents
- Represents the service in Change Advisory Board meetings
- Provides input in CSI
- Participates in internal service review meetings (within IT)
- Works with the CSI Manager to identify and prioritize service improvement
- Participates in external service review meetings (with the business)
- Responsible for ensuring that the service entry in the Service Catalogue is accurate and is maintained
- Participates in negotiating SLAs and OLAs.

To ensure that a service is managed with a business focus, the definition of a single point of accountability is absolutely essential to provide the level of attention and focus required for its delivery.

The Service Owner is responsible for continual improvement and the management of change affecting the services under their care. The Service Owner is a primary stakeholder in all of the underlying IT processes which enable or support the service they own. For example:

- **Incident Management** – Involved in or perhaps chairs the crisis management team for high-priority incidents impacting the service owned
- **Problem Management** – Plays a major role in establishing the root cause and proposed permanent fix for the service being evaluated
- **Release and Deployment Management** – Is a key stakeholder in determining whether a new release affecting a service in production is ready for promotion
- **Change Management** – Participates in Change Advisory Board decisions, approving changes to the services they own
- **Asset and Configuration Management** – Ensures that all groups which maintain the data and relationships for the service architecture they are responsible for have done so with the level of integrity required
- **Service Level Management** – Acts as the single point of contact for a specific service and ensures that the

Service Portfolio and Service Catalogue are accurate in relationship to their service

- **Availability and Capacity Management** – Reviews technical monitoring data from a domain perspective to ensure that the needs of the overall service are being met
- **IT Service Continuity Management** – Understands and is responsible for ensuring that all elements required to restore their service are known and in place in the event of a crisis
- **IT Financial Management** – Assists in defining and tracking the cost models in relationship to how their service is costed and recovered.

Table 6.8 Comparison of CSI Manager, Service Level Manager and Service Owner

P = Primary Responsibility *S = Secondary Responsibility*	CSI Manager	Service Level Manager	Service Owner
Focus			
IT services	S	P	P
IT systems	S		P
Processes	P	S	S
Customers	S	P	S
Technology	P	S	P
Responsibilities			
Responsible for development and maintenance of the catalogue of existing services		P	S
Responsible for developing and maintaining OLAs		P	S
Responsible for gathering Service Level Requirements from the customer	S	P	S
Responsible for negotiating and maintaining SLAs with the Customer	S	P	S
Responsible for understanding UCs as they relate to OLAs and SLAs	S	P	S
Responsible for ensuring appropriate service level monitoring is in place	P	P	S
Responsible for producing, reviewing and evaluating reports on service performance and achievements on a regular basis	P	P	P
Responsible for conducting meetings with the customer on a regular basis to discuss service level performance and improvement	S	P	S
Responsible for conducting yearly SLA review meetings with the customer	S	P	S
Responsible for ensuring customer satisfaction with the use of a customer satisfaction survey	S	P	S
Responsible for initiating appropriate actions to improve service levels (SIP)	P	P	P
Responsible for the negotiation and agreement of OLAs and SLAs	P	P	S
Responsible for ensuring the management of underpinning contracts as they relate to OLAs and SLAs	S	P	S
Responsible for working with the Service Level Manager to provide services to meet the customer's requirements	P		P
Responsible for appropriate monitoring of services or systems	P	P	S
Responsible for producing, reviewing and evaluating reports on service or system performance and achievement to the Service Level Manager and the Service Level Process Manager	P	P	P
Assisting in appropriate actions to improve service levels (SIP)	P	P	P

P = Primary Responsibility *S = Secondary Responsibility*	CSI Manager	Service Level Manager	Service Owner
Skills, knowledge and competencies			
Relationship management skills	P	P	P
A good understanding of IT services and qualifying factors in order to understand how customer requirements will affect delivery	P	P	P
An understanding of the customer's business and how IT contributes to the delivery of that product or service	P	P	P
Good communication skills	P	P	P
Good negotiation skills	P	P	P
Knowledge and experience of contract and/or supplier management roles	S	P	S
Good people management and meeting facilitating skills	P	P	P
Good understanding of statistical and analytical principles and processes	P	S	S
Good presentation skills	P	P	S
Good technical understanding and an ability to translate technical requirements and specifications into easily understood business concepts and vice versa	S	P	S
Innovative in respect of service quality and ways in which it can be improved within the bounds of the organization's limits (resource, budgetary, legal etc.)	P	P	P
Good organizational and planning skills	P	P	P
Good vendor management skills	S	P	S

6.1.5 Process Owner

The initial planning phase of any ITIL project must include establishing the role of Process Owner. This key role is accountable for the overall quality of the process and oversees the management of, and organizational compliance to, the process flows, procedures, data models, policies and technologies associated with the IT business process.

The Process Owner performs the essential role of process champion, design lead, advocate, coach and protector. Typically, a Process Owner should be a senior level manager with credibility, influence and authority across the various areas impacted by the activities of the process. The Process Owner is required to have the ability to influence and ensure compliance to the policies and procedures put in place across the cultural and departmental silos of the IT organization.

The Process Owner role is detailed in the ITIL Service Design publication.

6.1.6 Service Knowledge Management

Knowledge Management requires effective and authoritative ownership within an organization. The role of Knowledge Management process owner is crucial, in that it will design, deliver and maintain the Knowledge Management strategy, process and procedures.

The key activities of this role include:

- Undertaking the Knowledge Management role, ensuring compliance with the organization's policies and processes
- Architecting knowledge identification, capture and maintenance
- Identification, control and storage of any information deemed to be pertinent to the services provided, which is not available via any other means
- Maintenance of the controlled knowledge items to ensure currency
- Ensuring all knowledge items are made accessible to those who need it in an efficient and effective manner
- Publicity regarding the knowledge information maintained to ensure that information is not duplicated and is recognized as a central source of information etc.
- Acting as an advisor to business and IT personnel on Knowledge Management matters including policy decisions on storage, value, worth etc.

The Service Transition publication includes detailed information on Knowledge Management and the Service Knowledge Management System.

6.1.7 Reporting analyst

The reporting analyst is a key role for CSI and will often work in concert with the Service Level Management roles. The reporting analyst reviews and analyses data from components, systems and sub-systems in order to obtain a true end-to-end service achievement. The reporting analyst will also identify trends and establish if the trends are positive or negative trends. This information is then used in the presenting of the data.

Key responsibilities

- Participating in CSI meetings and Service Level Management meetings to ensure the validity of the reporting metrics, notification thresholds and overall solution
- Responsible for consolidating data from multiple sources
- Responsible for producing trends and provides feedback on the trends such as whether the trends are positive or negative, what their impact is likely to be, and if the trends are predictable for the future
- Responsible for producing reports on service or system performance based on the negotiated OLAs and SLAs and improvement initiatives.

Key skills and competencies

- Good understanding of statistical and analytical principles and processes
- Strong technical foundation in the reporting tool(s)
- Good communication skills
- Good technical understanding and an ability to translate technical requirements and specifications into easily understood reporting requirements.

6.2 THE AUTHORITY MATRIX

A key characteristic of a process is that all related activities need not necessarily be limited to one specific organizational unit. Configuration Management process activities, for example, can be conducted in departments such as computer operations, system programming, Application Management, Network Management, Systems Development and even non-IT departments like procurement, warehouse or accounting. Since services, processes and their component activities run through an entire organization, the individual activities should be mapped to the roles defined above. The roles and activities are coordinated by process managers. Once detailed procedures and work instructions have been developed, an organization must map the defined roles and the activities of the process to its existing staff. Clear definitions of accountability and responsibility are CSFs for any improvement activity. Without this, roles and responsibilities within the new process can be confusing, and individuals will revert to 'the way we've always done it' before the new procedures were put in place.

To assist with this task an authority matrix is often used within organizations indicating roles and responsibilities in relation to processes and activities. While there are many variations of the authority matrix, the RACI model, also supported by COBIT, is explained in Table 6.9.

Table 6.9 RACI authority matrix

R	responsibility – correct execution of process and activities
A	accountability – ownership of quality, and end result of process
C	consulted – involvement through input of knowledge and information
I	informed – receiving information about process execution and quality

Using the RACI model as an example there is only one person accountable for an activity, although several people may be responsible for executing parts of the activity. In this model, accountable means end-to-end accountability for the process. Accountability should remain with the same person for all activities of a process.

It is important to understand the distinction between a formal function within an organization and the process roles that the function is expected to carry out. A formal function may fulfil more than one specific Service Management role and carry out activities relating to more than one process. For example, a formal function 'network administrator' is 'Responsible' for carrying out 'Incident Management' as well as 'Capacity Management' activities. Although the network administrator may report to a functional line manager, he or she is also responsible for carrying out activities for the Service Desk and Capacity Management process owners.

Developing an authority matrix can be a tedious and time-consuming exercise but it's a crucially important one. The authority matrix clarifies to all involved which activities they are expected to fulfil, as well as identifying any gaps in service delivery and responsibilities. It is especially helpful in clarifying the staffing model necessary for improvement.

Experience teaches us that using an authority matrix helps with two major activities that are often overlooked or hard to identify. One is that all the 'Rs' on an RACI matrix typically represent potential OLA opportunities. The second is that identifying roles that must be kept informed helps to expose communication and workflow paths. This can be very helpful when defining the communication procedures in the CSI process.

Potential problems with the RACI model:

- Having more than one person accountable for a process means that in practice no one is accountable
- Delegation of responsibility or accountability without necessary authority
- Focus on matching processes and activities with departments
- Incorrect division/combination of functions; conflicting agendas or goals
- Combination of responsibility for closely-related processes, such as Incident Management, Problem Management, Configuration Management, Change Management and Release Management.

6.2.1 Process flows and RACI

In order to fully understand an authority matrix we must first begin with an example of a high-level process flow diagram. As an example see Figure 6.2 for a high-level process flow for Change Management.

Each of the major activities is then expanded into a detailed flow of specific procedures, tasks and work instructions. As an example, the fourth major activity (Authorize Change) is expanded in Figure 6.3.

Utilizing the detailed Change Management process flow shown in Figure 6.2, an example authority matrix is created based on the RACI model to illustrate the linkage between many of the roles we have discussed, the detailed procedures, and the level of responsibility assigned to each role in the successful execution of the procedure and, moving up, the process.

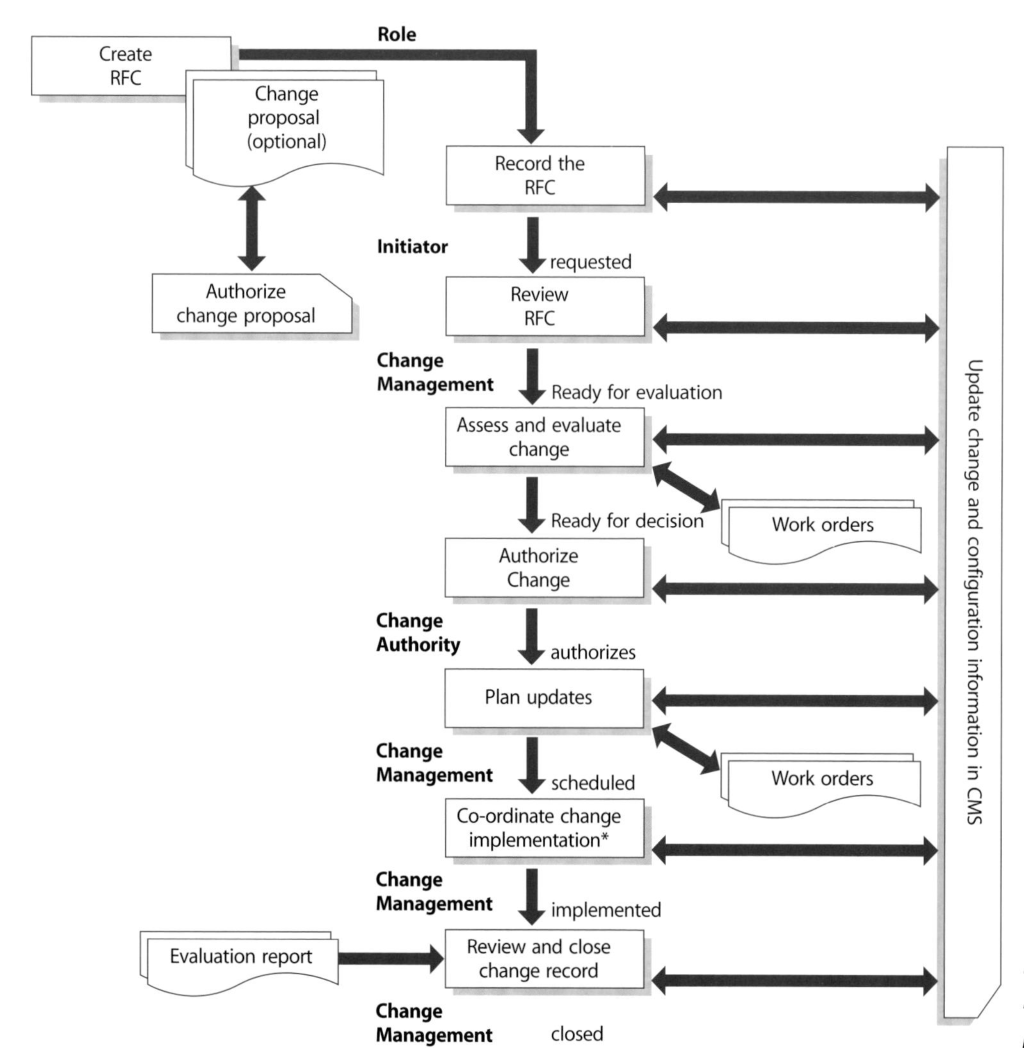

Figure 6.2 Change Management high-level process flow

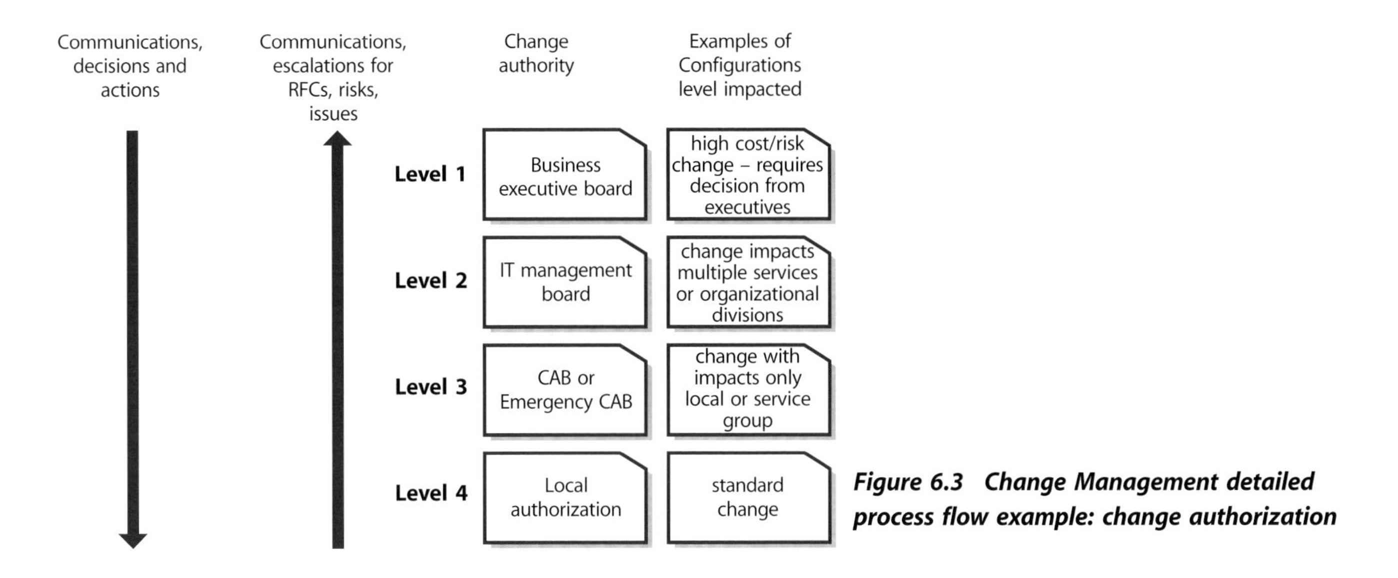

Figure 6.3 Change Management detailed process flow example: change authorization

Table 6.10 RACI matrix – sample Change Management authority matrix based on process flow

Flow #	Process Roles / Activity within process	Customer	Change Sponsor	Service Desk	Change Manager	Change Co-ordinator	CAB	CAB/EC	Change Builder	Change Tester	IT Manage -ment Board	Business Executive
1.0	Change Manager determines level of risk	C	C	C	R/A	C						
1.1	Level 4 – Standard change Local authorization		C		R/A	I						
1.2	Level 3 – affects only local or service groups RFC to CAB for assessment		C		R/A		C/I					
1.3	Level 2 – affects multiple services or organizational divisions RFC to IT Management Board for assessment		C		R/A		C				C/I	
1.4	Level 1 – high-cost/high-risk change RFC to Business Executive Board for assessment		C		R/A							C/I

	Process Roles	Customer	Change Sponsor	Service Desk	Change Manager	Change Co-ordinator	CAB	CAB/EC	Change Builder	Change Tester	IT Manage-ment Board	Business Executive
Flow #	Activity within process											
2.0	Endorsed? Yes – go to 2.1 No – go to 3.1				R/I		I					
2.1	CAB members estimate impact and resources, confirm priority, schedule changes				A		R		C			
3.0	Authorized? Not authorized – go to 3.1 Authorized – go to 3.2	I	I	I	A	I	R					
3.1	RFC rejected and closed (Initiator informed with a brief explanation of why it was rejected)	I	I		A	R	I	I				
3.2	Change builder builds change, devises back-out and testing plans	I	I		I	C			A/R	I		

Legend

R = Responsible	Responsible for executing the task
A = Accountable	Accountable for the final result
C = Consulted	Consulted about the task to provide additional information
I = Informed	Needs to be kept up-to-date on activities/tasks

6.3 SUMMARY

A number of new roles have been discussed in this chapter. These new roles are the embodiment of the concepts of a service-oriented organization. To run a traditional IT organization focusing on technical excellence, these roles will seem extraneous. To run a forward-thinking, service-oriented IT partner to the business, these roles are crucial. Improvement will not happen by itself. It requires a structured programme and mature processes. The roles shown below are responsible for that programme.

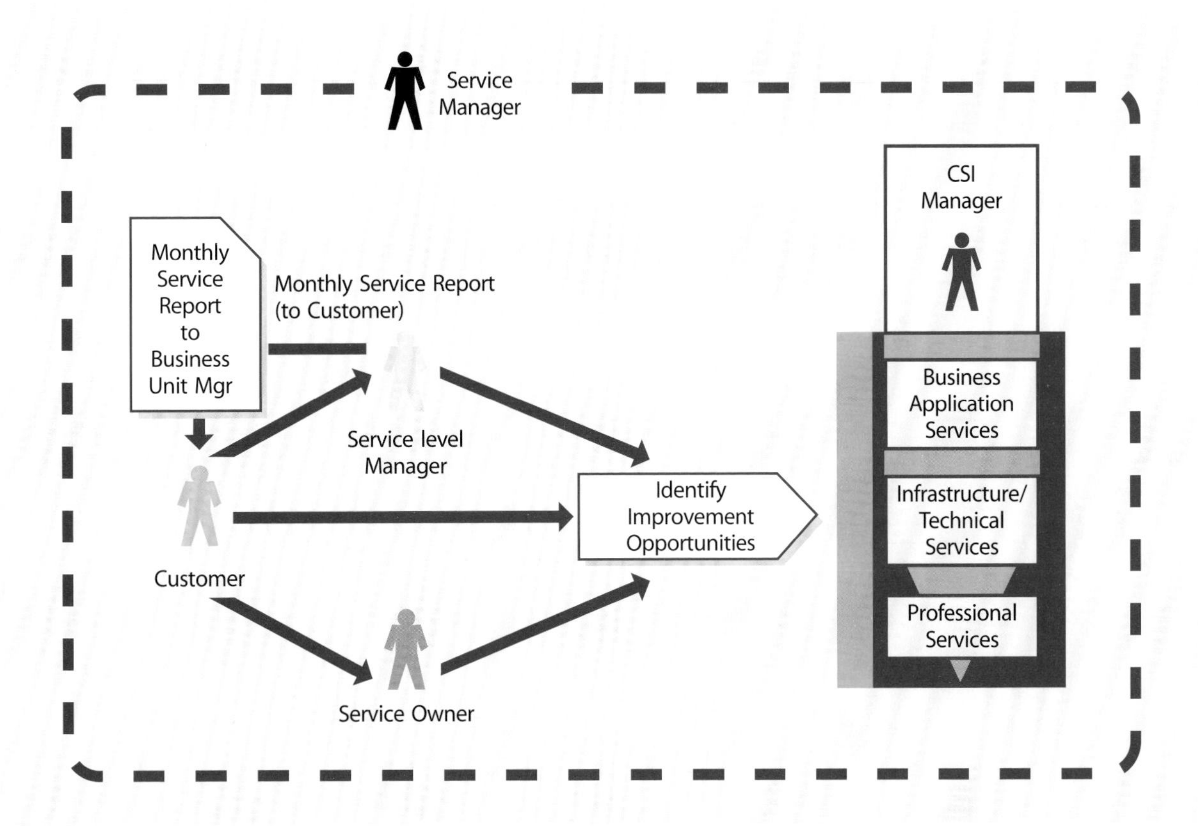

Figure 6.4 Service management roles and customer engagement

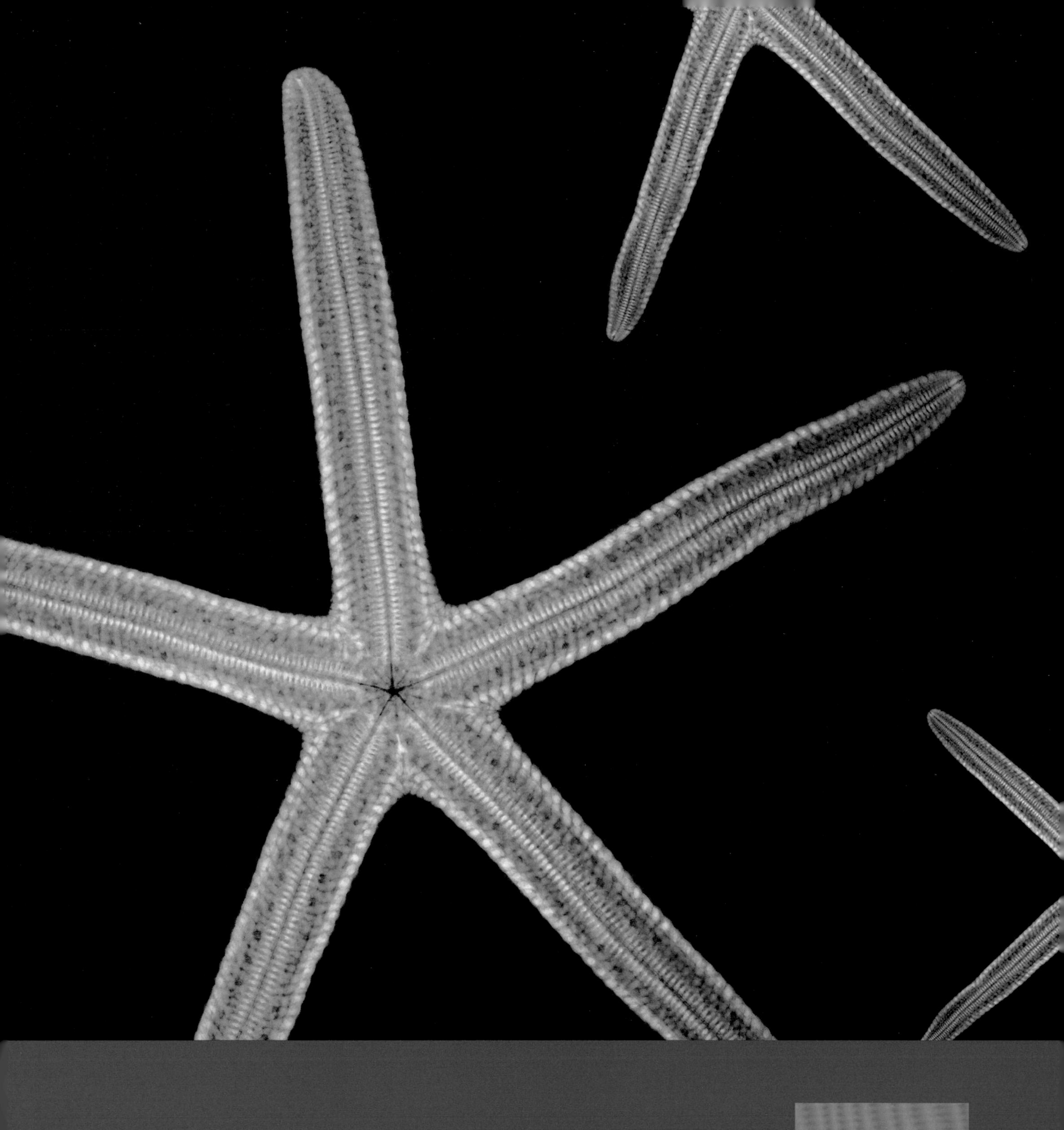

7 Technology considerations

7 Technology considerations

CSI activities will require software tools to support the monitoring and reporting on IT services as well as to underpin the ITSM processes. These tools will be used for data gathering, monitoring, analysis, reporting for services and will also assist in determining the efficiency and effectiveness of IT service management processes. The longer-term benefits to be gained are cost savings and increased productivity, which in turn can lead to an increase in the quality of the IT service provision.

From a service perspective the use of tools enables an organization to gain the ability to understand the health of its services from an end-to-end perspective. Even if an organization is not able to monitor end-to-end services it should be able to monitor, identify trends and perform analyses on the key components that make up an IT service.

From a process perspective the use of tools enables centralization of key processes and automation and integration of core service management processes. The raw data collected in the databases can be analysed resulting in the identification of trends. Preventive measures can then be implemented thereby increasing the stability, reliability and availability of the IT infrastructure.

The ITSM software tools of today have expanded their scope from mere 'point' solutions focusing on the Service Desk or Change Management to complete, fully integrated solution suites. Current tools represent a paradigm shift into the new era of ERP (enterprise resource planning) systems for IT. For decades, IT has provided systems to run the business; now there are systems to run IT.

7.1 TOOLS TO SUPPORT CSI ACTIVITIES

As part of the assessment of 'Where do we want to be?' the requirements for enhancing tools need to be addressed and documented. These requirements vary depending on both the process and technology maturity. Technology specifically means systems and service management toolsets used for both monitoring and controlling the systems and infrastructure components and for managing process-based workflows, such as Incident Management.

Without question, service management tools are indispensable. However, good people, good process descriptions, and good procedures and working instructions are the basis for successful service management. The need and the sophistication of the tools required depend on the business need for IT services and, to some extent, the size of the organization.

In a very small organization a simple in-house developed database system may be sufficient for logging and controlling incidents. However, in large organizations, very sophisticated distributed and integrated service management tools may be required, linking all the processes with systems management toolsets. While tools can be important assets, in today's IT-dependent organizations, they are a means, not an end in themselves. When implementing service management processes, look at the way current processes work. Each organization's unique need for management information should always be its starting point. This will help define the specifications for the tools best suited to that organization.

There are many tools that support the core ITSM processes and others that support IT governance as a whole which will require integration with the ITSM tools. Information from both of these toolsets typically needs to be combined, collated and analysed collectively to provide the overall business intelligence required to effectively improve on the overall IT service provision.

These tools can be defined into broad categories that support and annotate different aspects of the systems and service management domains:

7.1.1 IT service management suites

The success of ITIL within the industry has encouraged software vendors to provide tools and suites of tools that are very compatible with the ITIL process framework providing significant levels of integration between the processes and their associated record types. This functionality creates a rich source of data and creates many of the inputs to CSI including:

- **Incidents** that capture the service or the Configuration Item (CI) affected are a prime input to CSI enabling an understanding of the issues that are affecting the overall service provision and related support activities. Incident matching functionality allows the Service Desk to quickly relate like issues and create master records that highlight common situations that are affecting the users with associated resolution data to enhance problem identification and reduce the mean time to restore service (MTRS).

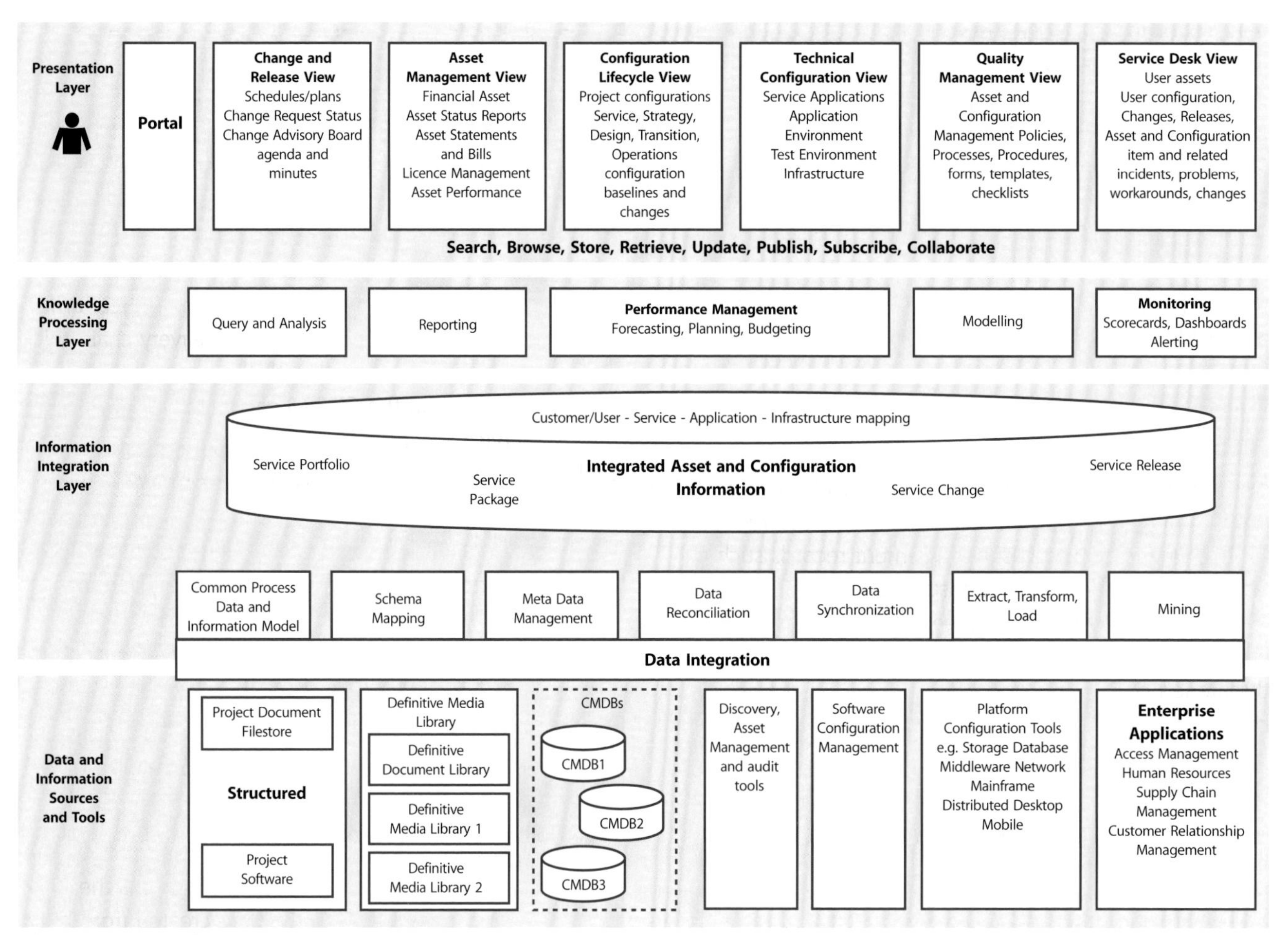

Figure 7.1 Configuration Management System

- **Problems** are defined with integrated links to the associated incidents that confirmed their existence. Using the configuration data from the CMS to understand the relationships, Problem Management now has a source of related data to enable the Root Cause Analysis process including change and Release history of the affected CI or service.
- **Changes** are often the first area of investigation following a service failure, again using the integration capabilities of the ITSM tool suite; it can be easier to trace the changes that have been made to a service or a CI. The Change Schedule and projected service availability can be automated using calendaring capabilities to ensure visibility of changes and calculated impacts to the Service Level Agreements. Recent improvements in the ITSM tools now allow for automated risk assessment and prioritization of changes, highlighting potential conflicts and reducing the administrative overhead for the Change Advisory Board.

Tool functionality in support of Configuration Management and the CMS has never been more advanced with extensive discovery and service dependency mapping capabilities. The CMS is the foundation for the integration of all ITSM tool functionality and is a critical data source for the CSI mission. While the service provider must still define the overall Configuration Management process and create the data model associated with their specific environment, the tools to establish and manage the CMS and the overall service delivery architecture have become very powerful. Key functionality includes: discovery and reconciliation capabilities to capture CI's within the environment, visualization of the hierarchy and CI relationships for ease of understanding and support, audit tools to streamline the verification activities and the ability to federate data sources where appropriate.

The ability to coordinate Releases and manage the contents of these Releases are also more mature with native support for the definitive libraries and key integration points to the CMS and to specialized version control software packages. Functionality typically includes support for Release records that consolidate and contain

Release contents enabling the attachment of related objects and documents pertaining to the Release. Integration is normally provided to enable hyperlinking to the associated Change records that are part of a Release and the related Incident, Problem or Service Request records that were the catalyst for the original RFC. Release versions are also supported with predefined naming and numbering standards that enhance the understanding of the overall process. Overall reporting of Release status and associated performance metrics are required as inputs to CSI ensuring that the deployment of new services are of the highest possible quality.

Service Level Management functionality is also well supported within the ITSM tool suites of today enabling the linkage of incidents, problems, changes and releases to associated Service Level Management records such as SLAs, OLAs and UCs. Most tool suites support automated SLAM charts (Service Level Agreement Monitoring) highlighting which agreements are within tolerance, are threatened or have been broken. This automation is driven by the ability to define key SLA criteria and use related operational support records to trigger thresholds (e.g. a priority one incident is about to break the one-hour resolution target time or a change has caused a longer downtime than was agreed). CMS functionality can also support the concept of prioritized CIs that underpin specific service levels highlighting a greater impact if a failed component supports a critical service or business process. Some suites also provide the ability to trigger Availability impacts to SLAs by capturing incident data related to service outages. Many of the suites also facilitate the definition of the service portfolio and the Service Catalogue while managing the workflow associated with the fulfilment of Service Requests. Some standalone point solutions support specialized functionality in this area (see below).

Reporting is one of the key benefits of an integrated ITSM suite with the ability to provide management information in a common format utilizing the combined data from all operational areas of the service lifecycle. This is of significant benefit enabling analysis of the relationships between service management events (e.g. incidents that result in problems, changes that cause incidents, releases that encapsulate certain changes) and all of the associated performance metric data that will feed the overall CSI initiatives.

7.1.2 Systems and network management

These tools are typically specific to the technology platforms that are under management and are used to administer the various domains but can provide a wide variety of data in support of the service management mission. These tools generate error messages for event management and correlation that ultimately feed the Incident Management and Availability Management processes. Utilization data from these platforms is the prime source for Capacity and Performance Management and the most accurate method for establishing true availability of components that will support improvements in the area of MTRS and MTBF. As the dynamic, real-time view of the current state of the service delivery chain this information can be integrated with the known service dependencies within the CMS to give enhanced visibility into the service provision to the end-user. Many of these tools also support technology proprietary methods for software deployment within their domains (e.g. Release of patches, pushing of firmware upgrades to remote components on the network) and, as such, can provide metric data in support of CSI for Change and Release Management and dynamic updates to the CMS.

7.1.3 Event management

Events are status messages that are generated from systems, network and application management platforms. These events are created when one of the above tools senses a threshold has been met or an error condition is discovered. The major issue with this capability is the significant volume of messages that are created from both the actual event and the up- and down-stream impact which can make it difficult to determine the real issue.

Specialized event management software can perform event correlation, impact analysis and root cause analysis to separate out these false-positive messages. Events are captured and assessed by rules-based, model-based and policy-based correlation technologies that can interpret a series of events and derive, isolate and report on the true cause and impact. These technologies support the CSI mission by providing information regarding availability impacts and performance thresholds that have been exceeded related to capacity or utilization. Well-correlated event management data provides a cost-effective method to improve the reliability, efficiency and effectiveness of the cross-domain IT infrastructure that supports the provision of business services.

7.1.4 Automated incident/problem resolution

There are many products in the marketplace that support the automation of the traditional manual, labour-intensive and error-prone process of incident and problem discovery and resolution. Utilizing data from proactive detection monitors, any component or service outage generates an alert that automatically triggers diagnosis and repair procedures. These procedures then identify the root cause and resolve the issue using pre-programmed and scripted self-healing techniques reducing the MTRS of many common causes of incidents and in some cases preventing service outages completely. These tools also document audit-related information within the incident or problem record for future analysis and identification of other potential proactive CSI opportunities.

7.1.5 Knowledge Management

There are specialist tools available that support and streamline the discipline of Knowledge Management. Providing efficient and accurate access to previous cases with proven resolution data, these tools address the symptoms associated with the current incident or problem. Capturing data throughout the Incident and Problem Management lifecycles enables a Knowledge Management engine to assign related keywords and service relationships that will enhance the search process providing a high percentage of hits, thus speeding up the overall resolution process. KM tools also generate significant metrics aimed at measuring the improvement process itself. Key CSI data adds transparency to incident recurrence and frequency, utilization rates, the effectiveness of the stored resolutions and the impact KM has on the efficacy of the overall support function.

7.1.6 Service Request and fulfilment (Service Catalogue and workflow)

As mentioned in the ITSM section, there are specialized tools that deal with Service Catalogue definition, request management and the workflow associated with the fulfilment of these requests. Some of these tools provide the workflow engines and some rely heavily on the capabilities of the companion ITSM suite. These tools provide the technology required to define the services within a catalogue structure in conjunction with the business customers and create a service portal (normally web-based) that allows users to request services. The request is then managed through the workflow engine assigning resources according to a defined process of tasks and related activities for each request type. These tools typically also capture related cost information to be fed to the financial systems for later charging activities. This functionality does much to support IT's integration with the business, defining services that underpin their mission and streamlining the delivery of commodity services that so often become a source of customer frustration. As in other tools, the true CSI benefit is the data that is collected and reported relate to the quality of the services delivered, any bottlenecks encountered, and the ability to track the achievement of related service levels

7.1.7 Performance management

Performance management tools allow for the collection of availability, capacity and performance data from a multitude of domains and platforms within the IT infrastructure environment. This data is used to populate the Availability and Capacity Management Information Systems (AMIS and CMIS) giving IT organizations a historical, current and future view of performance, resource and service usage for offline analysis and modelling activities. Capabilities of these tools generally include:

- Analysis of responsiveness, transaction and traffic throughput and utilization levels supporting the balancing of resources to optimize performance of the IT services
- Workload assessment with predictive trend analysis of future growth and required capacity for each of the IT services being provided
- The construction of performance, resource and data usage profiles enabling the comparison of actual utilization with planned models
- Predictive performance technology enabling the evaluation of tuning alternatives for systems, networks, databases and applications that support modelling of the expected outcomes
- Generation of the data required to report on SLAs and provide input to service Improvement plans.

There are many tools in the marketplace that support the overall CSI initiative across many aspects of performance management including business, service and resource capacity planning, feasibility analysis, modelling, solution development, implementation, management and on-going monitoring of the IT service provision.

7.1.8 Application and service performance monitoring

There has always been a challenge related to understanding the true user experience related to service provision. Recognizing this need, many vendors provide tools that monitor the end-to-end delivery of services, using either active or passive technologies, to fully instrument and probe the many components of the service delivery chain. The software provides key metrics such as availability, transaction throughput, transaction response time, network latency, server efficiency, database I/O and SQL effectiveness. This data provides system, application, Availability and Capacity Managers and Service

Owners the ability to analyse the delivery of services at all key points in the chain and look for potential improvements to streamline the overall delivery mechanisms. Usage trend data is vital for the Availability and Capacity Management processes providing the information required to assess current performance and plan for future growth. This capability also enhances Service Level Management's ability to accurately track conformance to SLAs and identify candidates for the service improvement process.

7.1.9 Statistical analysis tools

Most of the tools that are available to support the service management and systems management environments provide reporting capabilities but this is typically not enough to support robust Availability and Capacity Management capabilities. Raw data from many of the above tools needs to be captured into a single repository for collective analysis. This is the data that will provide input to the Availability and Capacity processes and support the analysis of MTRS, MTBFs, SFA, Demand Management, workload analysis, service modelling, application sizing and their related opportunities for improvement. This type of software provides the functionality to logically group data, model current services and enable predictive models to support future service growth utilizing a wide array of analysis techniques.

7.1.10 Software version control/software Configuration Management

These tools support the control of all mainframe, open systems, network and applications software providing a Definitive Media Library type repository for the development environment. Version information must seamlessly integrate with the CMS and Release Management.

7.1.11 Software test management

These tools support the testing activities of Release Management and deployment activities providing development, regression testing, user acceptance testing and pre-production QA testing environments. Typically, there is additional functionality to support testing of specific functional requirements that were captured early in the development lifecycle. These tools should integrate with Incident Management to capture testing-related incidents that may affect the production version of the same software.

7.1.12 Security Management

These tools support and protect the integrity of the network, systems and applications, guarding against intrusion and inappropriate access and usage. As in the systems and network management area, all security-related hardware and software solutions should generate alerts that will trigger the auto-generation of incidents for management through the normal processes.

7.1.13 Project and portfolio management

These tools support the registration, decision support, costing, resource management, portfolio visibility and project management of new business functionality and the services and systems that underpin them. These tools are typically used to manage the business-related aspects of IT. Integration points generally include: task assignments for development activities, change and release build information based on the agreed portfolio, capture of resource data from ITSM, TCO of portfolio and resource utilization data to Financial Management, request management linkage to ITSM etc. This tool is typically utilized to underpin the Management Board approval process related to strategic or major change projects.

7.1.14 Financial Management

Financial Management is a critical component of the IT services mission to ensure that there are enough financial resources to maintain and develop the IT infrastructure and professional capabilities in support of the current and future needs of the business. A balanced budget in IT through the recovery of IT costs, with a solid understanding of the fiscal aspects of their operations, will enable IT executives to justify their expenses in terms of the business services being supported.

In an increasing number of IT organizations this requires keeping track of resource and service utilization for the purpose of billing and chargeback of the shared IT resources. The costing and resource consumption measurement becomes critical to effectively and accurately charge business customers in an equitable, visible and auditable way.

Financial Management tools collect raw metering data from a variety of sources including operating systems, databases, middleware and applications associating this usage to users of services from specific departments. Data collectors gather critical usage metrics for each of the technologies being measured, links in the costing information from accounting software and then reports, analyses and allocates costs, enabling customers to evaluate the information in many dimensions.

Most tools will interface with the CMS to manage costs for each CI and resource to generate data related to billing, reporting, chargeback and cost analysis. These tools will typically federate with the organization's Financial Management applications and ERP system to acquire and share aggregate costs. Interfaces are also normally supported with project and portfolio management tools to facilitate the overall portfolio of investments.

Effective cost management is a basic requirement for the IT organizations of today, Financial Management tools will be required to ensure that customers can not only understand the IT costs of their business operations, but also more accurately budget and enable IT to evaluate the overall effectiveness of the services provision. Successful implementation and usage of these tools will support the continual improvement of cost management and drive ever-increasing IT value to the business.

7.1.15 Business intelligence/reporting

In addition to the statistical analysis environment that requires a toolset to support technical data, there is also a need for a common repository of all service information and business-related data. Often these tools are provided by the same vendors who support the statistical analysis software but the focus in this instance is on providing business-related data from all of the above toolsets representing a guide to direct the activities of IT as a whole in support of the business customer.

As the technology used to deliver IT services becomes increasingly complex, the distribution of services expands and the amount of centralized control we can apply is diminished, there will be a growing reliance on tools and software functionality to administer, manage, improve and ensure overall governance of IT service provision. As stated earlier, best-practice process should determine what support functionality is required but we can be assured that the software industry will continue to develop a wide and varied set of tools that can reduce the administrative overhead of managing our processes and improve the overall quality of IT service provision.

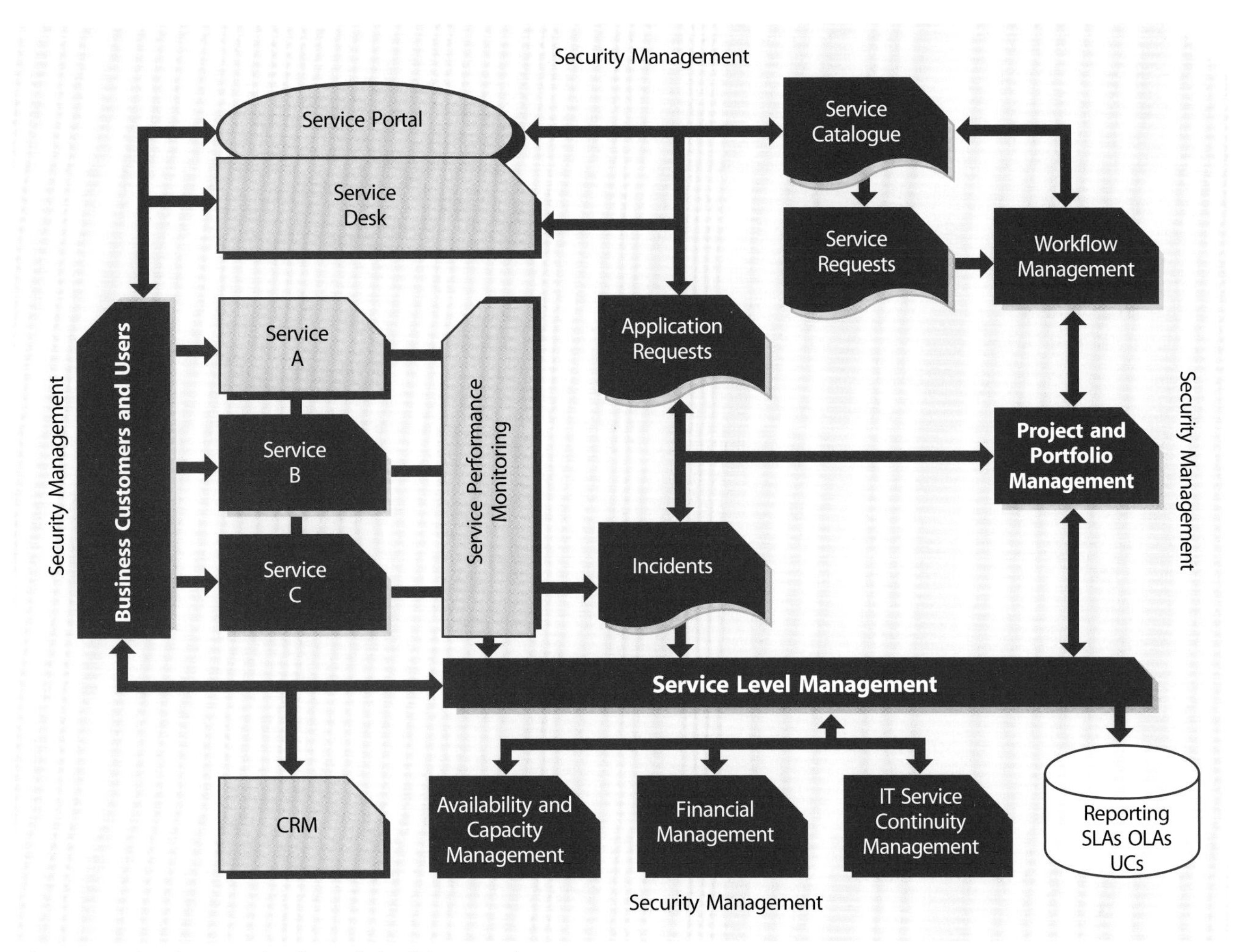

Figure 7.2 Service-centric view of the IT enterprise

7.2 SUMMARY

For effective CSI it is important for organizations to view their tool requirements from an enterprise perspective as shown below. Tools for CSI should support the key operational activities of the 7-Step Improvement Process: data gathering, data processing, data analysis and data presentation. Tools must provide for monitoring of each level of the service hierarchy: services, systems and components, as well as support the reporting activities for SLAs, OLAs and UCs.

8 Implementing Continual Service Improvement

8 Implementing Continual Service Improvement

This publication has discussed implementing CSI from two perspectives. First and foremost is the implementation of CSI activities around services. Second is the implementation of CSI around service management processes. However, if your organization does not have very mature service management processes then it is usually difficult to execute The 7-Step Improvement Process for services.

Immature processes usually have poor data quality if any at all. This is often due to no processes or very ad hoc processes. Other organizations have multiple processes working with multiple tools being used to support the processes. If any monitoring is going on it may be at a component or application level but not from and end-to-end service perspective. There is no central gathering point for data, no resources allocated to process and analyse the data, and reporting consists of too much data broken into too many segments for anyone to analyse. Some organizations don't have any evidence of reporting at all.

8.1 CRITICAL CONSIDERATIONS FOR IMPLEMENTING CSI

Before implementing CSI it is important to have identified and filled the critical roles that have been identified in Chapter 6. This would include a CSI Manager, Service Owner and reporting analyst. A Service Level Manager is really needed to be the liaison between the business and IT.

Monitoring and reporting on technology metrics, process metrics and service metrics need to be in place.

Internal service review meetings need to be scheduled in order to review from an internal IT perspective the results achieved each month. These internal review meetings should take place before any external review meeting with the business.

8.2 WHERE DO I START?

8.2.1 Where do I start – service approach

An organization can choose to implement CSI activities in many different ways. One way is to identify a certain service pain point such as a service that is not consistently achieving the desired results. Work with the Service Owner to validate the desired results and the trend results over the past few months. Review any monitoring that has been done. If there hasn't been any end-to-end monitoring in place but some component monitoring than review what has been monitored and see if there are any consistent issues that are leading to the lower-than-expected service results. Even if there hasn't been any component monitoring being conducted, review your Incident tickets and see if you can find some trends and consistent CIs that are failing more than others that impact the service. Also review the change records for the different CIs that together underpin the service.

Bottom line is that you have to start somewhere. If you don't feel you have adequate data from any monitor or other process than perhaps the first step is to identify what to monitor, define the monitoring requirements, put in place or begin using the technology required for monitoring.

Be sure to analyse the data to see if the trends make sense and to see if there are any consistent failures or deviation from expected results. Report findings and identify improvement opportunities

8.2.2 Where do I start – lifecycle approach

Another approach is to start looking at the handoff of output from the different lifecycle domains. Service Design needs to monitor and report on their activities and through trend evaluation and analysis, identify improvement opportunities to implement. This needs to be done by every part of the lifecycle especially Service Design, Service Transition and Service Operation. CSI is engaged in this activity. Until the service is implemented we may not know if the right strategy was identified, so we may not have input until later for Service Strategy improvement.

As Service Transition begins working with the product Service Design handed off, Service Transition may identify improvement opportunities for Service Design. CSI can be effective well before a service is implemented into the production environment.

8.2.3 Where do I start – functional group approach

Perhaps your organization is experiencing a lot of failures or issues with servers. If this is the case, one could argue a good case to focus CSI activities within the functional group responsible for the servers, as server failures have a direct impact on service availability.

This should be a short-term solution only as CSI activities should be reviewing services from an end-to-end perspective; however it is often easier to have a small group focused on CSI activities. Perhaps this could be a pilot of CSI activities before a full rollout across the organization.

8.3 GOVERNANCE

No matter if you are implementing CSI around service management or services it is critical that governance is addressed from a strategic view. Organizations are facing the need to expand their IT service management strategies from an operational level to tactical and strategic levels to address business process automation, market globalization and the increasing dependency on IT for the efficient and reliable management and delivery of core business services. To address this requirement formalized service management processes and specialized service and work management tools are being introduced to manage today's complex and distributed IT environments. Introducing service management processes into internal IT departments requires a transformation to the IT culture.

Most internal IT departments are system/technology-management-based organizations which are reactive in nature. Transforming to a service-management-based organization is more proactive in nature and is a step to aligning IT with business. It is also fundamental to achieving the goal of providing efficient and reliable management and delivery of core business services.

Implementing an ITSM process governance organization will support the development of and transformation to a process- and service-based organization and provide the organizational infrastructure to manage process improvement initiatives.

A comprehensive and integrated approach to the design, implementation and ongoing compliance to accepted ITSM standards includes:

- Organizational structures, roles and responsibilities
- IT processes, policies and controls.

8.3.1 ITSM programme initiative

Corporate initiative statement (The 'IT Service Management' Programme supports the IT Governance Institutes definitions of Enterprise Governance, IT Governance and COBIT)

8.3.2 Business drivers

The implementation of a standard ITSM process and governance is deemed as imperative to support current and future business plans:

- Support the organization's vision
- Provide standard IT processes and a stable and reliable IT environment to enable timely and efficient integration of new services and systems.
- Provide process policies, standards and controls to comply with internal audit and external regulatory and legislation requirements.

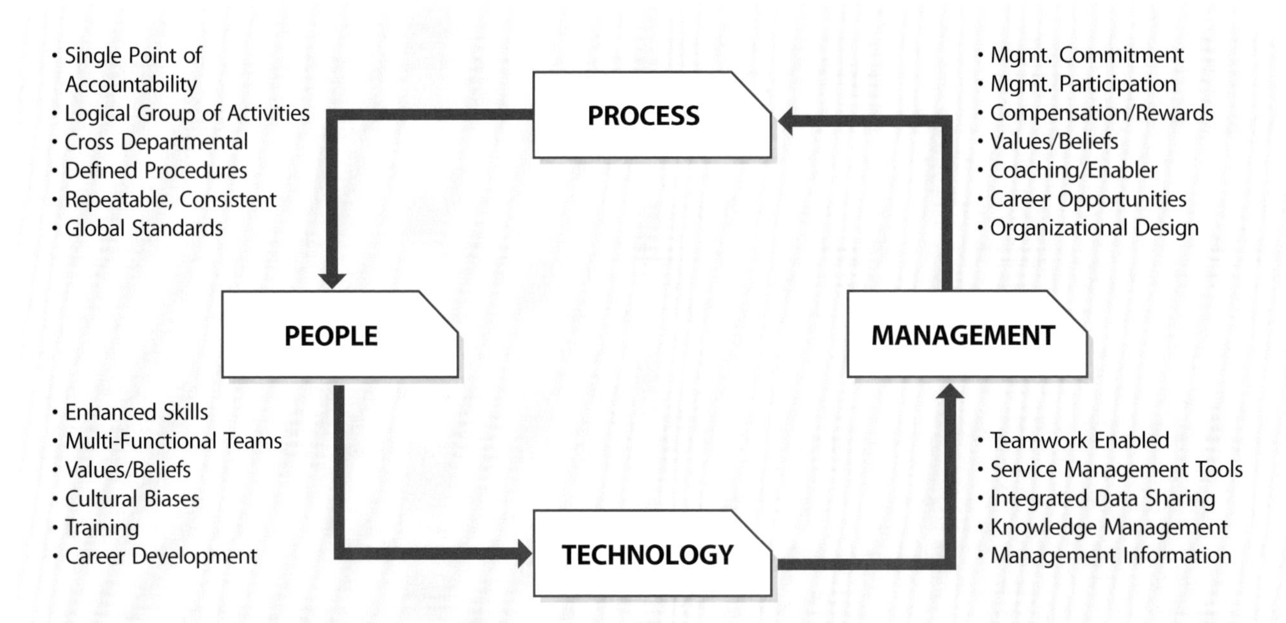

Figure 8.1 Process re-engineering changes everything

- Foster a climate of commitment to best practices.
- Provide a standard ITSM process across the IT organization to support the organizational transformation to an enterprise IT services model while maintaining operational stability and reliability to the business.

8.3.3 Process changes

Implementing CSI will have an impact on many parts of the IT organization. Processes, people, technology and management will undergo change. CSI needs to become a way of life within the organization. This may require new management structure, new technology, changes to processes to support CSI and people will need to be trained and understand the importance of CSI within the organization.

If you only focus on changing a process or technology CSI will not be effective. Figure 8.1 identifies some changes that may need to be addressed.

8.4 CSI AND ORGANIZATIONAL CHANGE

Project management structures and frameworks fail to take into account the softer aspects involved in organizational change such as resistance to change, gaining commitment, empowering, motivating, involving and communicating. Experience reveals that it is precisely these aspects that prevent many CSI programmes from

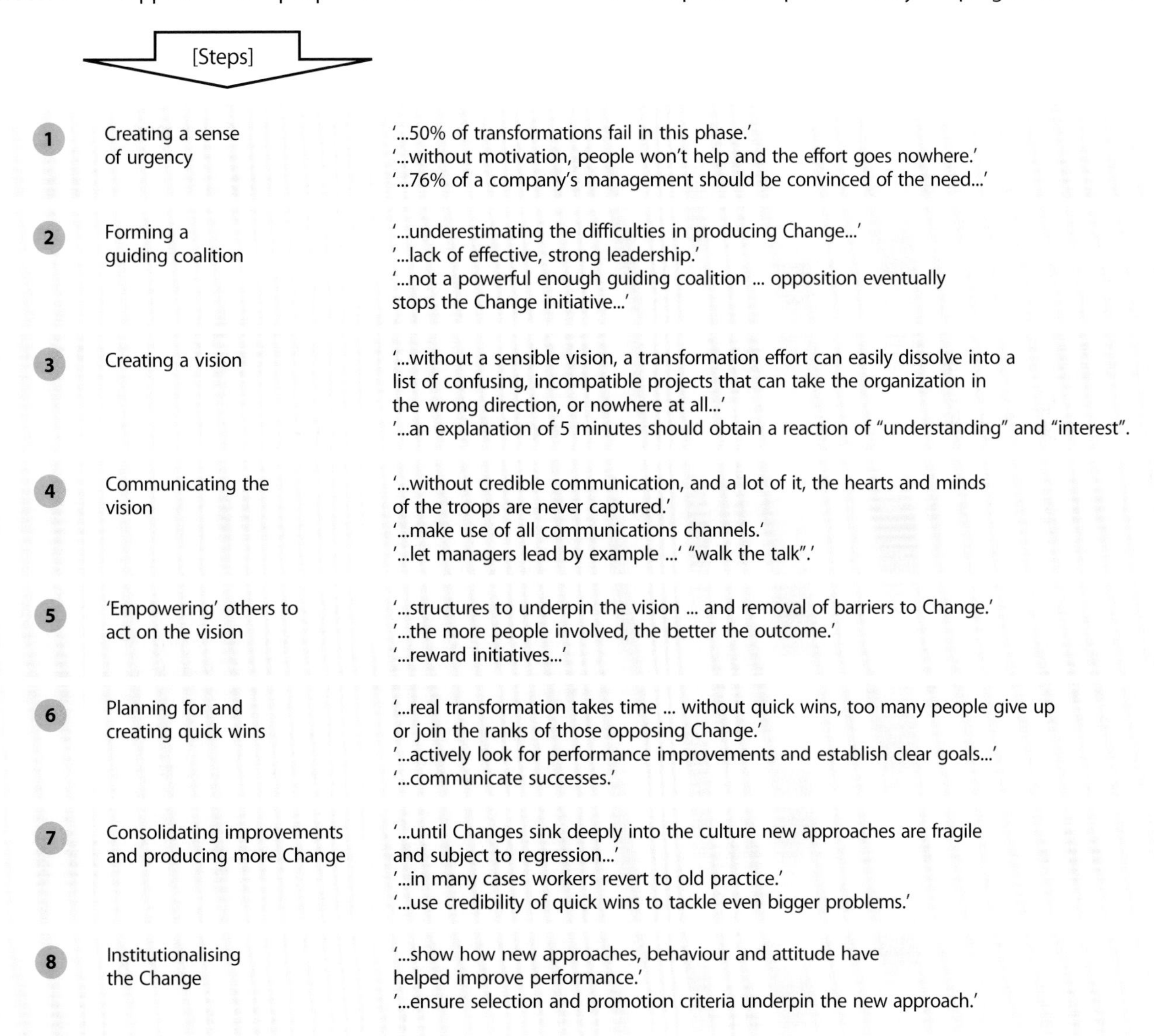

Figure 8.2 Eight main reasons why transformation efforts fail

(Source: Kotter)

realizing their intended aims. The success of a CSI programme is dependant on the buy-in of all stakeholders. Gaining their support from the outset, and keeping it, will ensure their participation in the development process and acceptance of the solution. The first five steps in Figure 8.2 identify the basic leadership actions required.

Those responsible for managing and steering the CSI programme should consciously address these softer issues. Using an approach such as John P. Kotter's *Eight Steps to Transforming your Organization*, coupled with formalized project management skills and practices, will significantly increase the chance of success.

Kotter, Professor of Leadership at Harvard Business School, investigated more than 100 companies involved in, or having attempted a complex change programme and identified 'Eight main reasons why transformation efforts fail'. The main eight reasons, which are shown in Figure 8.2 apply equally to ITSM implementation programmes.

8.4.1 Creating a sense of urgency

Half of all transformations fail to realize their goals due to the lack of adequate attention to this step. Not enough people buy into the fact that change is a must. Creating a sense of urgency is concerned with answering the question 'What if we do nothing?' Answering this question for all organizational levels will help gain commitment and provide input to a business justification for investing in CSI.

Examples of the consequences of doing nothing:

- The business will lose money due to outages of crucial IT services, systems and applications.
- The business finds IT costs unacceptable and may insist on staffing reductions as an easy option for reducing costs

The question 'What if we do nothing?' should be answered from the perspective of different stakeholders. This step could be taken in the form of one-on-one dialogues with stakeholders, workshops and team meetings. The aim is to create a real awareness and commitment that the status quo is no longer acceptable.

8.4.2 Forming a guiding coalition

Experience shows a need for assembling a group with sufficient power to lead the change effort and work together as a team. Power means more than simply formal authority but also experience, respect, trust and credibility. This team is the guiding coalition for the CSI.

It is important that the team leading the CSI has a shared understanding of the urgency and what it wants to achieve. A guiding coalition team does not have to be comprised solely of senior managers. A guiding coalition should ensure that the organization is motivated and inspired to participate. A single champion cannot achieve success alone. Those initiating a CSI should try to gain full support from the stakeholders, including the business managers, IT staff and the user community. The team must be prepared to spend time and effort convincing and motivating others to participate.

In the beginning this team will be small and should include an influential business or IT sponsor. As the programme buy-in grows, and throughout the programme itself when more and more successes are achieved and benefits realized, this team should be increased to involve a wider range of people and functions. Conscious attention should be given to managing a formal and informal network that forms the basis of a guiding coalition, asking the questions 'Do we have the right people on board?' and, if not, 'Who should we have on board?'

8.4.3 Creating a vision

The guiding coalition should be responsible for ensuring that a vision is produced describing the aim and purpose of CSI. A good vision statement can serve four important purposes:

- Clarify the direction of the programme
- Motivate people to take action in the right direction
- Coordinate the actions of many different people
- Outline the aims of senior management.

Without a sensible and easily understood vision, a CSI implementation can easily dissolve into a list of confusing, incompatible projects that can take the organization in the wrong direction, or even nowhere at all. A vision that is easy to understand is also easy to explain. As a rule of thumb, if one cannot explain the vision in five minutes, the vision itself is not clear and focused enough.

A sound vision statement is important when forming a business justification for CSI, if one is already underway then having clear aims will help set more specific goals. The goals of CSI should be SMART (Specific, Measurable, Achievable, Realistic and Time-bounded) as well as being addressed in terms relating to the business itself.

8.4.4 Communicating the vision

Although the vision is a powerful tool in helping guide and coordinate change, the real power is unleashed when the vision is effectively communicated to the stakeholders. Every stakeholder should understand the vision.

The sense of urgency ('What if we do nothing?') and the vision ('What's in it for me?') should form the basis of all communication to the stakeholders involved in or impacted by the CSI initiative. These messages should be aimed at motivating, inspiring and creating the necessary energy and commitment to buy in to the change programme. An important aspect of the communication is walking the talk – demonstrating by example.

It is important to make use of all communications channels to get the messages across. Use the organization's newsletters, intranet site, posters, theme and team meetings, and seminars. Aim the communication at the specific needs and wants of each target group. For example, a presentation to computer operators, stressing the benefits of lower management costs and increased business availability, may be less likely to inspire them than the idea that they will have the chance to gain new skills and opportunities, or that they will be supported by the latest advanced management technology so that they spend less time fire-fighting.

8.4.5 Empowering others to act on the vision

Establishing the urgency, creating a guiding coalition, creating and communicating a vision are all aimed at creating energy, enthusiasm, buy-in and commitment to enable successful change. In the empowering phase, two important aspects need to be stressed: enabling and removing barriers.

It is crucial to understand what is meant by empowerment. It is a combination of enabling people and removing barriers. Empowerment means giving people the tools, training and direction, and assurance that they will be given clear and unambiguous fixed goals. Once people are empowered, they are accountable. That is why confirming their confidence before going ahead is important.

8.4.6 Planning for and creating short-term wins

Implementing service management improvements can be a lengthy programme of change. It is important that, during the programme, short-term wins are realized and communicated. Short-term wins help to keep a change effort on track and help keep the energy and commitment levels high. Real transformation takes time. Without short-term wins, too many people give up or join the ranks of those opposing the change. Short-term wins can also be used to help:

- Convince change sceptics of the benefits
- Retain support of influential stakeholders
- Expand the guiding coalition and get more people on board and committed to the programme
- Build confidence to tackle even more complex implementation issues and process integration.

Try to identify some short-term wins for each service and/or process and plan these into the CSI. It is also important that short-term wins are made visible and are communicated to all stakeholders. When planning to communicate the short-term wins, obtain answers to the questions 'For whom is it a short-term win?' and 'To what degree does it support the overall aims and goals?' and work these answers into the communication.

8.4.7 Consolidating improvements and producing more change

The success of short-term wins keeps the momentum going and creates more change. In CSI it is important to recognize short-, medium- and long-term wins. Changes should sink deeply into the new culture or the new approaches will be fragile and subject to regression:

- **Short-term wins** have the characteristics of convincing, motivating and showing immediate benefits and gains.
- **Medium-term wins** have the characteristics of confidence and capability, and having a set of working processes in place.
- **Long-term wins** have the characteristics of self-learning and expertise, and fully integrated processes that have self-learning and improvement built into them; reaching this stage requires a baseline of confident, capable delivery and real understanding. Trying to reach this level before having gone through the other levels is like trying to win an Olympic medal before training has commenced.

8.4.8 Institutionalizing the change

Change needs to be institutionalized within the organization. Many changes fail because they are not consolidated into everyday practice. This is akin to buying a membership to a gym and not going. To institutionalize a change means showing how new working practices have produced real gain and benefits, and ensuring that the improvements are embedded in all organizational practices.

Often the CSI team is disbanded before the working practices are institutionalized; there is a danger that people may revert to old working practices. This has to stop. CSI must be a way of life not a knee-jerk reaction to a failure of some sort.

Some ways of institutionalizing changes:

- Look to hire people with ITIL experience or proven customer- or service-focused experience.
- Induction of new employees (both business and IT) includes service management familiarization: 'This is the way we do things.'
- Employee training plans and offerings include ITIL or service-management-focused training.
- Service goals and management reporting are matched to changing requirements, showing that they are used and requests are made for new sets of steering information.
- Clear action item are identified in meeting minutes and are acted upon in a timely manner.
- New IT solutions and development projects are integrated into existing processes.

Signs that the changes have been institutionalized include:

- People defend the procedures and declare, 'This is the way we work', rather than, 'This is the way I've been told to do it'.
- People make suggestions for improving procedures and work instructions to make them more effective or efficient.
- Service and process owners are proud of their achievements and offer to give presentations and write articles.

8.4.9 Organization culture

Organizational culture is the whole of the ideas, corporate values, beliefs, practices and expectations about behaviour and daily customs that are shared by the employees in an organization – the normal way of doing things. Component parts of the culture include:

- The way authority is exercised and people rewarded
- Methods of communication
- The degrees of formality required in working hours and dress and the extent to which procedures and regulations are enforced.

One could say culture is the heart of the matter or a key issue in implementing CSI. Culture could support an implementation or it could be the bearer of resistance.

Culture is continually named as one of the barriers in realizing any type of organizational change. When an organization has embraced CSI, the new organizational structure and technology receives overwhelming attention and almost no attention is paid to the effect on the culture. Culture isn't good or bad – it's just there.

An organization's culture can be immediately recognized by an outsider by the staff's attitudes and morale; their vocabulary – the phrases and buzzwords they use; and the stories and legends they tell of the organization's heroes. Continual improvement is about moving away from the hero mentality and focusing more on proactive planning and improving instead of always reacting to fix something when it breaks.

Key concept

One of the keys to changing the culture of an organization is to understand that you do not start out to change the culture. You start out to change the employee's behaviour. In other words, when implementing Continual Service Improvement around services and service management processes you are asking the staff members to change how they do things. You want them to follow the new CSI activities and procedures, and use the tools appropriately.

As you change employees' behaviour then over time this becomes the organization's new culture. Senior management plays an important part in changing behaviour. Senior management has to be the proper role model: if they don't follow a process then they are giving permission to others to follow their lead. Senior management has to ensure that people are rewarded for following the new process, and for Continual Service Improvement it means ongoing monitoring, analysing, reviewing, trend evaluation, reporting, identification of improvement opportunities and of course implementing those opportunities.

This will also require the help of your organization's human resource department, as changing employees' behaviour is directly tied to ensuring the job descriptions are up to date, employee's goals and objectives take into consideration service management responsibilities, and expectations include CSI activities. Also employee performance plans should be directly related to fulfilling these responsibilities and expectations. Whether an employee is performing an activity for service improvement or a Change Management activity, this should be recognized and employees rewarded based on the performance.

The following two statements are important when thinking about changing employee's behaviour.

- **What gets rewarded gets done**. This is why it is important to set up performance plans, performance appraisal systems and compensation plans to tie into

CSI activities as well as other service management activities. If you are rewarding an employee on who is keeping their box up and running and not on understanding the full end-to-end service management processes, than this is what you will get. It will be hard to change an employee's behaviour when they get rewarded for doing what they do today.

- **You get what you inspect not what you expect**. Organizations always expect employees to do certain things, but unless they are actually monitoring and checking to see if the tasks and activities are being done, there is little reason for an employee to change. Remember the State of North Carolina example. They achieved results through training, creating an awareness campaign and letting people know they were tracking results and would be discussing the results with the managers each month.

8.5 COMMUNICATION STRATEGY AND PLAN

Timely and effective communication forms an important part of any service improvement project. In an effort to transform an organization from performing CSI activities on an ad hoc basis to a more formal and ongoing CSI activities, it is critical that participants and stakeholders are kept apprised of all changes to the processes, activities, roles and responsibilities.

The goal of the communications plan is to build and maintain awareness, understanding, enthusiasm and support among key influential stakeholders for the CSI programme.

When developing a communication plan, it is important to realize that effective communication is not just based on a one-way flow of information, and it is more than just meetings. A communications plan must incorporate the ability to deal with responses and feedback from the targeted audiences.

The plan should include a role to:

- Design and deliver communications to the different CSI roles, stakeholders such as other ITSM process roles and identified target audiences
- Identify forums for customer and user feedback
- Receive and deliver responses and feedback to the project manager and/or process team members.

Key activities for the communications plan include:

- Identifying stakeholders and target audiences
- Developing communications strategies and tactics
- Identifying communication methods and techniques
- Developing the communications plan (a matrix of who, what, why, when where and how)
- Identifying the project milestones and related communications requirements.

In order to change behaviours and ultimately an organization's culture it will require a well-thought-out communication strategy and plan. An effective communication strategy and plan will focus on creating awareness as to why the organization is going down the path of implementing service management, why we want to formalize a CSI process, why ITIL was chosen as the best-practice framework. The plan will also need to address providing service management education through formal training programmes or internal meetings, providing formal training on the new processes and tool that sets new expectations as well as providing updates as to progress and achievements.

When developing your communication strategy and plan it is important to take into consideration how corporate communication works today. In some organizations if you want the CIO to communicate something on behalf of CSI or any service management project it may take a long time to get this accomplished. This needs to be planned for.

Also keep in mind the culture around communicating with the business. In some organizations there are strict guidelines on who can communicate with the business. Often times this is through the Service Level Management and Business Relationship Management processes. No matter what the method is, always have communicating with the business as one of your key communication activities.

8.5.1 Defining a communication plan

Defining your plan needs to take into consideration the following items:

- **Who is the messenger?** – This is often overlooked with regard to the importance of aligning the messenger with the message. There are times when it is appropriate for the CIO to deliver a communication. Another time it may be a Service Owner or Process Owner who should be doing the communicating.
- **What is the message?** – Define the purpose and objective of the message. This needs to be tailored to the target audience. Keep in mind the importance of communicating the benefits of the CSI programme. The WIIFM (what's-in-it-for-me) approach is still valid and needs to be addressed. Reporting can be a message that is provided.

- **Who is the target audience?** – The target audience for CSI could be senior management, mid-level managers or the staff who will be tasked with performing CSI activities. The target audience will often dictate who will deliver the message based on what the message is.
- **Timing and frequency of communication** – Be sure to plan and execute your communication in a timely manner. The one constant about managing change is that for communication to be effective it will take more than a one-time communication. If reporting is what is being communicated you will want to define your reporting timelines and frequency.
- **Method of communication** – The old standby of sending e-mails and putting something on the web can work for some forms of communication, but in order to effectively manage change it is important to have a number of face-to-face meetings where there is an opportunity for two-way communications to take place. Attending staff meetings, holding information meetings open to all of IT and conducting town hall meetings are all effective methods that need to be considered.
- **Provide a feedback mechanism** – Be sure to provide some method for employees to ask questions and provide feedback on the change initiative. Someone should have ownership of checking and ensuring responses are provided to the questions/comments that are provided.

Be sure to keep a record of your of all of your communications that go out as this represents how the communication plan has been executed.

You can develop a simple table for your communication plan as shown in Table 8.1. Keep in mind that you will be communicating to various groups within IT. Be sure to include senior management, mid-level managers, line contributors as well as those working or support CSI activities.

Communication transformation

The strategic management level usually initiates the communication about new initiatives and this should be true for implementing CSI within your organization. The CSI initiative is handed down from the strategic level to the tactical level and then to the operational level. It is more the rule than the exception that each level goes through its own transformation process. It is important that the same message is being sent and received as the vision is communicated down the organization. The outcome of this process is the cause and often the demand for the next level in an organization to transform. Information about this process and how people are dealing with it are seldom handed down. Unfortunately the higher level gives little feedback about this process to the next level.

What also happens is that the content of the vision and reasons for the organizational change becomes less understood as it moves down through the organization. Only parts of the rationale behind the organizational change come through to the operational level. The below figure depicts the fact that only part of the original content of the vision is handed down ('the shadow of the upper level') to the operational level. As the message is passed through the organizational levels, the clarity and content of the vision is blurred even further (see Figure 8.3).

Because each management level has its own separate transformation processes they fail to appreciate the feelings of the other levels. This is most evident for operational level staffs, who feel particularly vulnerable if they have not been involved in the discussions. And yet it is the commitment and energy of the operational level that are essential to the success of any organizational change.

Table 8.1 Sample table for communication plan

Messenger	Target audience	Message	Method of communication	Date and frequency	Status
CIO	All of IT	CSI initiative is kicking off	Town hall meeting	Month/day	Planned

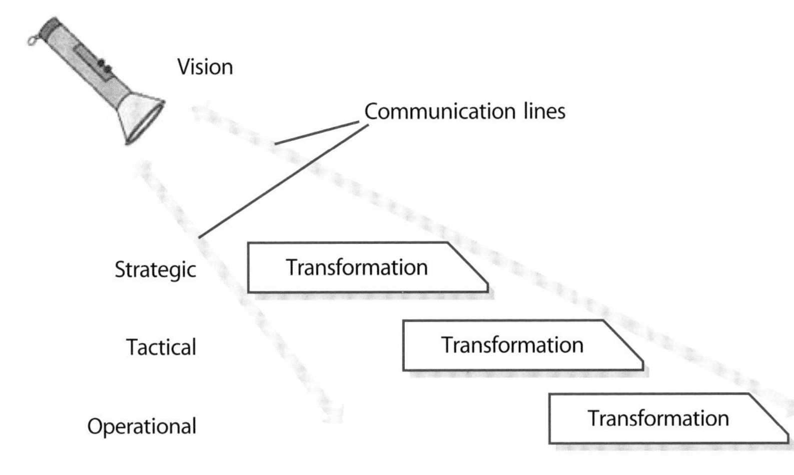

Figure 8.3 Vision becomes blurred

8.6 SUMMARY

Developing a governance structure is important for formalizing CSI in your organization. CSI will require that key roles are filled for trend evaluation, analysis reporting and decision making. Process compliance is critical for ensuring the proper output for process metrics to be used for identifying process improvement initiatives. Technology will need to be in place for monitoring and reporting.

Communication is critical to help change employees behaviour. Communication will require identifying the target audience, who the messenger is, what message is being communicated and what is the best way to communicate the message.

Figure 8.4 shows the roles and key inputs that are involved in the different phases of Continual Improvement.

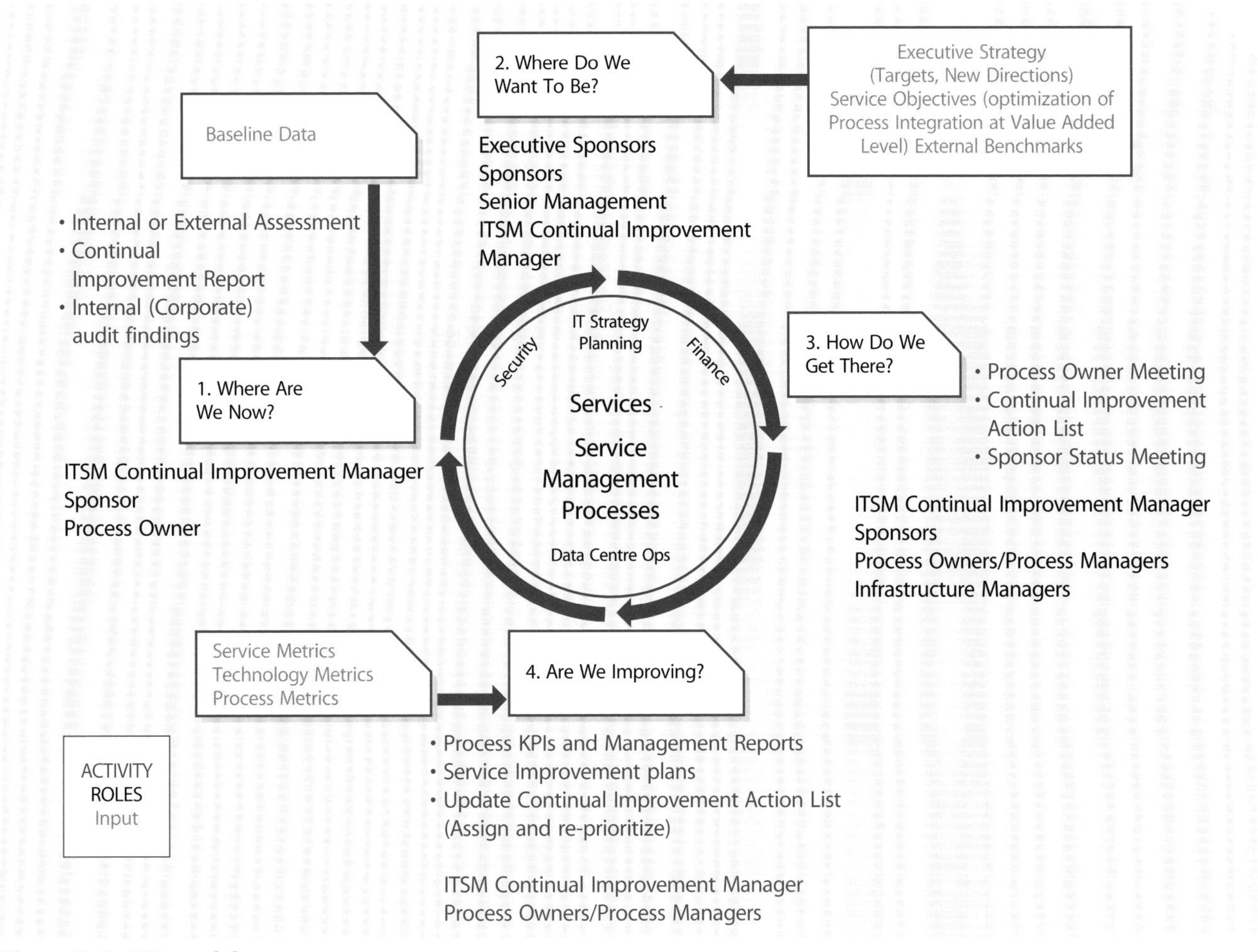

Figure 8.4 CSI model

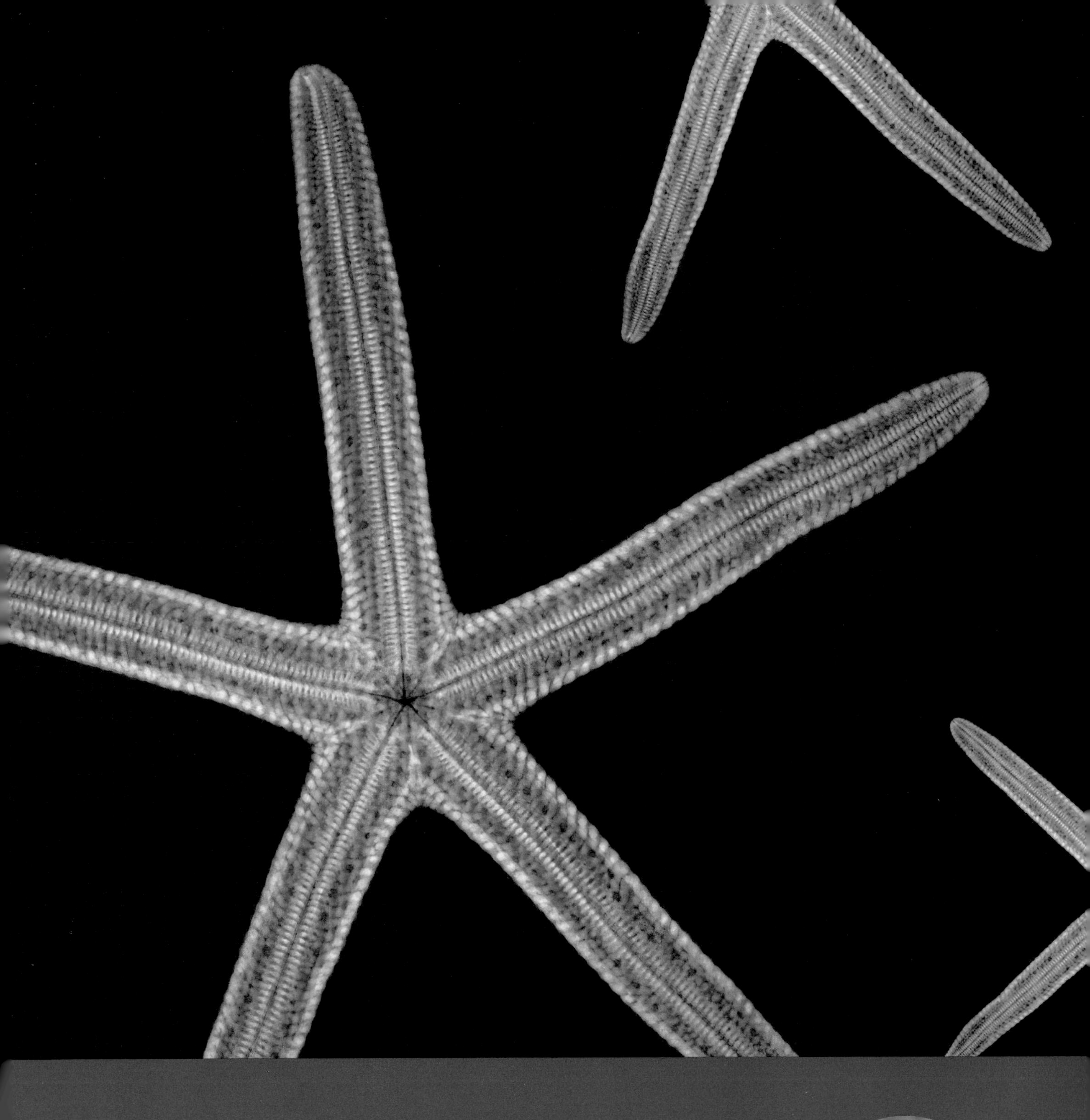

9 Challenges, critical success factors and risks

9 Challenges, critical success factors and risks

9.1 CHALLENGES

Every organization will have its unique set of challenges. As with implementing any type of change within an organization one of the major challenges will be managing the behavioural changes that are required.

The other issue is that CSI often requires adequate tools for monitoring and gathering the data, analysing the data for trends and reporting on the data. CSI does not happen only through automation but also requires resources to be allocated to CSI activities. The resources need to understand their roles and responsibilities and have the correct skill sets to execute the CSI activities.

Listed below are some of the common ones that you may encounter when implementing Continual Service Improvement:

- Lack of management commitment
- Inadequate resources, budget and time
- Lack of mature service management processes
- Lack of information, monitoring and measurements
- Lack of Knowledge Management
- A resistance to planning and a reluctance to be proved wrong
- A lack of corporate objectives, strategies, policies and business direction
- A lack of IT objectives, strategies and policies
- Lack of knowledge and appreciation of business impacts and priorities
- Diverse and disparate technologies and applications
- Resistance to change and cultural change
- Poor relationships, communication and a lack of cooperation between IT and the business
- Lack of tools, standards and skills
- Tools too complex and costly to implement and maintain
- Over-commitment of resources with an associated inability to deliver (e.g. projects always late or over budget)
- Poor supplier management and/or poor supplier performance.

9.2 CRITICAL SUCCESS FACTORS

- Appointment of a CSI manager
- Adoption of CSI within the organization
- Management commitment – this means ongoing, visible participation in CSI activities such as creating vision for CSI, communicating vision, direction setting and decision making, when appropriate
- Defining clear criteria for prioritizing improvement projects
- Adoption of the service lifecycle approach
- Sufficient and ongoing funding for CSI activities
- Resource allocation – people are dedicated to the improvement effort not as just another add-on to their already long list of tasks to perform
- Technology to support the CSI activities
- Adoption of processes – embracing service management processes instead of adapting it to suit their own personal needs and agenda.

9.3 RISKS

- Being over-ambitious – don't try to improve everything at once. Be realistic with timelines and expectations
- Not discussing improvement opportunities with the business – the business has to be involved in improvement decisions that will impact them
- Not focusing on improving both services and service management processes
- Not prioritizing improvement projects
- Implementing CSI with little or no technology
- Implementing a CSI initiative with no resources – this means that people must be allocated and dedicated to this
- Implementing CSI without knowledge transfer and training – this means educating first (acquire knowledge), then training (practice using the newly acquired knowledge). The training should be done as close to the launch of improvement as possible
- Not performing all steps of the 7-Step Improvement Process – it is important that all steps of the improvement process be followed; missing any one step can lead to a poor decision on what and how to improve

- Lack of making strategic, tactical or operational decisions based on knowledge gained – reports are actually used; people see that the reports are being used
- Lack of management taking action on recommended service improvement opportunities
- Lack of meeting with the business to understand new business requirements
- The communication/awareness campaign for any improvement is lacking, late or missing altogether
- Not involving the right people at all levels to plan, build, test and implement the improvement
- Removing testing before implementation or only partially testing. This means that all aspects of the improvement (people, process and technology) must be tested, including the documentation as well.

9.4 SUMMARY

Implementing CSI is not an easy task: it requires a change in management and staff attitudes and values that continual improvement is something that needs to be done proactively and not reactively.

Identifying the risks and challenges before implementing CSI is a critical first step. A SWOT analysis can help identify these items. It is important to define mitigation strategies for the risks and identify how to best overcome challenges that an organization may encounter.

Knowing the critical success factors before undertaking CSI implementation will help manage the risks and challenges. Don't try to change everything at once.

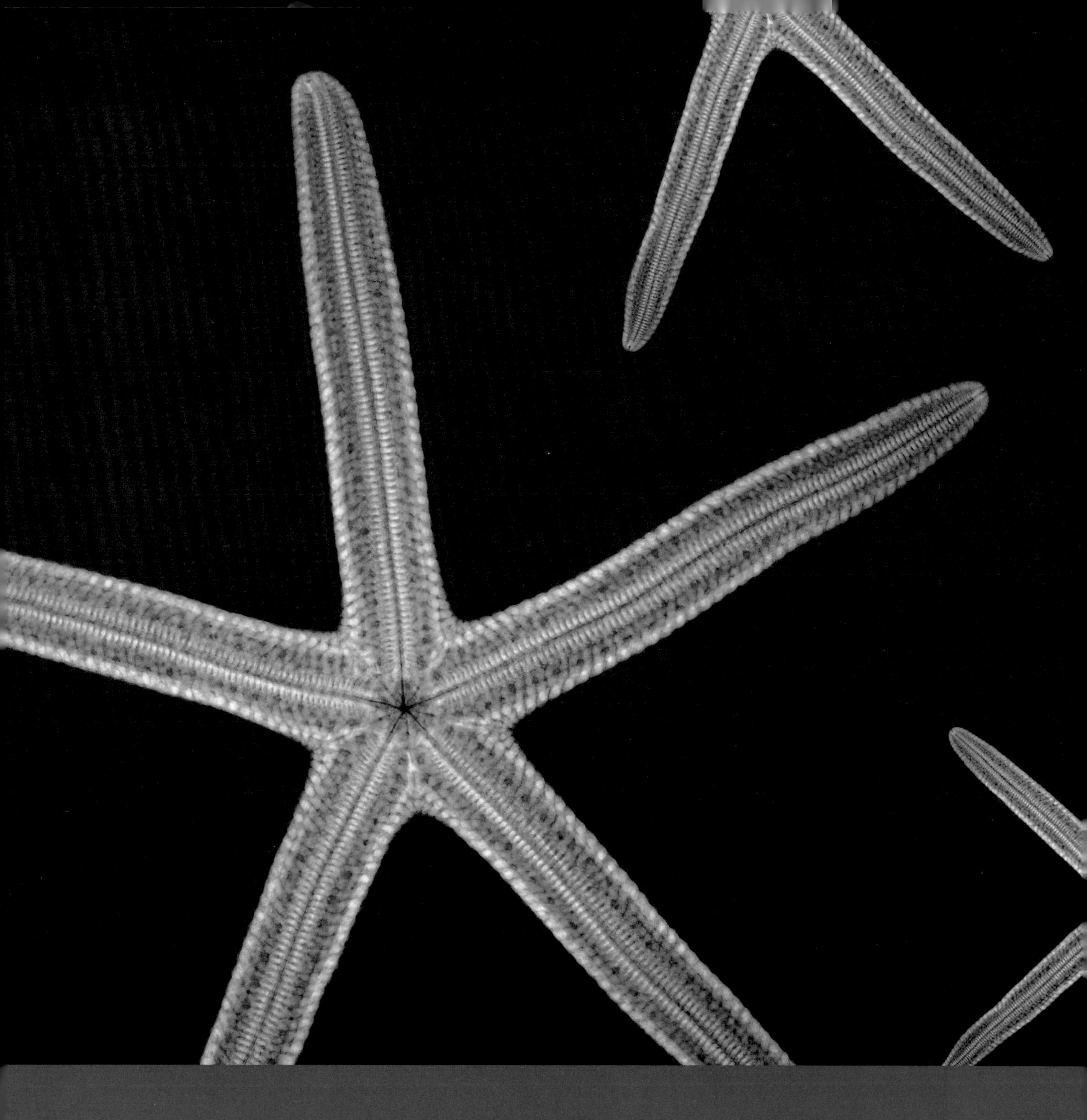

Afterword

Afterword

For centuries people have been sailing across the oceans in ships. While a very few have been intrepid explorers intent on charting new territory and new routes to far-off lands, most have simply set off on a journey from their home port to a distant destination. They plotted a course which would get them there safely in a reasonable time and then set sail. The risks were high, but the rewards were even higher. If the final destination was too far, they plotted a series of smaller journeys with stops at points along the way allowing them to get to their destination in steps. The course would often take them far from the sight of land, so each day they would need to check if they were still on course. In the beginning they used the stars, then the compass, the sextant, radio beacons and now global positioning satellites. The technology has changed radically but the goal is still the same, determine where you are right now and if the winds or the currents have moved you off course you must make adjustments in order to reach your destination. Continual Service Improvement is your journey. Your destination is your vision of a near-perfect future state. The vision may be far off, requiring you to set smaller goals along the way. You set the course for near perfection and continually check to see whether you are still on course. Continually making the necessary adjustments on your journey will enable you to reach your destination. Good sailing!

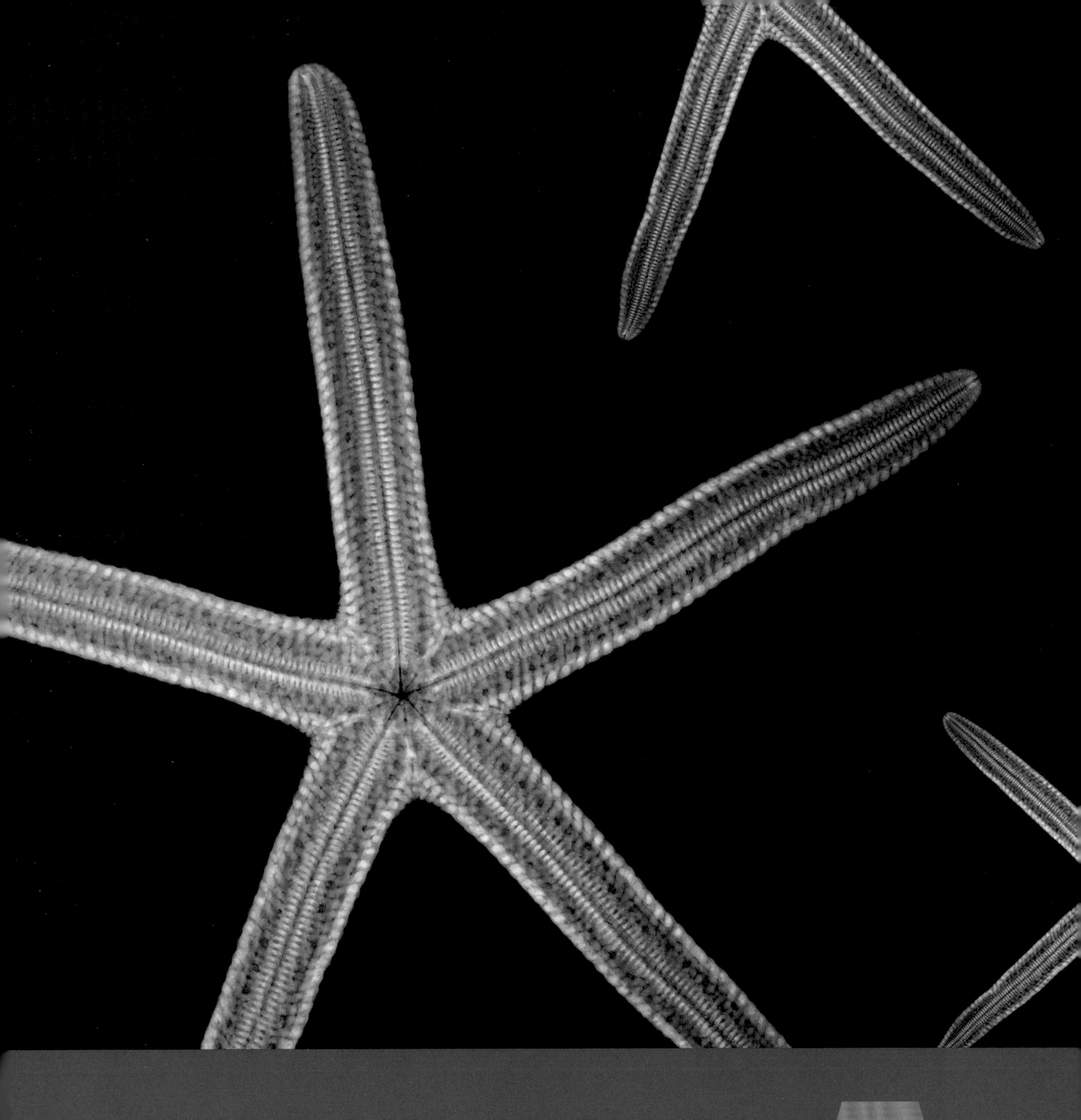

Appendix A: Complementary guidance

A

Appendix A: Complementary guidance

A1 INNOVATION, CORRECTION AND IMPROVEMENT

Within the service lifecycle it is important to remember that there are three distinct areas where services are touched. The first is service innovation: this is the whole lifecycle approach from Service Strategy to Service Design to Service Transition and into Service Operation.

The second is service corrections and this often involves Service Transition and Service Operation.

The third is service improvements and this also will impact the service from Service Design through to Service Operation. Service improvements impact Service Strategy. This publication has shared with you many critical elements of Continual Service Improvement. Figure A.1 shows a representation of service innovation, corrections and improvements.

Every publication within the lifecycle is important to fully understand the service lifecycle and to identify service improvements. This publication has talked about many different models, standards and frameworks. This chapter is a quick reminder on what other guidance can be used to support CSI activities.

A2 BEST PRACTICES THAT SUPPORT CSI

There are many best practices, standards, models and quality systems that are in use throughout the world that support CSI in one manner or another. Previous chapters introduced some of these best practices.

ISO/IEC 20000

Standards make an enormous contribution, although very often that contribution is invisible. If there were no standards, it would soon be noticed. It is when there is an absence of standards that their importance is brought home. When products and services meet expectations, there is a tendency to take them for granted. Few people are usually aware of the role played by standards in raising levels of quality, safety, reliability, efficiency and interchangeability – as well as in providing such benefits at an economical cost.

ISO/IEC 20000-1:2005 defines the requirements for a service provider to deliver managed services. It may be used:

- By businesses that are going out to tender for their services
- To provide a consistent approach by all service providers in a supply chain
- To benchmark IT service management
- As the basis for an independent assessment
- To demonstrate the ability to meet customer requirements
- To improve services.

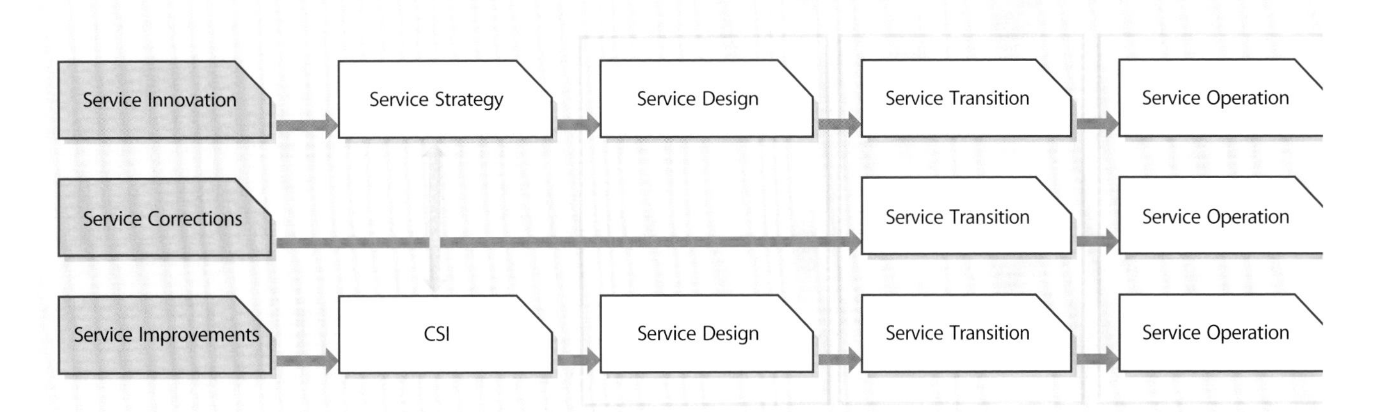

Figure A.1 Innovation, correction, improvement and CSI

There are many aspects of ISO/IEC 20000 that support CSI but the major ones are the following.

Service Level Management

The SLM process should ensure that the service provider remains focused on the customer throughout the planning, implementing and ongoing management of service delivery.

Key activities of SLM:

- Capturing initial business requirements and ongoing changes to volumes and expectations
- Defining and documenting services in a Service Catalogue
- Negotiating SLAs with defined targets
- Monitoring, measurement and reporting of the service levels achieved
- Initiation of corrective action
- Provide input to a SIP.

Service reporting

Service reports should be produced to meet identified needs and customer requirements.

Service reporting should include:

- Performance against service level targets
- Non-compliance and issues such as service level or security breaches
- Workload characteristics such as volume and resource utilization
- Performance reporting following major incidents and changes
- Trend information
- Satisfaction analysis.

Business Relationship Management

- The objective of Business Relationship Management is to establish and maintain a good relationship between the service provider and the customer based on understanding the customer and their business drivers. The customer business drivers could require changes in SLAs and thus becomes input into service improvement opportunities.
- The objective of supplier management is to ensure the provision of seamless, quality services. This will require monitoring, measuring and reviewing the performance of IT suppliers.

Management decisions and corrective actions should take into consideration the findings in the service reports and should be formally communicated.

ISO/IEC 20000 defines a requirement for continual improvement on the effectiveness and efficiency of service delivery and management. This is done through management establishing policies, objectives and the need for continual improvement. ISO follows the Plan-Do-Check-Act cycle. Checking involves monitoring, measuring and analysing, and acting is the continual improvement.

COBIT®

Control Objectives for Information and Related Technology (COBIT) is a globally recognized and adopted controls-based, value and risk management framework used to support overall IT governance. COBIT is a flexible framework that needs to be aligned to an organization's business requirements. It can be used by management, consultants and auditors to:

- Define the IT controls needed to minimize risks and add business value – and hence the development of a fit-for-purpose IT governance framework
- Create an IT measurement and CSI framework which is aligned to the business goals for IT
- Assess and audit against IT governance and ensure that IT governance aligns with overall enterprise governance.
- COBIT supports CSI in three ways:
- COBIT defines processes to support CSI
- COBIT provides maturity models that can be used to benchmark and drive CSI
- COBIT provides goals and metrics aligned to the business goals for IT, which can be used to create an IT management dashboard.

COBIT defines processes to support CSI

COBIT has defined four processes needed to support CSI. The COBIT process domain 'Monitor and Evaluate' (ME) defines the processes needed to assess current IT performance, IT controls and regulatory compliance. The processes are:

- ME1: Monitor and evaluate IT performance
- ME2: Monitor and evaluate internal control
- ME3: Ensure regulatory compliance
- ME4: Provide IT governance.

These processes take into consideration multiple factors that can drive the need for improvement, factors such as a need to improve performance and manage risks more effectively through better controls or regulatory compliance. These processes also ensure that any improvement actions are identified and managed through to their implementation.

An enterprise can therefore implement the processes needed to support CSI using COBIT processes. In addition, an enterprise can review the processes that support CSI periodically and improve them based on their associated maturity models within COBIT.

Six Sigma

Six Sigma is an IT-appropriate process-improvement methodology, though the fundamental objective is to reduce errors to fewer than 3.4 defects per million executions (regardless of the process). Given the wide variation in IT deliverables (e.g. Change Management, Problem Management, Capacity Management) and roles and tasks within IT operational environments, IT managers must determine whether it is reasonable to expect delivery at a Six Sigma level.

Six Sigma is a data-driven approach that supports continual improvement. It is business output driven in relation to customer specification and focuses on dramatically reducing process variation using Statistical Process Control (SPC) measures.

Six Sigma's objective is the implementation of a measurement-oriented strategy focused on process improvement and defects reduction. A Six Sigma defect is defined as anything outside customer specifications.

There are two primary sub-methodologies within Six Sigma: DMAIC (define, measure, analyse, improve, control) and DMADV (define, measure, analyse, design, verify). The DMAIC process is an improvement method for existing processes for which performance does not meet expectations, or for which incremental improvements are desired. The DMADV process focuses on the creation of new processes.

Defining, measuring and analysing are key activities of CSI.

Since Six Sigma requires data it is important to start capturing data as soon as possible. As previously mentioned if the data is questionable, this is not a problem as it provides the opportunity to analyse why the data doesn't make sense.

CMMI

Capability Maturity Model Integration (CMMI) is a process improvement approach that provides organizations with the essential elements of effective process measurement. It can be used to guide process improvement across a project, a division or an entire organization. CMMI helps integrate traditionally separate organizational functions, sets process improvement goals and priorities, provides guidance for quality processes and provides a point of reference for appraising current processes.

CMMI uses a hierarchy of five levels, each with a progressively greater capability of producing quality, where each level is described as a level of maturity.

CMMI Benefits

CMMI best practices enable organizations to do the following:

- More explicitly link management and engineering activities to their business objectives
- Expand the scope of and visibility into the product life cycle and engineering activities to ensure that the product or service meets customer expectations
- Incorporate lessons learned from additional areas of best practice (e.g. measurement, risk management and supplier management)
- Implement more robust, high-maturity practices
- Address additional organizational functions critical to their products and services
- More fully comply with relevant ISO standards.

Project management

It is also important to understand that a structured project management method, such as PMI (Project Management Institute) or PRINCE2 (projects IN Controlled Environments, v2) can be used when improving IT services. Not all improvements will require a structured project approach, but many will, due to the sheer scope and scale of the improvement.

Project management is discussed in great detail in the ITIL Service Transition volume.

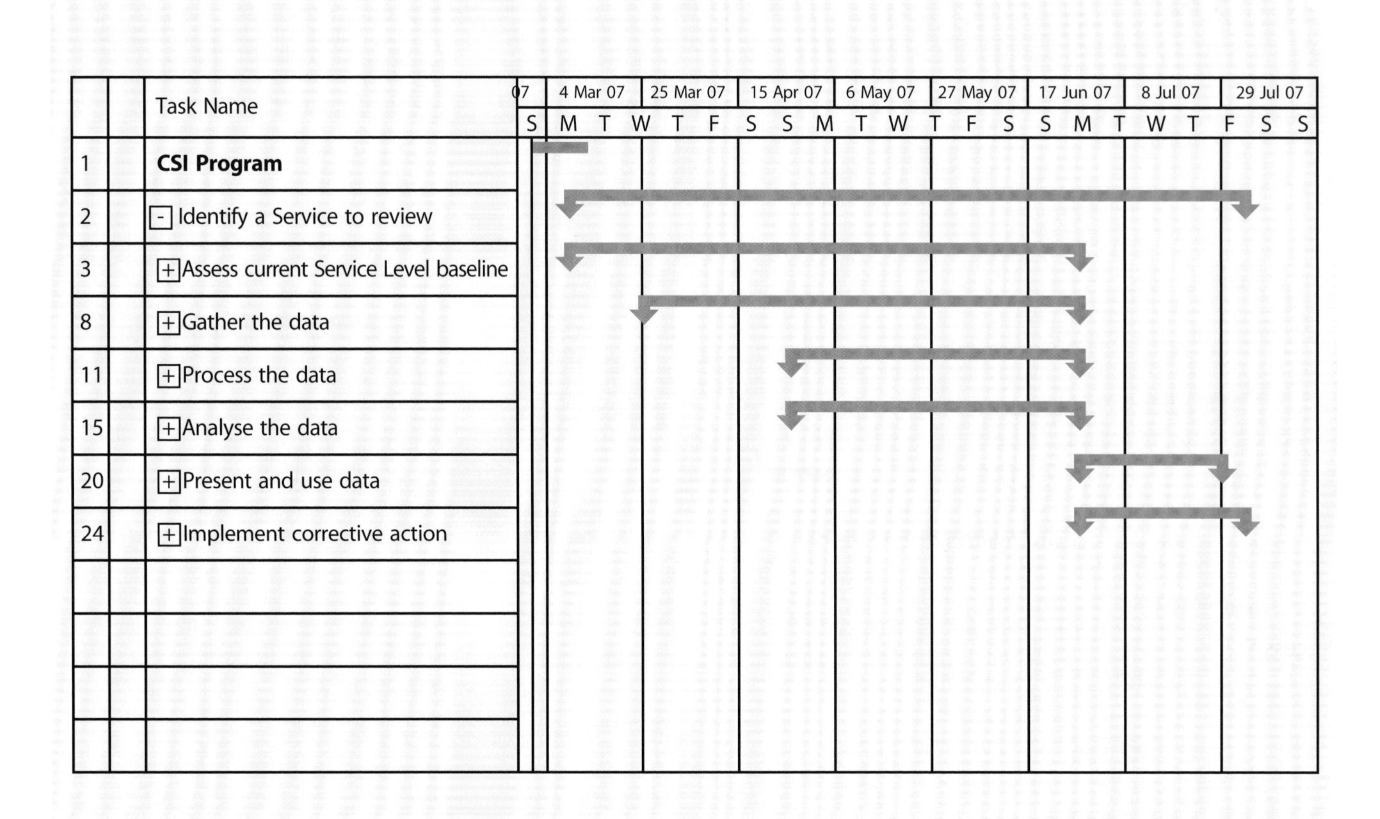

Figure A.2 Gantt chart

Gantt chart

Henry Gantt (1861-1919) created the Gantt chart in a setting and time which was deeply involved in exploring efficiency in manufacturing, time and motion studies, and the formulation of 'scientific management' (the foundation of modern management principals). Today many people see the Gantt chart as a project management tool, however its origins are completely intertwined with process.

Gantt charts use time-lengthened bars to represent tasks. Tasks are connected to each other according to predecessors and dependencies. Simple arrows are used to connect the task bars. See Figure A.2.

The simplicity of the Gantt chart makes it easy to use and read. It is especially legible to project managers and staff often engaged in project based work. It has been successfully used on highly complex projects such as the building of the Hoover Dam and the creation of the interstate highway network in the US. Its limitations are its inability to show organizational/departmental structures associated with tasks, an inability to include process/workflow rules, and inabilities to show split and join actions.

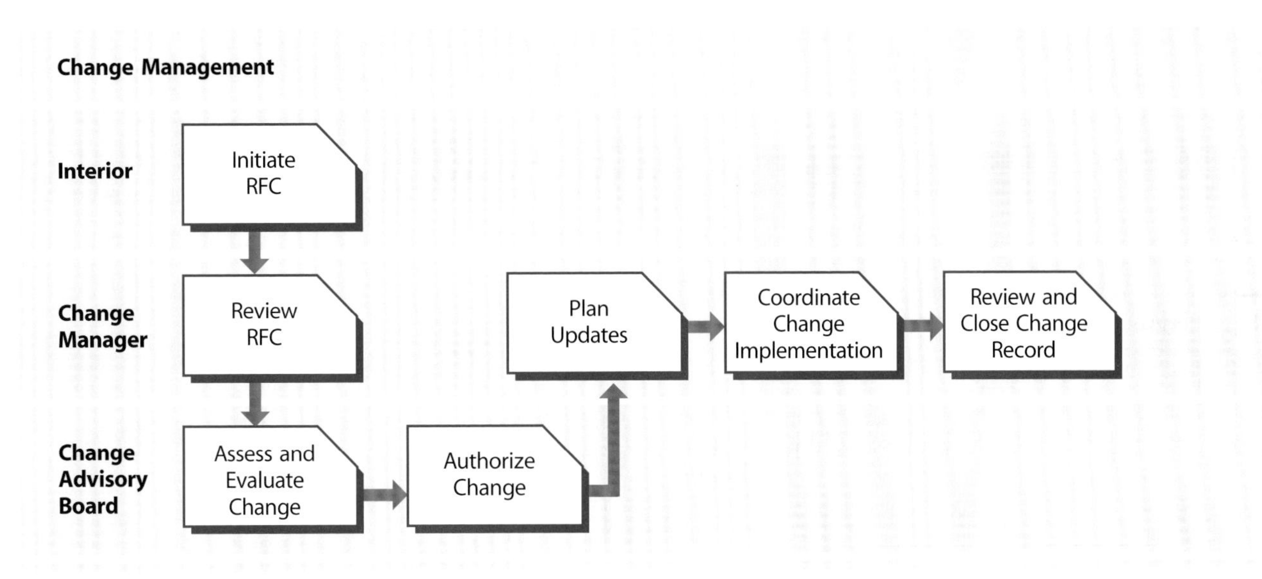

Figure A.3 Rummler-Brache Swim Lane example

Rummler-Brache Swim Lane

Process Swim Lanes were first described in Geary Rummler and Alan Brache's publication *Improving Performance*. Their impact in the process world is difficult to overstate. Their work has focused on helping companies improve their overall business processes, and thereby become more competitive and profitable. Process Swim Lanes have become the most ubiquitous term and method associated with their names.

It is a highly effective way to display the relationship between processes and organizations/departments. Swim Lanes are essentially flow charts which include horizontal or vertical bands to include customers, departments and technology.

Swim Lanes rely on rectangles for activities/tasks, decision diamonds, and arrows to represent flow. Central to the method is separating organizations with horizontal rows.

Each activity is placed in the row (Swim Lane) which represents the organization responsible for completing the task. See Figure A.3.

Swim Lanes are strong tools for communicating with business managers. Many managers are essentially organizational thinkers. They see the world in organizational terms. In the absence of those structures they will sometimes struggle. Swim Lanes describe a process from a viewpoint which is familiar and accessible.

The weakness of Swim Lanes stems from the fact that it is more of an approach than a standard. Managing complexity is generally done by including symbols from other standards within a Swim Lane diagram.

Value Stream Mapping

Value Stream Mapping is a hands-on method which comes from Lean Manufacturing (an approach to removing non-value-added work – originating with Toyota). It is traditionally a facilitation method done on whiteboards or on paper. The result is often a handmade, somewhat cartoonish representation of how a product is produced from inception to delivery to the customer. It includes process, information flow and a timeline separating value-add and non-value-add activities.

Value Stream Maps include handmade drawings for all types of mechanisms within the process: factories, trucks, people, documents, tasks etc. It is by its nature an eclectic and ad hoc method of diagramming a process.

Value Stream Mapping is a good tool for projects whose goal is to streamline a process. It ensures a high-level view which is broad and customer focused. It is not generally used as a tool for long-term documentation, but instead as a method of setting the right direction and staying on track. It can be a powerful tool when combined with other diagramming standards such as BPMN or IDEF. It is not a standard and as such does not have rigidity required for long-term documentation.

Total Quality Management

Total Quality Management (TQM) is a management strategy aimed at embedding awareness of quality in all organizational processes.

> TQM is a set of systematic activities carried out by the entire organization to effectively and efficiently achieve company objectives so as to provide products and services with a level of quality that satisfies customers, at the appropriate time and price.

At the core of TQM is a management approach to long-term success through customer satisfaction. In a TQM effort, all members of an organization participate in improving processes, products, services and the culture in which they work.

Quality management for IT services is a systematic way of ensuring that all the activities necessary to design, develop and implement IT services which satisfy the requirements of the organization and of users take place as planned and that the activities are carried out cost-effectively.

The way that an organization plans to manage its operations so that it delivers quality services is specified by its Quality Management System. The Quality Management System defines the organizational structure, responsibilities, policies, procedures, processes, standards and resources required to deliver quality IT services. However, a Quality Management System will only function as intended if management and staff are committed to achieving its objectives.

This section gives brief details on a number of different quality approaches.

Deming Cycle

The Deming Cycle of Plan-Do-Check-Act is an effective quality management system to follow.

A core concept in implementing TQM is Deming's 14 points, a set of management practices to help companies increase their quality and productivity:

1. Create constancy of purpose for improving products and services.
2. Adopt the new philosophy.
3. Cease dependence on inspection to achieve quality.
4. End the practice of awarding business on price alone; instead, minimize total cost by working with a single supplier.
5. Improve constantly and forever every process for planning, production and service.
6. Institute training on the job.
7. Adopt and institute leadership.
8. Drive out fear.
9. Break down barriers between staff areas.
10. Eliminate slogans, exhortations and targets for the workforce.
11. Eliminate numerical quotas for the workforce and numerical goals for management.
12. Remove barriers that rob people of pride of workmanship, and eliminate the annual rating or merit system.
13. Institute a vigorous programme of education and self-improvement for everyone.
14. Put everybody in the company to work accomplishing the transformation.

Juran

Joseph Juran became a recognized name in the quality field in 1951 with the publication of the *Quality Control Handbook*. The appeal was to the Japanese initially, and Juran was asked to give a series of lectures in 1954 on planning, organizational issues, management responsibility for Quality, and the need to set goals and targets for improvement. Juran devised a well-known chart, 'The Juran Trilogy', shown in Figure A.4, to represent the relationship between quality planning, quality control and quality improvement on a project-by-project basis.

A further feature of Juran's approach is the recognition of the need to guide managers; this is achieved by the establishment of a quality council within an organization, which is responsible for establishing processes, nominating projects, assigning teams, making improvements and providing the necessary resources.

Senior management plays a key role in serving on the quality council, approving strategic goals, allocating resources and reviewing progress. Juran promotes a four-phased approach to quality improvement, shown in Table A.1.

Table A.1 Juran's four-phased approach

Start-up:	creating the necessary organizational structures and infrastructure
Test:	in which concepts are tried out in pilot programmes and results evaluated
Scale-up:	in which the basic concepts are extended based on positive feedback
Institutionalization:	at which point quality improvements are linked to the strategic business plan.

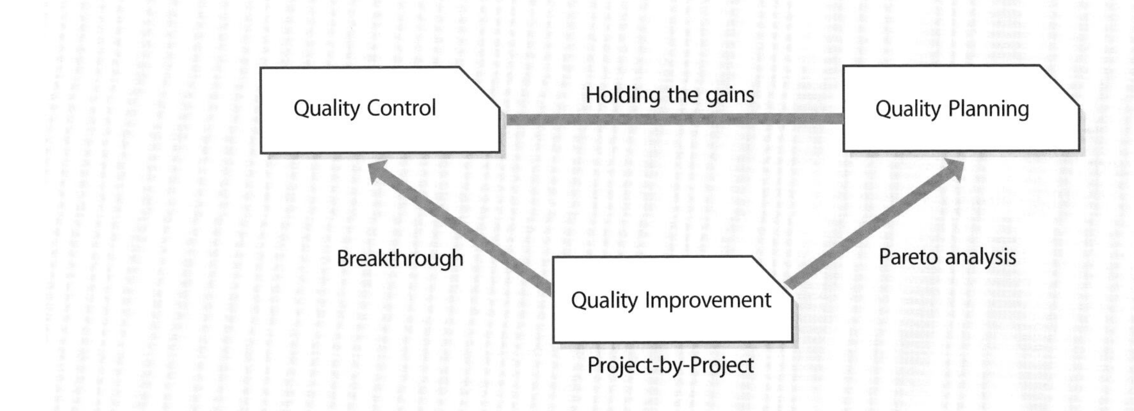

Figure A.4 The Quality Trilogy

Crosby

The Crosby TQM approach is very popular in the UK. The approach is based on Crosby's Four Absolutes of Quality Management:

- Quality is conformance to requirement.
- The system for causing quality is prevention and not appraisal.
- The performance standard must be zero defects and not 'that's close enough'.
- The measure of quality is the price of non-conformance and not indices.

The Crosby approach is often based on familiar slogans; however, organizations may experience difficulty in translating the quality messages into sustainable methods of quality improvement. Some organizations have found it difficult to integrate their quality initiatives, having placed their quality programme outside the mainstream management process.

Anecdotal evidence suggests that these pitfalls result in difficulties being experienced in sustaining active quality campaigns over a number of years in some organizations.

Management governance framework

The management governance framework and its processes are the means by which: 'A business directs, develops and delivers the products and services of the business.'

It is the way that the strategy is executed through business development products to develop product and service capabilities and through which day-to-day products and services are delivered and supported. It is the mechanism by which all the parts of the business and its supply chain partners work together on strategy, development and operation.

Figure A.5 illustrates the framework and what is involved in it. The framework is used to direct and run the business from left to right with feedback from right to left. Typically the strategy involves a long-term strategy; the business plan involves a short number of years with financial targets and budgets; the business architecture is the high-level design of the business, and so on.

The business needs to provide unified **direction** through disciplines and processes that involve strategy, business plans, budgets and business architecture.

The business needs to provide unified **development** through a shared business change plan and development programmes and projects disciplines under the control of operational change disciplines in the operational world.

The business needs to provide unified **delivery** of products and services through shared operational planning, operational delivery and operational support. The way the disciplines above are performed varies from business to business. Some businesses perform aspects formally and other aspects in an informal, ad hoc manner. In terms of best-practice business governance, the need for the individual disciplines above is crucial as is the way they interrelate. The governance framework formalizes the touch points between the value chains. From both business and IT viewpoints, the best-practice governance framework enables the processes and the relationships of the value chains to be formalized with each other across the governance model.

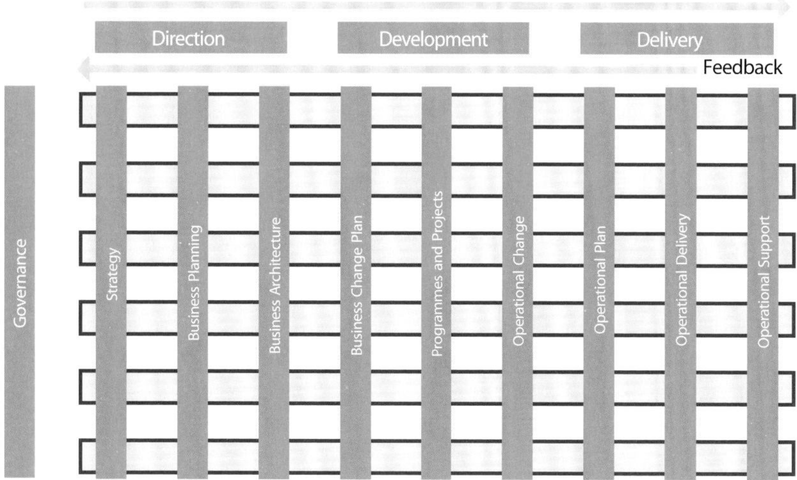

Figure A.5 Management governance framework

Further information

Further information

REFERENCES

Visit www.iso.org for more information on:

- ISO/IEC 20000 Information Technology Service Management
- ISO/IEC 27001 Information technology – Security techniques
  Information Security Management Systems
- ISO/IEC 17799 Information technology – Security techniques
  Code of practice for Information Security Management
- ISO/IEC 19770 Information technology – Software asset management
  Part 1: Processes
- ISO/IEC 15504 Information technology — Process assessment

Visit www.itgi.org for more information on COBIT.

Visit www.isaca.org for more information on IS Audit.

Visit www.sei.cmu.edu/cmmi for more information on CMMI (Capability Maturity Model Integration).

Visit www.johnkotter.com for more information on Kotter's 'Eight Steps for Organizational Change'.

- John P. Kotter, Holger Rathgeber, Peter Mueller and Spenser Johnson (2006) *Our Iceberg Is Melting: Changing and Succeeding Under Any Conditions*, St. Martin's Press
  ISBN-10: 031236198X
  ISBN-13: 978-0312361983
- John P. Kotter (1999) What Leaders Really Do, Harvard Business School Press
  ISBN-10: 0875848974
  ISBN-13: 978-0875848976
- John P. Kotter (1996) *Leading Change*, Harvard Business School Press
  ISBN-10: 0875847471
  ISBN-13: 978-0875847474
- John P. Kotter and Dan S. Cohen (2002) *The Heart of Change: Real-Life Stories of How People Change Their Organizations*, Harvard Business School Press
  ISBN-10: 1578512549
  ISBN-13: 978-1578512546

Six Sigma – www.ge.com/sixsigma

- Peter S. Pande, Robert P. Neuman and Roland R. Cavanagh (2000) *The Six Sigma Way: How GE, Motorola, and Other Top Companies are Honing Their Performance*, McGraw-Hill
  ISBN-10: 0071358064
  ISBN-13: 978-0071358064
- Pete Pande and Larry Holpp (2001) *What Is Six Sigma?*, McGraw-Hill
  ISBN-10: 0071381856
  ISBN-13: 978-0071381857

LEAN

- Michael L. George (2003) *Lean Six Sigma for Service: How to Use Lean Speed and Six Sigma Quality to Improve Services and Transactions*, McGraw-Hill
  ISBN-10: 0071418210
  ISBN-13: 978-0071418218

Visit www.deming.org for more information on the W. Edwards Deming Institute® and the Deming Cycle for process improvement.

Visit www.juran.com for more information on the Juran Institute.

- Joseph M. Juran and A. Blanton Godfrey (1998) *Juran's Quality Handbook*, 5th edition, McGraw-Hill Professional
  ISBN-10: 007034003X
  ISBN-13: 978-0070340039

Visit www.kepner-tregoe.com for more information on the Kepner-Tregoe method.

- Charles Higgins Kepner and Benjamin B. Tregoe (1997) *The New Rational Manager*, Kepner-Tregoe
  ISBN-10: 0971562717
  ISBN-13: 978-0971562714

Visit www.cimaglobal.com for more information on CIMA.

CIMA – The Chartered Institute of Management Accountants – is a leading membership body that offers an internationally recognized professional qualification in management accountancy, which focuses on accounting for business. CIMA, founded in 1919, is one of the oldest professional organizations devoted to Financial Management and cost accounting.

Visit www.sarbanes-oxley.com for more information on the Sarbanes-Oxley Act of 2002.

Sarbanes-Oxley provides a complete cross-referenced index of SEC filers, audit firms, offices, CPAs, services, fees, compliance/enforcement actions and other critical disclosure information.

Visit www.itil-officialsite.com for more information on all things ITIL.

- Office of Government Commerce (2007) *Service Strategy*, TSO
  ISBN-13: 978-0113310456
- Office of Government Commerce (2007) *Service Design*, TSO
  ISBN-13: 978-0113310470
- Office of Government Commerce (2007) *Service Transition*, TSO
  ISBN-13: 978-0113310487
- Office of Government Commerce (2007) *Service Operation*, TSO
  ISBN-13: 978-0113310463
- Office of Government Commerce (2007) *The Official Introduction to the ITIL Service Lifecycle*, TSO
  ISBN-13: 978-0113310616

M_o_R Management of Risk

- Office of Government Commerce (2007) *Management of Risk: Guidance for Practitioners*, TSO
  ISBN-13: 978-0113310388

Project management

Visit www.prince-officialsite.com for more information on PRINCE2™.

- Office of Government Commerce (2005) *Managing Successful Projects with PRINCE2*, TSO
  ISBN-13: 978-0113309467

Visit www.pmi.org for more information on PMI and PMBOK.

- Gregory T. Haugan (2006) Project management fundamentals, Management Concepts ISBN: 156726171X
  ISBN-13: 978-1567261714
- David I. Cleland and Lewis R. Ireland (2006) *Project Management: Strategic Design and Implementation, 5th edition*, McGraw-Hill Professional
  ISBN: 007147160X
  ISBN-13: 978-0071471602
- The Project Management Institute (2004) *A Guide to the Project Management Body of Knowledge* (PMBOK® Guide), 3rd edition, Project Management Institute
  ISBN: 193069945X
  ISBN-13: 978-1930699458

Visit www.msp-officialsite.com for more information on education and certification for MSP.

- Office of Government Commerce (2003) Managing Successful Programmes, TSO
  ISBN-13: 978-0113309177

Visit www.ogc.gov.uk for more information on the Office of Government Commerce, which owns the ITIL copyright.

Visit www.tso.co.uk for more information on TSO (The Stationery Office), which publishes the ITIL volumes, and www.best-management-practice.com.

Visit www.apmgroup.co.uk for more information on APMG, the accreditor of ITIL certifications.

Glossary

Acronyms list

ACD Automatic Call Distribution
AM Availability Management
AMIS Availability Management Information System
ASP Application Service Provider
BCM Business Capacity Management
BCM Business Continuity Management
BCP Business Continuity Plan
BIA Business Impact Analysis
BRM Business Relationship Manager
BSI British Standards Institution
BSM Business Service Management
CAB Change Advisory Board
CAB/EC Change Advisory Board/Emergency Committee
CAPEX Capital Expenditure
CCM Component Capacity Management
CFIA Component Failure Impact Analysis
CI Configuration Item
CMDB Configuration Management Database
CMIS Capacity Management Information System
CMM Capability Maturity Model
CMMI Capability Maturity Model Integration
CMS Configuration Management System
COTS Commercial off the Shelf
CSF Critical Success Factor
CSI Continual Service Improvement
CSP Core Service Package
CTI Computer Telephony Integration
DIKW Data–to–Information–to–Knowledge–to–Wisdom
ELS Early Life Support
eSCM–CL eSourcing Capability Model for Client Organizations
eSCM–SP eSourcing Capability Model for Service Providers
FMEA Failure Modes and Effects Analysis
FTA Fault Tree Analysis
IRR Internal Rate of Return
ISG IT Steering Group
ISM Information Security Management
ISMS Information Security Management System
ISO International Organization for Standardization
ISP Internet Service Provider
IT Information Technology
ITSCM IT Service Continuity Management
ITSM IT Service Management
itSMF IT Service Management Forum
IVR Interactive Voice Response
KEDB Known Error Database
KPI Key Performance Indicator
LOS Line of Service
M_o_R Management of Risk
MTBF Mean Time Between Failures
MTBSI Mean Time Between Service Incidents
MTRS Mean Time to Restore Service
MTTR Mean Time To Repair
NPV Net Present Value

OGC	Office of Government Commerce
OLA	Operational Level Agreement
OPEX	Operational Expenditure
OPSI	Office of Public Sector Information
PBA	Pattern of Business Activity
PFS	Prerequisite for Success
PIR	Post-Implementation Review
PSO	Projected Service Outage
QA	Quality Assurance
QMS	Quality Management System
RCA	Root Cause Analysis
RFC	Request for Change
ROI	Return on Investment
RPO	Recovery Point Objective
RTO	Recovery Time Objective
SAC	Service Acceptance Criteria
SACM	Service Asset and Configuration Management
SCD	Supplier and Contract Database
SCM	Service Capacity Management
SDP	Service Design Package
SFA	Service Failure Analysis
SIP	Service Improvement Plan
SKMS	Service Knowledge Management System
SLA	Service Level Agreement
SLM	Service Level Management
SLP	Service Level Package
SLR	Service Level Requirement
SMO	Service Maintenance Objective
SoC	Separation of Concerns
SOP	Standard Operating Procedures
SOR	Statement of requirements
SPI	Service Provider Interface
SPM	Service Portfolio Management
SPO	Service Provisioning Optimization
SPOF	Single Point of Failure
TCO	Total Cost of Ownership
TCU	Total Cost of Utilization
TO	Technical Observation
TOR	Terms of Reference
TQM	Total Quality Management
UC	Underpinning Contract
UP	User Profile
VBF	Vital Business Function
VOI	Value on Investment
WIP	Work in Progress

Definitions list

The publication names included in parentheses after the name of a term identify where a reader can find more information about that term. This is either because the term is primarily used by that publication or because additional useful information about that term can be found there. Terms without a publication name associated with them may be used generally by several publications, or may not be defined in any greater detail than can be found in the glossary, i.e. we only point readers to somewhere they can expect to expand on their knowledge or to see a greater context. Terms with multiple publication names are expanded on in multiple publications.

Where the definition of a term includes another term, those related terms are highlighted in a second colour. This is designed to help the reader with their understanding by pointing them to additional definitions that are all part of the original term they were interested in. The form '*See also* Term X, Term Y' is used at the end of a definition where an important related term is not used with the text of the definition itself.

Acceptance

Formal agreement that an IT Service, Process, Plan, or other Deliverable is complete, accurate, Reliable and meets its specified Requirements. Acceptance is usually preceded by Evaluation or Testing and is often required before proceeding to the next stage of a Project or Process.

Access Management

(Service Operation) The Process responsible for allowing Users to make use of IT Services, data, or other Assets. Access Management helps to protect the Confidentiality, Integrity and Availability of Assets by ensuring that only authorized Users are able to access or modify the Assets. Access Management is sometimes referred to as Rights Management or Identity Management.

Accounting

(Service Strategy) The Process responsible for identifying actual Costs of delivering IT Services, comparing these with budgeted costs, and managing variance from the Budget.

Accredited

Officially authorized to carry out a Role. For example an Accredited body may be authorized to provide training or to conduct Audits.

Activity

A set of actions designed to achieve a particular result. Activities are usually defined as part of Processes or Plans, and are documented in Procedures.

Agreement

A Document that describes a formal understanding between two or more parties. An Agreement is not legally binding, unless it forms part of a Contract. *See also* Service Level Agreement, Operational Level Agreement.

Alert

(Service Operation) A warning that a threshold has been reached, something has changed, or a Failure has occurred. Alerts are often created and managed by System Management tools and are managed by the Event Management Process.

Application

Software that provides Functions that are required by an IT Service. Each Application may be part of more than one IT Service. An Application runs on one or more Servers or Clients. *See also* Application Management.

Application Management

(Service Design) (Service Operation) The Function responsible for managing Applications throughout their Lifecycle.

Application Sizing

(Service Design) The Activity responsible for understanding the Resource Requirements needed to support a new Application, or a major Change to an existing Application. Application Sizing helps to ensure that the IT Service can meet its agreed Service Level Targets for Capacity and Performance.

Architecture

(Service Design) The structure of a System or IT Service, including the Relationships of Components to each other and to the environment they are in. Architecture also includes the Standards and Guidelines that guide the design and evolution of the System.

Assessment

Inspection and analysis to check whether a Standard or set of Guidelines is being followed, that Records are accurate, or that Efficiency and Effectiveness targets are being met. *See also* Audit.

Asset

(Service Strategy) Any Resource or Capability. Assets of a Service Provider including anything that could contribute to the delivery of a Service. Assets can be one of the following types: Management, Organization, Process, Knowledge, People, Information, Applications, Infrastructure, and Financial Capital.

Asset Management

(Service Transition) Asset Management is the Process responsible for tracking and reporting the value and ownership of financial Assets throughout their Lifecycle. Asset Management is part of an overall Service Asset and Configuration Management Process.

Attribute

(Service Transition) A piece of information about a Configuration Item. Examples are: name, location, Version number, and Cost. Attributes of CIs are recorded in the Configuration Management Database (CMDB). *See also* Relationship.

Audit

Formal inspection and verification to check whether a Standard or set of Guidelines is being followed, that Records are accurate, or that Efficiency and Effectiveness targets are being met. An Audit may be carried out by internal or external groups. *See also* Certification, Assessment.

Authority Matrix

See RACI.

Automatic Call Distribution (ACD)

(Service Operation) Use of Information Technology to direct an incoming telephone call to the most appropriate person in the shortest possible time. ACD is sometimes called Automated Call Distribution.

Availability

(Service Design) Ability of a Configuration Item or IT Service to perform its agreed Function when required. Availability is determined by Reliability, Maintainability, Serviceability, Performance, and Security. Availability is usually calculated as a percentage. This calculation is often based on Agreed Service Time and Downtime. It is Best Practice to calculate Availability using measurements of the Business output of the IT Service.

Availability Management

(Service Design) The Process responsible for defining, analysing, Planning, measuring and improving all aspects of the Availability of IT services. Availability Management is responsible for ensuring that all IT Infrastructure, Processes, Tools, Roles, etc. are appropriate for the agreed Service Level Targets for Availability.

Availability Management Information System (AMIS)

(Service Design) A virtual repository of all Availability Management data, usually stored in multiple physical locations. *See also* Service Knowledge Management System.

Balanced Scorecard

(Continual Service Improvement) A management tool developed by Drs. Robert Kaplan (Harvard Business School) and David Norton. A Balanced Scorecard enables a Strategy to be broken down into Key Performance Indicators. Performance against the KPIs is used to demonstrate how well the Strategy is being achieved. A Balanced Scorecard has four major areas, each of which has a small number of KPIs. The same four areas are considered at different levels of detail throughout the Organization.

Baseline

(Continual Service Improvement) A Benchmark used as a reference point. For example:

- An ITSM Baseline can be used as a starting point to measure the effect of a Service Improvement Plan
- A Performance Baseline can be used to measure changes in Performance over the lifetime of an IT Service
- A Configuration Management Baseline can be used to enable the IT Infrastructure to be restored to a known Configuration if a Change or Release fails.

Benchmark

(Continual Service Improvement) The recorded state of something at a specific point in time. A Benchmark can be created for a Configuration, a Process, or any other set of data. For example, a benchmark can be used in:

- Continual Service Improvement, to establish the current state for managing improvements
- Capacity Management, to document performance characteristics during normal operations.

See also Benchmarking, Baseline.

Benchmarking

(Continual Service Improvement) Comparing a Benchmark with a Baseline or with Best Practice. The term Benchmarking is also used to mean creating a series of Benchmarks over time, and comparing the results to measure progress or improvement.

Best Practice

Proven Activities or Processes that have been successfully used by multiple Organizations. ITIL is an example of Best Practice.

Budget

A list of all the money an Organization or Business Unit plans to receive, and plans to pay out, over a specified period of time. *See also* Budgeting, Planning.

Budgeting

The Activity of predicting and controlling the spending of money. Consists of a periodic negotiation cycle to set future Budgets (usually annual) and the day-to-day monitoring and adjusting of current Budgets.

Business

(Service Strategy) An overall corporate entity or Organization formed of a number of Business Units. In the context of ITSM, the term Business includes public sector and not-for-profit organizations, as well as companies. An IT Service Provider provides IT Services to a Customer within a Business. The IT Service Provider may be part of the same Business as its Customer (Internal Service Provider), or part of another Business (External Service Provider).

Business Capacity Management (BCM)

(Service Design) In the context of ITSM, Business Capacity Management is the Activity responsible for understanding future Business Requirements for use in the Capacity Plan. *See also* Service Capacity Management.

Business Case

(Service Strategy) Justification for a significant item of expenditure. Includes information about Costs, benefits, options, issues, Risks, and possible problems.

Business Continuity Management (BCM)

(Service Design) The Business Process responsible for managing Risks that could seriously impact the Business. BCM safeguards the interests of key stakeholders, reputation, brand and value-creating activities. The BCM Process involves reducing Risks to an acceptable level and planning for the recovery of Business Processes should a disruption to the Business occur. BCM sets the Objectives, Scope and Requirements for IT Service Continuity Management.

Business Customer

(Service Strategy) A recipient of a product or a Service from the Business. For example, if the Business is a car manufacturer then the Business Customer is someone who buys a car.

Business Impact Analysis (BIA)

(Service Strategy) BIA is the Activity in Business Continuity Management that identifies Vital Business Functions and their dependencies. These dependencies may include Suppliers, people, other Business Processes, IT Services, etc. BIA defines the recovery requirements for IT Services. These requirements include Recovery Time Objectives, Recovery Point Objectives and minimum Service Level Targets for each IT Service.

Business Objective

(Service Strategy) The Objective of a Business Process, or of the Business as a whole. Business Objectives support the Business Vision, provide guidance for the IT Strategy, and are often supported by IT Services.

Business Operations

(Service Strategy) The day-to-day execution, monitoring and management of Business Processes.

Business Perspective

(Continual Service Improvement) An understanding of the Service Provider and IT Services from the point of view of the Business, and an understanding of the Business from the point of view of the Service Provider.

Business Process

A Process that is owned and carried out by the Business. A Business Process contributes to the delivery of a product or Service to a Business Customer. For example, a retailer may have a purchasing Process that helps to deliver Services to its Business Customers. Many Business Processes rely on IT Services.

Business Relationship Management

(Service Strategy) The Process or Function responsible for maintaining a Relationship with the Business. Business Relationship Management usually includes:

- Managing personal Relationships with Business managers
- Providing input to Service Portfolio Management
- Ensuring that the IT Service Provider is satisfying the Business needs of the Customers

This Process has strong links with Service Level Management.

Business Service

An IT Service that directly supports a Business Process, as opposed to an Infrastructure Service, which is used internally by the IT Service Provider and is not usually visible to the Business.

The term Business Service is also used to mean a Service that is delivered to Business Customers by Business Units. For example, delivery of financial services to Customers of a bank, or goods to the Customers of a retail store. Successful delivery of Business Services often depends on one or more IT Services.

Business Unit

(Service Strategy) A segment of the Business that has its own Plans, Metrics, income and Costs. Each Business Unit owns Assets and uses these to create value for Customers in the form of goods and Services.

Call

(Service Operation) A telephone call to the Service Desk from a User. A Call could result in an Incident or a Service Request being logged.

Capability

(Service Strategy) The ability of an Organization, person, Process, Application, Configuration Item or IT Service to carry out an Activity. Capabilities are intangible Assets of an Organization. *See also* Resource.

Capability Maturity Model Integration (CMMI)

(Continual Service Improvement) Capability Maturity Model(r) Integration (CMMI) is a process improvement approach developed by the Software Engineering Institute (SEI) of Carnegie Melon University, US. CMMI provides organizations with the essential elements of effective processes. It can be used to guide process improvement across a project, a division, or an entire organization. CMMI helps integrate traditionally separate organizational functions, set process improvement goals and priorities, provide guidance for quality processes, and provide a point of reference for appraising current processes. See www.sei.cmu.edu/cmmi for more information. *See also* Maturity.

Capacity

(Service Design) The maximum Throughput that a Configuration Item or IT Service can deliver whilst meeting agreed Service Level Targets. For some types of CI, Capacity may be the size or volume, for example a disk drive.

Capacity Management

(Service Design) The Process responsible for ensuring that the Capacity of IT Services and the IT Infrastructure is able to deliver agreed Service Level Targets in a Cost Effective and timely manner. Capacity Management considers all Resources required to deliver the IT Service, and plans for short-, medium- and long-term Business Requirements.

Capacity Management Information System (CMIS)

(Service Design) A virtual repository of all Capacity Management data, usually stored in multiple physical locations. *See also* Service Knowledge Management System.

Capacity Planning

(Service Design) The Activity within Capacity Management responsible for creating a Capacity Plan.

Category

A named group of things that have something in common. Categories are used to group similar things together. For example, Cost Types are used to group similar types of Cost. Incident Categories are used to group similar types of Incident, CI Types are used to group similar types of Configuration Item.

Certification

Issuing a certificate to confirm Compliance to a Standard. Certification includes a formal Audit by an independent and Accredited body. The term Certification is also used to mean awarding a certificate to verify that a person has achieved a qualification.

Change

(Service Transition) The addition, modification or removal of anything that could have an effect on IT Services. The Scope should include all IT Services, Configuration Items, Processes, Documentation, etc.

Change Advisory Board (CAB)

(Service Transition) A group of people that advises the Change Manager in the Assessment, prioritization and scheduling of Changes. This board is usually made up of representatives from all areas within the IT Service Provider, representatives from the Business and Third Parties such as Suppliers.

Change Management

(Service Transition) The Process responsible for controlling the Lifecycle of all Changes. The primary objective of Change Management is to enable beneficial Changes to be made, with minimum disruption to IT Services.

Change Request

See Request for Change.

Change Schedule

(Service Transition) A Document that lists all approved Changes and their planned implementation dates. A Change Schedule is sometimes called a Forward Schedule of Change, even though it also contains information about Changes that have already been implemented.

Charging

(Service Strategy) Requiring payment for IT Services. Charging for IT Services is optional, and many Organizations choose to treat their IT Service Provider as a Cost Centre.

Client

A generic term that means a Customer, the Business or a Business Customer. For example, Client Manager may be used as a synonym for Account Manager.

The term client is also used to mean:

- A computer that is used directly by a User, for example a PC, Handheld Computer, or Workstation
- The part of a Client-Server Application that the User directly interfaces with. For example an e-mail Client.

Closed

(Service Operation) The final Status in the Lifecycle of an Incident, Problem, Change, etc. When the Status is Closed, no further action is taken.

Closure

(Service Operation) The act of changing the Status of an Incident, Problem, Change, etc. to Closed.

COBIT

(Continual Service Improvement) Control Objectives for Information and related Technology (COBIT) provides guidance and Best Practice for the management of IT Processes. COBIT is published by the IT Governance Institute. See www.isaca.org for more information.

Code of Practice

A Guideline published by a public body or a Standards Organization, such as ISO or BSI. Many Standards consist of a Code of Practice and a Specification. The Code of Practice describes recommended Best Practice.

Compliance

Ensuring that a Standard or set of Guidelines is followed, or that proper, consistent accounting or other practices are being employed.

Component

A general term that is used to mean one part of something more complex. For example, a computer System may be a component of an IT Service, an Application may be a Component of a Release Unit. Components that need to be managed should be Configuration Items.

Component Capacity Management (CCM)

(Service Design) (Continual Service Improvement) The Process responsible for understanding the Capacity, Utilization, and Performance of Configuration Items. Data is collected, recorded and analysed for use in the Capacity Plan. *See also* Service Capacity Management.

Component Failure Impact Analysis (CFIA)

(Service Design) A technique that helps to identify the impact of CI failure on IT Services. A matrix is created with IT Services on one edge and CIs on the other. This enables the identification of critical CIs (that could cause the failure of multiple IT Services) and of fragile IT Services (that have multiple Single Points of Failure).

Confidentiality

(Service Design) A security principle that requires that data should only be accessed by authorized people.

Configuration

(Service Transition) A generic term, used to describe a group of Configuration Items that work together to deliver an IT Service, or a recognizable part of an IT Service. Configuration is also used to describe the parameter settings for one or more CIs.

Configuration Item (CI)

(Service Transition) Any Component that needs to be managed in order to deliver an IT Service. Information about each CI is recorded in a Configuration Record within the Configuration Management System and is maintained throughout its Lifecycle by Configuration Management. CIs are under the control of Change Management. CIs typically include IT Services, hardware, software, buildings, people, and formal documentation such as Process documentation and SLAs.

Configuration Management

(Service Transition) The Process responsible for maintaining information about Configuration Items required to deliver an IT Service, including their Relationships. This information is managed throughout the Lifecycle of the CI. Configuration Management is part of an overall Service Asset and Configuration Management Process.

Configuration Management Database (CMDB)

(Service Transition) A database used to store Configuration Records throughout their Lifecycle. The Configuration Management System maintains one or more CMDBs, and each CMDB stores Attributes of CIs, and Relationships with other CIs.

Configuration Management System (CMS)

(Service Transition) A set of tools and databases that are used to manage an IT Service Provider's Configuration data. The CMS also includes information about Incidents, Problems, Known Errors, Changes and Releases; and may contain data about employees, Suppliers, locations, Business Units, Customers and Users. The CMS includes tools for collecting, storing, managing, updating, and presenting data about all Configuration Items and their Relationships. The CMS is maintained by Configuration Management and is used by all IT Service Management Processes. *See also* Configuration Management Database, Service Knowledge Management System.

Continual Service Improvement (CSI)

(Continual Service Improvement) A stage in the Lifecycle of an IT Service and the title of one of the Core ITIL publications. Continual Service Improvement is responsible for managing improvements to IT Service Management Processes and IT Services. The Performance of the IT Service Provider is continually measured and improvements are made to Processes, IT Services and IT Infrastructure in order to increase Efficiency, Effectiveness, and Cost Effectiveness. *See also* Plan-Do-Check-Act.

Contract

A legally binding Agreement between two or more parties.

Control

A means of managing a Risk, ensuring that a Business Objective is achieved, or ensuring that a Process is followed. Example Controls include Policies, Procedures, Roles, RAID, door locks, etc. A control is sometimes called a Countermeasure or safeguard. Control also means to manage the utilization or behaviour of a Configuration Item, System or IT Service.

Control Objectives for Information and related Technology (COBIT)

See COBIT.

Control Perspective

(Service Strategy) An approach to the management of IT Services, Processes, Functions, Assets, etc. There can be several different Control Perspectives on the same IT Service, Process, etc., allowing different individuals or teams to focus on what is important and relevant to their specific Role. Example Control Perspectives include Reactive and Proactive management within IT Operations, or a Lifecycle view for an Application Project team.

Cost

The amount of money spent on a specific Activity, IT Service, or Business Unit. Costs consist of real cost (money), notional cost such as people's time, and Depreciation.

Cost Centre

(Service Strategy) A Business Unit or Project to which costs are assigned. A Cost Centre does not charge for Services provided. An IT Service Provider can be run as a Cost Centre or a Profit Centre.

Cost Effectiveness

A measure of the balance between the Effectiveness and Cost of a Service, Process or activity, A Cost Effective Process is one that achieves its Objectives at minimum Cost. *See also* KPI, Return on Investment, Value for Money.

Cost Management

(Service Strategy) A general term that is used to refer to Budgeting and Accounting, sometimes used as a synonym for Financial Management.

Countermeasure

Can be used to refer to any type of Control. The term Countermeasure is most often used when referring to measures that increase Resilience, Fault Tolerance or Reliability of an IT Service.

Course Corrections

Changes made to a Plan or Activity that has already started, to ensure that it will meet its Objectives. Course corrections are made as a result of Monitoring progress.

Critical Success Factor (CSF)

Something that must happen if a Process, Project, Plan, or IT Service is to succeed. KPIs are used to measure the achievement of each CSF. For example a CSF of 'protect IT Services when making Changes' could be measured by KPIs such as 'percentage reduction of unsuccessful Changes', 'percentage reduction in Changes causing Incidents', etc.

Culture

A set of values that is shared by a group of people, including expectations about how people should behave, their ideas, beliefs, and practices. *See also* Vision.

Customer

Someone who buys goods or Services. The Customer of an IT Service Provider is the person or group that defines and agrees the Service Level Targets. The term Customers is also sometimes informally used to mean Users, for example 'this is a Customer-focused Organization'.

Dashboard

(Service Operation) A graphical representation of overall IT Service Performance and Availability. Dashboard images may be updated in real-time, and can also be included in management reports and web pages. Dashboards can be used to support Service Level Management, Event Management or Incident Diagnosis.

Data-to-Information-to-Knowledge-to-Wisdom (DIKW)

A way of understanding the relationships between data, information, knowledge, and wisdom. DIKW shows how each of these builds on the others.

Deliverable

Something that must be provided to meet a commitment in a Service Level Agreement or a Contract. Deliverable is also used in a more informal way to mean a planned output of any Process.

Demand Management

Activities that understand and influence Customer demand for Services and the provision of Capacity to meet these demands. At a Strategic level Demand Management can involve analysis of Patterns of Business Activity and User Profiles. At a tactical level it can involve use of Differential Charging to encourage Customers to use IT Services at less busy times. *See also* Capacity Management.

Deming Cycle

See Plan-Do-Check-Act.

Dependency

The direct or indirect reliance of one Process or Activity on another.

Deployment

(Service Transition) The Activity responsible for movement of new or changed hardware, software, documentation, Process, etc. to the Live Environment. Deployment is part of the Release and Deployment Management Process.

Design

(Service Design) An Activity or Process that identifies Requirements and then defines a solution that is able to meet these Requirements. *See also* Service Design.

Detection

(Service Operation) A stage in the Incident Lifecycle. Detection results in the Incident becoming known to the Service Provider. Detection can be automatic, or can be the result of a user logging an Incident.

Development

(Service Design) The Process responsible for creating or modifying an IT Service or Application. Also used to mean the Role or group that carries out Development work.

Diagnosis

(Service Operation) A stage in the Incident and Problem Lifecycles. The purpose of Diagnosis is to identify a Workaround for an Incident or the Root Cause of a Problem.

Document

Information in readable form. A Document may be paper or electronic. For example, a Policy statement, Service Level Agreement, Incident Record, diagram of computer room layout. *See also* Record.

Downtime

(Service Design) (Service Operation) The time when a Configuration Item or IT Service is not Available during its Agreed Service Time. The Availability of an IT Service is often calculated from Agreed Service Time and Downtime.

Driver

Something that influences Strategy, Objectives or Requirements. For example, new legislation or the actions of competitors.

Economies of scale

(Service Strategy) The reduction in average Cost that is possible from increasing the usage of an IT Service or Asset.

Effectiveness

(Continual Service Improvement) A measure of whether the Objectives of a Process, Service or Activity have been achieved. An Effective Process or activity is one that achieves its agreed Objectives. *See also* KPI.

Efficiency

(Continual Service Improvement) A measure of whether the right amount of resources has been used to deliver a Process, Service or Activity. An Efficient Process achieves its Objectives with the minimum amount of time, money, people or other resources. *See also* KPI.

Environment

(Service Transition) A subset of the IT Infrastructure that is used for a particular purpose. For Example: Live Environment, Test Environment, Build Environment. It is possible for multiple Environments to share a Configuration Item, for example Test and Live Environments may use different partitions on a single mainframe computer. Also used in the term Physical Environment to mean the accommodation, air conditioning, power system, etc.

Environment is also used as a generic term to mean the external conditions that influence or affect something.

Error

(Service Operation) A design flaw or malfunction that causes a Failure of one or more Configuration Items or IT Services. A mistake made by a person or a faulty Process that affects a CI or IT Service is also an Error.

Escalation

(Service Operation) An Activity that obtains additional Resources when these are needed to meet Service Level Targets or Customer expectations. Escalation may be needed within any IT Service Management Process, but is most commonly associated with Incident Management, Problem Management and the management of Customer complaints. There are two types of Escalation, Functional Escalation and Hierarchic Escalation.

eSourcing Capability Model for Service Providers (eSCM-SP)

(Service Strategy) A framework to help IT Service Providers develop their IT Service Management Capabilities from a Service Sourcing perspective. eSCM-SP was developed by Carnegie Mellon University, US.

Evaluation

(Service Transition) The Process responsible for assessing a new or Changed IT Service to ensure that Risks have been managed and to help determine whether to proceed with the Change.

Evaluation is also used to mean comparing an actual Outcome with the intended Outcome, or comparing one alternative with another.

Event

(Service Operation) A change of state that has significance for the management of a Configuration Item or IT Service.

The term Event is also used to mean an Alert or notification created by any IT Service, Configuration Item or Monitoring tool. Events typically require IT Operations personnel to take actions, and often lead to Incidents being logged.

Event Management

(Service Operation) The Process responsible for managing Events throughout their Lifecycle. Event Management is one of the main Activities of IT Operations.

Expanded Incident Lifecycle

(Availability Management) Detailed stages in the Lifecycle of an Incident. The stages are Detection, Diagnosis, Repair, Recovery, Restoration. The Expanded Incident Lifecycle is used to help understand all contributions to the Impact of Incidents and to Plan how these could be controlled or reduced.

External Customer

A Customer who works for a different Business to the IT Service Provider. *See also* External Service Provider, Internal Customer.

External Service Provider

(Service Strategy) An IT Service Provider that is part of a different Organization to its Customer. An IT Service Provider may have both Internal Customers and External Customers.

Failure

(Service Operation) Loss of ability to Operate to Specification, or to deliver the required output. The term Failure may be used when referring to IT Services, Processes, Activities, Configuration Items, etc. A Failure often causes an Incident.

Fault

See Error.

Fault Tolerance

(Service Design) The ability of an IT Service or Configuration Item to continue to Operate correctly after Failure of a Component part. *See also* Resilience, Countermeasure.

Fault Tree Analysis (FTA)

(Service Design) (Continual Service Improvement) A technique that can be used to determine the chain of events that leads to a Problem. Fault Tree Analysis represents a chain of events using Boolean notation in a diagram.

Financial Management

(Service Strategy) The Function and Processes responsible for managing an IT Service Provider's Budgeting, Accounting and Charging Requirements.

Fit for Purpose

An informal term used to describe a Process, Configuration Item, IT Service, etc. that is capable of meeting its objectives or Service Levels. Being Fit for Purpose requires suitable design, implementation, control and maintenance.

Fulfilment

Performing Activities to meet a need or Requirement. For example, by providing a new IT Service, or meeting a Service Request.

Function

A team or group of people and the tools they use to carry out one or more Processes or Activities. For example the Service Desk.

The term Function also has two other meanings:

- An intended purpose of a Configuration Item, Person, Team, Process, or IT Service. For example one Function of an e-mail Service may be to store and forward outgoing mails, one Function of a Business Process may be to dispatch goods to Customers.
- To perform the intended purpose correctly, 'The computer is Functioning'.

Gap Analysis

(Continual Service Improvement) An Activity that compares two sets of data and identifies the differences. Gap Analysis is commonly used to compare a set of Requirements with actual delivery. *See also* Benchmarking.

Governance

Ensuring that Policies and Strategy are actually implemented, and that required Processes are correctly followed. Governance includes defining Roles and responsibilities, measuring and reporting, and taking actions to resolve any issues identified.

Guideline

A Document describing Best Practice, which recommends what should be done. Compliance with a guideline is not normally enforced. *See also* Standard.

Help Desk

(Service Operation) A point of contact for Users to log Incidents. A Help Desk is usually more technically focussed than a Service Desk and does not provide a Single Point of Contact for all interaction. The term Help Desk is often used as a synonym for Service Desk.

Impact

(Service Operation) (Service Transition) A measure of the effect of an Incident, Problem or Change on Business Processes. Impact is often based on how Service Levels will be affected. Impact and Urgency are used to assign Priority.

Incident

(Service Operation) An unplanned interruption to an IT Service or reduction in the Quality of an IT Service. Failure of a Configuration Item that has not yet impacted Service is also an Incident. For example Failure of one disk from a mirror set.

Incident Management

(Service Operation) The Process responsible for managing the Lifecycle of all Incidents. The primary Objective of Incident Management is to return the IT Service to Customers as quickly as possible.

Incident Record

(Service Operation) A Record containing the details of an Incident. Each Incident record documents the Lifecycle of a single Incident.

Indirect Cost

(Service Strategy) A Cost of providing an IT Service, which cannot be allocated in full to a specific customer. For example, the Cost of providing shared Servers or software licences. Also known as Overhead.

Information Security Management (ISM)

(Service Design) The Process that ensures the Confidentiality, Integrity and Availability of an Organization's Assets, information, data and IT Services. Information Security Management usually forms part of an Organizational approach to Security Management that has a wider scope than the IT Service Provider, and includes handling of paper, building access, phone calls, etc., for the entire Organization.

Information Security Management System (ISMS)

(Service Design) The framework of Policy, Processes, Standards, Guidelines and tools that ensures an Organization can achieve its Information Security Management Objectives.

Information Technology (IT)

The use of technology for the storage, communication or processing of information. The technology typically includes computers, telecommunications, Applications and other software. The information may include Business data, voice, images, video, etc. Information Technology is often used to support Business Processes through IT Services.

Integrity

(Service Design) A security principle that ensures data and Configuration Items are modified only by authorized personnel and Activities. Integrity considers all possible causes of modification, including software and hardware Failure, environmental Events, and human intervention.

Internal Customer

A Customer who works for the same Business as the IT Service Provider. *See also* Internal Service Provider, External Customer.

Internal Service Provider

(Service Strategy) An IT Service Provider that is part of the same Organization as its Customer. An IT Service Provider may have both Internal Customers and External Customers.

International Organization for Standardization (ISO)

The International Organization for Standardization (ISO) is the world's largest developer of Standards. ISO is a non-governmental organization that is a network of the national standards institutes of 156 countries. See www.iso.org for further information about ISO.

International Standards Organization

See International Organization for Standardization (ISO).

Ishikawa Diagram

(Service Operation) (Continual Service Improvement) A technique that helps a team to identify all the possible causes of a Problem. Originally devised by Kaoru Ishikawa, the output of this technique is a diagram that looks like a fishbone.

ISO 9000

A generic term that refers to a number of international Standards and Guidelines for Quality Management Systems. See www.iso.org for more information. *See also* ISO.

ISO/IEC 17799

(Continual Service Improvement) ISO Code of Practice for Information Security Management. *See also* Standard.

ISO/IEC 20000

ISO Specification and Code of Practice for IT Service Management. ISO/IEC 20000 is aligned with ITIL Best Practice.

ISO/IEC 27001

(Service Design) (Continual Service Improvement) ISO Specification for Information Security Management. The corresponding Code of Practice is ISO/IEC 17799. *See also* Standard.

IT Infrastructure

All of the hardware, software, networks, facilities, etc. that are required to develop, Test, deliver, Monitor, Control or support IT Services. The term IT Infrastructure includes all of the Information Technology but not the associated people, Processes and documentation.

IT Operations Management

(Service Operation) The Function within an IT Service Provider that performs the daily Activities needed to manage IT Services and the supporting IT Infrastructure. IT Operations Management includes IT Operations Control and Facilities Management.

IT Service

A Service provided to one or more Customers by an IT Service Provider. An IT Service is based on the use of Information Technology and supports the Customer's Business Processes. An IT Service is made up from a combination of people, Processes and technology and should be defined in a Service Level Agreement.

IT Service Continuity Management (ITSCM)

(Service Design) The Process responsible for managing Risks that could seriously affect IT Services. ITSCM ensures that the IT Service Provider can always provide minimum agreed Service Levels, by reducing the Risk to an acceptable level and Planning for the Recovery of IT Services. ITSCM should be designed to support Business Continuity Management.

IT Service Management (ITSM)

The implementation and management of Quality IT Services that meet the needs of the Business. IT Service Management are performed by IT Service Providers through an appropriate mix of people, Process and Information Technology. *See also* Service Management.

IT Service Management Forum (itSMF)

The IT Service Management Forum is an independent Organization dedicated to promoting a professional approach to IT Service Management. The itSMF is a not-for-profit membership Organization with representation in many countries around the world (itSMF Chapters). The itSMF and its membership contribute to the development of ITIL and associated IT Service Management Standards. See www.itsmf.com for more information.

IT Service Provider

(Service Strategy) A Service Provider that provides IT Services to Internal Customers or External Customers.

ITIL

A set of Best Practice guidance for IT Service Management. ITIL is owned by the OGC and consists of a series of publications giving guidance on the provision of Quality IT Services, and on the Processes and facilities needed to support them. See www.itil.co.uk for more information.

Job Description

A Document that defines the Roles, responsibilities, skills and knowledge required by a particular person. One Job Description can include multiple Roles, for example the Roles of Configuration Manager and Change Manager may be carried out by one person.

Kepner & Tregoe Analysis

(Service Operation) (Continual Service Improvement) A structured approach to Problem solving. The Problem is analysed in terms of what, where, when and extent. Possible causes are identified. The most probable cause is tested. The true cause is verified.

Key Performance Indicator (KPI)

(Service design) (Continual Service Improvement) A Metric that is used to help manage a Process, IT Service or Activity. Many Metrics may be measured, but only the most important of these are defined as KPIs and used to actively manage and report on the Process, IT Service or Activity. KPIs should be selected to ensure that Efficiency, Effectiveness, and Cost Effectiveness are all managed. *See also* Critical Success Factor.

Knowledge Base

(Service Transition) A logical database containing the data used by the Service Knowledge Management System.

Knowledge Management

(Service Transition) The Process responsible for gathering, analysing, storing and sharing knowledge and information within an Organization. The primary purpose of Knowledge Management is to improve Efficiency by reducing the need to rediscover knowledge. See also Data-to-Information-to-Knowledge-to-Wisdom and Service Knowledge Management System.

Lifecycle

The various stages in the life of an IT Service, Configuration Item, Incident, Problem, Change, etc. The Lifecycle defines the Categories for Status and the Status transitions that are permitted. For example:

- The Lifecycle of an Application includes Requirements, Design, Build, Deploy, Operate, Optimize
- The Expanded Incident Lifecycle includes Detect, Respond, Diagnose, Repair, Recover, Restore
- The Lifecycle of a Server may include: Ordered, Received, In Test, Live, Disposed, etc.

Live Environment

(Service Transition) A controlled Environment containing Live Configuration Items used to deliver IT Services to Customers.

Maintainability

(Service Design) A measure of how quickly and Effectively a Configuration Item or IT Service can be restored to normal working after a Failure. Maintainability is often measured and reported as MTRS.

Maintainability is also used in the context of Software or IT Service Development to mean ability to be Changed or Repaired easily.

Managed Services

(Service Strategy) A perspective on IT Services which emphasizes the fact that they are managed. The term Managed Services is also used as a synonym for Outsourced IT Services.

Management Information

Information that is used to support decision making by managers. Management Information is often generated automatically by tools supporting the various IT Service Management Processes. Management Information often includes the values of KPIs such as 'Percentage of Changes leading to Incidents', or 'first-time fix rate'.

Management of Risk (M_o_R)

The OGC methodology for managing Risks. M_o_R includes all the Activities required to identify and Control the exposure to Risk, which may have an impact on the achievement of an Organization's Business Objectives. See www.m-o-r.org for more details.

Management System

The framework of Policy, Processes and Functions that ensures an Organization can achieve its Objectives.

Maturity

(Continual Service Improvement) A measure of the Reliability, Efficiency and Effectiveness of a Process, Function, Organization, etc. The most mature Processes and Functions are formally aligned to Business Objectives and Strategy, and are supported by a framework for continual improvement.

Maturity Level

A named level in a Maturity model such as the Carnegie Mellon Capability Maturity Model Integration.

Mean Time Between Failures (MTBF)

(Service Design) A Metric for measuring and reporting Reliability. MTBF is the average time that a Configuration Item or IT Service can perform its agreed Function without interruption. This is measured from when the CI or IT Service starts working, until it next fails.

Metric

(Continual Service Improvement) Something that is measured and reported to help manage a Process, IT Service or Activity. *See also* KPI.

Middleware

(Service Design) Software that connects two or more software Components or Applications. Middleware is usually purchased from a Supplier, rather than developed within the IT Service Provider.

Mission Statement

The Mission Statement of an Organization is a short but complete description of the overall purpose and intentions of that Organization. It states what is to be achieved, but not how this should be done.

Model

A representation of a System, Process, IT Service, Configuration Item, etc. that is used to help understand or predict future behaviour.

Modelling

A technique that is used to predict the future behaviour of a System, Process, IT Service, Configuration Item, etc. Modelling is commonly used in Financial Management, Capacity Management and Availability Management.

Monitor Control Loop

(Service Operation) Monitoring the output of a Task, Process, IT Service or Configuration Item; comparing this output to a predefined Norm; and taking appropriate action based on this comparison.

Monitoring

(Service Operation) Repeated observation of a Configuration Item, IT Service or Process to detect Events and to ensure that the current status is known.

Objective

The defined purpose or aim of a Process, an Activity or an Organization as a whole. Objectives are usually expressed as measurable targets. The term Objective is also informally used to mean a Requirement. *See also* Outcome.

Office of Government Commerce (OGC)

OGC owns the ITIL brand (copyright and trademark). OGC is a UK Government department that supports the delivery of the government's procurement agenda through its work in collaborative procurement and in raising levels of procurement skills and capability with departments. It also provides support for complex public sector projects.

Operate

To perform as expected. A Process or Configuration Item is said to Operate if it is delivering the Required outputs. Operate also means to perform one or more Operations. For example, to Operate a computer is to do the day-to-day Operations needed for it to perform as expected.

Operation

(Service Operation) Day-to-day management of an IT Service, System, or other Configuration Item. Operation is also used to mean any pre-defined Activity or Transaction. For example loading a magnetic tape, accepting money at a point of sale, or reading data from a disk drive.

Operational

The lowest of three levels of Planning and delivery (Strategic, Tactical, Operational). Operational Activities include the day-to-day or short-term Planning or delivery of a Business Process or IT Service Management Process. The term Operational is also a synonym for Live.

Operational Level Agreement (OLA)

(Service Design) (Continual Service Improvement) An Agreement between an IT Service Provider and another part of the same Organization. An OLA supports the IT Service Provider's delivery of IT Services to Customers. The OLA defines the goods or Services to be provided and the responsibilities of both parties. For example there could be an OLA:

- Between the IT Service Provider and a procurement department to obtain hardware in agreed times
- Between the Service Desk and a Support Group to provide Incident Resolution in agreed times.

See also Service Level Agreement.

Operations Management

See IT Operations Management.

Optimize

Review, Plan and request Changes, in order to obtain the maximum Efficiency and Effectiveness from a Process, Configuration Item, Application, etc.

Organization

A company, legal entity or other institution. Examples of Organizations that are not companies include International Standards Organization or itSMF. The term Organization is sometimes used to refer to any entity that has People, Resources and Budgets. For example a Project or Business Unit.

Outcome

The result of carrying out an Activity; following a Process; delivering an IT Service, etc. The term Outcome is used to refer to intended results, as well as to actual results. *See also* Objective.

Outsourcing

(Service Strategy) Using an External Service Provider to manage IT Services.

Overhead

See Indirect cost.

Partnership

A relationship between two Organizations that involves working closely together for common goals or mutual benefit. The IT Service Provider should have a Partnership with the Business, and with Third Parties who are critical to the delivery of IT Services.

Performance

A measure of what is achieved or delivered by a System, person, team, Process, or IT Service.

Performance Management

(Continual Service Improvement) The Process responsible for day-to-day Capacity Management Activities. These include monitoring, threshold detection, Performance analysis and Tuning, and implementing changes related to Performance and Capacity.

Pilot

(Service Transition) A limited Deployment of an IT Service, a Release or a Process to the Live Environment. A pilot is used to reduce Risk and to gain User feedback and Acceptance. *See also* Test, Evaluation.

Plan

A detailed proposal that describes the Activities and Resources needed to achieve an Objective. For example a Plan to implement a new IT Service or Process. ISO/IEC 20000 requires a Plan for the management of each IT Service Management Process.

Plan-Do-Check-Act

(Continual Service Improvement) A four-stage cycle for Process management, attributed to Edward Deming. Plan-Do-Check-Act is also called the Deming Cycle.

PLAN: Design or revise Processes that support the IT Services.

DO: Implement the Plan and manage the Processes.

CHECK: Measure the Processes and IT Services, compare with Objectives and produce reports.

ACT: Plan and implement Changes to improve the Processes.

Planning

An Activity responsible for creating one or more Plans. For example, Capacity Planning.

PMBOK

A Project management Standard maintained and published by the Project Management Institute. PMBOK stands for Project Management Body of Knowledge. See www.pmi.org for more information. *See also* PRINCE2.

Policy

Formally documented management expectations and intentions. Policies are used to direct decisions, and to ensure consistent and appropriate development and implementation of Processes, Standards, Roles, Activities, IT Infrastructure, etc.

Post-Implementation Review (PIR)

A Review that takes place after a Change or a Project has been implemented. A PIR determines if the Change or Project was successful, and identifies opportunities for improvement.

Practice

A way of working, or a way in which work must be done. Practices can include Activities, Processes, Functions, Standards and Guidelines. *See also* Best Practice.

Pricing

(Service Strategy) The Activity for establishing how much Customers will be Charged.

PRINCE2

The standard UK government methodology for Project management. See www.ogc.gov.uk/prince2 for more information. *See also* PMBOK.

Priority

(Service Transition) (Service Operation) A Category used to identify the relative importance of an Incident, Problem or Change. Priority is based on Impact and Urgency, and is used to identify required times for actions to be taken. For example the SLA may state that Priority 2 Incidents must be resolved within 12 hours.

Proactive Problem Management

(Service Operation) Part of the Problem Management Process. The Objective of Proactive Problem Management is to identify Problems that might otherwise be missed. Proactive Problem Management analyses Incident Records, and uses data collected by other IT Service Management Processes to identify trends or significant problems.

Problem

(Service Operation) A cause of one or more Incidents. The cause is not usually known at the time a Problem Record is created, and the Problem Management Process is responsible for further investigation.

Problem Management

(Service Operation) The Process responsible for managing the Lifecycle of all Problems. The primary objectives of Problem Management are to prevent Incidents from happening, and to minimize the Impact of Incidents that cannot be prevented.

Problem Record

(Service Operation) A Record containing the details of a Problem. Each Problem Record documents the Lifecycle of a single Problem.

Procedure

A Document containing steps that specify how to achieve an Activity. Procedures are defined as part of Processes. *See also* Work Instruction.

Process

A structured set of Activities designed to accomplish a specific Objective. A Process takes one or more defined inputs and turns them into defined outputs. A Process may include any of the Roles, responsibilities, tools and management Controls required to reliably deliver the outputs. A Process may define Policies, Standards, Guidelines, Activities, and Work Instructions if they are needed.

Process Control

The Activity of planning and regulating a Process, with the Objective of performing the Process in an Effective, Efficient, and consistent manner.

Process Manager

A Role responsible for Operational management of a Process. The Process Manager's responsibilities include Planning and coordination of all Activities required to carry out, monitor and report on the Process. There may be several Process Managers for one Process, for example regional Change Managers or IT Service Continuity Managers for each data centre. The Process Manager Role is often assigned to the person who carries out the Process Owner Role, but the two Roles may be separate in larger Organizations.

Process Owner

A Role responsible for ensuring that a Process is Fit for Purpose. The Process Owner's responsibilities include sponsorship, Design, Change Management and continual improvement of the Process and its Metrics. This Role is often assigned to the same person who carries out the Process Manager Role, but the two Roles may be separate in larger Organizations.

Production Environment

See Live Environment.

Programme

A number of Projects and Activities that are planned and managed together to achieve an overall set of related Objectives and other Outcomes.

Project

A temporary Organization, with people and other Assets required to achieve an Objective or other Outcome. Each Project has a Lifecycle that typically includes initiation, Planning, execution, Closure, etc. Projects are usually managed using a formal methodology such as PRINCE2.

PRojects IN Controlled Environments (PRINCE2)

See PRINCE2

Qualification

(Service Transition) An Activity that ensures that IT Infrastructure is appropriate, and correctly configured, to support an Application or IT Service. *See also* Validation.

Quality

The ability of a product, Service, or Process to provide the intended value. For example, a hardware Component can be considered to be of high Quality if it performs as expected and delivers the required Reliability. Process Quality also requires an ability to monitor Effectiveness and Efficiency, and to improve them if necessary. *See also* Quality Management System.

Quality Assurance (QA)

(Service Transition) The Process responsible for ensuring that the Quality of a product, Service or Process will provide its intended Value.

Quality Management System (QMS)

(Continual Service Improvement) The set of Processes responsible for ensuring that all work carried out by an Organization is of a suitable Quality to reliably meet Business Objectives or Service Levels. *See also* ISO 9000.

Quick Win

(Continual Service Improvement) An improvement Activity that is expected to provide a Return on Investment in a short period of time with relatively small Cost and effort.

RACI

(Service Design) (Continual Service Improvement) A Model used to help define Roles and Responsibilities. RACI stands for Responsible, Accountable, Consulted and Informed. *See also* Stakeholder.

Record

A Document containing the results or other output from a Process or Activity. Records are evidence of the fact that an activity took place and may be paper or electronic. For example, an Audit report, an Incident Record, or the minutes of a meeting.

Recovery

(Service Design) (Service Operation) Returning a Configuration Item or an IT Service to a working state. Recovery of an IT Service often includes recovering data to a known consistent state. After Recovery, further steps may be needed before the IT Service can be made available to the Users (Restoration).

Redundancy

See Fault Tolerance.

The term Redundant also has a generic meaning of obsolete, or no longer needed.

Relationship

A connection or interaction between two people or things. In Business Relationship Management it is the interaction between the IT Service Provider and the Business. In Configuration Management it is a link between two Configuration Items that identifies a dependency or connection between them. For example Applications may be linked to the Servers they run on, IT Services have many links to all the CIs that contribute to them.

Release

(Service Transition) A collection of hardware, software, documentation, Processes or other Components required to implement one or more approved Changes to IT Services. The contents of each Release are managed, tested, and deployed as a single entity.

Release and Deployment Management

(Service Transition) The Process responsible for both Release Management and Deployment.

Release Management

(Service Transition) The Process responsible for Planning, scheduling and controlling the movement of Releases to Test and Live Environments. The primary Objective of Release Management is to ensure that the integrity of the Live Environment is protected and that the correct Components are released. Release Management is part of the Release and Deployment Management Process.

Release Record

(Service Transition) A Record in the CMDB that defines the content of a Release. A Release Record has Relationships with all Configuration Items that are affected by the Release.

Reliability

(Service Design) (Continual Service Improvement) A measure of how long a Configuration Item or IT Service can perform its agreed Function without interruption. Usually measured as MTBF or MTBSI. The term Reliability can also be used to state how likely it is that a Process, Function, etc. will deliver its required outputs. *See also* Availability.

Repair

(Service Operation) The replacement or correction of a failed Configuration Item.

Request for Change (RFC)

(Service Transition) A formal proposal for a Change to be made. An RFC includes details of the proposed Change, and may be recorded on paper or electronically. The term RFC is often misused to mean a Change Record, or the Change itself.

Requirement

(Service Design) A formal statement of what is needed. For example, a Service Level Requirement, a Project Requirement or the required Deliverables for a Process.

Resilience

(Service Design) The ability of a Configuration Item or IT Service to resist Failure or to Recover quickly following a Failure. For example an armoured cable will resist failure when put under stress. *See also* Fault Tolerance.

Resolution

(Service Operation) Action taken to repair the Root Cause of an Incident or Problem, or to implement a Workaround. In ISO/IEC 20000, Resolution Processes is the Process group that includes Incident and Problem Management.

Resource

(Service Strategy) A generic term that includes IT Infrastructure, people, money or anything else that might help to deliver an IT Service. Resources are considered to be Assets of an Organization. *See also* Capability, Service Asset.

Response Time

A measure of the time taken to complete an Operation or Transaction. Used in Capacity Management as a measure of IT Infrastructure Performance, and in Incident Management as a measure of the time taken to answer the phone, or to start Diagnosis.

Responsiveness

A measurement of the time taken to respond to something. This could be Response Time of a Transaction, or the speed with which an IT Service Provider responds to an Incident or Request for Change, etc.

Restoration of Service

See Restore.

Restore

(Service Operation) Taking action to return an IT Service to the Users after Repair and Recovery from an Incident. This is the primary Objective of Incident Management.

Retire

(Service Transition) Permanent removal of an IT Service, or other Configuration Item, from the Live Environment. Retired is a stage in the Lifecycle of many Configuration Items.

Return on Investment (ROI)

(Service Strategy) (Continual Service Improvement) A measurement of the expected benefit of an investment. In the simplest sense it is the net profit of an investment divided by the net worth of the assets invested. *See also* Value on Investment.

Review

An evaluation of a Change, Problem, Process, Project, etc. Reviews are typically carried out at predefined points in the Lifecycle, and especially after Closure. The purpose of a Review is to ensure that all Deliverables have been provided, and to identify opportunities for improvement. *See also* Post-Implementation Review.

Risk

A possible event that could cause harm or loss, or affect the ability to achieve Objectives. A Risk is measured by the probability of a Threat, the Vulnerability of the Asset to that Threat, and the Impact it would have if it occurred.

Risk Assessment

The initial steps of Risk Management. Analysing the value of Assets to the business, identifying Threats to those Assets, and evaluating how Vulnerable each Asset is to those Threats. Risk Assessment can be quantitative (based on numerical data) or qualitative.

Risk Management

The Process responsible for identifying, assessing and controlling Risks. *See also* Risk Assessment.

Role

A set of responsibilities, Activities and authorities granted to a person or team. A Role is defined in a Process. One person or team may have multiple Roles, for example the Roles of Configuration Manager and Change Manager may be carried out by a single person.

Root Cause

(Service Operation) The underlying or original cause of an Incident or Problem.

Root Cause Analysis (RCA)

(Service Operation) An Activity that identifies the Root Cause of an Incident or Problem. RCA typically concentrates on IT Infrastructure failures. *See also* Service Failure Analysis.

Scalability

The ability of an IT Service, Process, Configuration Item, etc. to perform its agreed Function when the Workload or Scope changes.

Scope

The boundary, or extent, to which a Process, Procedure, Certification, Contract, etc. applies. For example the Scope of Change Management may include all Live IT Services and related Configuration Items, the Scope of an ISO/IEC 20000 Certificate may include all IT Services delivered out of a named data centre.

Security

See Information Security Management.

Security Management

See Information Security Management.

Server

(Service Operation) A computer that is connected to a network and provides software Functions that are used by other Computers.

Service

A means of delivering value to Customers by facilitating Outcomes Customers want to achieve without the ownership of specific Costs and Risks.

Service Asset

Any Capability or Resource of a Service Provider. *See also* Asset.

Service Asset and Configuration Management (SACM)

(Service Transition) The Process responsible for both Configuration Management and Asset Management.

Service Capacity Management (SCM)

(Service Design) (Continual Service Improvement) The Activity responsible for understanding the Performance and Capacity of IT Services. The Resources used by each IT Service and the pattern of usage over time are collected, recorded, and analysed for use in the Capacity Plan. *See also* Business Capacity Management, Component Capacity Management.

Service Catalogue

(Service Design) A database or structured Document with information about all Live IT Services, including those available for Deployment. The Service Catalogue is the only part of the Service Portfolio published to Customers, and is used to support the sale and delivery of IT Services. The Service Catalogue includes information about deliverables, prices, contact points, ordering and request Processes.

Service Culture

A Customer-oriented Culture. The major Objectives of a Service Culture are Customer satisfaction and helping Customers to achieve their Business Objectives.

Service Design

(Service Design) A stage in the Lifecycle of an IT Service. Service Design includes a number of Processes and Functions and is the title of one of the Core ITIL publications. *See also* Design.

Service Desk

(Service Operation) The Single Point of Contact between the Service Provider and the Users. A typical Service Desk manages Incidents and Service Requests, and also handles communication with the Users.

Service Failure Analysis (SFA)

(Service Design) An Activity that identifies underlying causes of one or more IT Service interruptions. SFA identifies opportunities to improve the IT Service Provider's Processes and tools, and not just the IT Infrastructure. SFA is a time-constrained, project-like activity, rather than an ongoing process of analysis. *See also* Root Cause Analysis.

Service Improvement Plan (SIP)

(Continual Service Improvement) A formal Plan to implement improvements to a Process or IT Service.

Service Knowledge Management System (SKMS)

(Service Transition) A set of tools and databases that are used to manage knowledge and information. The SKMS includes the Configuration Management System, as well as other tools and databases. The SKMS stores, manages, updates, and presents all information that an IT Service Provider needs to manage the full Lifecycle of IT Services.

Service Level

Measured and reported achievement against one or more Service Level Targets. The term Service Level is sometimes used informally to mean Service Level Target.

Service Level Agreement (SLA)

(Service Design) (Continual Service Improvement) An Agreement between an IT Service Provider and a Customer. The SLA describes the IT Service, documents Service Level Targets, and specifies the responsibilities of the IT Service Provider and the Customer. A single SLA may cover multiple IT Services or multiple customers. *See also* Operational Level Agreement.

Service Level Management (SLM)

(Service Design) (Continual Service Improvement) The Process responsible for negotiating Service Level Agreements, and ensuring that these are met. SLM is responsible for ensuring that all IT Service Management Processes, Operational Level Agreements, and Underpinning Contracts, are appropriate for the agreed Service Level Targets. SLM monitors and reports on Service Levels, and holds regular Customer reviews.

Service Level Requirement (SLR)

(Service Design) (Continual Service Improvement) A Customer Requirement for an aspect of an IT Service. SLRs are based on Business Objectives and are used to negotiate agreed Service Level Targets.

Service Level Target

(Service Design) (Continual Service Improvement) A commitment that is documented in a Service Level Agreement. Service Level Targets are based on Service Level Requirements, and are needed to ensure that the IT Service design is Fit for Purpose. Service Level Targets should be SMART, and are usually based on KPIs.

Service Management

Service Management is a set of specialized organizational capabilities for providing value to customers in the form of services.

Service Management Lifecycle

An approach to IT Service Management that emphasizes the importance of coordination and Control across the various Functions, Processes, and Systems necessary to manage the full Lifecycle of IT Services. The Service Management Lifecycle approach considers the Strategy, Design, Transition, Operation and Continuous Improvement of IT Services.

Service Manager

A manager who is responsible for managing the end-to-end Lifecycle of one or more IT Services. The term Service Manager is also used to mean any manager within the IT Service Provider. Most commonly used to refer to a Business Relationship Manager, a Process Manager, an Account Manager or a senior manager with responsibility for IT Services overall.

Service Operation

(Service Operation) A stage in the Lifecycle of an IT Service. Service Operation includes a number of Processes and Functions and is the title of one of the Core ITIL publications. *See also* Operation.

Service Owner

(Continual Service Improvement) A Role that is accountable for the delivery of a specific IT Service.

Service Package

(Service Strategy) A detailed description of an IT Service that is available to be delivered to Customers. A Service

Package includes a Service Level Package and one or more Core Services and Supporting Services.

Service Portfolio

(Service Strategy) The complete set of Services that are managed by a Service Provider. The Service Portfolio is used to manage the entire Lifecycle of all Services, and includes three Categories: Service Pipeline (proposed or in Development); Service Catalogue (Live or available for Deployment); and Retired Services. *See also* Service Portfolio Management.

Service Portfolio Management (SPM)

(Service Strategy) The Process responsible for managing the Service Portfolio. Service Portfolio Management considers Services in terms of the Business value that they provide.

Service Provider

(Service Strategy) An Organization supplying Services to one or more Internal Customers or External Customers. Service Provider is often used as an abbreviation for IT Service Provider.

Service Reporting

(Continual Service Improvement) The Process responsible for producing and delivering reports of achievement and trends against Service Levels. Service Reporting should agree the format, content and frequency of reports with Customers.

Service Request

(Service Operation) A request from a User for information, or advice, or for a Standard Change or for Access to an IT Service. For example to reset a password, or to provide standard IT Services for a new User. Service Requests are usually handled by a Service Desk, and do not require an RFC to be submitted.

Service Strategy

(Service Strategy) The title of one of the Core ITIL publications. Service Strategy establishes an overall Strategy for IT Services and for IT Service Management.

Service Transition

(Service Transition) A stage in the Lifecycle of an IT Service. Service Transition includes a number of Processes and Functions and is the title of one of the Core ITIL publications. *See also* Transition.

Serviceability

(Service Design) (Continual Service Improvement) The ability of a Third-Party Supplier to meet the terms of its Contract. This Contract will include agreed levels of Reliability, Maintainability or Availability for a Configuration Item.

Simulation modelling

(Service Design) (Continual Service Improvement) A technique that creates a detailed model to predict the behaviour of a Configuration Item or IT Service. Simulation Models can be very accurate but are expensive and time consuming to create. A Simulation Model is often created by using the actual Configuration Items that are being modelled, with artificial Workloads or Transactions. They are used in Capacity Management when accurate results are important. A simulation model is sometimes called a Performance Benchmark.

Single Point of Contact

(Service Operation) Providing a single consistent way to communicate with an Organization or Business Unit. For example, a Single Point of Contact for an IT Service Provider is usually called a Service Desk.

Single Point of Failure (SPOF)

(Service Design) Any Configuration Item that can cause an Incident when it fails, and for which a Countermeasure has not been implemented. A SPOF may be a person, or a step in a Process or Activity, as well as a Component of the IT Infrastructure. *See also* Failure.

SLAM Chart

(Continual Service Improvement) A Service Level Agreement Monitoring Chart is used to help monitor and report achievements against Service Level Targets. A SLAM Chart is typically colour coded to show whether each agreed Service Level Target has been met, missed, or nearly missed during each of the previous 12 months.

SMART

(Service Design) (Continual Service Improvement) An acronym for helping to remember that targets in Service Level Agreements and Project Plans should be Specific, Measurable, Achievable, Relevant and Timely.

Snapshot

(Service Transition) The current state of a Configuration as captured by a discovery tool. Also used as a synonym for Benchmark. *See also* Baseline.

Specification

A formal definition of Requirements. A Specification may be used to define technical or Operational Requirements, and may be internal or external. Many public Standards consist of a Code of Practice and a Specification. The Specification defines the Standard against which an Organization can be Audited.

Stakeholder

All people who have an interest in an Organization, Project, IT Service, etc. Stakeholders may be interested in the Activities, targets, Resources, or Deliverables. Stakeholders may include Customers, Partners, employees, shareholders, owners, etc. *See also* RACI.

Standard

A mandatory Requirement. Examples include ISO/IEC 20000 (an international Standard), an internal security standard for Unix configuration, or a government standard for how financial Records should be maintained. The term Standard is also used to refer to a Code of Practice or Specification published by a Standards Organization such as ISO or BSI. *See also* Guideline.

Status

The name of a required field in many types of Record. It shows the current stage in the Lifecycle of the associated Configuration Item, Incident, Problem, etc.

Storage Management

(Service Operation) The Process responsible for managing the storage and maintenance of data throughout its Lifecycle.

Strategic

(Service Strategy) The highest of three levels of Planning and delivery (Strategic, Tactical, Operational). Strategic Activities include Objective setting and long-term Planning to achieve the overall Vision.

Strategy

(Service Strategy) A Strategic Plan designed to achieve defined Objectives.

Supplier

(Service Strategy) (Service Design) A Third Party responsible for supplying goods or Services that are required to deliver IT services. Examples of suppliers include commodity hardware and software vendors, network and telecom providers, and outsourcing Organizations. *See also* Underpinning Contract, Supply Chain.

Supplier Management

(Service Design) The Process responsible for ensuring that all Contracts with Suppliers support the needs of the Business, and that all Suppliers meet their contractual commitments.

Supply Chain

(Service Strategy) The Activities in a Value Chain carried out by Suppliers. A Supply Chain typically involves multiple Suppliers, each adding value to the product or Service.

Support Group

(Service Operation) A group of people with technical skills. Support Groups provide the Technical Support needed by all of the IT Service Management Processes. *See also* Technical Management.

SWOT Analysis

(Continual Service Improvement) A technique that reviews and analyses the internal strengths and weaknesses of an Organization and of the external opportunities and threats that it faces. SWOT stands for Strengths, Weaknesses, Opportunities and Threats.

System

A number of related things that work together to achieve an overall Objective. For example:

- A computer System including hardware, software and Applications
- A management System, including multiple Processes that are planned and managed together. For example, a Quality Management System
- A Database Management System or Operating System that includes many software modules that are designed to perform a set of related Functions.

Tactical
The middle of three levels of Planning and delivery (Strategic, Tactical, Operational). Tactical Activities include the medium-term Plans required to achieve specific Objectives, typically over a period of weeks to months.

Technical Management
(Service Operation) The Function responsible for providing technical skills in support of IT Services and management of the IT Infrastructure. Technical Management defines the Roles of Support Groups, as well as the tools, Processes and Procedures required.

Technical Observation
(Continual Service Improvement) A technique used in Service Improvement, Problem investigation and Availability Management. Technical support staff meet to monitor the behaviour and Performance of an IT Service and make recommendations for improvement.

Technical Support
See Technical Management.

Tension Metrics
(Continual Service Improvement) A set of related Metrics, in which improvements to one Metric have a negative effect on another. Tension Metrics are designed to ensure that an appropriate balance is achieved.

Test
(Service Transition) An Activity that verifies that a Configuration Item, IT Service, Process, etc. meets its Specification or agreed Requirements. *See also* Acceptance.

Test Environment
(Service Transition) A controlled Environment used to Test Configuration Items, Builds, IT Services, Processes, etc.

Third Party
A person, group, or Business that is not part of the Service Level Agreement for an IT Service, but is required to ensure successful delivery of that IT Service. For example, a software Supplier, a hardware maintenance company, or a facilities department. Requirements for Third Parties are typically specified in Underpinning Contracts or Operational Level Agreements.

Threat
Anything that might exploit a Vulnerability. Any potential cause of an Incident can be considered to be a Threat. For example a fire is a Threat that could exploit the Vulnerability of flammable floor coverings. This term is commonly used in Information Security Management and IT Service Continuity Management, but also applies to other areas such as Problem and Availability Management.

Threshold
The value of a Metric that should cause an Alert to be generated, or management action to be taken. For example 'Priority 1 Incident not solved within four hours', 'more than five soft disk errors in an hour', or 'more than 10 failed changes in a month'.

Throughput
(Service Design) A measure of the number of Transactions, or other Operations, performed in a fixed time. For example, 5,000 e-mails sent per hour, or 200 disk I/Os per second.

Total Cost of Ownership (TCO)
(Service Strategy) A methodology used to help make investment decisions. TCO assesses the full Lifecycle Cost of owning a Configuration Item, not just the initial Cost or purchase price.

Total Quality Management (TQM)
(Continual Service Improvement) A methodology for managing continual Improvement by using a Quality Management System. TQM establishes a Culture involving all people in the Organization in a Process of continual monitoring and improvement.

Transaction
A discrete Function performed by an IT Service. For example transferring money from one bank account to another. A single Transaction may involve numerous additions, deletions and modifications of data. Either all of these complete successfully or none of them is carried out.

Transition
(Service Transition) A change in state, corresponding to a movement of an IT Service or other Configuration Item from one Lifecycle status to the next.

Trend Analysis

(Continual Service Improvement) Analysis of data to identify time-related patterns. Trend Analysis is used in Problem Management to identify common Failures or fragile Configuration Items, and in Capacity Management as a Modelling tool to predict future behaviour. It is also used as a management tool for identifying deficiencies in IT Service Management Processes.

Tuning

The Activity responsible for Planning changes to make the most efficient use of Resources. Tuning is part of Performance Management, which also includes Performance monitoring and implementation of the required Changes.

Underpinning Contract (UC)

(Service Design) A Contract between an IT Service Provider and a Third Party. The Third Party provides goods or Services that support delivery of an IT Service to a Customer. The Underpinning Contract defines targets and responsibilities that are required to meet agreed Service Level Targets in an SLA.

Unit Cost

(Service Strategy) The Cost to the IT Service Provider of providing a single Component of an IT Service. For example the Cost of a single desktop PC, or of a single Transaction.

Urgency

(Service Transition) (Service Design) A measure of how long it will be until an Incident, Problem or Change has a significant Impact on the Business. For example a high Impact Incident may have low Urgency, if the Impact will not affect the Business until the end of the financial year. Impact and Urgency are used to assign Priority.

User

A person who uses the IT Service on a day-to-day basis. Users are distinct from Customers, as some Customers do not use the IT Service directly.

Utility

(Service Strategy) Functionality offered by a Product or Service to meet a particular need. Utility is often summarized as 'what it does'.

Validation

(Service Transition) An Activity that ensures a new or changed IT Service, Process, Plan, or other Deliverable meets the needs of the Business. Validation ensures that Business Requirements are met even though these may have changed since the original design. *See also* Verification, Acceptance, Qualification.

Value Chain

(Service Strategy) A sequence of Processes that creates a product or Service that is of value to a Customer. Each step of the sequence builds on the previous steps and contributes to the overall product or Service.

Value for Money

An informal measure of Cost Effectiveness. Value for Money is often based on a comparison with the Cost of alternatives.

Value on Investment (VOI)

(Continual Service Improvement) A measurement of the expected benefit of an investment. VOI considers both financial and intangible benefits. *See also* Return on Investment.

Variance

The difference between a planned value and the actual measured value. Commonly used in Financial Management, Capacity Management and Service Level Management, but could apply in any area where Plans are in place.

Verification

(Service Transition) An Activity that ensures a new or changed IT Service, Process, Plan, or other Deliverable is complete, accurate, Reliable and matches its design specification. *See also* Validation, Acceptance.

Version

(Service Transition) A Version is used to identify a specific Baseline of a Configuration Item. Versions typically use a naming convention that enables the sequence or date of each Baseline to be identified. For example Payroll Application Version 3 contains updated functionality from Version 2.

Vision

A description of what the Organization intends to become in the future. A Vision is created by senior management and is used to help influence Culture and Strategic Planning.

Vital Business Function (VBF)

(Service Design) A Function of a Business Process that is critical to the success of the Business. Vital Business Functions are an important consideration of Business Continuity Management, IT Service Continuity Management and Availability Management.

Vulnerability

A weakness that could be exploited by a Threat. For example an open firewall port, a password that is never changed, or a flammable carpet. A missing Control is also considered to be a Vulnerability.

Work Instruction

A Document containing detailed instructions that specify exactly what steps to follow to carry out an Activity. A Work Instruction contains much more detail than a Procedure and is only created if very detailed instructions are needed.

Workaround

(Service Operation) Reducing or eliminating the Impact of an Incident or Problem for which a full Resolution is not yet available. For example by restarting a failed Configuration Item. Workarounds for Problems are documented in Known Error Records. Workarounds for Incidents that do not have associated Problem Records are documented in the Incident Record.

Workload

The Resources required to deliver an identifiable part of an IT Service. Workloads may be Categorized by Users, groups of Users, or Functions within the IT Service. This is used to assist in analysing and managing the Capacity, Performance and Utilization of Configuration Items and IT Services. The term Workload is sometimes used as a synonym for Throughput.

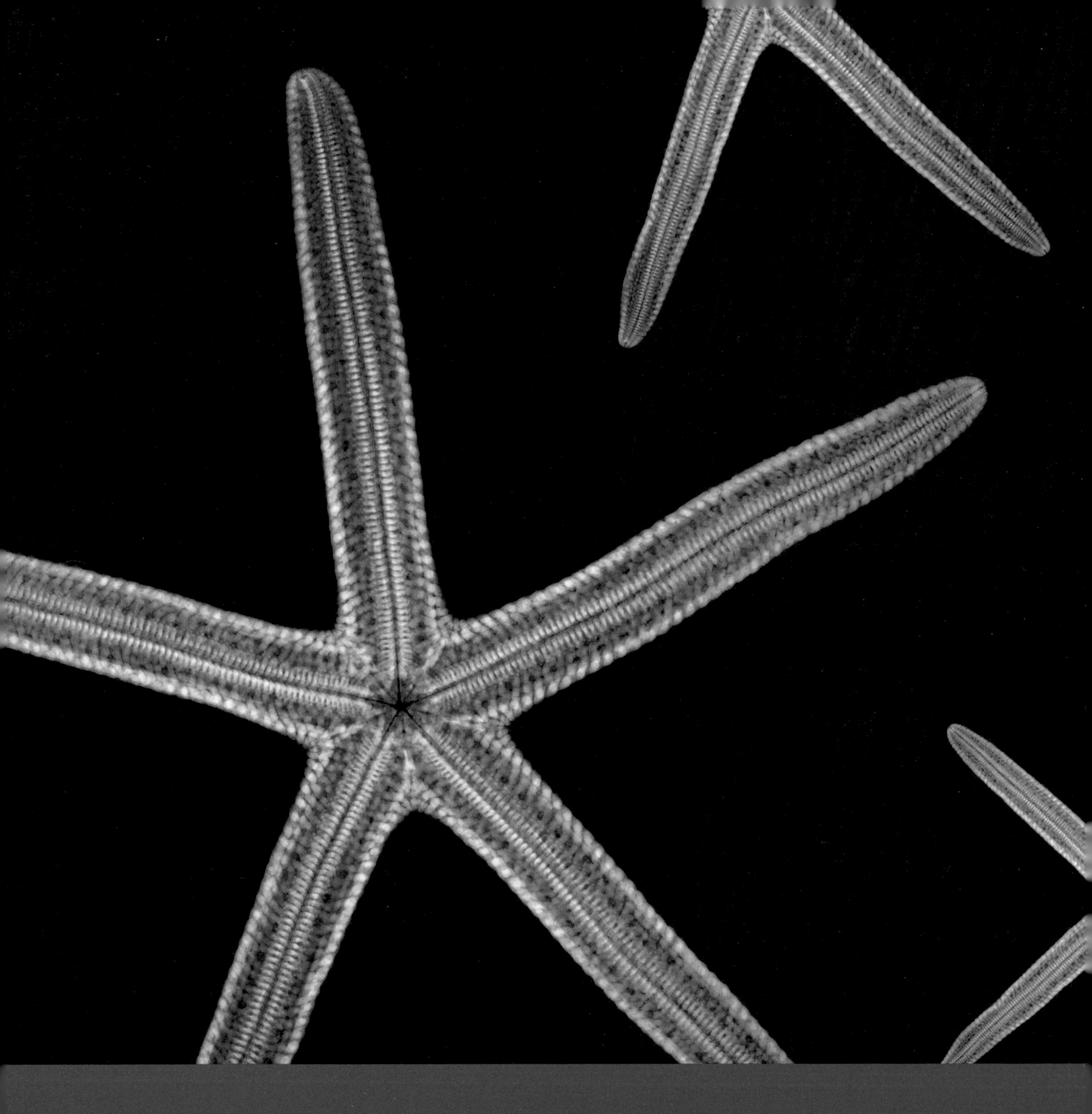

Index

Index

Figures are indicated by **bold** page numbers and tables by *italics*.